Czech Cultural
and
Community Center
(KULTURNI CENTRUM CESKE KOMUNITY)

Houston, Texas

In recognition of your contributions in preserving the culture, language, scholarship and the arts of Bohemia, Moravia, Slovakia and Silesia

CCCC • 2315 Del Norte • Houston, Texas 77018-1018, USA •
(713) 682-4608

INSTITUTE OF TEXAN CULTURES

This design, combining the emblem of Czechoslovakia with
the flag of Texas, portrays the real significance of this book.

CZECH PIONEERS
OF THE SOUTHWEST

By

HENRY R. MARESH

.. and ..

ESTELLE HUDSON

WESTERN LITHOGRAPH
HOUSTON, TEXAS

IN USA $14.95

For copies of *Czech Pioneers of the Southwest*
write to   CZECH CULTURAL AND COMMUNITY CENTER
2315 Del Norte
Houston, TX 77018-1018

Tel/Fax:713/682-4608

DEDICATION

To Those Of

Czech Birth and Descent
in Texas Who, Through Their
Labors in the Field of Agriculture and
Their Activities in the Sphere of Commerce and
Industry, Have Helped to Build Texas; Who, Through
Their Achievements in the Realm of Science, Literature and
Art, Have Added Laurels; Who, by Their Teaching,
Their Example and Their Influence, Have
Wielded Untold Good to Home and State,
Who Have Displayed Their Loyalty
to Flag and Texas in Time of
Peace and War . . .

This Volume Is Dedicated

This book is republished in memory of my beloved husband
DR. HENRY R. MARESH
TO CARRY FORTH HIS DREAM AND DEDICATION
FOR THOSE OF CZECH BIRTH AND DESCENT.

Thelma Burnett Maresh

CONTENTS

v

LIST OF ILLUSTRATIONS

WHERE IS MY HOME?

Where is my home?
Where is my home?
Waters through its meads are streaming,
Mounts with rustling woods are teaming,
Vales are bright with flowers rare,
Oh, earth's Eden, thou art fair,
    Thou art my home, my fatherland,
    Thou art my home, my fatherland.
    Where is my home?
    Where is my home?
By the towers of God 'tis bounded;
By the noblest sons surrounded;
True and light of heart are they,
Firm and bold in deadly fray;
Offspring grand of dear Bohemia,
    Thou art my home, my fatherland;
    Thou art my home, my fatherland.

From the works of
Josef Kajetan Tyl (1808-1856)

INTRODUCTION

DESPITE the floods of oratory on "America, the Melting Pot" that citizens of the United States listened to a decade or so ago, it is only occasionally that we actually realize that our United States is not peopled exclusively by persons of Anglo-Saxon descent and tradition. When the results of each federal census become available, those who read the statistics sometimes express amazement at the way in which this or that nationality bulks in the totals, and how "cultural pockets" are to be found scattered over the land. Those who read the sports columns are aware that the Lowells and the Cabots no longer supply the athletic heroes of even such institutions as Harvard; and when a man named Anton J. Čermak was elected mayor of Chicago it was called to the attention of every newspaper reader that non-Teutonic elements were rising to positions of power and leadership in many realms of American life.

The flow of immigration has subsided but the process of amalgamation is not yet complete. The first-hand records of the process by which a new American nationality is being evolved are still available, and historical interest and racial pride are working hand in hand to preserve the materials on which future historians must rely when they undertake to explain the racial structure of the new world. Studies such as this one serve to point out the rich field inviting investigation by the patient scholar. But they do more than that.

Racial pride is a fundamental emotion of every man. Whatever makes more complete a man's knowledge of his forbears, their background, temperament, characteristics, and achievements enriches that man's life and contributes to the enrichment of the cultural heritage of America.

This volume, then, in addition to making available to the historian many facts not elsewhere available, will be of especial interest to some half million Texans of Czech blood. Czechs migrated to this region during the decade of the Republic of Texas; they helped conquer the wilderness and to build a Southwestern empire; and today they continue their fruitful labor in the development of the region.

HERBERT P. GAMBRELL.

Southern Methodist University, 1934.

ix

PROLOGUE

"Hadst thou lived in days of old,
O, what wonders had been told."

TEXAS has been fortunate in attracting liberty-loving peoples. Both by birth and immigration her population has been increased, and through this, her expanding population, her natural resources have been developed until, in 1931, with taxable property in Texas assessed at $4,218,235,000, the State topped the combined total of the three neighboring states of Arkansas, Louisiana and Oklahoma, ranking at the time fourth in the nation with revenue receipts, her per capita debt given at 0.77.

For nearly one hundred years prior to the Civil War, 1861-65, the government of the United States fostered immigration by throwing wide the gates to all newcomers. The wave of immigration was especially high during the years of 1848-9, with the city of Galveston being the principal entrance by sea into Texas. As early as 1840 Czech immigrants arrived at Galveston and from this point took their way overland into the State, seeking locations for homes.

The shipping list from 1840-1860 was destroyed by the Galveston flood of 1900, wiping out much that would today make valuable and interesting history.

In 1864 Congress enacted a law authorizing the importation of laborers in large numbers. The fiscal year, however, ending June, 1931, records the lowest immigration to the United States in sixty-nine years.

This may be attributed in part to the Act of Congress, 1924, when the most sweeping immigration regulations in the history of the country were enacted. These laws became effective in 1929, fixing the total number of immigrants permitted to enter the United States at 153,714 yearly.

A standard based on the total population of each foreign country in America was fixed in connection for the purpose of arriving at the quota for each country. Germany's population at the time was one-sixth of the total allowance. Consequently the quota for German immigration was set at 25,000.

The United States Department of Labor, Bureau of Immigration, Washington, D. C., in the announcement of permanent residence immigration from Czechoslovakia into Texas during the year ending June 30, 1931, gave the total as 2,016. The preceding year the number was 4,438.

It is of interest to know that the approximate figures given for total Czech population in Texas in 1932 is between 350,000 and 500,000. This number includes families of the generations that have branched out from the pioneer stock. The native foreign-born citizenship is today comparatively small. The figures from the government immigration report of 1931 would indicate that the independent country of Czechoslovakia is holding her people at home.

But statistics are not half so important as the individuals who are responsible for them, and in this connection the words of Walt Whitman seem appropriate:

"Camerado. This is no book. Who touches this
        book, touches a man."

That all books are made from other books, as has been claimed, is not true in the present instance. As a matter of fact, the task has been doubly difficult for the very reason that there were no books from which material could be gathered.

"You are too late," was the pronouncement of one Texan, Dr. Rudolph E. Maresh of Houston, Texas, grandson of Czech pioneers, who deeply interested himself in the subject of the book, and deplored the lack of first-hand information.

"Fifteen years too late," he added, and there was a note of sadness in his voice for the lost opportunity—a plaint of regret for the passing of those pioneers who could have told the story in greater detail.

The men and women who could have told the story in all its fullness, have passed on, but they have left behind their influence, their achievements, and so, after all, the way is not trackless. There are the milestones they laid, the landmarks they builded, that the historian of the present might not be entirely lost.

Surrounded by these tangible evidences of the part the early Czech settler played in the struggle of pioneering, the pen moves to write, and, in writing, finds the impetus that drives it on and on, transcribing the deeds of courage and heroism of these sturdy patriots of the past.

Back when the infant Republic of Texas was born, Czech pioneers were present, taking their part, sharing the burdens of whatever had to be done. When the curtain rose in 1835 for the first act of the Texas Revolution, General Sam Houston issued the first call for volunteers from the United States.

"Come with good rifles and come soon," was the manner of the call—a battle slogan of liberty.

And there were Czechs listed among the soldiers in General Houston's army. And they "came soon," some of them from old North Carolina, many of them "with good rifles."

This is not, however, to be a history of Texas.

An eighty-year-old Texas pioneer said some years ago that there are few people who really know Texas history.

"Texas history," he said, "is unwritten; it cannot be written. In the years known as the '30s and '40s, even later, Texas history was being enacted chapter by chapter—the sort of history that makes nations."

And the story of the Czech settlement of Texas is a history, in part, of the great Lone Star State, for these Czech settlers were here when the first chapters were being enacted. They were in America when the first chapters of the Nation's history were being enacted, for William Pača of Maryland, one of the signers of the Declaration of Independence, was a Czech.

Taking up the thread of the present history, we go back through the years, through the stretching vista of a century. In those early pioneer days families were willing to live under trees; to endure loneliness, privation, and to suffer all the hardships of a new country in order that they might look to the future—a future in which not only they and the communities in which they dwelt might be benefited, but their families, and the coming generations.

It is well to remember that before the advent of the white man the country belonged to the Indian. He hunted, fought and maintained his wigwam.

In the coast plains territory of Texas, for a distance of some four hundred miles, as large an area as an average American state, these pioneer Czech immigrants settled in the early years.

Here, where the moss hung on the live oak trees and the fragrant white-flowered magnolia grew; where the sweet-gum and pine tree spread their branches; where the cape jessamine, oleander and palm tree flourished, these pioneers made their homes.

Here, in close proximity to the battle-grounds of Goliad, the Alamo, and San Jacinto, where Texas won the War of Independence, the liberty-loving immigrants took up their abode. Texas, before she was a Republic, and after she entered the United States, was a refuge for the oppressed of other lands.

It is conflict of the past and the modern progress that makes the Czech citizen of Texas today such an interesting American. There are no ghosts, no austere features of the puritan behind him. The hope of gain, the opportunity for accumulating wealth, a competency, whether it be a house or cultivated fields, or both, has ever been the basis of civilization. For this reason and because of religious oppression and politics, the Czechs came to Texas. It is written that before the outbreak of the Thirty Years' War the nation that is now Czechoslovakia contemplated a form of government not unlike that of the United States. This, however, is apart from the subject. They came to Texas, these early Czech settlers, accepting conditions as they found them.

The Battle of San Jacinto brought under the domain territory greater than the original thirteen colonies. The people were weak in the beginning. There were no resources, nor military power.

The country was harassed in her struggle for existence in those first days when order was being wrought out of chaos. Internal questions and dissensions, together with the dangers ever imminent in the new country, kept up the combative and aggressive spirit of the people.

Honorable Joshua Johnson, addressing the House of Representatives in 1850 in behalf of the preservation of the Union, said:

"Texas is just retrieving herself of the many difficulties and embarrassments that have long oppressed and cramped the courage of her people. For more than a quarter of a century she has been exposed to all dangers, endured all privations and submitted to all inconveniences incident to frontier life. As a pioneer of the wilderness, her life has been one of sacrifice, long suffering and peculiar hardships. She has had not only to subdue the wilderness, but tame the savage and beat back the Mexicans."

And this was the Texas to which pioneer Czech settlers had come. From the moment they lost sight of land on setting sail from the "old country," they were left to contemplation of what they would find in the new world.

With the boundless expanse of water, there were no changing scenes of travel—only the roll of the vessel and the stretch of days and nights which summed themselves up into weeks.

The good ship *Fortuna*, in charge of a Captain Fretag, docked at Galveston after one of these long voyages in 1856, having brought over a number of early settlers. But when these immigrants arrived they found that there were many already here before them, settled in homes from whence the spirit and the courage that overcame obstacles and made for development was already spreading abroad.

The first chapter of this chronicle attempts to set forth briefly something of what has come to pass within the past century in Texas, with the Czech settlers of the past and the Czech citizenship of today an integral factor in the State's development and progress.

The second chapter deals briefly with the history of Czechoslovakia, the beginning of the Nation before the Christian Era, the passing from the pagan to the Christian Era and thence on through the centuries down to the decades of commerce and industry.

In the third chapter, a brief outline of Texas history has been attempted by way of a background. The history of Czech settlement and development shows that Slavonic blood has enriched the State. These sturdy immigrants of Czech lineage brought along with them romance, not unmixed with tragedy.

With their pride, their ancient and illustrious lineage, the passionate desire for freedom which has ever characterized the Czech people, they came to settle in Texas. It is difficult to discover just how early they came, but the footprints lead backward into the very earliest years of Texas history.

The immigration that has come to Texas has been like a human stream which flowed hither from Czech land, bringing the best blood and enterprise as a contribution to the new home and country. From these pioneer homes and settlements intellectual activity as represented in the fields of science, literature and art, has spread across the State.

A chapter has been devoted to language and to the early Czech schools. Tomaš Štitny, sometimes mentioned as the "father of Bohemian literature," when attacked for his use of the Bohemian language for religious purposes, replied that St. Paul wrote his Epistles to the Jews in Hebrew; to the Greeks in Greek. "Why, then, should I, being a Bohemian, hesitate to write to my countrymen in Bohemian?"

In the famous "Law of Nationalities," adopted by the Hungarian Parliament in 1868, the wording of the section devoted to schools is interesting:

"Since, from the standpoint of general culture and wellbeing, the success of public instruction is one of the highest aims of the State, the State is therefore bound to ensure that citizens living together in considerable numbers, of whatever nationality, shall be able to obtain instruction in the neighborhood, in their mother tongue, up to the point where the higher education begins."

It is the plan and the purpose of this history to bring out in each chapter a phase, an incident or an epoch in the lives of the noble Czech citizenship.

The earliest history of the land of the Čechs is quite meagre, but it is believed that Slavs were the first inhabitants. The earliest proved historical writings state that in the second century B.C., this land was inhabited by the Boii, a people of ancient Gaul. Their domain extended, however, outside the present confines of Bohemia and Moravia. The Boii were a powerful, courageous, and warlike people. In the early part of the first century B. C., the Boii left the land of the Čechs. The footprints of these people remain in the names of rivers such as Labe and Jizer, as well as in the prehistoric name of the land of the Čechs, namely, Boiohemum (Bohemia, Böhmen, land of the Boii) ; in the excavations of their graves, bronze and iron implements are found. The land of the Boiohemum at this period extended to the River Danube.

About the year 60 B. C., the Marcomans, a branch of the Germanic race, subdued the Boii. A kindred tribe, Germanic Quadi, at the same time settled in the land of Moravia and Slovakia. The strongest king of the Marcomans was Marobud, who built a powerful kingdom, the seat of which he made the land of the present Čechs. Marobud came from Rome and, in true Roman style, organized a powerful army and built a large city surrounded by a stone wall. But some of the Germanic tribes rebelled and Marobud fled to Italy. The Marcomans and Quadi were weakened by constant warfare and eventually were subdued by kindred tribes.

These people lived there until A. D. 445, when Europe was invaded from the east by Attila and his horde. The nations of eastern Europe moved westward. The Slavs at this time were occupying the broad plains from the Black Sea to the Baltic Sea, and were forced by the invading Huns to move north and west. In leaving the regions north of the Carpathian Mountains they crossed the rivers of Vislu, Oder, and Labe, and joined their kindred tribes, who from time immemorial lived in the land of Bohemia, Moravia, Silisia and Slovakia. These people were closely related tribes of Slavs.

According to Čech legend, a leader of one of these emigrating Slavonic tribes was the famous Čech, a noble of Croatia (probably White Croatia or Galicia). When they reached the Řip Mountains, located on the plain between the rivers Vltava and Labe, the view of the surrounding country was very beautiful. Čech told his followers that they would settle there and asked them what they would call their new homeland. They immediately said that since he was their father they could not name the land better than to call it Čechy. And hence the name of the people and the land.

In the Čech language, whether it be written or spoken, the people are always referred to as Čechs, and in Čech literature there is no such expression as "Bohemian." It would have to be a Čech from Bohemia; or a German from Bohemia. It is only in some of the foreign languages that the people of Čechy or Bohemia are referred to as in German, Tscheche, or Böhmen; in French, Tchèque, or Bohèmien, in which language it also has a secondary signification, namely, a gypsy, because the first gypsies that entered France were believed to be Bohemians or Hussites, driven from their native country. In Russian it is Chekhŭ; in Slovak it is Cheh; in Hungarian it is Cseh; in English it is Czech or Bohemian. In the Čech language the land or country in the early records is generally referred to as Čechy, and in later years interchangeably as Čechy or Bohemia.

The native home of the Čechs lies today in the Czechoslovak Republic in which they are the dominating race, occupying about two-thirds of Bohemia, four-fifths of Moravia and the districts which were formerly known as Austrian Silisia. Since both names, Czech (the officially adopted English spelling of Čech) or Bohemian, and Čechy or Bohemia, will be used in this book and as there is much misunderstanding about the significance of either, it is deemed quite necessary to give an accurate and authentic explanation of the two names.

In writing the history, the authorized and officially adopted spelling of the names of *Czechoslovakia* and *Czechs* has been used, the letter "Z" given place following the "C" as in the spelling of the two words in italics. The authority for the spelling was received by letter from the Czechoslovak Legation at Washington, through the Secretary of the Legation, Dr. Aleš Brož.

—The Author.

CHAPTER I

A CENTURY OF PROGRESS

"Let me see; and let me write
Of the day, and of the night—
Both together . . ."
—KEATS.

A CENTURY OF PROGRESS. It is a simple matter to write the words. But their meaning—it is the days and the nights that make life. In them is war, deeds, struggles, disappointments, and achievements. A century of progress is behind every movement of the present.

The infant held close to the mother's breast in the chill of a stormy night in pioneer Texas, lived and grew to years of maturity, and in the course of time held in her arms, in the glow of the home-fire, another child, one of her own bearing. The wilderness was tamed. There were fields of drooping oats in which scarlet poppies rose up brightly. Men's voices were heard in song, in conversation in the fields, or as they called the cattle at eventide.

The desolation of fields cultivated in the wilderness was no more. There was food and clothes to wear, the products of the makers of a century. There was work for the laborer and a wage for his skill. There was supply and demand. The ox-drawn vehicle was no longer the means of transportation. Time and men wrought the change. The era of progress was at hand.

Transportation faster than the ox-cart was inevitable. Railroads were built. Land was provided by the State as a bonus for the builders. Land that came out of the vast unsurveyed, and, at the time, waterless public domain of Texas, inhabited by hostile tribes of Indians. The Czech pioneer helped to drive the spikes that held the rails in place, helped to make the grades and to build the bridges for this new means of transportation.

This was the renaissance, the humanism and the reformation in Texas, and the whole of the country became involved in the development, producing the modern type of man, freed from the fetters of absolutism, to become political and social equals. This

1

evolution may be traced back through the centuries, over the whole of America and into Western Europe, but Texas holds this vital position on the route of the century of progress.

The struggle of the small Czech farmer and artisan for an economic, national and cultural independence brought about results that are felt today, having lasted down through the years.

If Texas is great today after a century of development, the large population of Texas-Czechs has helped to make it so.

There is the regret that we can only recreate the pioneer days of Texas through the medium of legend and tradition and the stories told by sire to son and thus transmitted on to the third and fourth generations. If we could but listen today to the recorded voice of one of those early Czech settlers, if the radio had not waited so long to be with us, what joy it would be to "tune in" and hear the broadcasted story of life as it was being lived back in the pioneer days of Texas, fifty to one hundred years ago.

Texas, back in 1852, according to pioneer settlers, offered better opportunities for agricultural pursuits than any other state in the Union. In the Gulf Coast section crops matured earlier and with less labor. Frequently one working was all that was necessary to make a crop of cotton.

But droughts came, floods destroyed and the moth and the worm corrupted and damaged; and so the pioneers, with no harvest of the year before in their bins or storehouse, suffered both hunger, sickness and, sometimes, despair as they took up their residence in the new land. But they never lost their faith nor their courage. They believed in a Divine Providence and accepted what came.

This is the story, in so far as it is possible to record it, of a people who have played a splendid part in the progress and development of Texas. That there is no connected written record of their lives and labors, may be blamed possibly to conditions. There was a man, Judge Augustin Haidušek, a leader among men, a representative Czech citizen and an able statesman, who could have written the history of the pioneer Czech settlers of Texas because he was of their times, a pioneer himself. There have been others capable of the undertaking, but they, too, overlooked the value of keeping the recorded story of the lives, works and achievements of Czech citizens who pioneered.

Every Czech citizen in Texas shares by right of heritage in the story that is told in these pages. Those first settlers, as heads of families, left behind their progeny, bequeathed to posterity their accomplishments and their influence. Slavic blood flows today as yesterday in the veins of those whose ancestors came from their native land to Texas.

Galveston and Houston, when the early Czech settlers first set foot on Texas soil, were but straggling villages. Galveston was not even a safe port for a schooner, and Houston was far removed from the realization of the present $12,000,000 ship channel and port-of-entry for the ocean-going vessels that line her docks today.

The total cotton production in those pioneer days was hauled by ox-team to Old Mexico to be sold. The great sulphur industry and the Texas oil fields were then but buried treasure, awaiting the hand of the pioneer to be discovered and developed.

Coronado sought the fabled cities of Cibola. Other intrepid pioneers, among them the Czech immigrants, discovered, centuries later, the fields of liquid gold and built therefrom magic cities equal, it may be, to the "Seven Cities of Cibola" of which Coronado dreamed.

From the records of the New Orleans Cotton Exchange, covering a period of one hundred years, it is interesting to take account as of the varying prices of cotton. For the year 1842, using good middling as the base, cotton was quoted at 4½ cents per pound. In 1844 the price was 4¾, and in 1898 the quotation was 4¾. Houston records for this same year, 1898, gave the price as being 4⅝, showing a correspondingly similar price at both points in this year. In the record of the New Orleans Cotton Exchange covering the period of one hundred years, there was a notation that no record was available for the year 1860, but for 1863-4 cotton sold for as high as $1.80 per pound, the low being 52½ cents. In 1865 the price went up to $1.90 per pound and the low was 30 cents per pound.

The United States Government crop report for Texas, issued in May, 1932, gave the total acreage planted to cotton in Texas for 1931 as being 15,769,800, with 15,469,000 acres of this picked. The cotton acreage for the State in 1932 was considerably less than these figures for the previous year.

Taking this by way of comparison of the present with the past of seventy-five and one hundred years ago, interesting deductions with regard to progress and development are to be had. Texas produced in the year 1870 only 400,000 bales of cotton.

Those first settlers, the pioneers of Texas, when they had cleared the land and planted the cotton crop by hand, proceeded with the work of cultivation in the primitive fashion, getting down on hands and knees to pull weeds from the tender young plants and again using the hoe and the ox-drawn plow.

The Czech immigrants loved the soil. It was their first interest. To own some of it, to cultivate it and enjoy the profit of the yield, was not a purely mercenary urge. Rather it was the inborn love of home and freedom, the desire for progress.

To Czech pioneers belong, in large measure, credit for the possibility and reality of the millions of bales of Texas grown cotton that are exported each year. The Czech immigrant even before he had emigrated, had heard of the fertility of Texas soil. He had brought with him to the new country the desire to own land and cultivate it. The sight of the vast expanse of untilled acres when he set foot on Texas soil was indeed an inspiration. The possession of one tract of land brought the potent urge to add to it. Always as the story of the Czech pioneer unfolds there is the mention that he bought land, and that after a time he bought more land, and so on until he was a substantial land-owner and finally a developer of the State.

First the soil had to be wrested from the grip of the wilderness, then planted, cultivated and the crops gathered. Families were reared, new homes established. Schools and churches were started and with them came culture of mind and the development of the social and economic life of the communities. From the rural school the footprints of children blazed the trail to the urban academy and college, and thence on to the universities of the country. Ere many decades had passed there was a new generation, for, as the poet has written, "Where the soil is men grow." To these words he added in the same couplet, "Either to weeds or flowers," and from the result of the millions of bales of Texas cotton shipped into the great markets of the world, it would appear that it was not weeds that grew on Texas acres.

In the effort to record the history of these noble Czech pioneers, and that of their posterity, it is the achievement, the splendid influence of their lives, that seems all important. To each son and daughter of these pioneers and to those who have even a trace of the Slavic blood in their veins, the history belongs. And so, likewise, belongs credit for the Century of Progress in Texas.

It has been written that Texas should have monuments for its lusty fighters and patriots. It has been suggested that when Texas gets civilized enough to appreciate her heritage some sculptor will carve out fitting memorials to these illustrious ones. And then the question may arise as to what will be deemed a fitting tribute.

More than two thousand stone monuments extend in rows across the Breton country. Modern scientists are puzzled to know why they are there and who erected them. Some say as they delve into the centuries that these megaliths may have been set up by the Celtic civilization of sun-worshipers.

Tree rings tell their story better. They have been made to solve ancient mysteries and the Indian ruins of the great Southwest reveal tense dramas in the lives of prehistoric man. But withal, the theory of the giant stone megaliths in the land of Brittany, the making of the wooden calendar from the tree rings, or the Indian ruins, telling of prehistoric times—is it enough?

We would choose to do better than these by way of marking a century of progress made possible through the lives of the pioneers and their descendants. To weave into its noble design not only that which is tangible as marble and stone to the touch, but rather the spirit that lived in the pioneers, and still lives in Texas today in their children, even to the third and fourth generation. Weave in, too, that courage which gave them strength to bury their dead in unmarked graves, and still not falter in the tasks confronting them. And along with this courage weave in the life stories of these heroic pioneers, then add to the whole the spirit of the present to which hundreds of thousands of Texas-Czechs are contributing service, loyalty and zeal. If it were possible to turn back the hands of the clock for one hundred years, to get the actual facts as they were woven into the fabric of history, details would not crowd in on the subject. Instead there would be seen the colonists attracted by the liberal provision of the colonization laws of the country, presenting themselves for admission.

Following in the lead of these early settlers as the land was granted and surveyed, the trail would lead on to other developments which reach down through the years to the present. It is the truth of the beginning that makes all romance appear cheap. It is the actual facts that have contributed to history that offer the thrill.

In the new country labor had to be performed. The symbols of early character were the rifle, the axe and the saddlebag. Three things of which George Washington wrote in 1776 as prompting men to the regular discharge of their duty—natural bravery, the hope of reward and the fear of punishment were not the requisites for those first Czech pioneers to perform their duty, but instead it was for love of home and country that they carried on even in the face of great difficulty and distress.

As in the past, so in the long vista of the years to come, we will not see the honor of Texas fade, but instead the flowers will bloom more brightly where these dead heroes sleep, and the dawn will come and the day will end, leaving in the space other footprints of progress carrying on that trail first blazed a century ago.

CHAPTER II

Looking Backward—Czechoslovakia

Scientists have for years been on the trail of the first man. The written pages of history failed to hold the information which they sought. But buried far beneath the debris of the ages they seek and hope to find what this first man was like.

Before there was a language, so claims science, primitive man existed. When he haltingly stammered the first articulate words of the human tongue the sounds that came led to the creation of language which has been responsible for written history.

While these men of science are digging today after the primeval, the prehistoric, it is interesting to turn the written pages of history in recreating a background for the present.

We know too little of the small European nations set back from the coast and off the beaten tourist track.

The Republic of Czechoslovakia is today an independent nation of Central Europe, incorporating within its boundaries Bohemia, Moravia and Silisia of old Austria; Slovakia of old Hungary, and the autonomous territory of Carpathian Ruthenia. It is bounded on the north by Germany and Poland; on the west by Germany; on the south by Austria, Hungary and Roumania. It converges at the tip on the east where it projects into Roumania.

At the time the World War ended there appeared upon the stage of Central Europe the new Czechoslovakia. The territory occupied by this new republic had up until that time been a constituent part of the Austria-Hungarian Empire.

The new Czechoslovakia embraces about 55,000 square miles of territory which may be said to equal in size the combined areas of Maryland, Virginia and Massachusetts. In population it ranks tenth among the nations of Europe. Its population is estimated at 14,500,000 or about the same as the combined States of Alabama, California, Indiana, Maryland, Kansas and Iowa.

Years ago T. G. Masaryk, then a prominent Bohemian deputy, today the President of the Republic of Czechoslovakia, said: "A nation as vigorous and virile as our Bohemian Nation is bound, if persecuted, to seek new outlets for some of its surplus energy, and if while this process is going on we succeed in reclaiming some

6

of the ground that has been wrested from our forefathers, it is the law of compensation."

The earliest history of the Slavic nations is enveloped in a darkness which the investigations of diligent and sagacious historians and philologians have not been able to penetrate. The analogy between their language and the Sanscrit seems to indicate that their origin was from India, but to definitely state the time at which they first entered Europe has been impossible. It is estimated, however, to have been seven or eight centuries before the Christian Era. Because of the over-population of the Ganges, Heroditus mentioned a people he called "Krovyzi," who lived on the Ister. Strabo, Pliny and other classical writers, as well as several Oriental historians, occasionally alluded to the Slavic nations.

The first distinct intelligence does not seem to be older than the middle of the sixth century. From this time they are traversing the Danube in multitudes, settling on both banks of the river. They are frequently mentioned by Byzantine historians as allies, sometimes as conquerors, but chiefly as emigrants or colonists thrust out of their own countries by the pressure of the more warlike Germans or Teutons. The name Slavi, derived from "Slava," means "glory." Slovo means "word," or "speech."

In the course of the years the Slavic nations took specific names, as, for instance, Russians, Poles, Silesians, Czechs, Moravians. Early historians sometimes spelled it "Czekh." The earliest Slavic historian, Nestor, was a Russian monk, born in 1056.

It has been recorded that wherever the Slavic people established themselves, they began to cultivate the earth and to trade in the productions of the country. The early cultivation of language belongs to the Slavic nations. It has been set forth by these early writers that in the second half of the eleventh century no people on the globe, with the exception of the Arabs, had extended themselves so far. The earliest data on the Slavic race is found in their own mythology. The practice of females in burning themselves with the corpses of their husbands seems to have been brought from India.

Among the popular songs of the Bohemians and Serbians and Russians are to be found some derived from the pagan period; these, however, being preserved through tradition, have naturally undergone changes as the language has changed.

A single circumstance, such as that of the Bible translation into the Slavic language by Cyril, serves as an illustration. That language was evidently the expression of thinking men through the centuries.   Dobrovsky of Praha, the Bohemian Abbott, examined the opinions of his predecessors with more exactness and erudition and investigated the differences of Slavic dialects more deeply, it is claimed, than any other philologist, and was of the opinion that no language in the world will resist the influence of its neighbors.   He was of the opinion that the Serbian, Bulgarian, and Macedonian dialects of the Slavs in Thessalonica, the birthplace of the two Slavic apostles, Cyril and Methodius, was the old Slavic in which Dobrovsky counted 1605 radical syllables.   Schloyer, historian and linguist, observed that among all modern languages the Slavonic (Old Slavic) was one of those most fully developed.   Its model was the Greek language in the days when Greece was the most cultivated nation in the world.

The alphabet as arranged by Cyril (Constantine) is founded on the Greek-Thessalonica alphabet at the time of the Romans. The brothers, Cyril and Methodius, were born of a noble family in a country inhabited by many Slavs.

Through the centuries that have gone into the making of the country of the Czechs, there have been crises through which the people passed on to other epochs, each leaving in its wake lasting impressions, but through different periods every phase of existence has been represented.

The historian has by way of preface to the story mentioned that there was no written history of Bohemia during these early centuries—that what is known comes by legend and tradition, both colorful and gripping mediums for the transmission of the things that have to do with a mystic past.

Going back yet a few centuries earlier, the student will encounter in reading of Caesar's Gallic wars mention of the "Boings," said to have been esteemed highly for their valor. The name "Boii" means "brave warrior." These Boings came formerly from across the Rhine and had passed over and settled in Noricum, possessed themselves of Norei, the capital, and were associated with the Helveitians in the design to gain entire sovereignty of Gaul. At the request of the Aeduans they had settled with them in the territory, where they were given lands and admitted to all rights and privileges. In a roll which Caesar had from the camp of the Helveitians, enumerating the tribes of the country, the number of the Boings was placed at 32,000.

Passing along to the later centuries, the coming of Saints Cyril and Methodius, bringing Christianity, is recorded. Then Jan Žižka of Troconov, the great military leader of 1417, is encountered, to be succeeded by other epochal eras, which include the Hussite Wars, following the death of King Vaclav in 1419, and the Battle of White Mountain in 1620, when the imperial troops of Ferdinand II defeated the rebel army of Bohemia. At an earlier date, 1040, Henry II of Germany had met defeat while trying to invade Bohemia. The "Robota" requiring enforced personal service, was the cause of the revolution of 1040. A patent issued by Emperor Joseph in March, 1848, freed the peasants from all obligations of this kind, which had to do with service rendered to feudal landlords.

Looking backward, gathering material from these early chroniclers, some slight discrepancies may appear, but it is conceded that the Czechs have inhabited what has been known as Bohemia and Moravia as early as the beginning of the Christian Era. Samo, a Czech chieftain in the middle of the seventh century, invaded adjacent territory, defeating the Avars and the Franks in two decisive battles, thereby establishing a kingdom which included the Slovaks, who at that time seem to have covered the greater part of the Danubian Plain.

In the course of the fifth and seventh centuries, there were in the present territory of the Czechs, known in English as Bohemia, a Slavonic people differing from the previous inhabitants who were of Gaelic origin, because of the fact that they burned their dead. Prehistoric graves in Central Europe tell of cremation that is ascribed to the Slavs.

"Czechoslovakia" is popularly believed to be a term invented in 1918 to describe the newly-formed republic, but the inhabitants of the territory now included in the republic were referred to as "Czechoslavs" by Šafařik as early as 1818, and even before this.

A "Českoslovenka Gramatyka," (Czechoslovak Grammar) was published at Bratislava in 1805. The Slovak poet, Tablic, translated a collection of English poems into the "Czechoslovak" in 1831.

Since the beginning of the nineteenth century the Czechs and Slovaks together have been referred to as Czechoslovaks and thus Czechoslovakia was the most appropriate title for the new state, which united the ancient Kingdom of Bohemia, inhabited by the Czechs, to Slovakia, inhabited by the Slovaks.

Passing now from the abundant traditions of the early centuries of these people, whom historians of the period designated as Bohemians, we find them increasing in influence, with educa-

tional interest never waning, their political ideals held fast, and ever industrially progressive.*
And so in 1934 we find the young republic on the frontiers of Europe.

Today the Czechoslovak Republic, which was established by the Peace Treaties as one of the succession of states of the late Austro-Hungarian Monarchy, consisting of five parts, Bohemia, Moravia, Silisia, Slovakia and Carpathian Ruthenia, has sprung Phœnix-like, not from dead ashes, but from the live and burning coals of undying love of country.

The Czechoslovakian Constitution is interesting, as showing the spirit in which the republic regards responsibilities, for instance:

"We, the Czechoslovak Nation, desiring to consolidate the perfect unity of our people, to establish the reign of justice in the Republic, to assure the peaceful development of our native Czechoslovak land, to contribute to the common welfare of all citizens of this state and to secure the blessings of freedom to coming generations, have in our National Assembly this twenty-ninth day of February, 1920, adopted the following Constitution for the Czechoslovak Republic; and, in so doing, we declare that it will be our endeavor to see that this Constitution, together with all the laws of our land, be carried out in the spirit of those modern principles embodied in the idea of self-determination, for we desire to take our place in the Family of Nations as a member at once cultured, peace-loving, democratic and progressive."

The economic reconstruction of Czechoslovakia provides a most interesting and instructive chapter in the industrial and commercial history of Europe, and holds also an important place in the affairs of America.

Rich in natural resources, strong in the valuable qualities of its citizenship, it is not strange that this young republic was the first country to emerge from the post-war chaos.

In the naming of epochs, the list is not complete without the "Masaryk epoch." Thomas G. Masaryk's name is vitally associated with the Czechoslovak Republic. This man has been likened to our own Washington, for he is called the "Father of His Country." Likened also to our Thomas Jefferson, because the Declaration of Independence was the work of his hands.

---

*Further information concerning early history of Czechoslovakia will be found in a speech by Judge Augustin Haidušek, reprinted in full in the Appendix.

Likened to our Abraham Lincoln, because he rose from the depths of obscurity to the pinnacle of popular adoration. His Excellency, Dr. Thomas G. Masaryk, elected by the popular consent of the people, President of the Republic of Czechoslovakia for life, married an American, the marriage taking place at Boston in 1878. His son also married an American girl, the daughter of Charles R. Crane, a close friend of President Woodrow Wilson.

The Declaration of Independence of the Republic of Czechoslovakia was drafted by Thomas G. Masaryk in our own national capital on October 18, 1918, and was first read by President Masaryk in the courtyard of the historic Independence Hall, Philadelphia.

Although the country occupies seventh place among European states in respect to density, with an average population of 248 per square mile, still it is far from being over-populated, especially Slovakia and Carpathian Ruthenia, where a future increase of population could easily be taken care of through the development of natural resources, according to Paul Einzig, Director of Political and Economic Sciences, University of Paris.

The country is rich in mineral waters whose curative effects have attracted hundreds of thousands of visitors from abroad. The fame of her watering places, Karlovy Vary (Carlsbad), Marianske Lazně, (Marienbad) and Františkovy Lazně (Franzenbad) reach far beyond the frontiers of Czechoslovakia and even beyond Europe.

Agriculture and forestry are of paramount importance in Slovakia and Carpathian Ruthenia, which are among the most richly-wooded territories of Europe. The arable land is forty-five per cent of the total area, which is slightly inferior to the proportion in France and Germany. The distribution of the arable land among by-products is: Rye, 17 per cent; potatoes, legumes and other vegetables, 15 per cent; oats, 15 per cent, and on through a variety of food products with the proportion of fallow land estimated at 7 per cent.

The country is in the favorable position of being able to produce the raw material for the greater part of its manufacturing industries. Sugar, alcohol, beer, porcelain, and glassware are among the exclusively Czechoslovak raw materials. Among the agricultural industries, that of sugar production occupies first place, there being approximately 186 factories in operation. Bohemian hops have an international reputation. Although the Czechoslovak beer brewing industry consumes every year about 30,000 to 40,000 tons of hops, there is a considerable surplus available for export.

The Republic of Czechoslovakia has 260 leather factories. The Bata Shoe manufactory, located at Zlin, is one of the largest in the universe. It has received world-wide publicity and recognition. Its founder, Thomas Bata, made a fortune in the business and, in achieving his own success, provided employment for hundreds of people and consumed the raw leather product of the republic, which helped not only to enrich the individual but the country as well. Bata shoes have been sold in Texas for a number of years, and Texas, before the sudden death by airplane accident, July 12, 1932, of the great shoeman, anticipated having a branch plant of the manufactory located in the state.

The quality of gloves made in Czechoslovakia gives them an excellent reputation.

The country possesses a great variety of metal resources. Its mountains contain iron, lead, tin, copper, uranium, antimony, graphite, zinc, gold and silver. The importance of these products, however, as well as that of kaolin and precious stones, is overshadowed by the coal production, which is one of the national assets. Czechoslovakia possesses the richest radium mines in the world. To Madam Curie is given the honor of having made the discovery of this very precious element in the republic.

The production of kaolin and quartz is the basis of the world-famed porcelain and glassware industries. Granite, limestone and cement are also produced in large quantities.

Of the precious stones, the Bohemian garnets and Slovakian opals are known abroad for their beauty.

The first railway on the continent of Europe, opened for public transportation in 1833, was the line from Česke Budejovice, in Bohemia, to Linz in upper Austria, the cars being drawn by horses. The idea was first advanced in 1813, but it took nineteen years to execute the idea and eight hundred horses to put the first railroad into operation. Steam power was substituted for horse-power in 1872. The railroads are state-owned.

In looking backward thus briefly into the history of Czechoslovakia, past and present, it is not hard to visualize the patriotism that engendered the spirit and the courage of those who fought for the independence of the country, not only in the World War, but throughout the centuries that have made the history of what we are pleased today to call the Republic of Czechoslovakia.

Czechoslovakia is an agricultural and industrial country, well harmonized. The agricultural population of the republic forms a sound basis for harmonious development in the economic, cultural and moral spheres.

The production of seeds in Czechoslovakia is regulated and protected by laws which enable the seed improvement establishments to develop freely. In many countries there is a great demand for Czechoslovakian red clover seed, famed for its great power of resistance against frost, and for the large amount of hay produced. The sugar beet seed industry is carried on in five large improvement stations which, during the last thirty years, have cultivated sugar beet seed equal to the best obtainable.

The economic capacity of the poorer areas is increased by the agricultural spirit-distilling industry. In the republic there are some 940 agricultural spirit distilleries, which make use mainly of potatoes, and 70 industrial spirit distilleries which make use mainly of molasses. Starch-making comes next to spirit-distilling, the most important industry in the hilly regions. Starch is made chiefly from potatoes, in some 140 plants and from cereals in six establishments. The largest demand for starch comes from highly-developed textile industries.

Czechoslovakia still has its flourishing folk-art. Especially is this distinctive industry carried on in the mountain districts, where many of the inhabitants earn their living by lace-making, embroidery, hand-weaving, pottery-making and the production of the large assortment of trinkets for which a world market has been developed.

The Czechoslovakia glass industry is filled with traditions which has made these products sought after all over the world.

In recounting and reciting these things about the Republic of Czechoslovakia, the thought carries the subject on to comparison with other countries and other peoples, and finally to the Czech immigrants who came to Texas with the centuries of all these things behind them. They brought with them seed from their native land to plant in virgin soil.

They brought with them their folk art, and their agricultural skill to put into the development of new homes. These which have been in process of development for centuries past together with their spirit, their courage and their genius, begotten under the varying tempos of the centuries, and preserved throughout the generations, they brought into the new country. So naturally it would come to pass that through looking backward into this land of Czechoslovakia inspiration would guide the vision forward into Texas where the Czech has played such an important part in the development and progress of the American Union's largest state.

CHAPTER III

TEXAS

Where Pioneers saw the many-million-acre land
Won from the desert by their hand,
Swiftly among the nations rise—
Texas a sovereign state,
And on her brow a star.

—HENRY VAN DYKE.

THE total population of Texas on April 1, 1930, was 5,824,715, comprising 2,965,994 males and 2,858,721 females. The total number of farms in Texas was 495,489, having a total acreage of 124,707,130, with a total value, including land, buildings, implements and machinery, of $3,779,593,795.

And so Texas is called "The Billion Dollar State."

When Texas declared its independence in 1836, the Congress of the new republic defined the territory as being bounded on the south by the Río Grande, and by a line running northward from the source of the Río Grande to the forty-second parallel of latitude, the northern and eastern boundaries coinciding with the western border of the United States as fixed by a treaty with Spain in 1819, and reaffirmed with Mexico January 12, 1828, at the time Mexico won her freedom from Spain.

This territory, in addition to covering all that which is now Texas, extended nearly half way across New Mexico and sent a long "panhandle" into Colorado to a point about one hundred miles northwest of Cheyenne, Wyoming. About 96,000 square miles of the Republic of Texas was formerly a part of the Louisiana Purchase, but had been ceded to Spain by the United States under the Treaty of 1819. Various surveys were made during the following years through boundary disputes. Texas, annoyed by so many changes in the position of the meridian, hired an astronomer in 1892 to fix it. He added a strip about a mile wide to the territory of the State as compared with the survey of 1859. In 1927 the Supreme Court took the matter in hand and ordered a final survey. This was finished in 1929 and the starting point was

14

found to be a mile east of the mark set in 1859. So now the boundary of Texas is officially described as:

"Beginning in the Gulf of Mexico at the outlet of the Sabine Lake, the line passes through the middle of Sabine Lake and up the middle of Sabine River to the point where the river intersects the parallel of 32 degrees; then along the meridian of that point northward to the point where the meridian intersects the Red River; then up the south bank of the Red River, along the south fork to the one hundredth meridian west of Greenwich; thence north on that meridian to the parallel of 36 degrees 30 minutes; west on that parallel to the meridian of 103 degrees as marked; then south along the meridian to the parallel of latitude 32 degrees; thence west on that parallel to its point of intersection with the Río Grande; thence down the mid-channel of the Río Grande to the boundary line between the United States and Mexico; thence following that line to the Gulf of Mexico."

The area of Texas within this boundary is 265,896 square miles, 262,398 of which are land and 3,498 are water, making the state the largest in land area and only surpassed by Florida and North Carolina in water area.

The exact geographical center of Texas is fifteen miles northeast of Brady in McCullough County. The highest point is El Capitan, 8700 feet above sea level in Culberson County. The lowest is, naturally, the Gulf of Mexico.

On an old Texas map, drawn about 1810, not a single town or settlement in Texas appears as it is known today.

San Fernando de Béxar is now known as San Antonio; La Bahía is today the old town of Goliad. Texas as a whole was referred to as the "New Philippines." It has been estimated that if the land of Texas was divided among every male citizen in the United States, each would have an acre and a half.

President Anson Jones of the Republic of Texas, on the occasion of his valedictory address at Austin, February 19, 1846, said:

"Industry and enterprise have received new impulse. A market is found at home for nearly everything our citizens have to dispose of and a large and very desirable immigration to the country is now taking place."

On the delivery of this address the cannon proclaimed the admission of Texas into the Union, the flag of the United States was unfurled and the Republic of Texas was no more.

The story of the annexation of Texas to the United States of America covers a decade of history, that period comprising the historical years between 1836 and 1846 when annexation was finally effected.

Old records and papers and public letters of state, give dramatic accounts of how statesmen and patriots carried on through these years, the work of settling all questions that arose in connection with the making of a satisfactory Treaty of Annexation.

President Tyler, zealous in the cause of Texas, is accredited with having felt at the time the necessity of reorganizing his Cabinet, and in 1843 asked Mr. Upshur of Georgia to occupy the place held by Daniel Webster as Secretary of State. The sudden death of Upshur in February, 1844, on the steamer *Princeton,* led to the appointment of John C. Calhoun of South Carolina as Secretary of State, and so negotiations for annexation were promptly renewed.

In the letters and public documents of Calhoun, considerable publicity was given to the account of how the British government stood ready to throw its protecting shield over the harassed and embarrassed Republic of Texas.

The question of slavery was of considerable importance from the British conception. The abolishment of slavery was the desire of Great Britain, according to these old letters and whether or not, according to the principles of international law, a nation had the right to interfere with the domestic relations of another country, no matter what might be the motives in this instance it brought about on the part of the United States a more intensive exertion to consummate the treaty of annexation.

In the Treaty of Annexation that was finally adopted, signed and ratified with the sanction of both governments, Texas went into the Union retaining all her vacant and unappropriated land. A summary of the public lands of Texas at this time, as included in a report of the Commissioner of the General Land Office to the President of the Republic of Texas, is of interest:

	Acres.
The aggregate estimate was	203,520,000
Lands appropriated	67,408,673
Remainder unappropriated	136,111,327

In a report of a committee of the House of Representatives of the Congress of Texas, made to that body on January 12, 1841, the debt and liabilities of the republic were as follows:

Funded debt, bearing 10 per cent interest____$1,650,000

Bonds sold and pledged, bearing 10 per cent
    interest _____$1,350,000
Treasury notes without interest _____ 3,000,000
Debts of various description, say, audited
    drafts and other claims without interest__ 1,000,000

            Total debt _____$7,000,000

The revenues of the government following this statement, had nearly equalled the expenditures so that the debt had not materially increased, except for the interest that had accrued. The Treaty of Annexation in joint session of the Senate and House of Representatives of the United States of America in Congress assembled, resolved that Congress agreed that the territory properly included within and rightfully belonging to the Republic of Texas, "may be erected into a new State to be called the State of Texas, with a republican form of government to be adopted by the people of the said republic, by deputies in convention assembled, with the consent of the existing government in order that the same may be admitted as one of the States of this Union.

"And be it further resolved: That the foregoing consent of Congress is given upon the following conditions and with the following guarantee, to-wit: 'This had to do with the settling of boundary, proper adoption of a Constitution by the people of the Republic, same to be transmitted to the President of the United States to be laid before Congress for final action.' "

The third item of resolution has been through the years a subject of speculation and discussion, and this had to do with dividing the state.

"New states of convenient size not exceeding four in number, in addition to said State of Texas, and having sufficient population, may hereafter, by the consent of said State, be formed out of the territory thereof, which shall be entitled to admission, under the provisions of the Federal Constitution. And such states as may be formed out of that portion of said territory lying south of 36 degrees, 30 minutes north latitude, commonly known as the Missouri Compromise line, shall be admitted into the Union, with or without slavery, as the people of each state asking admission may desire."

Those who came to settle in Texas did so to improve, cultivate and render productive, wild and almost uninhabited wastes; and to make valuable that which before was worthless. All this was effected at a heavy cost and with great danger and difficulty.

It is of interest in looking backward to note that the people of Texas were not agriculturalists in the early days. The Indians kept up a constant warfare. At the end of the French regime in Louisiana, 1803, there were only three settlements in Texas— San Antonio de Béxar, the presidio of Bahia del Espiditue Santo and the pueblo of Nacogdoches. The population of Béxar at the time was 2500, Bahía 618, Nacogdoches 770, with other settlers at the various missions, making a total of 4000 civilized persons in Texas. Slight attention was paid to the cultivation of the soil. Starvation was warded off on occasions by the use of wild-horse meat.

When the United States took possession of Louisiana by purchase in December, 1803, interest in the colonization of Texas grew, especially in view of Napoleon's plan for world conquest. The way to defend Texas was to develop it into a strong province through the introduction of settlers.

In 1808, Napoleon by the cession of Bayonne, had gained complete ascendency over Charles IV and King Ferdinand VII and secured from them title to the throne of Spain and the Indies under pretext of settling family dissensions and establishing order in the revolution-harassed domain. It is recalled that he took steps to make his brother Joseph King of Spain, sending emissaries to America to announce the change.

Under these circumstances Texas was one of the most vital spots in the Spanish Dominion of America. It was during the year 1809, owing to rumors of the greater activity on the part of the United States and Napoleon, that instructions for closing the door to European immigration from foreign countries was given. It was feared that Napoleon would introduce emissaries in the guise of settlers. Again when the United States declared war on Great Britain in 1811, the Spaniards became alarmed and proceeded to guard zealously the Texas frontier.

New Orleans was prepared for defense. President Madison had sent a message to Congress dealing with the revolt of the Spanish-American provinces. The fall of Bahía and Béxar came in 1813. Texas was in a deplorable condition. The fields were untilled and yielded not a "tortilla."

A lone star in a field of blue joined in a field equally divided between red and white—the Texas Flag.

Behind the evolution of the flags that have flown over the state of Texas lies history which in many respects is without parallel. Romance, patriotism and sentiment are crowded into the record. Texas under six flags has been the theme for both song and story, and some day there will be one who will write a great history, the pages of which will recount the whole as a magnificent drama—a drama in which the nations of the world will play the leading rôles. The curtain will rise and fall even as did the flags, and the acts of the drama will comprise the history of the great Empire State of the Southwest.

In 1684 Texas was claimed by right of discovery by Spain and the Spanish flag of King Charles II was raised.

With the first colonization, when Robert de la Salle entered Matagorda Bay in January, 1685, he took possession in the name of his king, Louis XIV of France, planted the French flag, built a fort, a small church, and sowed a crop for the families and animals he had brought with him.

Two years later the Spanish governor of Coahuila came and found no trace of the French. Thus ended the first attempt at a European settlement. And the Mexican flag flew over the domain. When the Spanish colonies in America threw off the yoke of the mother country over a period of years, 1810-21 to 1846, it was an independent Republic, and then flew the Lone Star Flag. When Texas joined the United States as a sovereign state, she raised the Stars and Stripes. When she seceded in 1861, and during the years of the war between the north and the south, 1861-65, the flag of the Confederate States floated over the state. Since Texas has been under the "Stars and Stripes," and because of this, seven flags have been at times claimed for the state.

It is recorded among the legends and traditions in which Texas is indeed rich, that an Indian Chief told General Sam Houston with regard to the name "Texas," that when the Spaniards over-ran Mexico, the Indians crossed the Río Grande and traveled eastward through the salt-marshes until they reached the Colorado and found it a beautiful stream. Beyond the stream they saw a country dotted with trees whereupon the Indians in their joy cried out, "Tehas." "Tehas," according to the old chief, meant "paradise."

All public lands in Texas belonged to the State, being sold for fifty cents per acre through the issuance of "script," the land going to settlers under the term of "headrights" during first days of settlement.

After the close of the Civil War, it was estimated that Texas had about 120,000,000 acres. This land began to attract the attention of capitalists and schemes were soon in operation to acquire large tracts of the land. In the Sixteenth Legislature patriotic members are accredited with having opposed the opening of the doors to these outsiders. The "Patriots" succeeded in passing a law setting apart one-half of the "Public Domain" for educational purposes. Subsequently, this law was broken down and lands sold for fifty cents an acre, as originally prescribed.

An Act of the Legislature, supplementing an Act of March, 1848, entitled "Better defining the marital rights of parties," was placed on the statute. "Be it resolved by the Legislature of the State of Texas, that the common property of the husband and wife shall be liable for all debts contracted during marriage except such cases as are especially excepted by law, and in settlement of community estates it shall be the duty of the survivor, executor, or administrator, to keep separate and distinct account of all community debts allowed to be paid in the settlement of such estates."

It is also interesting to know that the "Homestead Law" originated in Texas. It was passed by the Congress of the Republic of Texas. From this act has sprung the American system of homesteads. All states in the Union have since passed some law to protect the home to the family. Texas exemptions of property from forced sale include the following: The homestead, household and kitchen furniture, lots in cemetery, implements of husbandry, tools, apparatus and books belonging to any professions, library and portraits of family. Also five milch cows and calves, two yokes of oxen, with yoke and chains; two horses or mules and one wagon; one gun; one carriage or buggy; twenty head of sheep; all saddles, bridles or harness for family use; all provisions and forage on hand for family consumption; all current wages for personal services. The proceeds from the sale of the homestead are not subject to garnishment or forced sale within six months after sale. Limitation judgment of ten years; promissory notes, four years; open accounts, two years.

An amendment to the Constitution to exempt Texas homesteads valued at $3,000 or less from taxation, was voted on by the people of the State, in the November election of 1932. This exemption is intended to encourage home ownership in Texas. The vote ratifying the homestead exemption amendment gave Texas the distinction of being the first state in the world to adopt a constitutional amendment of this character.

Going back to the early efforts to wrest Texas from Mexico, it is a matter of historical record that Louisiana was ceded by France to Spain in 1762 and restored to the former power in 1800. Three years later it was ceded by France to the United

States. In none of these cessions were there any specifications of boundary. The territory was a vast undefined region east of the Mississippi; and with rare exceptions untenanted by civilized inhabitants. It of course adjoined the Spanish domain of Mexico, but the dividing line could not easily be ascertained. As the American settlements in Louisiana extended, the question of boundary necessarily became a matter of discussion between governments of Spain and the United States. This question was finally settled in 1819 by a treaty with Spain in which the contracting powers ceded to each other all claims to territory beyond their respective sides of a defined line.

In 1820 the State of Missouri, formed out of the Louisiana territory, was admitted into the Union as a slave state. To facilitate its admission, and to overcome the formidable opposition of the Northern States to the incorporation into the Confederacy of another slave-holding state, the slave-holders proposed and effected the celebrated Missouri compromise, a law declaring that in future slavery should be prohibited north of 36° 30″ north latitude.

It was not long, however, before it was discovered that this Missouri compromise, together with the southern boundary of the United States, as defined in the Spanish treaty of 1819, had reduced within comparatively narrow limits the area from which slave states might thereafter be formed. With the exception of Florida, the territory south of the Missouri compromise line was not sufficient for more than two states.

The State of Louisiana was separated from the Spanish province of Texas by the Sabine River and the soil, climate, and position of that province rendered it a desirable acquisition to slave-holding interests.

The plan of colonization was adopted with Moses Austin of Missouri obtaining in 1821 permission from Spanish authorities to introduce three hundred families into Texas on certain conditions. The permission was granted, as is recorded, on the representation of Austin that Catholics were oppressed in the United States, and it was agreed that all settlers to be introduced by him should be of the oppressed religion. Austin dying, the grant was in 1823 renewed to his son Stephen F. Austin, who commenced a colony on the Brazos River with emigrants from Tennessee, Mississippi and Louisiana. By the renewed grant the settlers were to be exclusively Catholics.

In 1826 a body of immigrants from the United States settled near what is now Nacogdoches, and again there was a declaration of independence, but this was crushed by the Mexican forces. The first attempt at settlement had been at this same place as early as 1819, when James Long had come from Natchez, Mississippi, with about seventy-five people.

The independence of Texas fluctuated from one point to another. Hopes of acquiring the province by purchase were abandoned in the process of elimination of plans and measures. President Andrew Jackson had authorized the offer of five million dollars for the purchase of Texas in 1829. Rumors had previously been afloat that the province was to be placed under protection of Great Britain.

About this time Mr. Samuel Houston of Tennessee made known his intention of coming to Texas. He was at the time organizing an expedition with recruits from the United States and his plans had been communicated to President Jackson. Of this expedition a Louisiana newspaper announced that Houston had gone to Texas, the editor adding: "We may expect shortly to hear of his raising his flag."

On May 10, 1836, General Gaines of the United States military forces transmitted to the President of the United States the news of the victory of the Texans at San Jacinto. He indulged the anticipation that it would some day be a magnificent acquisition to the Union.

In 1846, Mexico declared war on the United States. After the few eventful and stormy years of existence as a Republic, Texas had been added to the Union. The Mexicans who had been camped at Matamoros, exchanging epithets with General Zachary Taylor's men at Brownsville, just across the river, were let loose by orders from Mexico City. Almost before they knew what was happening, they were soundly thrashed at Palo Alto and Resaca de la Palma.

The war had been expected, but it came so suddenly that Washington was rather taken by surprise. Arrangements had not been altogether perfected and there had been at this time certain conditions not unlike those experienced in 1916 when Major General Funston and Brigadier General John J. Pershing entered Mexico at the identical spot where, in 1846, Colonel Doniphan and his troopers from Missouri had crossed the Río Grande. Here, however, progress had changed the situation, and the generals of the later invasion had rapid fire guns, rifles that would carry a mile. They had airplanes to locate the enemy, and railroads and automobile trucks to carry water and commissary supplies; also the telegraph, telephone and wireless to keep them in touch with their base, with each other and with Washington. Those other generals eighty-six years before had to operate with so-called "pop-gun" cannons and rifles that carried only a quarter of a mile. Ox-teams carried their supplies, and only a rainstorm putting in prompt and opportune appearance could save them from dying of thirst in a desert section of the country. Lack of communication left them without word of advice or endorsement from their own government at Washington.

Looking thus backward through the pages of this early history we move in a circle to the present when Texas, with her five hundred thousand Czech citizens, has left behind these years of struggle and suffering in the new country, to take part in making new progress by way of modern invasion into new industry.

One hundred years ago Mary Austin Holly, cousin of Stephen F. Austin, wrote the first book ever printed in English about Texas. She classified Texas at the time as "Terra Incognito."

The book was written while she was a member of the Stephen F. Austin Colony at Bolivar, its purpose being to inform the people of the United States and England what life was like in this then unknown territory designated as the "Southwest." The book also set forth the possibilities the land held out to colonists from the United States and Europe.

The book presents a weird and at the same time comprehensive picture of the pioneer life of these first colonists and is today one of the most prized items in all the hundreds of books and pamphlets that have been written on Texas.

This first writer of Texas history wrote successfully and lastingly because—shall we say?—she was a woman and intuitively grasped conditions. She realized the value of detail and envisioned also the great possibilities of the then unknown southwest. She has left to posterity the story of Texas as she saw and lived it.

The wonderful possibilities recounted by Mary Austin Holly one hundred years ago have become the realities of today. The Czech settlers accepted these possibilities and called them opportunities and have caused to be brought forth greater results therefrom than were ever dreamed of a century ago—results that stand like milestones along the great highway of progress that stretches throughout the vast area of Texas.

In 1881 the Texas State Capitol burned and a session of the Legislature designated as "Extraordinary," was called for the purpose of providing a new building. By an Act of the Legislature in 1879, 3,000,000 acres of land in Northwest Texas had been set aside for the purpose of building a State Capitol. The new building was begun in 1886 and completed in 1888 and immediately took rank as one of the largest and handsomest state buildings in the whole of the United States. The material from which the building was constructed came from Texas quarries and Texas forests. The passing of the half century since the completion of the building has made for more progress and development.

Judge Augustin Haidušek, Czech pioneer, was a member of the Texas Legislature when the three million dollar state capitol building was authorized for Texas. There will doubtless be other Czech representatives in the Texas Legislature when the time arrives to build a new state capitol.

It is interesting to note that before the establishing of a general land office in Texas the archives had to be kept in seven different communities, these, according to the records being San Patricio, Nacogdoches, San Felipe, San Felipe de Béxar, Liberty, Refugio, and Viesca, the latter settlement being in Falls County.

The old Texas Land Office Building in Austin was erected in 1853, occupying the southeast corner of the State Capitol grounds. When the State Office Building was completed in 1919, the Land Office and Archives were moved into this building, occupying the entire fourth floor.

The old Land Office Building is maintained as a State Museum, the Daughters of the Texas Republic using the second floor and the Daughters of the Confederacy the ground floor. Valuable historical relics of both the Republic of Texas and the Confederacy form a part of the two museum collections. William Sidney Porter, better known as "O. Henry," short story writer of worldwide fame, worked in the old Land Office Building in the draughting department, in 1887. On many of the old maps will be found pen sketches he made on the margin after he had completed the making of the map.

The Bloodless Battle, as the incident is designated, is one among the interesting events taking place in the course of the making of Texas history. This battle without bloodshed took place in 1842 on the occasion of the attempt to transfer the records from Austin to Houston. It followed the invasion of General Vaquez with 1,200 Mexican troops into San Antonio. President Houston having been apprised of the invasion by refugees from San Antonio, eighty-three miles to the south, removed the seat of government from Austin to Houston. In the haste of departure, the archives of the Land Office were left behind.

Some months later President Houston sent agents to transport these to Houston. According to the story, the citizens, about fifty families of Austin, enraged at being, as they thought, deserted, refused to surrender the archives. Again President Houston sent an armed force to secure the documents, and on a cold December day while residents of Austin were sitting by the warmth of their home fires, the records were hastily loaded on three wagons and the departure stealthily made. Before nightfall, however, the wagons were overtaken by pursuing citizens and the documents recovered without bloodshed.

So it became known as the "bloodless battle."

CHAPTER IV

Who Was the First?

Who was the first?

He was a valiant man, whoever he may have been, to bring the blood of his illustrious race into the wilds of the vast land we know today as Texas. His name, we fear, may be lost in those annals of the past, buried in the onward rush of time.

William Pača, one of the signers of the Declaration of Independence, and a member of the Maryland Convention that ratified the Constitution of the United States, was of Czech ancestry. He was born at the paternal manor on the eastern shore of Maryland in 1740, his parents having presumably come from England, where many of the Czechs migrated in the course of centuries of unrest in their own country.

The Pača family was eminent in Maryland through several generations, distinguished for the good use of their wealth and influence. The family supported, prominently and honorably, the affairs of state and country.

Maryland, as the history of the times reveals, did not want to declare her independence and refused to be bound by a vote of majority of Congress, making strong profession of affection and loyalty toward King George and the mother country. When, however, the delegates were left free to vote without restrictions, Mr. Pača cast his vote in favor of independence and subscribed his name to the Declaration.

John Wesley, whom Georgia claims as one of her most illustrious pioneers, was, it is said, of Czech descent. His name passed through various changes, having been originally spelled "Vesely," even as the small Texas town first named Vesely was finally spelled Wesley.

As these two, the great statesman and the religious reformer are found in the list of those among the first, so others might be added.

August Heřman, one of the first Czech emigrants to America, made the first map of Maryland, copies of which are preserved in the archives at Richmond, Virginia.

26

Upper Left:
JOSEPH L. LEŠIKAR

Top Center:
House built by Mr. Lešikar in
1856, near New Ulm (New
Bremen Settlement), Texas.

Upper Right:
JOSEPH PETER
and his Pioneer Home,
High Hill, Texas.

Lower:
Front and side view of the
Peter pioneer home.

It has been generally conceded that Dr. Anthony M. Dignowity was the first Czech to come to Texas.

As recent as 1932 there have come to Texas official letters of inquiry as to the life and history of one of the early settlers, Arnošt Bergman. He was in Texas, according to the meagre records at hand, as early as 1848. Honorable Wenzel Matejowski, born in Nechanitz, Bohemia, in 1829, came to Texas in 1850, landing at Galveston.

First settlers of Praha, Fayette County, came in the early fifties, and the names of these include a Mr. Novak, F. Branitzy, Joseph Vyvjala, George Morysek, Joseph Hajek, a Mr. Jareš, John Bača, and are perpetuated in the families that have descended. Tom Batla settled at Fayetteville in 1853, Vinc Rypl in 1854, both coming from Bohemia to Texas. Josef, Jan and Pavel Wychopeň, Josef Laštovica, Josef Ječmenek, Paul Ječmenek and Josef Hlavaty, came from Moravia to Fayetteville in 1855. John Hruška, John Odloželik, Frank Horak immigrated to Fayetteville in 1856. And so it may be found all through the early years of the settlement of Texas that Czech pioneers took prominent places in the affairs of state and community development.

Other early Texas-Czech settlers included:

Karel Joseph Rypl, born 1824 in Zlomu near Landškron, Čechy. Came to Texas in 1854, died in Wesley 1877.

Jan Baletka, born 1825 in Ratiboři, Moravia. Came to Texas in 1855, died in Wesley 1894.

Jiři Chupik, born May 7, 1815, in Hoštalkově, Moravia. Came to Texas in 1856. Died in Wesley September 30, 1881.

Arnošt Schuerer, son-in-law of Reverend Opočensky, born June 24, 1832, in Schneeberg, Silisia. Came to Texas 1854, died at Wesley February 5, 1895.

Josef Ježek, born February 2, 1817, in Čermne, by Landškron. Came to Texas 1854. Died November 23, 1898, at Caldwell, Burleson County.

Frank Šebesta, born December 23, 1826, in Lipě by Vyzovic. Came with his brother Pavel to Texas in 1856.

Jiři Pšenčik, born November 25, 1813, in Vyzovicich. Came to Texas in 1854. Died at Welcome, Austin County, July 9, 1887.

Pavel Šebesta from Zadueřic, near Vyzovic. Came to Texas in 1856.

Petr Mikeska, born 1811 in Zelechovicich, Moravia. Came to Texas in June, 1854. Died in Wesley, March 8, 1886.

Josef Skřivanek, born in Zelechovic by Vyzovic. Came to Texas in 1855. Died in Hallettsville, 1882.

These, along with many other names of Czech pioneers, are preserved for posterity. They had the strength and the genius to rise above circumstances of life, acquire knowledge, however opposed by difficulties, and to advance their station in life. Some achieved positions of affluence and eminent usefulness, and altogether they participated in the common affairs of the days of early settlement in Texas.

Josef Lešikar, who came to Texas with seventeen other families from eastern Moravia, from the sections of Vsetin and Vyzovic, in writing his memoirs, stated that he claimed for himself the distinction of being the instigator of emigration to Texas. As early as 1851, he wrote: "Sixteen families sailed from Hamburg for Texas." He explained in this connection, however, that the records for years before had been censored so that it would be difficult to say for a certainty just when the first immigrants had sailed for Texas.

The fate of the sixteen families which sailed in 1851 was not a happy one, they having fallen into the hands of an agent who shipped them on faked contracts through England to Liverpool, where they received other and different contracts. The food was raw, the families having to do their own cooking. The sailboat *Victoria* was already overloaded with Irishmen, and about half the people died en route. The voyage lasted seventeen weeks. One year elapsed before the friends and relatives left behind heard a word of their fate. It was in September, 1852, that news of them was received.

In the meantime, Josef Lešikar had been corresponding with a Mr. Klacel, a publisher, and to him was sent one of the Arnošt Bergman letters written from Cat Springs, Texas.

*   *   *   *

Through the world's decisive battles, some fifteen or more, Texas may lay claim to one—her Battle of San Jacinto, fought and won on April 21, 1836.

When General Sam Houston formed his army for attack, young Frederick Limsky, musician, in Captain Henry Teal's company, put his fife to his mouth and played the air of an old love song, "Come To My Bower." Young Limsky was accredited with being a Czech. It is a Czech name. A letter from J. H. Walker, State Land Commissioner, General Land Office, Austin, Texas, written under date of June 29, 1932, gives the name of Limsky as being on the Muster Rolls on file in the General Land Office, showing the list of those engaged in the battle of San

Jacinto. And thus has the State of Texas kept on record the name of the Czech musician who played the fife at the decisive Battle of San Jacinto.

* * * *

Arnošt Bergman was an enthusiastic believer in the opportunities to be had in Texas. He was a prolific letter writer and his letters never seemed to be without results. He wrote in glowing terms of the state to which he had immigrated in 1848. On the publication of the Bergman letter in *Moravske Noviny,* at the time published by Klacel, the news spread throughout Moravia about the great country of Texas.

In the year 1853 Josef Lešikar and family accompanied a party of seventeen immigrant families to Texas. On September 9, 1853, they left their homes, boarding the ship, *Savanna,* waiting for two weeks at Grage for the vessel, and on Christmas Day docked at Galveston, having been seven weeks en route. The voyagers were happy, however, in anticipation of the new home and country. They had made arrangements with service by Bedeker from Bremen, and this was good, considering all the hardships that immigrants encountered in those early days.

"We were fortunate," recorded this immigrant who claimed credit for having brought about immigration to Texas from his homeland. "Fortunate in having a short rest in Galveston and then being carried to Houston on a steamboat."

From this point the immigrants were transported slowly up-state by ox teams. This trip lasted two weeks, the distance covered being about sixty miles. All told, the trip to Texas from the native land of Moravia, to what this early immigrant designated, "the land of promise," lasted fourteen weeks.

Near New Ulm these eighteen families stopped, finding at this place friends who had preceded them. Some of the newcomers hired themselves out to do whatever kind of labor they could find. Others proceeded to build a community. The children of the Lešikar family hired out while their parents remained with a friend, Karel Shiller. In this same year, 1854, "with a friend we bought a farm," recorded Josef Lešikar. This was the beginning of the evolution that brought order out of chaos in the lives of these early immigrants. It came by slow stages, but from a piece of raw land there eventually evolved a cultivated field with a house and a roof over it.

Such early settlers as Josef Lešikar, Josef Petr, Valentin Haidušek, the Reymershoffer family, the Šebestas, Mikeskas,

Shillers, Hruškas and those others which go to make up the list of the pioneers, have just claim to the picturesque background and primitive setting that belongs with pioneer days in Texas. Josef Kopecky of Hallettsville, stated in 1931: "Czech immigrants came to Texas about seventy-five years ago, settling at Fayetteville, Dubina, Praha and Hostyn. Later the immigrants drifted as they came into other sections of Texas, and so today there are many prosperous communities where these people are dominant. Czechs are good farmers, but do equally well in all professional lines. We have a large number of physicians, lawyers, bankers, educators, musicians, as well as those engaged in mechanical industries. The Czech people are industrious and thrifty, and it is a recognized fact that wherever they settle in large numbers, they build up the community. This has been true in the instances of West, Granger, Ennis, Cameron, Caldwell, Sealy, Wallis, East Bernard, Rosenberg, Ganado, El Campo, Shiner, Flatonia, Sweet Home, Jourdanton and dozens of other localities."

"As for myself," explains Professor Kopecky, "I was born in Lavaca County. My parents came here in the early seventies, and married here. I received my education in our Czech schools. I was graduated from the Shiner High School in 1894, and from St. Edward's University, Austin, in 1896. All the early years of my life I lived on a farm. I taught in the country schools for several years. I married in 1898. In 1906 I bought the weekly newspaper *Novy Domov* at Hallettsville and during a twenty-five-year ownership, built up a large circulation, and changed the publication from a weekly to a semi-weekly. I sold the newspaper plant in 1931."

Professor Kopecky has been a member of the Board of Directors of the Agricultural and Mechanical College, College Station, for some years, to which position he was appointed by Governor R. S. Sterling. In holding this position of educational trust in the State, Professor Kopecky is himself one among the first Czechs to become actively associated with the higher educational affairs of Texas.

Josef Lidumil Lešikar, one of the first Czech pioneers, in a letter written to his children some time before his death, October 21, 1887, gave an interesting sketch of his life. His father, Josef Lešikar, was born about 1767 near Čermna, Czechoslovakia, and died in 1823. His mother, Rosalie (Prokop) Lešikar, was born between the years 1770 and 1775, in Crhov, Czechoslovakia, the date of her death not being recorded, but it is known that she lived a number of years after the death of her husband. These, the

parents of the early Czech pioneer in Texas, were farmers in both
Bohemia and Hungary.

Josef, the son, was sent to school at the age of six years. The
first years were spent in a church school. He received a fair
education in both the Czech and the German languages. He
graduated as a tailor, at the age of seventeen, soon after the
death of his father.

After his graduation he traveled and worked for two years
in Hungary, where, as he wrote in the sketch, he enjoyed life
very much, especially the freedom of the country. He intended
settling in that country, but being a Czech and a subject of
Bohemia, he had to return to his native land. Here he lived
for some years at home with his mother in a city called Nepomuk
(near Landškron, its county seat). He married Theresie Šiller
before being drafted into the military service, "in order," he
wrote, "to evade the draft." The marriage, however, proved one
of life-long happiness, according to the story.

After his marriage he opened a tailor shop of his own, and
was soon honored with the appointment of Notary Public of
Nepomuk. He was also made secretary to the Justice of the
Peace. In 1848 he was elected as representative from a district
including four counties, to the Czech Parliament, but on account
of the bombardment of the city of Praha at the time by
Windischgratz, he did not attend.

It was in 1851 that he read one of the Bergman letters about
Texas. The climate especially came in for fulsome praise. The
pioneer Texas letter writer mentioned also that Texas had a
great quantity of timber, and that it was an ideal place to live.

The contents of the letter were widely discussed. Seventeen
families decided to come to Texas on the strength of the letter.
These families sold all their goods and property and prepared
for the voyage. J. L. Lešikar, wife and four sons, were listed,
but the wife before sailing begged that the voyage contract be
cancelled because she preferred remaining in a land that she knew
rather than move to a strange country in which she would be an
alien. This was done and the other sixteen sailed in the fall of
1851. The trip across the Atlantic ended after much distress and
sorrow. Almost half of the number died before reaching the
shores of Texas. The survivors settled near what is now New
Ulm, where they started life in the new country by tilling its soil.

It was in 1853 that Josef Lešikar and family—wife and four
sons—Josef, Charles, Vinc and John, set sail for Texas on the
ship *Sava*. After a rough voyage they landed at Galveston on

Christmas Day, 1853. Remaining a few days in Galveston, the family proceeded by schooner to Houston, and there bought supplies for the journey inland which was made by ox-teams for a distance of sixty miles. This took fourteen days, there being at this early date no roads. The route lay often through swamps and frequently weather conditions were unfavorable. The adult members of the family walked the entire trip by the side of the ox-drawn wagons. A relative of Mrs. Lešikar, Charles Šiller, had come with the immigrant party in 1851, and it was at his home that the Lešikar family remained for a time on their arrival.

In 1854 Josef Lešikar bought a tract of farm land near New Ulm, and with the help of the four sons, built a log house for a family residence. This house was still standing in a good state of preservation in 1933, owned by Mrs. John Štalmach, née Theresie Lešikar, granddaughter of the pioneer builder.

This one of the early Texas-Czech pioneers, having had a good education in Europe, was in a position to be of valuable help to those of his people less fortunate in the matter of education. He kept open house on Sundays and, according to old family records, often had as many as fifteen and twenty neighbors in the home.

He wrote for a number of Czech publications in Bohemia and Moravia about conditions in Texas. These articles brought about more immigration to Texas, especially after the Civil War, when the largest number of Czech immigrants arrived. This Texas pioneer was one of the founders and stockholders of the St. Louis *Narodni Noviny,* one of the first papers printed in the Czech language in the United States. During the Civil War the paper took sides with the Union cause and the Texas founder and stockholder was subjected to severe criticism, together with all Texas readers of the paper. In the stress of the times there were threats about hanging the Czech pioneer. He explained that he was a loyal, law-abiding Texas citizen and not responsible for the editorial policy of the St. Louis newspaper.

Three of the sons were drafted for service in the Confederate Army, the youngest, John, seventeen years old, going as a teamster helper, hauling freight to and from Mexico. While in Mexico on one of these trips he got a job on a cotton platform, handling bales of cotton. For a time he was a clerk in a store in Mexico. Tall for his age, and of sturdy build, with the physical strength begotten in part through contact with danger and the hardships of the life, he was called on for too great physical exertion, which was the final cause of his death. He died either in Mexico or while on his way home, from injuries thus incurred.

*   *   *   *

Josef Mašik, born March 30, 1810, at Jacarech, Moravia, has given in a brief sketch of his life a graphic pen picture of early immigration to Texas. It was while he was in Čermne, Czechoslovakia, in the year 1851, where he had been a teacher for twenty-three years that he heard favorable talk about America and Texas. A letter at this time had just been received from Arnošt (Ernest) Bergman, written from his Texas home at Cat Springs, in which praise in no small measure was given to Texas, which, the writer said, was rich in natural resources and afforded unlimited opportunities for the pioneer. The liberty and freedom to be had was not the least of the advantages and, naturally, was one of the strongest pleas for immigration.

In 1851 many Czech and Moravian families sold their estates and prepared to come to Texas. Josef Mašik was dissuaded from joining the party by an uncle and he, instead, bought an estate in his home land, which was offered for sale cheap. The land was not good. He soon became dissatisfied and wanted more than ever to emigrate. There were many friends who wanted to accompany him, and this gave publicity to the project which brought down upon them government censure. Suspicion finally centered on Professor Mašik, with the result that he was arrested as a "Tory" and accused of seducing the subjects. His belongings were searched and all papers confiscated, among them his passport. He was carried to Vsetin, where his wife, much alarmed, followed, arriving just in time to see him being carried to jail where he remained for several weeks before he was given a hearing. In the meantime, others of the party who had planned to leave for Texas were arrested and questioned, but were later released.

The papers in which his passport was included being confiscated, Professor Mašik had to remain behind and see his friends embark for Texas. He had been the one on the previous date who waited for them to prepare for the exodus, but fate decreed that he should remain behind. Moving to Čechy after this, he again requested a pass for emigration, but was refused. In November, 1854, he finally set out with his family for the land of promise. The party suffered untold hardships on the voyage which lasted eight weeks.

The Mašik family were fortunate in having enough bread and dried fruit to keep them from starving, and to the fruit Professor

Mašik always gave the credit for their avoiding the scurvy with which others were afflicted. There were on board about ninety passengers, in addition to the fifteen Czech and one Moravian families, mostly German and Polish. New Year's Day was spent at sea and on January 2, 1855, the party landed, the vessel docking at Galveston. From this point the families were taken by water to Houston and went thence into the state by ox-teams.

The fifteen Czech families were bound for Cat Springs, and a bargain was made with an American teamster to take them to the point of destination, one hundred and ten miles from Galveston.

On the start the weather was clear and fine. The first night out, however, darkness brought omnious clouds, which were soon followed by a heavy downpour. Fortunately there were plenty of feather beds in the family baggage, but Mrs. Mašik, in looking after the comfort of her family, exposed herself and contracted a severe cold. They traveled on the following day, but slowly, with mud and water to combat. In some places ten yoke of oxen were required to pull a wagon out of the mud. The third day of the trip a river had to be crossed and it was already at the flood stage.

When the party camped for the night Mrs. Mašik was stricken with cholera and on the third day died. She was buried there, just as she had reached the threshold of the land of promise to which she had looked in behalf of her family for deliverance from oppression and distress.

The trip from Galveston to Cat Springs required two weeks, and the Mašik share of the teamster's price for hauling was $23.00. Professor Mašik, while in Bremen just before sailing, had met a friend in distress who owed six weeks' board bill and was being threatened with being sent back and not permitted to come on with the party. To him Mašik loaned all the money he had, enough to pay the board and half the fare of the trip to America. This loan placed him in the position of having to borrow from a friend in order to pay the teamster in Texas.

But for the young daughter, Terezia, later Mrs. Skřivanek—and Rosa Skřivanek, niece of the pioneer, Josef Mašik, this chronicle of events would not be preserved, for to them goes the credit for having recorded the data before it was lost with the passing of the years.

CHAPTER V

THE TRAIL-BLAZERS

*"When we build let us think that we build forever.
Let it not be for present delight nor for present use alone.
Let it be such work as our descendants will thank us for.
And let us think, as we lay stone on stone, that a time is to come
when those stones will be held sacred because our hands have
touched them, and that men will say as they look upon the
labor and wrought substance of them:
'See this our Fathers did for us.' "—*JOHN RUSKIN.

IN THE absence of documentary evidence, fancy may at times
supplement the break in the story—not with the idea of giving
more drama than the history would permit, but rather to visualize
the subject in the fullness of detail.

When there are no published or unpublished records to draw
from, instead only the contact with the people whose ancestors
were of the pioneer days—pioneers who laid stone on stone—the
historian must at times reach the subject by way of a detour
which leads through the third and fourth generations.

Few Czech parents have ever had cause for disappointment
in their children, or their children's children. The sons and
the daughters of the pioneers are found today holding positions
through the whole of the state and the United States with every
line of business activity represented—lawyers, doctors, merchants,
bankers, farmers, teachers, statesmen, realtors, musicians, artists,
builders, inventors and actors.

In visualizing the structure of the history of the Czech settlement we follow the procession of the ox-drawn vehicle which
carried the first settlers to chosen home-sites in the new country.
This primitive means of transportation had its bearing on the
location of the first settlement, holding the pioneers near to the
point where the sea meets the land. The journey inland from the
coast, tortuous and frought with all the dangers and discomforts
of a wild and unsettled country, left along the way many monuments to the zeal of these trail-blazers. In some instances a mound

of earth marked the spot beneath which lay the body of a pilgrim whose strength was not equal to the hardship of the journey. With the rising smoke from the first campsites, and later the lighted home fires, one may vision the shadowy outline of the pioneer's home in the making. Today it is easy to forget that this development came slowly. Before there were growing fields, there had to be the toil, the sweat of the brow, the cutting into the wilderness to obtain space for fields. The axe and the felled tree marked the route toward progress. When the tree had been limbed and dragged away to be cut into logs and stancions, and fashioned into a primitive cabin home, then home-making in Texas began. The first signs of community building are to be found in the setting up of the first blacksmith shop, locating the first saloon, building the first church and opening the first general merchandising store. The saloon was recognized as a legitimate part of every settlement. These pioneers were not prohibitionists—not in those first days of settlement— nor in the years that have followed. The saloon passed on with the advent of the Eighteenth Amendment, but the belief in the doctrine of personal rights and privileges still remained.

As the Czech pioneers took citizenship in the new country they asked no favors for themselves, neither did they come with reservations as to what they would or would not do. They had left the homeland to be free of oppression and the demands of militarism, but many of them were called to take up arms in defense of the country in the war of 1861-65. In some instances this call came almost as soon as they arrived. They knew nothing of the underlying causes of the conflict between the North and the South, and were opposed to anything that had to do with slavery, but most of them took sides with the Confederacy and fought in the Southern Army through loyalty to the land of their adoption.

Pioneer schools brought families into closer touch. The pioneers got a clearer idea of the qualities of the new country, its capacity for development, and the work of building took on greater impetus. As St. Guys Cathedral in Czechoslovakia has been the tomb of the Bohemian Kings, so the composite structure moving forward to completion through the years in Texas has been and will be the home of the Czech kings of finance and industry.

In a newspaper column devoted to happenings "Fifty Years Ago" (1882) a Texas publication carried the incident of a Waco preacher who had just returned from the frontier, in this instance Buffalo Gap, Leon County, Texas. Today this is a territory served by modern highways. Motor bus transportation is available almost hourly to all points in the State and out. The sign of prosperity is found in the cultivated fields and the towering derricks not far away, marking the spot where the fountain of liquid gold pours forth its golden stream.

* * * *

When one has come to the gateway, dividing the past and the present, the hand lingers on the latch and the feet pause in the passing. The patriots, those Czech pioneers who blazed the trail over which the way has come, are to be left on the other side.

Plumes of soft gray moss sway with the winds, descending from the branches of the Texas live oaks. A mocking-bird sings in the deep recesses of the majestic tree. Silently, as if fearful of breaking the impressive spell that hangs for the instant over the sacred spot where past and present meet, a lone Texas "cotton-tail" emerges from the friendly underbrush to cross the roadway to another rendezvous.

It is a holy hour at a sacred shrine.

Why did they, the pioneers, come to suffer so many privations —so many discomforts and so many hardships? They left a native country which had been established and civilized for centuries to cross the great Atlantic and put in at a strange harbor where they were beset with every obstacle and subjected to every danger, including pestilence and warfare.

"I had it," says Dr. Henry R. Maresh, a son of the second generation, "from my ancestors. I absorbed it when a child in my grandfather's log cabin home in the new country. They came in order to live their lives as they wished, free from oppression, political, religious and class. They wanted not only to enjoy their own freedom, but to have it for their children and their children's children. They wanted to put class behind them and breathe the air as free men and women. In the old country one was never able to get away from being a cabinet-maker if his father before him had been one. Once a tradesman of a specific branch, it was always the same. No chance to climb, no opportunities for the children.

"And so it was that they decided to be pioneers. They wanted to take up residence in the free, broad open country of Texas and they were willing to give their all in return. They brought with them no grudges nor ill-will; rather, they wanted to forget everything but that they were going into a new homeland, where they would put off the old and take on the new."

It is an historical fact that the tendency of class to harden into caste was more evident in Germany in these former years. The tendency and endeavor was seemingly to crush out Slavism. The Slavs at one time looked toward Russia as the one state in whom they saw a possible protector against the situation in which they found themselves—a situation which robbed them of their heritage, which forced on them a foreign tongue.

During a period of some years, dating from 1850, the German language was made the language of the administration of the courts and the schools, with the police arbitrary, interfering frequently with the ordinary courts.

Following the Battle of White Mountain in 1620, when Germany gained control of the government of Austria, the Germanization movement was strong. After the establishment of the dual monarchy, Austro-Hungary, the work of exterminating the non-German peoples continued. In Austria it was to Germanize, and in Hungary to Magyarize. It was possibly the misfortune of these rulers at the time that they failed to have the conception of the principles of self-determination which is recognized as the fundamental principle of mankind in the advancement of civilization.

It is not the purpose of this history to recount at length the story of Central Europe and the Slavs in their native land, nor the chronology that went toward the making of the history in which centuries are involved. Recognized historians have dealt comprehensively with the subject in order that a record might be available. A brief mention of some of the reasons for immigration which brought the early Czech pioneers to America and Texas is made in order to show that the first pioneers came not with the idea of material gain, but rather to have the privileges and the rights of the American Constitution. "Certain inalienable rights," among them those of "life, liberty and the pursuit of happiness."

Whole communities in Texas were founded by the Slavonic emigrants, who came seeking freedom. They did not come because they felt that the United States had been founded to provide a free home, but they did feel that the United States of America was founded so that human rights might be asserted.

The venture of emigration was given long and serious consideration. All the disadvantages of the homeland and the opportunities believed to exist in the new land were taken into account, including the matter of religion—a state religion as against the chance to worship according to the dictates of their own hearts and consciences. The matter of the sanctity of the home—a home free from the surveilance of government, searched at times for suspected seditious literature.

How they suffered, how they endured and then passed on into the great beyond without having tangible reward for their privations, is a matter of history. It is when one knows of the drastic political conditions in the old country—of the conflict that existed between race and language—of the universal annoyances arising from the differences of religion and racial culture between the rulers and the ruled, that the life and home-making of the Czech in the new country is appreciated.

And so the great American dream of the Czech pioneer was not composed of the fabric of material wealth and plenty, but rather it took for substance an unhampered existence, one not shut in by barriers of class distinction.

The dream has been realized in the course of the century of progress. Possibly not fully and perfectly, but the Texas-Czech pioneer will tell you:

"The endless ages have indeed throbbed through my blood, but a new rhythm dances in my veins."

When for an evening the time was given to some homely entertainment as a respite from the labors of the day—when families in a community enjoyed a neighborhood dance—the pioneer forgot for the time the cares and weariness of the day's toil, and danced through the hours of the evening to the old familiar music of his native land, played by musicians in the families of the pioneers.

On such occasions there were refreshments provided by the mothers, wives and daughters of the pioneer families. Beer was cheap and legally available and the refreshment of both food and the drink was for everyone present. No one, not even the children were forbidden to eat and drink—and no one was drunk! Occasionally an old man or several of the older men got a little tipsy, but they only enjoyed themselves the more, talked more and bestowed more applause to the playing of their favorite tunes.

As he listened to the folk-songs of his native land, the Czech pioneer dreamed his American dream of a land in which there was opportunity for each man according to his ability or achievement.

During the middle of the nineteenth century this had been a difficult dream for the European ruling class to interpret. At present it may even not be possible to interpret in truth the meaning of the dream which did not include merely motor-cars and high wages, but rather a dream of a social order in which each man and each woman would be able to attain to the fullest their individual ambitions, and, in so doing, to be recognized by others for what they are, regardless of the fortuitous circumstances of birth and family estate.

And so it came to pass that the Czech immigrants came and took homesites, selecting them in consideration of the soil. Fundamentally a village and small town people, naturally in the beginning they sought the rural sections to found their homes.

It has been estimated that nineteen-twentieths of the Czechs in Texas live in small towns and rural sections and about ninety-eight per cent of them own their own homes.

The Texas-Czech population possesses the real Czech as well as the real American spirit which combines to make a splendid citizenship. There is never heard any radical outbursts among these loyal Texas-Czechs. They are not led or swayed by any such sentiment. Strong of character and purpose, they hold to that which they believe to be sane and normal.

About one-twentieth of the Texas-Czech population reside in Houston, the largest city in the State. It was through Galveston and Houston that the pioneers passed on their inland routes when they came to take up residence in Texas.

The past is today behind the gate that divides the generations. After seventy-five and one hundred years of pioneering the early Texas-Czech settlers have not left off their labors, but their ambitions and their aspirations live, and the influence is not to be shut away and left behind with the closing of the gate that locks away the past.

That desire to attain the finer things of life, refinement, culture, knowledge of life in all its fullness, will not die in Texas any more than it will die in Czechoslovakia.

CHAPTER VI

THE FIRST CZECH PIONEER.

"A land without memories is a land without liberties."
—FATHER RYAN.

ON OCTOBER 8, 1832, after a voyage of forty-eight days, the *Ship of Good Hope* with young Anthony Michael Dignowity aboard, sailed up New York harbor.

Two men who were to play a vital part in the history of Texas had turned their faces toward the Southwest. Sam Houston of Tennessee and Anthony Michael Dignowity of Czechoslovakia. Two men, born in widely separated countries, en route to Texas where they were to become important figures in the great drama of empire building.

In 1833 the young Czech immigrant, Anthony Michael Dignowity, who had set sail one memorable day from Hamburg, with a duly signed passport for America, rode on horseback into San Antonio de Béxar.

About the same time Sam Houston, former governor of Tennessee, was taking up his residence at Nacogdoches. Neither of the men remained long in these Texas localities.

Sam Houston rode westward toward San Antonio de Béxar, and Anthony Michael Dignowity, after a brief sojourn in San Antonio, turned his face toward Natchez, Mississippi, from whence he had come, and where he was living.

Thus did Dr. Anthony Michael Dignowity, first Czech settler of Texas, first cast eyes upon the land that was to become his home.

In 1833, Dr. Dignowity again rode into San Antonio de Béxar, this time with a prospecting party with which he had traveled the entire distance on horseback from Mississippi.

As he strolled over the straggling village of adobe houses and through the open plazas, we may vision him paying a visit to the old Spanish Missions, he being a devout Catholic. He may have left the town proper to ascend some of the near-by hills. From the vantage point which may have been what was later called "Dignowity Hill," and years afterward, "Dignowity Park," he may have stood to observe the surrounding country.

41

He may on this occasion have had a mental picture of that ancestral home at Kutna Hora, called for centuries "Dignowity House." While he stood on the Texas hill, carpeted with Texas wild flowers, looking to the north and the south and the east and the west, around and about the historic city of San Antonio, he may have visioned another house, his own "Harmony House," erected years later on Dignowity Hill.

The vengeance of men poured out on chosen victims was but a part of the tragic era when a state and a country was in the process of being born. Anthony Michael Dignowity, pioneer settler, was probably not the exception, but nevertheless he suffered much at the hands of men who, too, were pioneers. According to memories that still linger around the broken links and from the words of this first Texas-Czech pioneer settler, written in his autobiography, we learn that he suffered too heavily.

Was it possible, we wonder, that this first Czech pioneer, standing on an eminence overlooking San Antonio, had the gift of prophetic vision? Again, as he strolled leisurely through the open plazas of the city, did he dream that just at dusk one evening in years to come an old negro mammy was to fall panting at his threshold with the message that he was that very night, with two other men, to be hanged in the Plaza? And was there, in this same year of 1833, the vision that he would be the friend and companion of governors and statesmen?

Dr. Dignowity, in his autobiography, published in 1859, told the story of his life. The manuscript for the book was prepared during the winter of 1857 while the author was recovering from a serious illness at his home, Mount Harmony, in San Antonio. It was, he stated, written at the request of his wife in order that a true record of his life might be left to his children and friends.

Part first of the book, "Bohemia Under Austrian Despotism," is devoted to what the author was pleased to designate "My Nativity." Among other things the writer presents a description of Kuttenberg, or Kutna Hora, as it is called in the Bohemian or Slavic language.

The city, according to the autobiography, was founded about the eighth or ninth century, during the reign of the celebrated seeress, Libuša, Queen of Bohemia, who is said to have seen in a vision in the locality, rich mines of silver and gold. A monk, on discovering the gold, hung his cowl on the limb of a tree while he hastened to the convent for necessary tools with which to work, and gave the spot the name, "Kutna Hora," hora meaning a hill.

"From the heights of the city," writes Dr. Dignowity, "is one of the most magnificent views in Europe. One standing at this vantage point may count as many as fifty cities and some hundreds of market places and villages."

At Kutna Hora is to be seen the sarcophagus of Jan Žižka, the blind but terrible leader of the Hussites, whose wars lasted some ninety-five years. The frontispiece of the book is an engraving of "Kuttenberg from the level grade," as it was at the time the book was written.

"This book," according to the author, "is not written from information derived from other books, but from actual experience."

Dignowity House at Kutna Hora, so called for centuries because it had always been the abode of a family of miners of that name, occupied a commanding position. The name Dignowity was an honorary title bestowed on the family for some heroic deed.

Anthony Michael Dignowity, the last of ten children of Wenceslaus and Catherine Dignowity, was born in January, 1810. He was baptised on the day of his birth at the Catholic Church near by, being given the name Anthony Michael. In family records it is related that he was born with a veil over his face, with which went the gift of prophecy.

The story of his life as told by himself, near to a half century after his birth, reads like a chapter from the "Arabian Nights."

The father of this first Texas-Czech settler was a man of mighty and powerful stature, six feet, five inches tall, weighing 245 pounds. He was an only son, in fact, an only child of the last of the historic House of Dignowity. He had, when a small boy, lost the sight of one eye through illness. This defect incapacitated him for work in the mines, but offered, through the leisure imposed, opportunity for study and travel. He was a musician, a poet, a man of trades and a wielder in consequence of strong influence in his home and community. He found much time and occasion for travel, and gathered a store of information that made him almost an oracle both at home and abroad.

It was while on one of his trips into a distant part of the country that he met Catherine, the young daughter of a miller, who later became his wife and the mother of ten children, the youngest of these being Anthony Michael.

The student of Texas history may trace with interest the route of the first coming of Dr. Anthony Michael Dignowity to Texas from Natchez, Mississippi. The incidents of the trail may be gathered from such brief accounts as are to be found in the early

writings of Dr. Dignowity. He recorded of himself in his autobiography which he dedicated "To the philanthropic and practical
reformers—to all seekers after truth," that he had been a traveler.
Born in Kutna Hora, Czechoslovakia, in 1810, he was put in the
Jesuit College at the age of six years, being led by the hand of his
father to the threshold of the institution of learning and placed
in the care of the masters of the institution. Of his school days
Mr. Dignowity wrote with great feeling. He loved his school and
his teachers, the Jesuits, who took great interest in his welfare
both physical, mental and spiritual. He came of a family distinguished for intellectual endowments in addition to the possession of some material wealth, but while the boy was yet in his
young and tender years, his father, through an unwise investment lost everything he had and his financial loss put the family
in destitute circumstances.

To contribute to the support of the mother and father, the boy
began working after school hours. His first venture into the business world was as a vendor of home-made hooks and eyes, which
he fashioned with his own small hands from bits of wire with the
help of a pair of pliers he found in his father's tool chest. These
crude bits of wire fastenings were tacked on a bit of pasteboard
and offered for sale from house to house, but without success.

Another venture proved more lucrative. This was the manufacture and sale of sulphur matches. He learned the art of
making them from a neighbor girl, but forgot about the sulphur
fumes penetrating his clothes and, on entering his classroom after
his first job of match-making, he was severely reprimanded
because of the odor he diffused. Thinking that he might be
afflicted with some kind of an itch, his small jacket was removed
so that his arms might be examined.

Not to be discouraged in his efforts, the boy sought other ways
to take home to his mother a few pieces of money. At the Lenten
season one year he got a job with a baker delivering and selling
pretzels, the special bread used during this season. All the years
of his youth were filled with hardships, and the boy became more
and more a student, and at the age of seventeen became a traveler,
visiting many parts of his own as well as adjoining countries.

In 1826, when he was sixteen years old, his mother died and in
the following year he became a mechanical engineer, traveling
through Germany, Čechy, Prussia and Poland in order to gain
experience. During the Revolution of 1830, Russia against
Poland, he joined the Polish army. The uprising was soon suppressed, however, and young Dignowity, with other Polish

soldiers, fled to Hamburg. From this point he sailed on the *Ship of Good Hope* for New York, arriving, according to his own record, October 8, 1832, at the age of twenty-two. Here again in the New World, as in the old, he traveled, visiting most of the states and living for a time in a number of them. One interesting incident recorded by Dr. Dignowity was the historical falling of the stars in 1833 which he witnessed in Athens, Georgia.

As he traveled in those first years, Dr. Dignowity studied not only places but the people, and the Constitution of the United States. It was the Constitution which in later years, when he had taken up his permanent residence in Texas, controlled his destiny in that he became a Unionist and a Republican. When the tragic days of the war between the North and the South were at hand, tragedy and distress came into his life.

Even years before this critical period in the nation's affairs, Dr. Dignowity suffered at the hands of those who differed with him. Looking back over three-quarters of a century, it is difficult to visualize the situation that existed. Incidents that occurred in the life of this pioneer Texas-Czech might best be left unrecorded and thus forgotten, but for the part they hold in the chronology of events.

Dr. Anthony Michael Dignowity played a part in the development of Texas which will never lose its place in history. The name of Dignowity will long be remembered in San Antonio, where he built his home, Harmony House, on Dignowity Hill.

He entered into the spirit of the country, adopted the manners and the customs, engaged in various lines of business endeavor, even that of newspaper making. No matter in what part of the country he found himself, he proceeded to make the most of opportunities, and when in the course of his travels he made his way south, locating for a time at Natchez, Mississippi, he turned his attention to the things that belonged with the south.

There he worked on plantations and soon invented a cotton gin. He saw the vast timber areas and built a sawmill. Also during the time of his residence in Natchez he owned a hotel, later destroyed by a tornado.

He read medicine in Natchez under Doctors Stone and Carothers and attended lectures, as was the custom, in Cincinnati, Ohio. He adopted the Eclectic system of medicine, at that time in the early stages of its development. He began his practice in Mississippi.

Soon after the tornado which destroyed his property, he gathered up what was left of his hotel fixtures and furnishings, chartered a little steamer called the *Lady Morgan* and moved to

Talequa, then the recently established seat of government of the Cherokee Nation, where he practiced medicine and studied the Indian language. During this time he made frequent visits to Little Rock, where he met Miss Amanda McCann, daughter of an Irish pioneer, Francis McCann, who had settled in Arkansas but two years prior to their acquaintance with Dr. Dignowity.

In February, 1835, Dr. Dignowity and Miss McCann were married and moved to a place called Illinois Falls in the western part of Arkansas, close to the border of Indian Territory. There they lived for several years, Dr. Dignowity continuing his practice of medicine.

It was early in the Spring of 1846 that he volunteered under Ex-Governor Yell of Arkansas, for service in the war between the United States and Mexico. With ten other volunteers he made his way across the country to San Antonio, it being their intention to form a connection with the Texas Rangers, or some branch of the military, and proceed to join the armies of Generals Scott and Taylor.

From the time in 1830, when he was a Polish soldier, through the middle forties, when he was a volunteer, hastening to offer his services to his government, and finally in 1861, when he left his homeland, Texas, on account of war in which he did not wish to take part, it must be conceded that Anthony Michael Dignowity never once thought of anything but what he considered his conscientious duty.

Within a few hours after Dr. Dignowity and his companions arrived in San Antonio that day in 1846, and while he was at the table partaking of his first meal in the place, he was hastily summoned to attend a Mexican and an Indian who had sustained injuries in a street affray. It becoming known that this newcomer was a physician, and there being at the time urgent need for his professional services, he was prevailed on to remain in San Antonio and devote himself to the practice of medicine.

Soon he had a good practice and decided to locate permanently in San Antonio. He sent for his wife and family, and at once devoted himself to his chosen profession.

Passing again along the years we find Dr. Dignowity at the Capitol in Austin with Governor Houston when the talk of Secession was being discussed. Opposed to Texas' withdrawal from the Union, Dr. Dignowity at the time threatened to leave the country if such should come to pass. Following his conference with Governor Houston, he left the Capitol and proceeded to his plantation near Waverly.

When the vote in favor of Secession foretold the final outcome, Dr. Dignowity put into effect his threat, previously made, to leave the country, and early in 1861, telling his wife and family good-bye, he started north, making his way through the State toward the Red River and Indian Territory. He traveled on horseback, passing through Arkansas, suffering all the hardships of the long overland journey, and finally reaching his destination, Washington City, where he secured employment with the government. There he remained during the entire period of the war. Impoverished both in health and material wealth, he returned to Texas in 1869. He did not resume the practice of medicine, but, instead, devoted himself to the task of gathering together the fragments of his depleted fortune, and his confiscated property.

That day of his leaving Texas was the one on which the old negro woman became a self-imposed courier to carry the message to the Dignowity house in San Antonio that the master of the house was to be hanged on the Plaza that very night. The young son, Anthony Francis, oldest of the children, was at home at the time, his mother being at the ranch located in the hills somewhere between Austin and Comfort.

"Is yo' pa comin' home tonight?" asked the colored woman in a frenzy of fright. And when the boy replied in the affirmative she wailed out in broken sentences the story of how three men were to be hanged that night. "An' your pappy is one of 'em!"

The boy, typical son of his father, and grandson of that intrepid ancestor who stood in his might, six feet and five inches, took the situation in hand, and when his father came he had a horse in readiness, hidden in the shelter of the brush. It was on this animal that the trip north was made.

Following their fortunes and activities we find that the two men, General Sam Houston and Anthony Michael Dignowity, had much in common. Both were men of genius and both were soldiers of fortune and soldiers of the battlefield. Both had varied experiences which included the misfortune of having their names under a cloud during the period of the Civil War. They were agreed upon the question of preserving the Union of States, and accordingly opposed Secession. Both men lived for a time among the Indians. Both studied the Indian language. Both rode out of Arkansas to Texas and adopted it as their native land.

When the great tragedy came into his life in 1856 and he was accused and found guilty of what was at the time claimed to be a land fraud offense, and received a penitentiary sentence of one year, Governor Sam Houston pardoned him. Again when trouble came to him it was another staunch friend, Governor Pease, who came to his aid.   When all matters were straightened out, he, with his family, was taken to Austin, where they were guests at the Governor's mansion for one whole month.

The story of the life and family of Dr. Anthony Michael Dignowity is crowded into one chapter of Texas-Czech history. Naturally it is but a brief outline.   Some ambitious and serious writer will possibly find the subject of a biography in this first Czech settler of Texas, and will record the achievements and the part this early settler played in the development of the State.

Dr. Dignowity was an ardent advocate of education and believed zealously in the protection of state school lands. On several occasions he devoted himself to the process of restoring school lands to the State.   He reared a family in Texas which has gone out into varied lines of activity, each member contributing his or her share to the welfare of the community in which it has been their lot to reside.

The name of Anthony Francis Dignowity, oldest son of the pioneer, stands indelibly written on the scroll of State and National activities.   Being a civil engineer he found a wide scope for his activities.   He has to his credit the founding of several towns and communities and one county in the State.   He laid out the town of Brackettsville in Kinney County, founded the town of Del Rio, and was instrumental in organizing Val Verdi County, acting first as deputy sheriff, then as sheriff of this county.

He was appointed by President William McKinley as a special agent of the United States in civil affairs to Porto Rico. During their stay in Porto Rico, Mr. and Mrs. Dignowity were the recipients of many honors, social and otherwise. Returning from this post of duty in 1909, Mr. and Mrs. Dignowity took up their permanent residence in San Antonio, building about this time the present home.   Mr. Dignowity engaged in the insurance business. Mrs. Dignowity was Mary Catherine Dulnig of the pioneer Dulnig family, associated with the early development of San Antonio.   They had no children.

Incidents in the life of Dr. Dignowity, which gave rise to the writing of several books, published in 1859, have long since lost their bitterness and much of the ill-feeling which at that time existed.

Dr. Dignowity's express concern and deep regret was that his name should be forever recorded in a Texas law record book as a criminal.   Strange as it may seem, there are to be found but one or two of the books written in 1859 by this first Texas-Czech settler. One volume only is preserved in the State Library at Austin. This is as a "chained volume," permitted to be read only under supervision of the library officials because of its value as a Texas historical item. Another book, the first one, "Bohemia Under Austrian Despotism," an autobiography of his life, reposes in the public library at San Antonio.

Many of the early Texas newspapers took occasion to offer editorially and in news articles, congratulations and expressions of satisfaction when the trouble was settled and Dr. Dignowity regained his freedom. Among the newspapers carrying these articles were the Austin *Intelligencer*, 1856; San Antonio *Ledger*, December 27, 1856; the *Sun*, San Antonio, December 20, 1856, and many others in various parts of the State. Invariably they were profuse in words of commendation in behalf of this pioneer settler and citizen.

Dr. Dignowity's career was an exceptional one, made so by his mental and moral organization. He was not only a successful physician, but a successful business man. As a student, his mind was both practical and philosophical. His philosophy was to live within the boundaries of fairness and moral rectitude, seeking to do that which was right because it was right, and not from motives of selfish gain. He became a Republican on the organization of the Republican Party and remained ever afterward an ardent advocate of the principles of his party. He was reared a Catholic and, during the earlier years of his life, was an active communicant of the Church, but his views gradually underwent a change and he closed his life by a leaning toward spiritualism.

One less courageous than Dr. Dignowity would not only have faltered, but would have succumbed under the stressful events of his time. But this Czech pioneer carried on through all. He took pride in being able to overcome obstacles cheerfully, and withal remain true. His death occurred in San Antonio, April 22, 1875, forty-two years after the date of his arrival in Texas.

He was a great sufferer through the war of 1861-65, having had his property swept away and his health impoverished. Surviving at his death were the widow, five sons and one daughter. The sons were Anton Francis, Edward Lucein, Henry Louis, Charles Leonard and James Victor; the daughter, Imogene Teresa. One son, Albert Wentzel, the second in age, was killed February 25, 1872, at Piedras Negras, Mexico, while a soldier in the army of the Patriot Juarez, and a daughter had died in childhood, bitten by a rattlesnake. The daughter, Mrs. Imogene Teresa Dignowity

Hambleton, resides with her daughter, Imogene Teresa, in Houston.

A grandson, Captain Henry Dignowity, was stationed at Fort McIntosh, Laredo, Texas, in 1933.

The literary activities of Dr. Dignowity, as previously stated, included several published volumes. He wrote in 1859 "Bohemia Under Austrian Despotism." It was said of this book that the material was poorly arranged, but depicted conditions as existing at the time in Austria. Thoughout the whole of the writing, in every line, the author breathed his love for his people, the Czechs.

He wrote another book, "American Despotism," in which he depicted conditions as he saw them through the eyes of a European, which is described as being the rendering of justice by bought jurists along with the haughtiness of the Anglo-Saxons.

Finally he wrote "Crimes and Cruelties Committed by the So-Called Courts of Justice on the Sacred Rights of Individuals." In this volume he included his own experience with the laws of the land, which made a sad chapter as he associated it with American Courts.

The incident which brought about the writing of this book was the case which is recorded in Volume 17 of Texas Reports, page 522.

It has been related in connection with the case that enemies incited the feeling against him, making the accusation that he had tried to cheat an Irish widow out of a piece of land which she had bought from him. For this, in 1856, he was sued and sentenced to the penitentiary for a period of one year. Governor Sam Houston pardoned him. The story told of the matter was that the land had been sold to a man and his wife on credit, the money consideration being only a couple of hundred dollars. The husband died before the purchase price had been paid, and the widow asked Dr. Dignowity to take back the property. This he did and finally sold it for a little more than the price contracted for by the first purchasers. It was this that brought about the suit. Times were at the crucial point in these pioneer days, and many things occurred that possibly would not have under other and less strenuous conditions.

Mrs. Dignowity was the daughter of Francis M. McCann, born in County Tyrone, Ireland. Her mother was Sara Kramer, a native of Lancaster County, Pennsylvania. Her father came to America at the age of nine years with an uncle and settled at Baltimore, Maryland, where he grew to maturity. At the age of twenty-one, he enlisted in the United States Army under Captain

Hale Hamilton and fought through the War of 1812, taking part in the Battle of New Orleans under General Andrew Jackson. He was mustered out of service at the close of hostilities with a lieutenant's commission. In August, 1817, he married Miss Sara Kramer, of Pennsylvania, niece of Congressman Kramer, of that state, and moved to the mountains of Western Virginia, where the wife of Anthony Michael Dignowity was born. The family afterward moved to Hagerstown, Maryland, and moved several times during a period of a few years. The daughter, Amanda, was in the meantime sent to the convent school at Loretta, where she remained for four years. With the tide of the emigration from the south to the west, the McCann family drifted to Mississippi and finally, in 1840, went to Little Rock, where they settled with servants, quartered on a headright some miles outside of the town. This headright had been received for services in the War of 1812.

Speaking of her early years, Mrs. Dignowity related much that is of interest to Texas-Czechs. Her experiences and life in Texas as the wife of a pioneer physician were both thrilling and colorful. Her childhood had been spent largely in travel with her parents. Her father was a merchant as well as a planter and, as there were no railroads, all travel was by carriages and wagons. The young daughter accompanied him on many trips which took her through the States of Virginia, Pennsylvania, Kentucky, Ohio, Mississippi and Arkansas. In these states she had opportunity to see and practice the primitive ways of living. Being the oldest daughter in a large family of girls, and there being many servants to care for, she had to take charge of the medicine chest, one of the necessary adjuncts of every large household in those days.

"I had to administer the physics prescribed," said Mrs. Dignowity, in recalling her life as a pioneer. "I took a fancy to the study of medicine, and although women of that period were not permitted to practice medicine, I determined to learn something about the subject. I began to read medicine under Dr. J. Coombes, of Mississippi, and after my father moved to Arkansas I continued my studies under Doctors Tucker and Prayther. Meeting Dr. William Byrd Powell, then president of the Medical College of New Orleans, and afterward State Geologist of Arkansas, I continued my studies under him, he teaching me the reform system known as the Eclectic."

Her marriage to Dr. Anthony Michael Dignowity, friend and partner of Dr. Powell, put an end to the career.

"Whatever ambition I may have had for an independent career

as a medical practitioner, if indeed I ever had any, was now laid aside, although I continued my studies and often in after years joined my husband in his researches and lent him what aid I could in his professional labors."

Dr. Dignowity, having located in Texas in the early spring of 1846, Mrs. Dignowity remained with her parents in Little Rock until the following fall when she joined her husband. The account of the trip as related by Mrs. Dignowity is deeply interesting, as pioneer days are brought closer through seeing them in the words of the woman who shared the life of the first Texas-Czech citizen.

She said: "After masses, offered by Archbishop Byrens and the prayers of the congregation for my safety in the land of war and desperadoes were said, I left relatives and friends, some of whom I was never to see again, and others not for many years, and took a steamer for New Orleans. At that place I waited thirty days for a vessel sailing for Texas. I took passage on the bark *William* in the latter part of January, and after being driven much out of our way at sea, suffering for days without water, we finally put in at Matagorda Bay.

"Here a supply of food and water was obtained, and the vessel proceeded to Indianola. At this point I was fortunate in meeting Mr. Van Rensselaer, of New York, and Judge Stuart of Texas, both friends of my husband. We chartered a lighter and the two gentlemen, myself and babies, and the captain left for Port Lavaca, which I was told was distant only a few hours' sail. But we had gone scarcely a mile when a Texas 'norther' sprang up and we were driven out to sea. We battled the storm until the next evening before we reached Port Lavaca. I remained overnight at the hotel. The next morning one of the gentlemen asked me to step out and look at the fine United States mail coach that was waiting to take us overland to our destination. Imagine by astonishment to see a large wagon without cover or seats. Six Mexican mules were attached, each mule held by a Mexican peon (the latter as strange-looking to me as the mules), until we got in. I procured a rocking chair and a roll of carpeting from my baggage and made myself as comfortable as possible with my babies.

"The word to start was given, the Mexicans springing out of the way of the mules. These animals stood first on their hind feet, then plunged forward in response to yells from the driver and the Mexicans, and we were on our way. We faced the north wind for miles. Nearly frightened to death, I could only hold myself in readiness for anything that might come.

"At last we arrived at Victoria. 'Limpy' Brown, well known in Texas history, kept the hotel there. After dinner we had a relay of bronchos and started on, facing toward evening a sleeting norther. We arrived late at Seguin, half frozen, hungry and tired out. My baby, not a year old, suffered with the croup. Our faces were blistered with the sleet and cold. There I met, for the first time, Captain Jack Hays, on his way to Washington City, and others who were going to San Antonio, among them Mr. William Vance, Captain Shaw and Mr. A. A. Munsey, all of whom I knew at home before coming to Texas. Our hostess was Mrs. Calvert and residing with her were her beautiful daughters, who afterward became respectively Mrs. Johnston, Mrs. Hays and Mrs. John Twony.

"The journey was continued without further suffering or the occurrence of any event to break the monotony of travel until eight miles east of San Antonio when we reached the Salado crossing. Here we were startled by a fearful war whoop. The men seized their guns, pistols and Bowie knives and prepared for battle with a determination that so frightened me that I slid from the chair to the bottom of the wagon, covering my babies with the carpeting. Soon a voice called out:

" 'No fightie, much *amigo;* plenty whiskey; plenty drunk.' What a relief! As we descended the hill we saw in the bend of the creek over a hundred Indians. They had been to San Antonio for rations and all were beastly drunk except the three watchers.

"When we reached the top of the hill east of the city, where my residence later stood, Mr. Van Rensselaer remarked: 'Mrs. Dignowity, you must not be surprised at the appearance of the town. There has been a fearful norther and all of the houses have been unroofed,' which I verily believed was so until I got fairly into the town and more closely inspected the buildings. The hotel at which we stopped, a typical jackal with the flat roof, dirt floor and grated windows, seemed to be the chief place of rendezvous of the town, but I paid very little attention to its appearance or the inmates.

"My husband, though absent at the time, being on duty among the soldiers at Mission La Purissima Concepcion, had prepared a room for me and had a nurse waiting. I repaired at once to my apartment, which seemed a haven of rest, and awaited his return. When we went out to dinner there were about thirty persons at the table and I was told that seven languages were being spoken. There was not one American lady in the number, I was told, and later found this to be true. Also that there were very few American women in the city. I recall meeting at the hotel beautiful Mrs. Glanton, Prince Solms, Don Castro and a number of United States officers, some of whom I had known at home. The next day I rode with my husband to the camps and visited the sick.

"The family baggage was delayed five months, arriving in July following our arrival in January. Dr. Dignowity had purchased a home on Acequina Street and the family took up permanent residence there.

"After this I saw much of the city, came to know the few American ladies, also made acquaintance with some of the Mexican ladies and so had a very pleasant life. All visiting was done after sundown. The Plaza from ten o'clock in the morning until four o'clock in the afternoon was empty. All doors were closed. Every one took a siesta. After four o'clock and on until midnight, the Plaza and streets were gay with men and women in full dress and elegant toilets engaged in shopping, visiting and enjoying the evening air.

"About one year after my arrival some of the ladies formed a class and engaged Dr. Winchell, who had been a tutor in Santa Anna's family, to teach us Spanish. The authoress, Augusta Evans Wilson, then a young girl, was one of the number. I visited some of the Spanish ladies, joined them in visiting the church during their festivals and fiestas and thus became much interested in the devotions to the Señora Guadeloupe, the great patroness. Later when German immigration began pouring into the city, I found it necessary to study German.

"Street fights between Mexicans and Indians were frequent occurrences, and my husband was many times called to attend the wounded on both sides. Sick and disabled soldiers from the Río Grande were also frequently brought to our house for treatment, so that for years we were almost constantly in the midst of affliction. But in spite of all this we had our pleasures and enjoyed life. I recall that we had many distinguished visitors in our home, among them Generals Kearney and Doubleday of the United States Army; Ex-Governor Yell of Arkansas; President Sam Houston; Archbishop Lamy, Bishop Odin and Reverend Mark Anthony.

"The incidents of the Alamo and the invasion under Vasquez and Woll were then fresh in the minds of the people, and I heard many interesting accounts of those stirring times. After the establishing of peace, in company with my husband and sometimes with lady friends, I visited the old missions. Concepción Mission was used for a considerable time as a stable by the soldiers who were quartered there after the Mexican War. This was a terrible desecration, it seemed to me, but not more shocking than the vandalism since exhibited by tourists in breaking and taking away the lovely decorative work. The missions then were by no means in so dilapidated a condition as at the present. Every sculptured flower, leaf, fruit and face was in perfect preservation.

"The Civil War brought a new era of trials and suffering. My husband was a Union man. He left the country on account of his views on slavery and secession and remained in the North until the restoration of peace. My two eldest sons, aged sixteen and nineteen, were conscripted into the Confederate Army, but subsequently, while on a furlough, swam the Río Grande, made their escape and joined the Union forces at Brazos de Santiago. They later went to Washington City where they secured positions in the Department of the Interior and remained until 1868. Most of our property was swept away during the four years' struggle, some of our losses being caused by the Indians who made frequent incursions into the country and stole cattle, horses and sheep from the ranches, sometimes murdering the ranchmen."

Many valuable possessions of the Dignowity home were stolen. Dr. Dignowity had a splendid library and the books became widely scattered. Mrs. Dignowity carved the massive mantle that was at the great open fireplace in the spacious living room at Harmony House on Dignowity Hill. The mantle was of mahogany, sent to her as a gift from Mexico. This valuable old mantle disappeared some years ago when the old home was torn down in the process of converting Dignowity Hill into Dignowity Park.

Mrs. Mary Dignowity, the widow of Anthony Francis Dignowity, oldest son of Dr. and Mrs. Dignowity, who lives in San Antonio on a part of the old Dignowity Hill, recalls many rare and valuable pieces of furniture that once belonged to the Dignowity household. She has in her home a small table carved in an acorn and oak leaf pattern by her mother-in-law, Mrs. Anthony Michael Dignowity. On the table is also an old pottery vase which was a gift from her husband's mother. The old table with its vase is kept somewhat as a shrine to the memory of this pioneer Texas settler. A patchwork quilt on which is embroidered Texas' wild flowers in colors, the material of the quilt being that from which men's suits were made, is also another prized possession of Mrs. Dignowity. The quilt was the handiwork of the mother-in-law.

Mrs. Dignowity has had an interesting life. She has traveled extensively with her husband, who held positions of state including an appointment under President William McKinley to Porto Rico as has been previously mentioned. Her husband spoke many languages and in consequence held positions of wide import and influence. He was a skilled surveyor and artist in oil paintings. When but a young boy, he received the commission to paint and decorate the carriage of General Bee in San Antonio. The ornamentations consisted in part of bouquets of flowers painted on the carriage body.

Anthony Francis (Frank) Dignowity was the oldest child of Dr. and Mrs. Dignowity, born before they came to Texas, at Illinois Falls, Arkansas. As a boy in Texas he knew General Sam Houston and recalls visiting him in Austin at one time in company with his father. He always treasured the memory of General Houston, who said to him: "My boy, push your hat off your forehead. One who has the splendid brow that you have, should never cover it by wearing the hat pulled down."

During the years that Frank Dignowity was engaged in his profession of civil engineer, he founded and laid out the towns of Del Rio and Brackettsville. He acquired large tracts of ranch land and sold to the railroad the site for the high bridge across the Pecos near Del Rio. He laid out a town site near the railroad at this point which he named Pecos, but which never developed.

Locating in San Antonio in 1909, he and Mrs. Dignowity built their home on Dignowity Hill.

During the war, 1861-65, all of Dr. Dignowity's property in Texas was confiscated, but he recovered it later and sold to the Government the tract of land located in San Antonio on which the present Army Post of Fort Sam Houston is located.

Dignowity Hill in the early days was as if in the country. It was covered by the native growth which included a carpet of Texas wild flowers. One little daughter but five years old, while gathering flowers, was bitten by a rattlesnake and died within a few hours. A brother with her at the time was also bitten, but ran quickly to the house where the older brother Frank was, calling to him that he had been bitten by a snake. The brother with presence of mind took out his knife and cut open the wound, sucking out the blood. The baby sister came later and said that she, too, had been bitten, but it was too late to counteract the deadly poison. The father was hastily summoned from his office and he came, bringing with him another physician, but the child died within a few hours.

These were important incidents connected with Czech pioneer

life in Texas. They form an interesting commentary on the progress and development of the country.

When this old home was torn down in 1926, the workmen found it to have been very substantially built. The outside walls were of rock and the interior walls were built of wood, lath and plaster. It was two stories in height. Floor joists, roof joists and stairways were of wood. The house had a shingle roof. The old building was erected many years ago and the material used was the very best obtainable in those days. The walls were very heavy, and the whole structure was built in a thoroughly substantial manner.

Honorable Phil Wright, Commissioner of Fire and Police, San Antonio, wrote this in description of the historic old Dignowity home in 1933. Commissioner Wright had under his supervision the tearing down of the building when the ground on which it stood was turned into what is now Dignowity Park. It has been since regretted that the old house had not been preserved and used for a recreation center in connection with the park.

CHAPTER VII

The Family Šebesta

Like the Pilgrims who landed at Plymouth on December 22, 1620, those first Czech immigrants who landed in Texas a century ago had two objects in view: to enjoy religious freedom and to acquire land for themselves. They were followed during succeeding years by others whose primary purpose was also the acquiring of land and the establishing of homes, as the many Czech settlements, towns and communities in Texas attest. Texas received a large number of her immigrants between the years of 1850-60. These pioneers took up homesteads and went at once to the work of establishing residence, breaking the prairies and tilling the virgin soil.

Arnošt (Ernest) Bergman, born in 1797, at Zapudov, near Mnichove Hradište, Bohemia, emigrated to the United States in 1848, settling in this same year at Cat Springs, Austin County, Texas. He was so impressed with the country that he wrote numerous laudatory letters to friends back home who were so impressed with the promising future depicted as awaiting them in Texas that numerous Czech families set out for this new land of promise.

Throughout the Czech settlements in Texas are to be found the paternal names of these pioneer families. In almost every one of the early settlements such as Mill Creek, settled in 1834, Cat Springs, 1834, Industry, 1838, Dubina, High Hill, Bluff, Praha, Frydek and the many other Czech communities settled by these early arrivals, there are to be found the names of Leshikar, Shiller, Holub, Kubal, Petr and Šebesta, the latter the progenitor of the large Šebesta family.

There are many other pioneer names—Chupik, Žabčik, Hruška, Stojaňik, Adležilec, Škopik, Precechtel, Smetana, Reymershoffer and Dignowity. Little social or industrial unrest is or has ever been found among the Czech citizens. While they have contributed both thought and money to the cause of the liberation of the Czechoslovak nation, they have never in the least degree weakened in their devotion to Texas. When the United States entered the World War they volunteered for service in the army and invested

58

in Liberty Bonds, their interest in the mother country being only a matter of sentiment.

Frank Šebesta, father of the big Texas Šebesta progeny, was born December 26, 1826, in Lipa, Moravia. Together with two brothers, Jan (John) and Pavel (Paul), he came to Texas in 1855, landing at Galveston from where he sailed on a raft to Houston, described as being at the time "a mere village." From Houston they journeyed on to Cat Springs, their destination. The voyage across the Atlantic had been in a sailing ship and had lasted three months. The vessel was blown far out of its course by storms, the ship rocking like a shell, the immigrants suffering intensely from sea-sickness. Fearing that the frail vessel would not withstand the onslaught of the mountainous waves, the pilgrims read their Bibles and sang hymns to keep up their courage. The food through these dreary days was not conducive to cheerfulness nor good spirits. Beans, bacon and wormy bread constituted their diet during the voyage.

Landing at Houston, via the raft, the baggage and children were loaded on ox-drawn wagons. Adults and older children walked behind these crude vehicles. It was winter time and the roads were bad, owing to constant rains.

Crossing the Brazos River on the ferry at San Felipe (where today is located the Czech settlement of Frydek), the further continuation of the journey was impossible on account of the heavy rains, impassable roads and biting cold weather. There was no shelter and the rain prevented them from making a fire by which to warm and dry themselves. Alone, homeless, friendless, in a land not as yet beyond the wilderness stage, Frank and Rosalie Šebesta, fearing that they and their children would freeze to death, went in search of shelter.

Rosalie Šebesta, wife and mother, carried in her arms a baby almost four months old who had been born in Roudnice, Bohemia, en route to the new country. The baby had been baptised there, receiving the name of Catherine. Holding the infant close to her breast in the effort to keep it warm and protect it as best she could from the rain, she came just before dusk to a lonely hamlet where she begged for shelter. She was unable to understand the language, but was made to understand that the man of the house refused to give up the only bed which he occupied; neither would he permit their remaining overnight in the house. The woman of the house, to her credit be it said, interceded in behalf of mother and baby, begging that they might not be turned away, but to no avail. The two immigrants, husband and wife with their children, wet through and through, numb and trembling with the cold, crouched near a fence at the mercy of the elements.

During the night a lone horseback rider came that way and stopped at the house. He was told by the woman there of the plight of the family who spoke a strange language. Lantern in hand he began a search which led to the distressed pioneers. The stranger took them with him to his own house which stood some distance further, and there they were given welcome. The wife of the Texas householder took the baby from the mother's arms, put dry clothes on it and held it near the open log fire while the mother and father warmed and dried themselves in front of the rude fireplace. For three days the Šebestas remained in this home where they were given both food and shelter.

The other members of the immigrant caravan suffered intensely during this time, having remained in an improvised camp. Paul Šebesta had a large family and two of the children died from the exposure.

As soon as the weather permitted, the trip was continued until their destination was reached. An uncle of Frank Šebesta, who likewise bore that name, was located at Cat Springs, having arrived a year before, and the three other Šebesta families on their arrival made their home with this relative for the remainder of the year, helping with the farm work.

Surrounded at the present with the achievements of progress, with modern highways and railroads, automobiles and airplanes, it is difficult to vision the distress of these pioneers in an uncharted wilderness. The time from Houston to Cat Springs by railroad or automobile is but a matter of a couple of hours. In the days of the Šebesta pioneers the way was but a trail through a section fraught with all the dangers that beset an unsettled country. The name Cat Springs had been given to the settlement in the early days of its founding because a boy had killed a wild cat near one of the springs on the San Bernardo.

Here the early settlers suffered all the hardships and privations of pioneer life. They built log houses and planted corn and cotton. The prairie of Bernard extended from the Brazos to the Colorado River and was a free ranch for the cattle of the settlers. Wolves were plentiful and made constant depredations on the sheep. The rich and fertile lands of this section, possibly, attracted the large number of the early Czech immigrants. They were mostly farmers. The farm-laborer received his board and fifty cents per day, according to records of the early years, when employment was to be had.

The Šebesta brothers, Frank, Jan and Pavel, were sons of fairly well-to-do parents in their native country—parents who were fortunate in owning a larger piece of land than was ordinarily the case, it being known as "*Na lipskich pasekach.*" The wife of Frank Šebesta, she to whom was born the baby daughter on the way to the new home and country, was herself born in 1831 in Hosčalkov, County Čestin, Moravia. Her mother had been one of a large peasant family. Two of the brothers were protestant ministers, another a choirmaster and teacher, one a farmer and another, according to family chronicles, "just a careless happy-go-lucky fellow." The little girl who was later to become the wife of Frank Šebesta and come to Texas, always helped her grandmother Kateřina of the large Kovařova family with her weaving. She of the large family was the one to inherit the family estate, heavily encumbered, however, with debt. So it was sold and a smaller place known as Na Haluzic purchased. There the family fared well with the good management of the maternal grandmother.

Little Rosalie helped at nights, holding the torch so that the work of the weaving might go on. On one occasion when there was a large stock of woven linen on hand as a dowry for the sons and daughters, robbers broke in and stole it. This, the family history records, so grieved the mother and weaver that she became ill and died. Rosalie was at that time eleven years of age, her sister Anna, ten, and a brother, Martin Jančalek, was in the army, his military service lasting fourteen years, taking him through the Italian campaign under Field Marshal Radetzy. A second wife came into the home, and Rosalie left the place at the age of sixteen to marry Frank Šebesta. The young couple bought a small place at Bohuslavice with a large incumbrance on it and this, together with heavy taxes and general dissatisfaction with life in Austria, brought the decision to emigrate to what they pictured as "The Golden America."

And so they reached Texas on that memorable day in 1855 with their Austrian passport papers which are yet preserved in the family.

At this time there were no farms for rent. Texas was yet undeveloped, was in the main an open country. Buffalo, deer, antelope, bear and other wild game were free to roam at large. American-owned farms were cultivated by negro slaves. In some places a German farmer had built a poor makeshift of a home for some of the immigrants. The Czechs were not acquainted with the farming methods of the new country, and worse, a terrible drought this first year was responsible for a very poor crop yield. There was no opportunity for earning even a scant wage. Frank Šebesta built a primitive place of abode for his family, the frame of poles, the roof of sod and grass. Leaving the family in this rude structure he went to seek work where a railroad was in course of building. The wife with the little family lived for two months on hickory nuts gathered from the trees in the woods. On one occasion, forced by the great hunger which came with the scant nourishment of the wild nuts, the mother went to an American family to ask for food. Not understanding her at first these Texans were inclined to laugh on hearing the foreign tongue, but finally grasping the meaning of the call they gave the help requested.

She awaited longingly the return of the husband, trusting that he would bring money to buy some of the things so badly needed, but he came finally empty-handed, penniless, having had his earnings stolen. It was yet early afternoon when he got home. There was wild game to be had in the open country so he went hunting and soon returned with quail, which provided food for supper and breakfast.

Soon they were able to rent a farm from a German settler who helped the family to get some cornmeal. In cooking and baking the meal into bread the housewife used suet. Rabbits were plentiful and provided the larder with meat. Some wild plant was used for green vegetables and coffee was made from the parched corn. With these provisions the family felt rather well supplied, especially after existing for two months on hickory nuts.

Everything was scarce in those first days of settlement. Frank Šebesta must plow the land, but needed a clevis for the plow to which he could hitch the traces. He bought a steer which he slaughtered. The family ate the meat, and from the skin was fashioned the plow clevis, which served its purpose well. The only implements in those days were the hoe and the plow. Convenient limbs of trees were used for harrows, and cotton was planted by hand. All cultivating of the crops had to be with the hoe.

Frank and Rosalie Šebesta worked hard, devoting long days and part of the nights to the labor of the farm. Their first year's crop on this rented farm was seven bales of cotton and enough corn for their needs. Half of the crop had to be given to the landowner, but they were able to buy a barrel of flour, which luxury pleased them more than anything since their arrival in the new country.

Later they planted for themselves some rye and wheat. This they had to harvest with the sickle and thrash with a flail. With the harvesting of this crop the family began to live better.

Having rented several years, they finally bought some land near the settlement of Vesely, Washington County, or Wesley as it is called today, paying $10.00 per acre, this being considered quite an exorbitant price at the time, as the land was not of the best quality.

A log house was the beginning of the development of the property. The roof was of rough hand-made shingles. On one side of the rude log cabin was built a primitive stone hearth where all the cooking for the family was done for seventeen years. Prosperity had been coming during these years, as there were horses and cattle and poultry, but very little money. But with the prosperity came the Civil War. During the time when there was talk of the abolishment of slavery and the possibility of war, the Czech immigrants, only a few years in Texas, not owning slaves, loving liberty with all the ardor of their Slavic temperament, resented the idea of slave-holding and in consequence, there were many who sympathized with the North. There were naturally exceptions, as in the case of the late Judge August Haidušek who fought in the Confederate Army.

Frank Šebesta, his health impaired through years of pioneering and the result of the hardships encountered, not wishing to join with the cause of the Confederacy, kept in hiding, but was caught and forced into the army. When the division in which he served was encamped near Hempstead, Waller County, the longing to see his family overcame him and he left to go home. He was again caught, being found as soon as he had reached the friendly shelter of his own fireside. He barely escaped hanging for desertion.

The women of Civil War days, as recalled by early Czech settlers, suffered much while the men of the family were in the army. Especially was this true of those women who had young children. The Czech women were successful in raising tobacco which they sold to the American women in exchange for cloth. The American women wanted the tobacco to send to their menfolks in the army. During these turbulent times flour could not be had, and coffee cost one dollar per pound.

After the close of the war, conditions were almost intolerable. Chaos and disorder reigned throughout the whole country. Armed bands of maurauders raided peaceful settlements, making life far from safe, especially among the foreign-born population, unable to speak the English language.

Stealing, burning and general destruction of life and property went on without penalty, there being for a time no law for protection of either life or property, no means for enforcing such a law. After the war, however, immigration to Texas increased and the aged father of Rosalie Šebesta came to spend his declining days in Texas, where he died at the age of ninety-four. Frank Šebesta died in 1874 and was buried in the cemetery at Wesley for which he had donated the land. The wife and mother continued after his death to carry on the farm work, as she knew well how to manage and look after business. She only retired from active work at an advanced age to make her home with her children and died at the home of a daughter, Mrs. Julia Škarpa of Snook, Texas, April 15, 1907, at the age of seventy-six. She was buried in the Snook Cemetery. As the mother of twelve children she had from her youth laid her hand to the distaf and took hold of the spindle that the welfare of her household might be well attended.

The pathos of the story of the establishing of this home in the seemingly unbearable hardships endured, has earned the Šebesta family a prominent place in the annals of Texas-Czech history.

The Šebesta name is found again twenty years later among the Czech immigrants coming to help settle Texas. George Šebesta, a younger brother of these earlier pioneers, Frank, Jan and Pavel, came with his wife and three children, John, aged ten, Joe, younger, and the daughter Fannie, from the native country of Moravia, in 1875. George had married Annie Nedbalek in the Old Country and, with their children, they settled at Wesley, Washington County, Texas. A later residence was established in Austin County. Three other children, Frank, Rosie, and Charley, were born in Texas. The father of the family being one of the successful farmers of his section, the family had the opportunities of education and the advantages of choosing professions and occupations in keeping with their ambitions.

The sons and daughters, with the exception of Fannie, who remained unmarried until her death, all have families residing in Texas. John, who was only ten years old when his parents reached Texas, married Mary Škrabanek and moved to Burleson County, near Snook, where he still lives. Mr. Šebesta has been successful as a farmer, and has reared a family of five children. Fannie remained at home with her parents and Jerry E., who married Mary Louise Patterson, resides in Houston. Henry Warren Šebesta, another son, married Esther Lešikar, daughter of a pioneer Texas-Czech family of this name, and resides in Houston, where he holds a position in the legal department of one of the large trust companies, having studied law and qualified himself for this particular position. A daughter, Stannie, married W. S. Lewis of La Porte. Another daughter, Vlasta, married T. V. York of Lyons, Texas.

Joe, another brother in the pioneer Šebesta family of 1875, born in the Old Country, married Annie Čermak and had six children—Johnnie, Vlasta, Albina, Libbie and twins, Ben and Bessie. This family resides at Bellville, Texas. Frank Šebesta, one of the sons born in Texas, married Albina Jančik. They reside also at Bellville, where their five children, Jerry, Frank, Arthur, Edmund and Ethel were born. Charles Šebesta married Annie Stephan, and they have seven children—Henry, Edwin, Charles, Alvin, Esther, Raymond and Gladys. Family home, Bellville.

The daughter, Rosie, married John Surovik of Bellville. They have five children—Annie, Walter, Olga, Rosalie and John. Walter married Lydia Pomykal. Annie married Albie Barnett.

The pioneer George Šebesta of 1875, father and grandfather of the large family named, died June 14, 1888, at an advanced age. The wife, Annie Nedbalek Šebesta, died April 28, 1920, aged eighty-five.

And through this progeny the family name of Šebesta in Texas will live and be perpetuated in the establishment of new homes through the State. The children of these generations may look back with pride to their ancestors, who kindled the first hearthstone fire in the new land of Texas.

CHAPTER VIII

THE REYMERSHOFFERS

In the year 1854 a three-masted sailing vessel, the *Ammerland*, docked at the quarantine station at Galveston. For eight weeks she lay anchored on the bar under strict quarantine. In full view of the harbor of "the land of promise," the vessel, which had been en route for nine weeks, rocked and swayed in the restless waters of the Gulf.

Jan Reymershoffer, wife and five children, Clara, Zdeňka, Otilii, Jan and Gustav, were among the passengers. The wife lay ill with smallpox, contracted on the voyage.

With the distress of the fevered body, endured under the trying conditions of little comfort and inadequate accommodations, the mind of the young mother must have turned back to her native land. There she had met Jan Reymershoffer, the dashing young knight, who had paid her most gallant attention. Clara Holly, daughter of an evangelical minister, was woed and won by young Jan and soon became his wife.

Jan Reymershoffer came from an old and prominent family of Holešově on Hane. The family had come to Moravia originally from Virtemberg in the sixteenth century, the name having once been Reimer zu Hoffer. The father of Jan Reymershoffer signed his name Frank Reymershoffer. He had married Innocencii Klašterňik. They had two sons, Jan and Jiřik. Jan was born on December 27, 1808. After finishing the public schools his ambition was to become an artist, but his parents wanted him to study for the clergy. When he would not follow their suggestions, and found that he could not become an artist, he went into trade.

After spending several years in Vienna, where he engaged in various branches of business, he returned to his native town and opened a general merchandise store. There he met Clara Holly at the fair and over the protest of both families they were married. Jan Reymershoffer was a good citizen and an ardent nationalist in his native country, which he loved. He took an active part in politics and in the year 1848, when not only his own country, but the whole of Europe, was rocked with disturbances, he found

66

UPPER LEFT: *Three generations, (seated) Clara Holly Reymershoffer, who came to Texas in 1854; her daughter, Clara Inocencii, and her daughter, Clara Sedonia.*

UPPER RIGHT: *Jan Reymershoffer, member of the Austrian Reichstag, 1848, and Czech pioneer of Texas, 1854, settling at Cat Springs; established a general store there the same year.*

LOWER: *The pioneer, Jan Reymershoffer and family. This picture was made in Matamoros, Mexico, at the close of the Civil War.*

himself in the midst of both opportunities and difficulties. He was elected a representative to the Austrian Reichstag. There is still to be seen among old documents in possession of the family at Galveston a black and white drawing showing the assembly quarters with the names and places of the members of the Reichstag. The name of Jan Reymershoffer is included.

It was in the Ministry of Schwarzenberg when Dr. Alex Bach became minister of the interior that he felt very deeply the oppression to which his people were subjected. All Czech political publications were suppressed, and in addition a constant watch was kept, through police and gendarmes, over all their activities, the heads of the more prominent families being under especial surveillance.

It was at this time that a letter from Arnošt Bergman, evangelistic minister located at Cat Springs, Texas, fell into the hands of Jan Reymershoffer. Immediately he started a correspondence with the Reverend Bergman and finally decided that he would leave his native soil for Texas. Eventually he arrived at Galveston as has been previously mentioned. When released from quarantine with his family he started immediately for Cat Springs.

There they were cordially received by Reverend Bergman. But with all the cordial welcome and kind greetings, the conditions that prevailed at the time in this primitive settlement were not conducive to peace, happiness and contentment. Possibly but for the horrors of the long voyage across the Atlantic, the Reymershoffer family would have returned to their native land of Moravia. Mrs. Reymershoffer admonished each one to have patience. They had brought with them several barrels of goods, intending to engage in the merchandising business. A shack was rented, the goods unpacked, and everything was then ready for customers. Business was good and it was not long before Jan Reymershoffer bought a farm on which he built a nice home and store. The farm was soon sold, however, as it was not easy to manage a farm and a general merchandising business too.

In an old china cupboard in the home of Miss Clara Reymershoffer of Galveston, daughter of one of the five children who came to Texas on the *Ammerland,* are several pieces of the chinaware brought over from Moravia in 1854.

An old silver candlestick, a beautiful hand-decorated beeswax candle, made in thread-like strands to be unwound and used threaded through a special holder, are as perfect and beautiful today as when made, possibly a century ago. Old china teacups and small pieces of bric-a-brac, remain as mute evidence of one of the first commercial enterprises of pioneer Texas—the first store of imported merchandise established in the State.

In 1859 the Reymershoffers decided to enlarge their business interests. They moved to Alleyton, Colorado County, which at the time had a promising outlook and did eventually become one of the most prosperous and thriving communities of that section, being recognized as an important cotton market.

Soon after the Civil War began. Jan Reymershoffer was in sympathy with the North, and consequently suffered much censure and criticism from his neighbors who were "southern sympathizers." His business declined, and his son Jan, Jr., obtained a position with a firm of German wholesale merchants named Dause at Matamoros, Mexico. The boy proved himself so honest and industrious that he was later made a partner in the enterprise. Gustav, the other son, soon followed his brother, leaving the father alone with his business at Alleyton.

After the war both Jan and Gustav moved to Galveston where their father soon joined them. They first established a glass and porcelain business, importing the goods from the Old Country. Later they sold this business and established a steam flour mill. About this time—October, 1876—Jan Reymershoffer, Sr., died.

The younger Reymershoffers exported Texas-made flour to England, Bremen and other European ports. In 1897 Gustav quit the business and Jan took over the management, being in addition Texas Consul for Austria at Galveston. He died on December 12, 1899. His wife, Mrs. Clara Clausen Reymershoffer, died in November, 1900, at the age of eighty-nine years. Gustav died in Galveston in November, 1903, being at the time a City Commissioner. His widow continued the family residence in Galveston and was still living at the old homestead on Post Office Street in 1934.

The Reymershoffer family tree, which was started in 1698, has always carried the family name of John. The daughters were always given three names, as Clara Innocencii Barbara, and Clara Sedonia Anna. Clara Innocencii was the daughter of the pioneers, Jan and Clara Holly Reymershoffer. She married František Nešetřil, but in the latter years of her life, took back her maiden name of Reymershoffer. Her daughter, also Clara, resides at the family home in Galveston. An only son, brother of Clara, died in his early young manhood.

The visitor to the office of J. Reymershoffer in Galveston will find the story of the pioneer family graphically told in old family records. In fireproof steel vaults these priceless mementos are kept. With the turn of the knob and the swinging open of the heavy vault door, files upon files and locked drawers in rows are exposed to view. With an index in his hand, J. Reymershoffer takes from a file document after document. One is the old citizenship papers granted to his grandfather at Cat Springs, Texas.

An interesting coincidence in the Reymershoffer family of Texas is that the three generations, the father, son and grandson —who is the present J. Reymershoffer III—have each held commissions and appointments under the late Emperor Franz Josef of Austria. It was in 1848 that Jan Reymershoffer held a seat in the Austrian Reichstag, his commission coming from the Emperor. In Texas, many years later his son, Jan Reymershoffer II was appointed Consul for Texas, representing the countries then under Austrian rule. At his death, his son, J. Reymershoffer III, received the appointment as consul and served until the United States entered the World War. These official documents of appointment are preserved in the Reymershoffer archives.

On the occasion of the Sixtieth Jubilee anniversary of the rule of Franz Josef, 1908, Mr. Reymershoffer, at the time consul for Austria, was made a Knight of the Order of the Iron Crown. Accompanying the announcement of the honor was the badge of the order. It is an exquisite example of the jeweler's art and is preserved in the original velvet, satin-lined casket. On the inside cover lining, embossed in gold, is the name of the crown jeweler. The history of the Order of the Iron Crown dates from the year 1815, when the order was created. It is said that the original crown was made of a nail of the Cross of the Crucifixion. The emblem, a solid gold and jeweled badge, has a fragment of iron within the gold, jewel-studded crown. The order was conferred on J. Reymershoffer "for valuable services rendered."

In addition to this honor, Mr. Reymershoffer received a gold memorial coin, one hundred kronen, equal in value to the American twenty-dollar gold piece. The piece, a medallion coin, was issued in commemoration of the Sixtieth Jubilee. A seal ring, over 150 years old, which belonged to Jan Reymershoffer, the first, which he wore on the index finger and used in putting a signature seal on letters and documents, is still in use by J. Reymershoffer III.

Several old Reymershoffer seals which have been in use in the family for generations are to be found in Mr. Reymershoffer's office, and are used when the occasion requires.

This member of the family, representing the third generation, has held a place in the affairs of Galveston for many years.

His name has been associated with many important enterprises, including real estate development, oil interests, and various business projects entailing large financial investments. He has traveled extensively, both in Europe and the United States. In his office he has a number of prized trophies of the hunt, two large mooseheads, mementos of two hunting trips in Canada. A caribou head, mounted and occupying a position over his desk, attests to his skill in marksmanship.

A large picture of his father, Jan Reymershoffer II, hangs on the wall of the office. There is a smile in the eyes as though life had been kind to him. This picture, the son recalls, was taken on the occasion of his departure for Europe to join Mrs. Reymershoffer and accompany her home. He had neglected to have his suit pressed, however, and no sooner had she seen the photograph than she discovered the omission, and another picture had to be taken in which this detail was correct.

The mother was descended from a long line of doctors and philosophers, men of scholarly attainments. She came to Texas for a visit to an uncle, a Dr. Aschoff, druggist in Galveston, and on the visit met and married Jan Reymershoffer, II. She spent much time after her marriage in Europe.

The oldest Moravian settlement in Texas was at Cat Springs, Austin County. It is not an historical fact that all Moravian and Czech immigrants of the period 1850 to 1854 came to Cat Springs. Some of them went to other localities. It is believed, however, that the first Czech settler in Cat Springs was the Reverend Arnošt Bergman, born August 12, 1797, in Zapudov, near Mnichova Hradiště, in Čechy. He moved with his family to Cat Springs in March, 1849. It is claimed that at the time there were no Czechs at this place. Not knowing what else to do, he bought land and began farming. In order to exist, his entire family had to work from daylight to dark. The head of the family found time for letter writing, and all early data pertaining to Czech immigration makes a mention that it was through the reading of a Bergman letter that a family or a group of families emigrated to Texas. That the Bergman letters were responsible for much of the early Czech immigration to the State is an accepted fact.

In the instance of Jan Reymershoffer I, wife and five children, it was a Bergman letter that was responsible for their immigration. When they arrived in Cat Springs, Reverend Bergman received them most cordially and did all that he could to make them feel comfortable. In turn, when the Reymershoffer family had become settled in their own Texas home, they too, extended hospitality to other Czech pioneers, offering whatever assistance they could in the matter of providing a home and comforts.

"There were many Czech families already settled in Cat Springs and Texas when my people came," J. Reymershoffer of Galveston relates. "Josef Šiller and his brother-in-law, Josef Maresh, and several other families from Nepomuk in Landskřon, had come to Cat Springs in 1852."

One of the Bergman letters had fallen into the hands of Josef Lešikar. This letter depicted conditions as being most favorable to settlement, so much so that several families who had previously decided on moving to Banat in Hungary changed their plans and made arrangements to sail through Hamburg for Texas. From Liverpool to Galveston they came on the ship *Victoria.* Josef Lešikar did not come until 1853, however, sailing at this time with a number of families on the ship *Savu,* the voyage lasting seven weeks.

Josef Tauberg, Bohumil Kolačny, Jan Kraulik and Anton Štupl, came to Cat Springs in 1854.

These names are given by way of establishing the residence of pioneer Czech immigrants at Cat Springs. The names and date of arrival in Texas, when thus authenticated, confirm other matters connected with the Czech settlement of Texas.

The question has been asked, why the early settlement by Czech pioneers at Cat Springs?

Ferdinand F. Doubrava, in an article printed in the *Wisconsin Magazine of History,* June, 1925, entitled "Experiences of a Bohemian Emigrant Family," gives a reason. A group of Moravian Brethren, led by a man named Koch, emigrated to the United States. When the Mexican War came, one of the members of the Koch family enlisted in the United States Army, and so valuable were his services, that after the close of the war he was granted a square league of land in Austin County, Texas. The Koch family had never broken off relations with their kinsmen in the Old World. In course of time correspondence spread in Moravia among the Czech Protestants and a large number were induced to seek homes in Texas, locating in the vicinity of the Koch grant.

In this connection Mr. Doubrava takes occasion to mention the Reymershoffer family. Speaking of the early settlers in the Koch vicinity he states that the people prospered abundantly in material ways, but had no schools or churches and no preachers to minister to them.

A Czech merchant named Reymershoffer who was living in

Alleyton, Texas, had a brother-in-law who was a pastor of a Calvinistic church at Miroslav, Moravia. His father was then a member of that congregation. Reymershoffer, strongly urged by the Czech community, implored his reverend brother-in-law to come to Texas and establish among the Czechs such a church as they desired, promising him liberal rewards. This was responsible for the coming of Reverend Opočensky to Texas about the year 1858.

The Doubrava family came to Texas in a "two-masted tub," a freighter out of Bremen for Galveston. When within sight of Galveston harbor, after weeks of storm and splintered masts at sea, and putting back into port for refitting, a nor'wester sent the ship prancing back over the storm-tossed Gulf, after fourteen weeks and two days at sea.

The family took a Buffalo Bayou boat at Galveston, boarded a train at Harrisburg and finally arrived at Alleyton, where they were welcomed by the Reymershoffers. They remained in the Reymershoffer home until they were rested from the voyage, then set out to visit the Reverend Opočensky who lived about twenty miles away. There being no stage coach or other means of travel, Ferdinand Doubrava and father started to walk the distance. On the way they were overtaken by a four-yoke ox-team and were given a ride to the end of the journey. Reverend Opočensky is said to have embraced his old friends, kissing them in the old country manner.

The war between the North and the South had by this time begun and Galveston, the only point of exit by water, was blocked, so the Doubrava family, who wished to return to Moravia, had to remain in Texas.

In writing of this experience, Ferdinand Doubrava states: "Never before had I held a plow handle in my hands. Never had I driven a yoke of oxen. I knew less about ploughing than did the oxen themselves, but being of stubborn disposition, we stuck to the work and had fair success."

Unaccustomed to the climate, the family suffered from typhoid fever and malaria.

"Doctors were scarce. Their visits cost twenty-five dollars each and medicines were worth a small fortune," he writes. "Flour was a dollar a pound and scarce at that. Sugar, tea and coffee were not obtainable at any price. Even salt was a precious item. In addition the danger to life and property was great and almost continuous."

Mr. Doubrava also mentions that he had the experience of being rounded up by bloodhounds, unleashed by a troop of guerrillas, and when captured was taken before a captain with the object of being forced into the Confederate Army. Through an interpreter, after much excited conversation and the producing of passports, showing that he was a subject of the Austrian Empire, he was released.

Many youthful Slovaks, Moravians and Bohemians were forced into the Confederate Army, most of them engaged at the siege of Vicksburg. After the fall of that city they were paroled and returned to Texas.

Another item of interest in connection with those trying days in Texas, as chronicled by Mr. Doubrava, was that their four years' cotton crop, which they had managed to conceal, was sold to a northern firm for a large sum of money, the payment being in United States gold. The Doubrava family moved from Texas to Wisconsin.

The hospitality of the Reymershoffers, previously mentioned, was a bright chapter of pioneer days. They founded a home and dispensed the generous hospitality which has brought the Reymershoffer name into prominence throughout the more than three-quarters of a century's residence in Texas.

So often in the memoirs of a Czech pioneer is found the statement, "The Reymershoffers helped us." As the Reymershoffer family helped others, they also helped themselves and in so doing, helped to build and develop Texas. Old documents and records show the care with which the family affairs and business operations were managed.

Looking back through the years to the days of the membership in the Reichstag, to pick out the name and seat set apart for the honorable member, Jan Reymershoffer, and trying to vision him in the wilds of Texas seventy-five years ago, we find it almost impossible to fit him in with the conditions of the time. And yet his training in his native country must have equipped him for the task he undertook and carried through in the land of his adoption.

He had wanted to be an artist—a painter—but fate had decreed otherwise; but in old records and papers in the possession of members of the Reymershoffer family are to be found his writings, drawings and sketches used in carrying on the every day affairs of life in the Texas home.

A cow in the pioneer days cost some $16.00 and for this reason was a valuable piece of property. The cows in the Reymershoffer herd were not only named, but pictures of them were drawn and kept for identification. In a book somewhat yellow with age, but well preserved for the more than half-century of its service, are to be found the names of cows, such as "Lillie," who was red and white; "Jenny," who was brown; "Flower," who had white feet; "Rosie," who was white, yellow and brownish. And there was an "Old Brindle" and a "Young Brindle." In some instances a pencil-drawing of the cow accompanied the name and description. A complete chart of all the neighborhood cattle brands and their owners was made by pioneer Jan Reymershoffer.

With merchandise brought over in 1854 the Reymershoffers became the first importers. And in this modern age when in most of the display windows of the big department stores of Texas are to be found goods from Czechoslovakia, it is interesting to turn the pages backward to the little village of Cat Springs and Jan Reymershoffer's first place of business.

Business was good in those pioneer days. Money was plentiful and not much to spend it for. Pioneer Reymershoffer prospered and soon there was talk of enlarging the business.

And now, eighty years after the establishing of the Reymershoffer store at Cat Springs, the few pieces of the imported stock of merchandise which remain, are as good as when unpacked from the shipping cases, fresh from the historic land of the far-famed "Bohemian Glass," embroideries, garnets and opals.

A sketch made in pencil by Gustav Reymershoffer, second son, of the pioneer home and estate at Cat Springs, soon after it was founded and improved, is being used in this history by permission of Miss Clara Reymershoffer, granddaughter of Jan Reymershoffer. The house was built soon after the family reached Cat Springs in 1854. The drawing was made not long afterward, according to Miss Reymershoffer.

And so it came to pass that the son of the father who wanted to be an artist and paint pictures in the Old World inherited the talent and the same inclination, and drew with his pencil pioneer Texas scenes including the first home of the Reymershoffer family. More than three-quarters of a century later the work of this pioneer Texas artist is brought forth to receive an award of honor. But for the pencil sketch, mellowed with age, historic scenes in the first Czech settlement in Texas at Cat Springs, would not have been preserved for historical record.

Another sketch by Gustav, that of a street scene in the pioneer village, appears on birthday greetings, made for his mother.

The value of these pencil drawings lies in the fidelity to detail, which include the fence, the cattle, the ox-drawn wagon, loaded with the bales of cotton, the cowboys, lariats in hand, and long-horn cattle on the open prairies.

It is a long step from the Austrian Reighstag to the old and tattered paper on which are to be found the brands and cattle marks of all settlers at Cat Springs. The record of these brands and marks was made by a member of the Reymershoffer family soon after the arrival of the family in 1854, the probable date being given by Miss Clara Reymershoffer as 1856. Miss Reymershoffer comments: "A cow was valuable in those days, being worth as much as fifteen or sixteen dollars, and hogs, sheep and goats, having their own relative value, and so it was a part of good business to have a record of all the Cat Springs cattle brands and marks."

The John Reymershoffer brand was an "Anchor and an R." Many pioneer names are to be found on the old document, among them that of Arnošt Bergman, who wrote the splendid letters which "sold" Texas to the hundreds of Czech immigrants who settled not only at Cat Springs, but in many other communities in the State.

CHAPTER IX

Judge Augustin Haidušek
Pioneer Statesman and Jurist

"If Judge Haidušek were living he could tell you—"
Not once, but again and again has come this lament in response
to the quest for early historical data.

In every section of the State where there are communities
settled by Czech citizens, the mention of pioneer days in Texas
brings to mind the name of the illustrious Czech statesman, jurist
and philosopher.

When he had lived in Texas for half a century, he stood where
he had spent his boyhood days and looked backward. As he
visioned the days when his people had first come to this new land,
he saw a country just emerging from the wilderness. A lad of
eleven years, when he came with his parents to Texas, his conception of the great state, whose limits are spanned by ten degrees
of latitude and as many of longitude, must have had lasting
influence.

In September, 1856, Valentin Haidušek with four children,
Theresa, John, Augustin, and Hynek, half-brother of the former,
left their native country for Texas. From the village of Mišši,
which had been the home of the family for generations, the
Haidušeks, with several other families, set sail for the new home
and country. The story of the voyage, with the subsequent journey
overland from Galveston and Houston to LaGrange, was graphically told in the address given by Judge Haidušek at Dubina on
the occasion of the fiftieth anniversary celebration and which is
reproduced in another chapter.

The village of Mišši, where Augustin Haidušek was born, is
situated in the northeast part of Moravia, near the Carpathian
Mountains. Here the Haidušek family, always agriculturists,
owned considerable land, which Valentin Haidušek had inherited
from his father, George Haidušek.

The mother of Augustin died in 1847, when he was but two
years old, and after her death he was placed in the care of an
aunt who took charge of him until his father married again in
1848. There were two other children by the first marriage, Theresa

76

Augustin Haidušek
La Grange, Texas

and John. John died on February 14, 1863, while stationed with Captain Alexander's company at Brownsville, Texas.

Having had some educational training before leaving his native country, Augustin Haidušek's education was continued under the direction of his father until the establishment of the first school. He knew nothing of the English language, however, until in the early sixties when he attended an English school. In 1863 he went with a drove of cattle to Louisiana. These animals were forced to swim the Mississippi River in order to be delivered to the Confederate Army at Port Hudson. On his return to Texas he enlisted in the Confederate Army, Company F, Bates Regiment, stationed at Fort Velasco. On June 6, 1865, he returned home and helped his father make a crop. The year 1866 found him farming and going to school. He clerked in a store in LaGrange for several months in 1867. In the fall of that year he cut and split 4,000 post-oak rails for a neighbor, George Morysek, continuing his English studies by firelight.

During the year 1868 he farmed and taught school, settling in LaGrange in 1869, where he began the study of law. On December 22, 1870, he was admitted to the bar. This was an event of paramount importance, both to himself, and his fellow-Czechs, he being the first Czech in the United States to earn such an honor.

Again he set a precedent when he was made mayor of LaGrange at the city election of 1875, being the first Czech to be elected mayor of an American city. In 1884, a little more than a quarter of a century after his arrival as a small immigrant boy in Texas, he was elected County Judge of Fayette County. In 1880 he was elected a member of the Seventeenth Legislature, representing Lee and Fayette counties.

During his administration as judge of Fayette County, much constructive work was planned and carried into execution. Nineteen iron bridges were built in the county and the bridge across the Colorado River at LaGrange was purchased, the vote of Judge Haidušek being the decisive one in the transaction. The contract to build the handsome courthouse at LaGrange was made and the foundation laid during his administration.

In 1885 Judge Haidušek established *Svoboda,* a newspaper which later had the largest circulation of any similar publication.

When the First National Bank of LaGrange was in need of a head, Judge Haidušek accepted the presidency and under his official administration the bank paid handsome dividends.

It fell to this early settler and community developer to carry through to completion many undertakings. He had the privilege of building during his term of office a bridge over Navidad Creek, where his boyhood home had been.

From this creek he had carried water to cool the fevered brows of the settlers who, unaccustomed to the privations of the new country, had fallen ill. In the waters of the historic creek he had often thrust his own small bare feet to cool and rest after the labors of the day.

The courage of the boy lasted through the years of a useful and prolific lifetime. His energy was pronounced "indefatigable." Strong of will, but not obstinate, he was ever an outstanding figure in promoting the welfare of his people, and that of the state of his adoption. Believing as the years brought progress and development that English should be the language of the Czech schoolroom, he urged its adoption and the employment of English teachers.

Augustin Haidušek believed in teaching the younger generation the lesson in the pioneering spirit which laughed at hardships and forged ahead toward perfection. He never lost the perspective of a wilderness that had been changed into a prosperous commonwealth.

The mere routine manner of citing the achievements and activities of this Texas-Czech pioneer falls short of being a fitting tribute, but his long life, with its full record, is one of the most inspiring chapters in the Texas-Czech history of the State.

Recalling in later life the rail-splitting days, and the studying at evening by firelight, he related that a small Webster's dictionary constituted his library; that he read this book through many times. He was a methodical man and kept accurate record of matters that pertained to business and his professional career.

From that day, August 15, 1856, when as a lad he embarked on a small sailing vessel at Bremenhaven, to the day October 30, 1856, which marked his arrival at Galveston after many weeks at sea, he held every incident in memory. The voyage to Texas, however, was but the preface to the story of a long and eventful life.

In the city election at LaGrange in February, 1876, he received one hundred and one votes. In the second election, 1878, which gave him the office for another term, he received one hundred and thirty-one votes, the two other candidates for the office receiving respectively eighty-one and forty-eight votes.

There was but a bare quarter of a century between that little immigrant boy of eleven years, and the Texas statesman who journeyed to Austin, taking with him the baggage of a well-to-do gentleman, the wardrobe befitting a man of affairs of the time.

These things did not come by accident, but were instead the result of studious endeavor and honest effort, coupled with the courage of a sturdy pioneer.

Judge Haidušek was throughout his long life an avowed Democrat. On one occasion, when addressing an audience in his home community, he took occasion to stress this point of his party policy, saying in the opening remarks of his speech that he was not a Democrat for office-seeking purposes, but from principle. At this time he was being urged to run for Congress, and said in part:

"Fellow-citizens, I appear before you not as a candidate for office, nor as an office-seeker, but as a citizen who feels a deep interest in the prosperity and welfare, not only of the particular party and people to which we belong, but to the whole of the people of the country.

"As one who loves this country, the people and the institutions above all else, who is ready to do all in his power for the whole people not by policy alone, but by principles, as such I appear before you today or at any time when I am called upon for service."

This fragment of an address given to his people while he was yet in the prime of his career, illustrates the spirit of the man. His whole life was spent in service in behalf of his fellow-man. Speaking on another occasion about administering justice, he said:

"It is often said that jurors when they retire to consider a verdict should be governed by common sense. I warn you against that idea. It is erroneous. While common sense is a desirable and advisable quality in man, and exceedingly useful in all the practical affairs of life, including the duties of jurors, it cannot be a better guide to them in the discharge of their duties than the rules of law. Indeed, the rules of law are generally the condensed common sense of ages. But the common sense of twelve jurors would not likely be all alike. If each juror were to act upon his common sense instead of the rules of law, there might be as many different opinions as there were jurors."

Throughout the whole of his life, which ended September 28, 1929, at the family home in LaGrange, after he had reached his eighty-fourth year, this pioneer was always a student. He never forgot a favor. During the years in Texas when the "Know-nothing Party" was strong, and sought to wage warfare on the so-called foreign element in the State, the Democratic Party came to the rescue, fighting the cause of the rights of the immigrant population. Judge Haidušek never forgot this. He espoused the cause of Democracy and fought in the ranks, carrying with him the almost solid vote of his people. The part he played in politics in Texas belongs elsewhere, however. The life work and the influence of Judge Haidušek may not be confined to any one chapter, nor to any specific period in the history of the Czech settlement of Texas. The efforts of the man, together with his achievements, are as a permeating influence that binds past, present and future.

Judge Haidušek was an ardent scholar, and his extensive library, which may still be seen in the family home in LaGrange, included a variety of books by authors past and present, all indicating a wide taste in reading throughout a busy life. In his law office were those volumes you would expect to find in any well-selected legal library. He was a close student of political economy, and attacked with an analytical mind any subject on which his interest became focused.

Following his legislative work as State Representative in the Texas Legislature, Sixteenth and Seventeenth sessions, his interest in his fellow-man stands foremost.

He advocated reform measures in the State penitentiary system. Opposed to any form of peonage or slavery, Judge Haidušek objected to the State leasing out the convicts for long periods.

In reviewing the outstanding incidents in the life of the man, attention is drawn to those early years when he was a small, barefooted immigrant boy, carrying the grass for thatching the roof of the pioneer home. Again when he hurried with water from the little stream to bathe the fever-scorched brows of his loved ones. Again as, after the day's labor, he sat at night with that small worn Webster's dictionary in the firelight, storing his memory with the words that were to serve him so well in the days to come, when he became the legal advisor of his people, the judge of his county, the mayor in his home town, a member of the Texas Legislative body, and finally the owner and editor of a newspaper that had the distinction of having the largest weekly circulation of any publication in the Southwest. In 1888 he assumed the management of the publication, rescuing it from indebtedness and building up the circulation from a few hundred to several thousand. In 1890 Judge Haidušek became the owner of *Svoboda* and published the paper in the interest of the Democratic Party.

The influence that Augustin Haidušek wielded through the columns of his newspaper is not shut away in dusty files. The boys and girls who read *Svoboda* are today men and women, and they remember how through its columns this Texas-Czech builder advocated self-culture and the practice of temperance in all things. While he did not oppose the dance, nor any kind of decent and wholesome amusement, he besought that all should be indulged sanely and not to exclusion of educational matters. A student himself, he wanted his own people to aspire to do that which fostered nobility of character and improvement of the mind.

An incident in the life of Judge Haidušek recalled by one of his lifelong friends, Judge L. D. Brown of the Texas bar, illustrates not only the intellect of the man, but gives an insight into his forceful character and splendid qualifications.

The occasion was a national meeting in Chicago in 1907 of Bohemian organizations, fraternal lodges included. In the evening a banquet was held on the roof of the LaSalle Hotel and Senator Choate was guest-speaker for the occasion. He had been invited because of his recognized knowledge of the Constitution of the United States, and his ability to interpret it. After he had finished speaking there were calls from the banqueteers for Judge Haidušek. Judge Haidušek rose, with the poise and dignity for which he was ever noted, from his seat at one of the banquet tables. After addressing Senator Choate, the speaker of the evening, he began talking as he was qualified to do. With every word his eloquence took on greater richness. He spoke of the Constitution of the United States as he knew and interpreted it. He spoke of America, the land of his adoption, with the respect and reverence of the citizen who loved it dearly for the privileges it provided, the personal liberty it gave and the protection the Government guaranteed every citizen in the pursuit of life and happiness.

The address was spontaneous and therefore there was no copy kept, but Judge Brown recalls the fervor of Senator Choate's congratulations and his confession to this Texas-Czech that he had given him (Choate) a better understanding of the Constitution of his country than he had ever had before.

Judge Haidušek was married in May, 1872, to Miss Bečka, native of Austin County, Texas, who was born near Bellville, on June 27, 1856, just a few months prior to arrival of the Haidušek family in Texas. She was the daughter of John and Catherine (Zgabay) Bečka, natives of Moravia. This family had come to Texas in 1855, according to old records, and settled in Austin County. Judge and Mrs. Haidušek had five children. Two of them, George L. and Vlasta (Mrs. Koss) reside in LaGrange.

Mrs. Haidušek wielded a wonderful influence over the life of her husband and children. In the family home at LaGrange she was surrounded by the happy family circle, to which was drawn the social and educational element of the entire town and community.

CHAPTER X

AFTER FIFTY YEARS

CZECH immigrants to Texas shipped in whatever vessel they found available as they turned their faces toward free America. The names of many of the ships of the pioneers are lost to present-day historians. Of small importance at the time, they were soon forgotten, being but the means to an end, and yet these now-forgotten sea-going craft hold a place of vital importance in the story of immigration.

Storm-tossed, rocked by the ever-restless waves, the small sailing ships with their cargo of pioneers, found harbor in Texas ports. We think of them with reverence and silent admiration.

At Dubina in 1906, on the occasion of the fiftieth anniversary celebration of the first Moravian settlement west of the Colorado River in Fayette County, Judge Augustin Haidušek was among the speakers. He spoke in the Czech language, but through the courtesy of Dr. Henry R. Maresh of Houston, the address has been translated for use in this history. It is a literal translation and presents conditions of the time in a colorful and realistic manner.

"It was in the early part of September, 1856, when my father, who was living in the small village Mišši, between Frenštat and Přibor in northwestern Moravia, moved with the determination of settling somewhere in America. With him from the same village came Ignac Pustějovsky and Valentin Holub, all going in wagons to Bohumin, and were there joined by families who were also going to America. At Bohumin we boarded a train and went to Bumen; there we stayed several days. Then we boarded a small boat and sailed down the river to Bremenhaven. There we were transferred to a larger sailboat and this carried us to Galveston, Texas.

"This sailboat was about one hundred feet long and had only two masts. This was a mere rowboat when compared to the steamships which present-day emigrants come in. The very first night we ran into a storm, the waves tossed our boat as if it were a piece of wood, and to my dying day I will not forget the suffering and sea-sickness of the travelers, especially of the women. This lasted a whole night and a day; after this the sailing was fair, but it was fourteen weeks before we reached Galveston Harbor. At that time Galveston was a very small town. A small steamboat towed our sailboat to a larger steamboat on which all of our belongings were loaded and then carried us up the Buffalo Bayou to Houston, which we reached early the next morning on the Day of All Saints. The following families landed: "Konstantin Chovanec, Josef Janda from Trojanovic, Bejamin Klimiček, Alois Klimiček, Valentin Kolibal, Vojtěch Kněsek, from Frenštat; Ignac Šramek, Josef Kalich, Ignac Mužny, Josef Petr, Frank Marak from Tiche; Frank Šugarek from Klokočova, Ignac Pustějovsky, Valentin Holub and my father Valentin Haidušek from Mišši and Frank Kosa from Skenov, John Konvička, who were single. Several young ladies, Johana Brož, Rosalie Mužny, Rosalie Holub, and two from Frenštat whose names I have forgotten, were in the party. There were also several families of Germans.

"That very same day our belongings were loaded on wagons and to each wagon was five yoke of oxen. In this manner we started on our trip. There were no railroads. We left Houston in the early afternoon and a few miles from town we spent our first night. It was a nice picture to see each family build individual fires and prepare the evening meal. Some of them had their small children with them who became cross and irritable. It was six days before we reached Cat Springs in Austin County. There we camped that night in a small grove of trees where we were visited by a man whose name, I think, was Matuštik. He talked about Texas so badly that several families decided to return to Galveston and from there go to the State of Iowa, where lived a Mr. Holub, also from our village. But then a Mr. Hirsch, a Czech who lived at Cat Springs, came to see us and persuaded us to stay in Texas, saying that we would reach Iowa in the time of the greatest cold; that it would be as cold there as it was in our home in the old country. We then decided to stay.

"We were there about two weeks and during that time my father, with Josef Petr, Josef Kalich and Frank Marak, explored the surrounding country. When they returned they could not say too much about Fayette County. They said the country was beautiful, the soil was rich and that they had contracted for some land. With them came two wagons and in these we traveled to LaGrange where we stayed a few days, while Marak, Kalich, Šramek, Petr, Holub, Mužny, Janda and my father bought land in East Navidad. To this point we were carried in wagons by Joe and Charlie Brasher. This piece of land is here, at Dubina, and on it we settled; not all of us, only Petr, Šramek, Kalich, Mužny, Holub and my father. Janda did not move but remained at Bluff, selling his land to Mužny. Marak moved the coming year, having stayed at Bluff the first year.

"It was in the latter part of September, 1856, when the Brasher brothers brought us here and unloaded us under liveoak trees on Holub's land, in the early afternoon. A strong north wind was blowing and it was sleeting. We were wet through and through. The only shelter we had was the trees. For many miles around no one lived. There was much crying and lamenting for fear that we would perish. Shortly the fire was made and the evening meal was prepared, but during the night no one slept as it was raining and sleeting. The next day was clear so that everybody who was capable of manual labor had to work. By the evening of that day there was a house built on our land in which we lived for the next six months, and that comfortably. On the morning of this day my father found two forked trees that stood close together. He cut a long pole which he placed between the forks of these two trees. Then other poles were cut and placed, one end into the ground, the other end against the cross pole. Across these poles smaller poles were placed and these were fastened with vine twigs. While the men were doing this work the women were cutting grass which was several feet high. This was tied into bundles and I carried this on a horse. This grass was made into flat bundles similar to boards and out of this the roof was made. It was put up so securely that even during the hardest rains the roof did not leak. In this kind of hut we lived; and we loved each other. There was no quarreling and fussing, but instead, we worked together peacefully.

"Mr. Frank Kosa later built a house for us out of shaped logs, and I am sure that it is still standing as it was built. We lived in this house until 1867 when father sold this farm and bought another one about three miles west of Schulenburg, on which Brother Hynek Haidušek is still living. As soon as the huts were built we began to clear and plow the land and make rails so that by planting-time everybody had a few acres of land prepared. We planted the corn about twelve feet apart, leaving three and four stalks together, thinking that in this way we would gather a bigger yield. We also left the cotton very close together in rows about two feet apart. When the corn began to bloom an American citizen, John Prude, visited us. We were just then plowing the corn for the last time. He pulled up stalks of corn, leaving the spaces as it should be. We did not like this, thinking that he had ruined a lot of corn for us. While he was doing this he was talking and showing, but we did not understand what he said, because we did not know the English language. The corn that was spaced by Mr. Prude had very good ears, while the ones that we left did not have anything but shucks. The total yield of cotton of the six families amounted to one bale and this was not heavy. We loaded this on a sled and carried it to LaGrange for sale. At that time we bought all of our needs in LaGrange.

"The first year was a sad one as there was not a single family that was well. They all became ill at the same time with chills and fever, which illness stayed with them for a long time. I, however, did not get sick and this certainly was good, because even at that time, I was very hard-headed and bad, too, and evidently for this reason the fever left me out. And it was well as I knew a few words in English so that I went after the doctor and interpreted as much as I could. Also I administered the medicine and carried cool water to refresh the sick. This sickness as I learned later was caused by heavy work and impure drinking water. We all had shallow wells from which we got our water. After the first year everybody was well from then up to now. The second year was worse than the first, in a way, because there was nothing to eat and no money to buy food with. During the first year all the money that was brought from Europe was spent. However, we did not remain altogether hungry. We bought our corn from the miller, Mr. Němec, in LaGrange. Dr. Meyenberg at Bluff was our doctor. For the corn we paid two dollars per bushel, and it was not the best. For the flour we paid twenty dollars per barrel. Meat was cheap, however, and altogether everything else was very high. The second year we knew how to farm and the young people could talk English. The Americans came to us from afar so that they could see the emigrants. They were polite and kind and taught us how to do things. The second year we made a good crop, both of corn and cotton and every year after that first year, so we soon forgot the hard times we experienced in the beginning.

"When four years later new emigrants came, some of them expressed surprise at the buildings we were living in. Several families stopped with us, among them Valentin Gallia, a classmate of my father. After he looked at our building, which was fairly good, he said 'My dear Valento, you had a better pig-sty at home,' and my father answered, 'I had rather live in this hut as an American citizen than to live in a palace and be under the

Austro-Hungarian oppression.' I remembered these words although I did not understand their significance then, but later I understood and I certainly do value their meaning today. Thanks to the Lord, there are only a few of us who do not realize the importance of being an American citizen. We appreciate these privileges even though we got them without effort, while our brothers across the ocean, to obtain these same privileges, offered not only their property, but even their blood and lives. These privileges were denied for hundreds of years for the reason that their forefathers did not uphold their rights.

"It should be our desire that our sons become good citizens, that they should be able to attend to their affairs and while doing this we should not forget ourselves.

"We were the first Czech citizens to settle on the west side of the Colorado River and, out of these first settlers, there are still living Valentin Holub, Frank Kosa, Mrs. Janakova and Mrs. Syřinkova. The others have passed on and left us as young people, but some of us are now old, so it will not be long before we will follow them. Our places, however, will be taken by the younger generation."

                    *   *   *   *

This one of the early Czech settlements had been first called Navidad owing to the proximity of Navidad Creek. Judge Haidušek substituted Dubina, a Bohemian name, meaning "Oak Grove."

On the fertile prairie of Navidad, bordered with liveoak and postoak trees, the pioneer Czech settlers found their first homes. There were no railroads in the county, freight had to be hauled by wagon from Houston, and from this point transported by team throughout the country. The wagon was the home of the driver who went into remote parts of the country for a "consideration."

Those early days, as reviewed by Judge Haidušek, presented the hardships, the sufferings and privations endured, but withal, there was happiness.

Konstantin and Apolen Chovanec and family, two sons and four daughters, one, Johanna, a baby of three years, were among those who came to Texas with the Haidušek immigration party.

This family settled in Fayette County, renting first a farm on the Colorado River from a resident named Bell. The two sons died at this place. The family then moved to Ross Prairie, near Fayetteville, where after a few years they bought a farm.

Johanna, whose death occurred on January 19, 1932, at the

age of seventy-eight years, had an eventful life, the story of which might read like a true adventure in a wilderness country.

When she was twenty years old she wished to marry, but her parents objected because the man of her choice, Alois Polansky, did not own a farm. Love has been accredited through the ages with always finding a way, so with the aid of his parents, the young man purchased a farm, giving his note for $100.00 as the initial payment. No cash money was involved in the transaction. When this important deal was attended to, Johanna Chovanec and Alois Polansky were duly married. The groom was given a horse and a strip of bacon by his folks. Johanna owned three cows and two calves, but soon after the wedding a thief took one of the cows. Alois carried corn to a mill owned by his parents, to be ground into meal, and with the sale of poultry and eggs the couple bought sugar and coffee.

Their first year's store-bought supplies amounted to $2.00 worth of coffee and one sack of flour, for which they paid $1.00. They lived on cornbread, corn mush, and occasionally bread made from a precious sack of wheat flour. The farm they purchased was grown-up in weeds, but with a good pair of oxen, also bought on credit, they worked. From daylight until dark the two were in the field. Johanna cooked the meals after dark. The husband's health failed under the strain of this excessive toil, and he contracted what was thought to be consumption.

He was told that he had but a short time to live, that his left lung was gone. Remembering the healing virtue ascribed to some old herbs, he began taking medicine which he prepared from these. The story handed down through the years is that in seven months he was able to be back at the plough in his fields.

During these months the young wife added a baby daughter to the family.

Their next venture was the purchase of a building in the town of Fayetteville. Also some tinner's tools were bought, and the husband opened a tin-shop. The farm had been rented and the cotton was being eaten up by the seemingly ever-present boll-weevil, so the young tinner in his new shop invented a sprinkler which would sprinkle eight cotton rows at the time. He obtained a patent and began making the sprinklers on a commercial basis. From this enterprise the couple were able to save several hundred dollars, and with the money bought an adjoining building, known as a hotel, in which a general merchandising store was opened along with the tin-shop. The farm was sold and the family located permanently in business in town.

At this time a brother of Johanna Polansky, Konstantin Chovanec, who owned a gin at Fayetteville, died. His father was made the administrator and put the son-in-law, Alois, in charge to operate the gin. Johanna, the wife, was left in charge of the business of tin-shop and store.

Misfortune seemed to have been lying in wait around the corner. Polansky had sold a plot of ground adjoining his property to Vetter Brothers, supposedly for a saddlery business and a saloon. Polansky had his business in the front part of the building and the family lived in the rear, the upstairs being rented to a doctor. One night Vetter's caught fire and the whole block burned with the exception of one building, which was saved by a sudden rainfall. The merchandise that was carried out of the burning building was stolen overnight. Mrs. Polansky became overheated, got wet and chilled, which permanently impaired her health.

She and her husband went to California where at a sanitarium he began the treatment of soldiers for tuberculosis from which he had miraculously cured himself. The wife returned home to Texas, where she continued to decline in health.

They lived together, however, for fifty-eight years. Two sons now live in California, and two in Taylor, Texas. One daughter, Matilda, married Frank Špan; one, Albina, married Frank Bača, of Bay City; another daughter, Mary Chalupka, lives in Fayetteville, and Sofie Kučera lives in Dallas.

In looking back through the years, as Judge Augustin Haidušek did on the occasion of the fiftieth anniversary of the founding of Dubina, it would seem that there was more of sacrifice and trial than there was of luxury and the leisure which modern life demands as essential to peace, happiness and comfort. But they are not quoted as ever having complained. They labored for future generations, that they might enjoy some of the things which the pioneers doubtless only dreamed of.

CHAPTER XI

The Schiller Family

Mrs. Alvina Matějka, of Caldwell, Texas, widow of the late Frank Matějka, was born in Texas during the tragic era, 1861-64.

She says of herself: "I am the seventh child of Vincent and Frances Schiller, born April 17, 1863, during the height of the Civil War. My father left with cotton on a trip to Old Mexico. I was not there when he left. When he returned, months later, I was three months old."

Referring to the eventful lives of the pioneers, Mrs. Matějka continued:

"In spite of all hardships my parents also enjoyed a lot of happiness. They accumulated considerable property, reared a large family, and lived to an age where they were able to enjoy the fruits of their endeavors. Now they are both dead, buried by the Moravian Brethren Church at Industry, Austin County, in which church and community they lived and labored.

"There were twelve children. Some of them died young, but they reared nine, seven daughters and two sons, to years of maturity.

"My father, Vincent Schiller, was born on March 18, 1829, in Čermne. My mother, Frances Schiller, was born on November 18, 1834, in Čermne. They were married August 13, 1850, my father being twenty-two and my mother sixteen. Father died February 11, 1899, and mother died May 12, 1906.

"When my father married, his parents, Pavel and Kateřina Schiller, desired that he take charge of the estate, according to the custom of the times, but the young married couple did not wish to do this, as the property was not fully paid for. They lived for a time with the wife's parents, then heard of some families leaving for America, and they decided to join the immigrant party.

"Mother's oldest sister, a Mrs. Marek, had been in Texas for three years, having left the native country in 1850. While on the ocean her husband died, and she found herself alone with two young sons. Both sons died in Galveston, leaving her

JOSEPH H. SHILLER of Rowena, Texas
Eighty-four years old in 1933

This pioneer Texas-Czech citizen is the oldest living Czech immigrant in Texas, having been in the State for eighty years, settling at New Ulm in Austin County. Grandfather of John G. Bubak of Dallas.

destitute, alone and friendless in a strange land. She finally reached Industry, Austin County, and there looked for work, finding domestic duties in a family by the name of Nagle. She did all the housework, including the washing and ironing, for three dollars per month. Not being able to speak English she found it hard to remain in this employment.

"Later she met a widower with two children, Henry Ginzel, and they were married. The Ginzel home was comfortable and the husband provident, so she invited my parents and my mother's parents to come to Texas, as she was very lonesome and homesick. So in the year 1853 they decided to emigrate. They had two children at this time, the youngest a baby only six weeks old. With them was a young man, Josef Maresh, and the Elšik, Kořinek, Štěpan, Ignac Schiller, Hrdlička, Rypl, Patka, Hanka, and Slováček families.

"They embarked in a sailing ship and were nine weeks envoyage, being many times off their course, which made it necessary to battle with the waves on a trackless expanse of water. Their provisions ran low. They had only black bread, which got so hard it was almost impossible to eat it.

"At Galveston my parents and members of the family were met by my brother-in-law, Henry Ginzel. He came with a wagon of two wheels which he had made himself, the wheels being fashioned from a large tree, having been sawed from the body of the tree and holes cut through the center for the axle. To this primitive vehicle he had hitched a yoke of oxen. It was, of course, impossible to haul all the members of the family by this crude means of transportation, so the result was that they started for Industry, getting separated in the meanwhile, which resulted in each one going a different route, and arriving at different places. Some of them arrived finally at Industry. As much of the baggage and personal belongings as possible had been loaded on the two-wheel ox-drawn wagon which proceeded along the pioneer road toward Industry. Young Josef Maresh died on the way.

"When my parents reached Industry they found my aunt, Mrs. Ginzel, living in a small log house. My mother's parents remained with her, but my parents went in search of a place of their own. A short distance from the Ginzel place they found a small log cabin belonging to a German named Patlcove, who offered to rent it. The house consisted of one room, no windows, a hole for the entrance and a dirt floor. It was only partly finished, so my father completed the construction, making a roof out of grass and cornstalks. The cracks between the logs were filled with the same material. In the absence of a door for the entrance, a quilt was hung. Four poles were fastened into the wall in such a way that they served as a bed. Mother was provident enough to have plenty of bedding and bedclothes. In the middle of the room, on the dirt floor, the fire was built. There all cooking was done in a big iron pot, the fire also supplying the family with light at night. There were no matches, the fire being lighted from an old flint brought from Europe along with the family household goods.

"Some of the pioneers brought with them small mills in which they ground the corn. Others, who had no mills, beat the corn, boiling it into corn mush. Water was the only drink, except in the instance of a few families who had some rye which they roasted, using it instead of coffee. Some of these first pioneers dried the skins of the sweet potato and used this as a substitute for coffee.

"There was no milk, all the cattle being wild. There were plenty of prairie chickens and sometimes a nest of their eggs was found in the prairie grass. There was plenty of wild game. Tallow served as a lard substitute.

"An improvised light at the time was a wild gourd filled with tallow into which a cotton string was placed, wick fashion. It was necessary to keep a constant watch over the wick to prevent the gourd catching fire.

"Work was hard to find. Those who owned slaves did not hire help. Father split rails and fence posts for twenty-five cents a day. Crops were poor and there were very few farm implements. Ploughs were made of wood to which was attached a small piece of steel which served to break the soil. There being no way to sharpen the steel, it wasn't a very successful means for cultivating the crop or breaking the hard prairie soil.

"There was an epidemic of cholera in which mother's brother died while she held him in her arms. The body was wrapped in a clean white sheet and, with the saying of a short prayer, was buried. The members of the family present at the time left as quickly as they could as everyone was so much afraid of the disease. The other members of the family had been in close contact with him during the illness, but not one became ill. My mother attributed this to her prayers.

"Then came tragedy—the Civil War. My father, to keep from going into the service, agreed to haul cotton to Old Mexico. On each trip there would be six and seven wagons, each drawn by four or more yokes of oxen. These trips lasted as long as three months. The oxen moved so slowly that my father has often related the story of how, after traveling all day across the prairies, they could in the late evening look back over the route and see the place where they had camped the previous night. On one trip father became seriously ill. Mother was notified. The message said to come and get him, as he was dying. At this time Reverend Josef Opočensky was in Industry, having come from Czechoslovakia in 1861. My mother pleaded with him to take her to the place where my father was ill. Reverend Opočensky owned a horse and buggy and in this they made the trip. How far they had to go, I do not know, nor when they returned home.

"Women did all the farming in those days of war time. They were not able to produce good crops, as their strength was not sufficient to cope with the hard, dry prairie soil. If they were fortunate enough to make a few barrels of corn, this was taken by the soldiers to feed their horses. The surrounding country was uninhabited, so there was no one to ask help of. If anyone had cattle or milch cows, the soldiers slaughtered them for food, without asking. They laughed when my grandmother shook her fist at them. The family water was procured from a near-by creek and in order to have a clear supply, a barrel was placed in the creek deep enough to permit the water to seep into it.

"On one occasion my father purchased a wild steer, hoping to tame and train it to the yoke, but it became necessary to kill it. This was done in the middle of a prairie and, being unable to carry the meat, it had to be left unless there was the price of the hire of a wagon in which to haul it.

"During the war some of the young men wanted to evade army service. They had immigrated to America to escape military duties and the story of wars. On one occasion a young boy came to my mother and proposed that if she would give him a dress and a bonnet, he would plow and work for her in the fields. She agreed and it was arranged that if mother saw the officers coming she would call out the warning, 'Volkama gee' in a loud voice, thus giving the boy time to hide.

"Religious services were held in some of the homes. The singing was from one song book. Great distances were traversed in order to attend these services, and when the children had to be taken to be christened, a makeshift sled was rigged up consisting of a cowhide stretched across the box frame of the vehicle. Father walked alongside to drive the oxen. It was necessary on one occasion to cross a stream, the banks on either side being steep.

In order to climb up the opposite bank father whipped up the oxen, spilling us into the water. It was considered only a part of the trip and was not considered an accident.

"After the war, conditions were better. Father purchased some land and built a home for the family, which had increased during the years since the first arrival in Texas. They were able to make payments on the homestead in spite of the fact that they had a lot of bad luck. They lost their horses and cattle. The cotton gin burned and with it five bales of their cotton and a lot of cotton bagging. They had to forget these misfortunes and work a little harder.

"In those days people sowed rye and oats for their own use. There were no implements for the cultivation of grain, it being necessary to cut it by hand. Harvest time was an enjoyable occasion, for all the neighbors gathered to help each other. The grain was threshed by hand after being hauled to the house from the field. It was carried to a large barn on a wagon sheet, a bundle of wheat was placed in the middle of the sheet, and men with flails stood on each side and threshed it out.

"Weddings were the great events of the time. My three sisters had grand weddings. The best cooks that could be had were hired for four days before the weddings to prepare the feasts. Chickens, turkeys, ducks, hogs, geese, beef and mutton were included in the meat course, as many people were invited to attend the festivities. The bride selected several attendants whose duty it became to invite the guests. Each bridegroom had a beautiful horse especially selected for the occasion, gaily caparisoned as to saddle and bridle, with a green twig and flower placed on the bridle, just behind the horse's ears. The groomsmen had flowers in their hats. In those days it was not an offense to carry firearms, and each groomsman had with him his pistol, which he fired on riding to the home where there were guests to be bidden to the wedding. On the report of the pistol he would be greeted by the friends of the household who would serve some light refreshments. Then the courier would proceed to the next neighbor's home where the ceremony would be repeated. The weddings were beautiful. The brides wore full bridal toilets with long veil and orange wreath.

"A beautiful old custom, which it would be well to emulate today, was the part of the ceremony where the bride and groom went to the outside of the home, at which spot they were met and welcomed by a band of musicians. After this attention they entered the house where only the parents of the couple awaited their coming. The bride thanked her parents for their care in

having reared her and begged their forgiveness for whatever she
had done to cause them sorrow or worry. The bridegroom did
likewise with his parents, and then asked the parents of the bride
to receive and accept him as their own son. They then received
the blessings of all parents and immediately approached the altar
improvised for the occasion, and were united in wedlock.

"The bride was presented with clothing and household furnishings by her mother. There was no silk available and the material
used was fine linen. There was no thread to be had when my
sisters were married, but my mother had a white sheet which
she had brought from the old home and from this she drew the
threads used in making the wedding garments. The hats were
woven from corn shucks.

"In those early days there were few schools. A Czech teacher,
Josef Mašik, taught at Wesley, Washington County. Our parents
sent us to school there. They had to pay tuition as well as board.
It is no wonder that we older children received so little schooling,
but we are grateful for what we have. The younger children had
better opportunities and were given good educations, both in
Czech and English. One brother, Vincent, studied bookkeeping
in New Orleans. My brother, William, studied pharmacy for
three years at Louisville, Kentucky. A younger sister attended
school in Brenham, Washington County. The children of my
parents, who are yet living beside myself are Mrs. Marie Ustynik; Mrs. Matylda Schiller; Mrs. Little Glenn, and one brother,
Vincent Schiller. I have four sons living, John C. Matějka of
West, Ladimir K. Matějka of Harlingen, Captain Jaroslav Matějka
of New Jersey, and Franklin Matějka of Brownsville, Texas.
My daughter, Gardenia Lešovsky, died in 1909."

*   *   *   *   *

Josef H. Shiller, Texas-Czech Pioneer, presents a vivid picture
of early days in the Southwest.

"It is hard to write about things that happened more than
eighty years ago," says Mr. Schiller. "I do not remember much
from my childhood years, but I will try to give my experiences
in chronological order.

"I was born on April 27, 1849, in Nepomuk, Čechy. I was a
little over four years old when my father and several other families decided to emigrate to America. This was in the fall of 1853.

"My oldest sister, Anna, with her husband, Vincenc Schiller,
had gone to America two years earlier. They were located at New
Ulm, Austin County, Texas, along with several other Czech fami-

lies. My father was Jan Schiller; my mother Terezie (née Jirasek) Schiller. Their children were Anna, Rosalie, Jan and I, Josef. I was at that time the youngest. Vincenc was born in Texas.

"As well as I remember, this group of emigrants consisted of the following: Jan Schiller, my father, and family; his four brothers, Karel, Vincenc and Franta with their families and Bernard, single; Josef Lidmuil Lešikar, with wife and four sons, Josef, Karel, Vincenc and Jan; Jan Coufal and family; Josef Mareš and family. All of these settled at New Ulm. There were more in this group, but I do not remember their names.

"The voyage across the ocean was made in a sailboat and lasted thirteen weeks. I do not remember the voyage, but I was told later that the boat was blown from its course by a storm, which was the principal cause for the long voyage. I remember only one incident. An elderly German lady, wearing wooden shoes, was walking down the steps when she slipped and fell. In later years, during the World War, when I heard the rat-tat-tat of a machine-gun it carried me back to the time of my voyage to the United States, the sound being similar to the noise made by the German lady's wooden shoes on each step as she fell.

"We landed in Galveston. There we were transferred to a barge and towed up the Buffalo Bayou to Houston where we were loaded into wagons drawn by many yokes of oxen and thus carried to Cat Springs. The trip from Houston to Cat Springs lasted over two weeks, but it was an extremely pleasant one. We soon left Cat Springs and later reached New Ulm.

"The first year, 1854, we lived with Anna and Vincenc Schiller; the second year we lived with the family of Rosalie Ježek, where also lived Josef Mareš and family. The Ježek home was a log house, one large room and a small side room, called the 'back room.' During warm weather the cooking was done out in the open. In cold weather the fire was built in the middle of the big room, the floor of which was composed of packed dirt. There was no fireplace. The third year father bought a farm of 144 acres, two miles east of New Ulm, at that time on the main road to Houston.

"About this time father was taken ill. Shortly after he died, at the age of sixty-six. I was ten years old at the time and remember well this sad incident. The neighbors gathered and made a box coffin out of unplaned post-oak boards. The hearse was a two-wheeled cart, drawn by oxen. Father was buried at New Ulm.

"After father's death mother divided her time with her children, Rosalie, Jan, Vincenc and myself. We lived this way through the Civil War, until 1865, when sister Rosalie married Karel Rippl. Brother Jan also left home.

"Our experiences during the Civil War were hard. The Czech emigrants left the Old Country to escape wars, and when they came here, they did not understand the cause for the conflict. To them it seemed that it was brother killing brother. Consequently, they did not feel like taking part, so evaded the draft whenever possible and went into hiding. The solicitors were mainly slave-owners. I remember when they came after Tomaš Wotypka. He ran and was shot and killed. Vinc Schiller also was shot while running away, but received only a scalp wound. He was held captive under guard in his father's home, but before his wound healed, he escaped and was not captured again. There were many such escapes of Czech and German boys, but I cannot recall their names.

"Life was simple and yet there was contentment among our people, even if they had just escaped Austrian oppression. Our family cultivated about twenty acres. The farm implements consisted of one plow with a wooden mold board, a wooden three-prong harrow, and a few hoes to chop cotton. It would be interesting to observe a modern farmer cultivating his crops with such equipment.

"Neither were we very selective in our foods. There was plenty of milk, meat, butter, cheese and bacon, as hogs roamed wild in the woods. Sweet potatoes were plentiful as they grew well in the sandy soil. The only bread we had was made from corn. During the war, on account of the blockade, it was impossible to buy coffee, so the housewives, being resourceful, experimented with different ingredients; some parched rye, others parched sweet potatoes, and still others parched acorns. So, you could have your choice, according to taste.

"Clothing was usually made at home from any material obtainable. I wore pants made out of a ripped ducking sack. Hats were made of palm leaves. I do not recall that the Czechs or Germans wove any cloth, but the Anglo-Saxons did.

"During the war all ports in the Gulf were blockaded, so that cotton was sent to Matamoros and Laredo. Several wagons formed a caravan, each wagon being drawn by five or more yokes of oxen. I was a member of one of these caravans. On September 2, 1864, I went on one of these trips. There were six wagons; two older men, A. D. L. Jones and Gottlieb Maroň, each about fifty years of age, and four boys, Baltazar Hill, George Hill, Paul Eckert and myself. I was fourteen. We left New Ulm empty, but loaded cotton somewhere in Jackson County. This same cotton was being hauled by the Miller Brothers, but they were stopped and made to unload the staple by Confederate soldiers. Then they, with their teams and wagons, were forced to haul for the Confederate Army. We reloaded the cotton and carried it on to Mexico.

"From New Ulm we traveled in the direction of Eagle Lake, where we forded the Colorado River. The road was not marked well and in some places we went through grass waist high. We reached Victoria after a heavy rain. The Guadaloupe was out of its banks. When the water subsided, the ground in the valley was soaked, so that the wheels sank to the hubs. We crossed the river on a ferry. After we got out of the river bottoms we had no trouble until we reached Nueces in San Patricio County. Here the road was very rough from previous traffic.

"At this crossing we had an accident, a real misfortune. The steel tire on one of the wagons broke. The nearest town was San Patricio, four miles up the river. Two of the boys mounted horses and dragged the tire to San Patricio. When they reached there, they found no blacksmith, and the next nearest town was thirty-five miles farther. On the way they broke the tire in another place. But they found a good blacksmith, who welded the tire. For the trip back they made better preparations to avoid an accident. They made a sled out of a small mesquite tree and on this they tied the tire.

"While we were waiting for the tire, sixteen soldiers came along, saying that they were looking for deserters. Without asking any questions they exchanged their tired and worn-out horses for ours, and left without a thank you.

"After we left the Nueces River, everything went well until we reached the Davis Ranch. From here we had forty miles of sandy road. This was such hard traveling that we could not make more than five miles a day. The second day in this desert our water supply gave out. The nearest water was at the Davis Ranch. Everybody was eager to go, but I won. I was sent on a horse with two five-gallon kegs. I do not remember of ever being so happy to go after water.

"My happiness did not last long, however, because as soon as I had my refreshing drink the problem of loading the two kegs on the horse loomed before me. The kegs were already tied together, so that they would fit across the back of the animal. I was only fourteen years old, so you can imagine that the task was difficult. At first I tried to load both kegs at the same time, but that was too much, so I untied the kegs, lifted one and tied it to the saddle, but then I had no rope to tie the other. So I took the one keg down, tied the two together and, with what seemed a superhuman effort, I finally lifted both onto the horse.

"On the third day we reached a place where our leader knew of a good well, but we found it filled with sand. As we had no spade we used a tin pail and dug out the sand and mud. Then we had plenty of water. But again we ran into trouble. There was no trough. Sand will not hold water, and we had no large vessel, so that we could not water our horses and oxen. We dug a hole in the sand and over this we spread a raw hide from which we watered over thirty oxen and six horses. Ordinarily animals would not drink from such a trough, but thirst lasting several days will make them do even this. A few days later, at night, four horses were stolen. This made it very difficult to herd the oxen each morning. From here to Brownsville, a distance of sixty miles, the trip was easy.

"We started back in the second week of January. At this time, salt sold in the interior at ten cents a pound. Somewhere east of Brownsville, we bought salt at twenty-five cents a bushel. In crossing the desert, we had great difficulty. In one place we had to pay twenty cents a head to water the animals. When we finally reached Nueces River we decided to rest as there was plenty of water and grass, but our animals were too worn out and many died.

"We spent two months there before we could get enough oxen to continue our trip. We bought wild steers from a rancher named Randolph at $10.00 and $12.00 a head. These had to be tamed and trained. Out of our old lot we picked the tamest and strongest oxen and to each we tied one of the new animals. One of these wild oxen was so powerful that he killed the tame one. We left the wild one tied to his tame, dead mate, for two days before we tied him to another tame one and drove him to the camp. This one gave us a lot of trouble. Only those who have had similar experience can comprehend and appreciate how much hard work it required to tame and train such wild animals for use.

"To the north of our camp was a prairie of several hundred acres, encircled by mesquite woods. This prairie was covered with fine grass. Here we grazed our oxen. Several times a day we encircled the prairie to keep watch on the oxen. Late one evening, a friend and I started out afoot. Before we turned back to camp, it suddenly became dark and began to rain. We lost the beaten track. There were large bunches of cactus and cat claws, so that our progress was slow, as well as dangerous. We broke off mesquite limbs and with these felt our way, but we lost our direction. In our groping we stumbled across a group of hogs that were huddled together, asleep for the night. As they were not used to such nocturnal visits, they were terribly frightened, perhaps more than we were, as they ran away.

"We resumed our tramp and after a short distance fell again. This time we thought we were in a well, but it was a creek. We were happy because we had an idea that this would lead us to the camp. But which way to go? I suggested that to go in one direction would bring us luck. My friend, who was a German, after some hard words, said that we had no luck, and wanted to know my plan, and I told him that if we would join both right hands we would go to the right and if the left hands, we would go to the left. In our first try we joined our right hands, and that way we went. After walking a long distance we saw a light flicker. As we advanced, the light was lost to sight many times, but we held to the course as near as possible, and we finally reached the camp, tired and wet through and through. Supper was waiting for us and we needed no tempting. After supper we dried our clothes.

"While in this camp our flour supply gave out, so that for many days we lived on beef and coffee. Finally I was able to buy, in San Patricio, a quart of corn meal for fifty cents. Later we bought a bushel of corn and had it ground. The negro that ground this corn on a hand-mill charged us one dollar, so that our corn bread proved expensive.

"From here the trip home was uneventful. We reached New Ulm in May, 1865. The reunion with mother was a very happy one, as I had not seen her for six months. I had written to her only one time, and for this writing I used ink made from gunpowder and water. For the six months, not one time did I sleep under a roof.

"From two years after the war we lived on the farm that father bought. Then mother sold the farm so that she could give the share from her estate to Anna, Rosalie, and Jan. Her share was $1,200, and this she loaned without any security to one of her kin, and he, a good fellow, forgot to pay it back. Then it happened that we were again penniless.

"In 1869 I married Rosalie Jirasek, who came to Texas from Čermne, Čechy, in the fall of 1867. When I married I owned one horse and had $60.00 in cash. With this money I bought a yoke of oxen. The horse and oxen comprised our entire equipment, but we started farming. The household furnishings we purchased on credit from Ernst Knolle, a merchant at Industry. My dealings with this man convinced me that he was one of the noblest gentle-men I had ever met.

"The first crop of cotton was eaten up by worms, so that we gathered only one and one-half bales. I sold the cotton to Mr. Knolle and after adding up the amount, which was for the entire crop, and looking on the books to see how much I owed him for the year, he found that I had a small difference coming to me. He suggested that I take the whole amount and let him carry the debt for another year. He felt that I needed the money and he wanted to help me, saying he was once poor himself.

"For the first two and one-half years we lived in a log house, eight-by-ten, then our landlord built us a box house, twelve-by-fourteen. This was the largest house on the plantation. Two children were born here. The first died at the age of four. The second was a daughter, Rosalie, who is married to Josef Hošek, and now living in Victoria County.

"From Industry I moved to Nelsonville, Austin County. Here, with John Mikeska, I opened a grocery store with a bar and a dance hall, as was the custom at that time in small country towns. Business was good, and we thought we had found a gold mine, but our good beginning had a bad ending. We opened up in January, and in May I was stricken with typhoid fever. At first it seemed that I would soon be well, but a turn for the worse changed the course. I was unconscious for twenty-one days. The attending physician, Dr. Thompson, called in consultation two other doctors and the verdict was that I would not live over eighteen hours. But I lasted longer. A few days later another consultation was held and this time I received a sentence of six hours, but it was not my time to go, and I am still here. After my illness I was unable to attend to business for many months. My partner, who was very lenient, sold much on credit, and as crops were poor that year, when fall came there was no collections and our business went bankrupt. We lost not only the $1,500 in gold we put in, but an additional $300.00. During this time one of my mules died, so again I had less than nothing.

"Just as I was recovering from typhoid, our boy was stricken with spinal meningitis, and died in a few days. One misfortune after another came our way. This same year, daughter Anna was born, who later married John Bubak, and lived in Dallas until the time of her death, in 1929. The second year I rented a farm near Nelsonville from a man named Williams, and then for two years, 1875-76, I rented from Jan Schiller. In 1875 another boy was born, but he died from yellow jaundice at the age of ten months.

"Thus being pursued by the grim reaper, and the loss of property, my wife and I were anxious for some kind of a change. At this time there were two Czech families in Williamson County, both my friends—V. S. Schiller, near Round Rock and Joset Mikeska, near Rice's Crossing. In 1876 I made a trip to Williamson County and rented a place from J. E. Robinson, half mile from Rice's Crossing, on the south side of Brushy Creek. In January, 1877, I moved a distance of seventy-five miles. I hauled two wagon loads and the rest I shipped by train to Elgin, at that time the nearest railroad point.

"We had plenty of bacon, flour and coffee, but no molasses. I took a gallon jug and went to Rice's Crossing. This also was our postoffice. The merchant was very obliging, and asked what I wanted. I told him a gallon of molasses, but that I had no money. He told me that if my landlord would stand good for my debt I could have what I wanted. This hurt my pride terribly, as I had always paid my debts, and here was he asking security for one gallon of molasses. It was hard to come home to the children without molasses, but there was no alternative and they had to learn to eat butter, bread and milk. Soon, however, I passed my neighbor, an American, who was making molasses in an old-time three-pot equipment. I got off my horse and went to see his contraption. He immediately asked me if I needed molasses, and I told him yes, but that I had no money. He said that he did not ask me if I had money, but whether I needed molasses. So I went home after the empty jug, and when I went back, my children, rejoicing, met me half way down the road. I have not experienced such want since.

"Our first year, 1877, was not very kind to us. The year I rented the farm the prairies were covered with grass, but that fall this was eaten by grasshoppers, so that cattle died from starvation. Many died in the very stream from which we obtained our drinking water, which we had to strain through a cloth in order to separate the dead animals' hair from the water. Today we would not think of taking such a risk, but in those days we had no choice.

"The year was a dry one. We made five bales of cotton, and enough corn for our use. This same year, Jan, who now is living in Rowena, was born. We lived on this farm three years, and then rented from John Tyler, near Taylor. When I went through Taylor in 1876 there was not even a crossing. The town, besides the name, had two wooden homes. On John Tyler's farm I lived for two years, and then moved back to Robinson's farm for one year. So you see I also experienced the benefits of renting, moving from one place to another, according to inclination, for when you once buy a piece of dirt, you are stuck, and have to stay in one place.

"This year I bought my first farm, near New Sweden, in Travis County. Here Josef Marek, Michael Štiba, my brother Vincenc, and myself bought a section of land, 640 acres, which we divided into four parts. Others that bought land here were Josef Lešikar, Frank Lešikar, Vinc Lešikar, Ludvik Dušek, V. S. Schiller, Josef Matějka, and Vinc Mareš.

"Today not one is living there, not even their descendants. This land was a bare prairie. Breaking such raw land without proper equipment was a hard task. I was again confronted with the training of oxen for work. By this time I had a large herd of steers, and out of this herd I trained five yokes of oxen. For a novice this would be very hard, but I utilized the experience from my younger days. With this team I first hauled all building material from Taylor, a distance of twelve miles, and then the cedar posts from Elgin, a distance of fifteen miles. This always required two days, one day to go and one day to come.

"I first built a barn of two rooms and a stable, all under one roof. The corn and cotton we put into the rooms, and the family moved into the stable, which was open on one side. Then I began building my home. Immediately a blizzard blew up, with sleet. The temperature was eight degrees above zero. This lasted for several days. Our three children stayed under the feather beds day and night, as our building did not offer much protection. It took a long time to build the home, as I had no money to hire help. Consequently, I had to do all the building. Then the breaking of the raw land was difficult, but I managed so that I was able to plant twenty acres in cotton.

"Here my sons, Henry and Josef, were born. Henry graduated from the Agricultural and Mechanical College at Oklahoma City and he is now teaching in Runnels County. Josef finished in medicine from the University of Texas, Galveston, and is a prominent physician at Rowena. On this farm also my mother died at the age of seventy-two. In 1897 I moved to Victoria County, where I had purchased some land two years before. So, it happened that again I was breaking new prairie land for a farm, but this time it was much easier, as I had plenty of horses and mules to haul building material. But for the breaking of the prairie I again relied on the trustworthy oxen.

"The organizers of the Czech colony in Victoria County were Jan Mikeska, Tomaš Janota, Jan Hošek, Josef Hošek, Jan Bubak, Josef Marčak, Jan Marčak, Jan Schiller, Vinc J. Schiller, Vinc Lešikar, Josef Lešikar, Ludvik Dušek, Frank Lala, Mrs. Anna Marek, Petr Faltysek, Jan D. Dušek, Mikšik, and myself. On this farm we lived for twenty years. The first years here were hard. Wet weather and bugs destroyed the crops. At this time the bollweevil appeared. But perseverance wins, and as conditions changed, crops were good for many years.

"In 1913 we again moved, this time to the new town of Placedo, situated at the junction of the Southern Pacific and Missouri Pacific railroads. Here we built a comfortable home and remained until 1921, when my wife became ill. She died on December 1, 1923, at the age of seventy-seven. From the time of her death I have lived with my children. At the present I am with John at Rowena. I am eighty-five and fairly healthy. I still drive my car, as I have been doing for the past fourteen years. I am a charter member of Č. S. P. S., Lodge Jižni Bratrstvo, Taylor. I was the charter member of the following lodges in the S. P. J. S. T.: Jan Žižka, Elgin; Našinec, DaCosta; Placedo, Placedo. At present I am an active member in the Placedo lodge.

CHAPTER XII

The Holik and Jančik Families

On New Year's night, 1861, Josef Holik and wife, Anna Mikeska Holik, and their children, a year-old son, Josef, and a three-year-old daughter, Anna, slept in an immigrant's camp on the banks of the Brazos River by the side of an ox-drawn wagon. The ground was covered with snow.

This family had set sail for Texas from Zadveřicich, Moravia, in 1860, and after a seven-weeks' voyage, arrived at Galveston where they were entertained for a few days in the Reymershoffer home. They spent the Christmas holidays in Houston at the home of Thomas Krajča. Taking the train at Houston the family went as far as Hempstead which was at this time the end of the railroad, where a wagon to which was hitched several yoke of oxen, was waiting to carry them to their destination. New Year's night found them beside the muddy waters of the Brazos. Morning came and the little company of pioneer settlers resumed their journey, coming finally to the home of Jan Mikeska at Industry.

Josef Holik, the baby son, who celebrated his first birthday on the ocean on the way to Texas, said in after years that, "Jan Mikeska must have been in Texas a long time because he owned his farm."

Josef Holik, Sr., on the arrival at Industry, 1861, rented a farm near New Ulm from Josef Šiller (Shiller) who was at the time living in Houston. With one yoke of oxen, one plow and one sled his work began. Hard times also beset them. The Holik cash capital was only fifty cents. And to add to all these discouragements, the Civil War broke out.

Josef Holik was not in sympathy with slavery, having left Europe because of conditions which he remembered as "oppression" and slavery.

With the war hard times became harder for Josef Holik and family. He did not want to go to war and so hid in the woods while his wife with two children tried to carry on the farm work. Enough corn and rye was grown to furnish something to eat, but there was nothing for clothes. The mother, under stress, and to provide for the family, ripped the covering from the feather beds brought from the Old Country and made shirts for the children as long as the material lasted.

Frank Mikeska, a brother of Josef Holik's wife, was a shoemaker and was thus not required to go to war. He made shoes for the family. But the daily food and clothing were not the only worries. Officers and soldiers of the army were zealous in their lookout for men evading army service. Many times the Holik home was searched, but "always they were gentlemen," recalls Josef Holik in his recollections. "They did not trouble mother in any way."

After three years Josef Šiller left Houston and returned to his farm. The house, a one-room log building, could not accommodate the two families, so the mother, with the two children, had to move. The Holik family found a place with Karel Šiller in a kind of a shed attached to the Šiller residence. The roof was of three limbs, covered with gray Spanish moss. This location was between New Ulm and Krekental. Later another location was found close to New Ulm. While the family always raised enough corn and rye for home use, it had to be ground or crushed in some fashion before it could be eaten by the mother and children.

One day this pioneer Texan mother loaded several sacks of corn on a sled to which she hitched a yoke of large oxen preparatory to going to the mill to have the corn ground into meal. She hoped to return by nightfall, but the distance to Alleyton, where the primitive corn mill was located, was long and the oxen slow.

It was in the summer and when the oxen, dragging along the lumbering sled, loaded with bags of corn, reached the Bernard River they waited for no ceremony but went at once into the cool river, submerging the sled and corn sacks. When they had quenched their thirst they lazily drew their load on through the water behind them.

Finally the place of Miller Vrla was reached. The corn had to be dried before it could go into the hopper. Night came on and the mother could not get back to her children. Bears, she knew, were in the habit of approaching the house at night. The children, Anna and Josef, cried themselves to sleep. Morning came and the mother was not there, and again they cried until finally she arrived.

At this time it was rumored that the war was over. Josef Holik dared to leave his hiding and approach the house and his wife and children. One day when he came nearer than usual he found the house surrounded by soldiers. With the cries of his wife and children ringing in his ears he was taken away. The son later said of it that he "was driven as if he were a steer going to the slaughter."

The army camp was located not far from the home of the Holik's and here the father was placed under guard for the night along with several other prisoners, one of whom was Jan Wotipka. The following night the guard was removed, leaving only one soldier on duty. Josef Holik took advantage of the opportunity and made his escape. He sensibly left the locality and his wife and children did not see him until after the end of the war.

The story of the Holik family as related by the son, on whose memory every incident of those distressing days of the early life in Texas has been indelibly inscribed, makes a colorful chapter in the history of the Czech pioneers in Texas. They came seeking freedom and found warfare in which they had no sympathy. It is not strange that they tried to keep from joining in the conflict.

Of the occasion Josef Holik, Jr., comments:

"During the war mother raised cotton. Out of black moss she plaited sacks to cover the cotton she kept for her own use, selling the surplus for four and five cents per pound. At this time cotton had to be hauled to Mexico for a higher price. Clothing for the family was a serious problem. On one occasion mother was able to buy some cloth from cotton haulers who passed our house on their way home from Mexico. She paid fifty cents a yard for it. It was made of jute, about the quality of the inner sacks for coffee. From this I had my first pair of pants and felt very much dressed up.

"After the war cotton brought a much higher price and the gin nearest to our place was operated by horsepower. We had two bales of cotton ginned there and the covering was from the bagging made from the black Spanish moss. Father loaded the last bale on a sled and took it to New Ulm, where he sold it for twenty-six cents a pound, being paid the whole amount in silver. It made a huge pile. With some of the money he bought two wheels and made what we called an ox-car. We felt rich, for in this vehicle we went visiting on Sundays, and to weddings and other special functions.

"Cotton continued to bring good prices, so that in three years father bought some bare prairie land near Nelsonville. On this he built a log house with four walls and one door. He bought for the construction only some nails. The other materials were all hand made at home.

"It was hard in those days to turn the native sod, but mother broke the ground while father split the rails to fence in the field. The plow was made at home all of wood except the ploughshare. There was a blacksmith at Industry who made plows that had a little more iron in their construction than these hand-made ones.

"While the sod was being broken for the field, the rails being split for the fence, our prized ox-car broke down and there was no means for hauling the rails. Another wagon had to be bought. Things went along pretty well, however. Splitting the rails was hard work and I often cried because I was so tired from pulling the saw.

"We were lucky in cattle-raising. At this time we had five yoke of oxen of our own. I could manage them easily and could drive them anywhere. I often hauled logs to the mill to have boards made.

"Hunting was about the only pleasure I had as a boy. Four hound dogs added to my pleasure on the hunt. One day, when about a half mile from home, the dogs found something in a dense thicket. Being curious myself to know what it was, I crawled through the brush and when I stuck my head through some moss that had obstructed the view, I came face to face with a big black bear, his red tongue and a row of white teeth showing. I could feel the hot breath of the animal in my face. I did not tarry long, but back through the brush I jerked myself and ran with the speed of an Amazon, never once looking back, although I felt that the bear was following. Only when out of breath did I stop, when, to my relief, there was no bear behind me, only my dogs. They were badly damaged, however. One had an eye missing, another a large piece of skin from the side of his head.

"Time passed quickly. I was growing fast. Father wanted me to be in school, but there was no school for me to attend. The distance to schools was great for that time. Finally he found room and board for me at Industry. All the pupils there spoke German. I could speak German well also, but in school I studied English. I read, but did not understand the meaning of a single word. This I knew would not do, as father wanted me to learn English, so I was sent to school at Nelsonville. Here there were eighty pupils, large and small, some twenty years old, and more, and I among them not understanding a single word of English.

"It was not long, however, before I began to grasp the meaning of words. I liked the school. I rode a mule the distance of four miles each day. I had learned to ride well so that neither horse nor mule could throw me. I had some bones broken once when a horse fell with me. When I was seventeen years old, I measured six feet, two inches, which proved to be full growth.

"Several years before this date there was a celebration at Wesley on the occasion of the raising of the flag. Mother and father went, riding horseback. My sister and a younger brother were to remain at home, but I did not like this arrangement. Mother said that I did not have suitable clothes to wear to such a celebration, but I wanted to be there, suitable clothes or not. There was no way to get there, but fate was kind, as the Dřevojanek family came along in their ox-drawn wagon and I asked for a ride. They were obliging, so I hastily put on a pair of father's pants, three times too large for me, old shoes and a torn hat and off to the celebration I went.

"There was a large gathering, so I passed in the crowd unnoticed. I was much interested and wanted to see everything. The time came for the raising of the flag. Someone made a short talk and then a small girl stepped on the platform and, after a few words, nailed the flag to the pole. Following this there were several other speakers, and then I saw for the first time Augustin Haidušek and heard his speech. At the time he was quite young, but his eloquence impressed me.

"Feeling by this time quite at ease, I was mixing freely with the crowd when I accidentally came in contact with my mother. She was surprised to tears—mortified to see me there in such clothes. Even in those days I had often heard that clothing did not make people good, so I tried to console her and myself at the same time.

"My delight was in breaking wild horses. There was plenty of work to do on the farm, but father wanted me to study, to learn to read Czech, but I did not care to study.

"About this time František Zdrubek was the pastor of the church at Wesley. He taught both Czech and English, so father sent me to his school. My enunciation of English was better than the teacher's and I did not care much about reading Czech. When the school money gave out, I went to pick cotton. As I was quite a distance from home, I felt that father would not find out, and as I reasoned that I could not learn figures, all would be well.

"One day Mr. Zdrubek told me that I had to remain after school, for what reason I did not know. He began dismissing the children. I did not like this and realized that quick action was necessary. One window was open, so I grabbed my books and hat and out that window I went. When the teacher finally saw me, I was out of reach. I thought of the whipping that would come Monday. No one but my mother had ever whipped me. My cousin Maryška Mikeska and her cousin, Františka Kopa, went to school with me, and when Mr. Jiři Kopa came after the girls, there being too much work in the field to leave them longer in school, I asked for a ride and with my bedding and clothes went home. On my arrival I said that school was over. Father was real glad that I had come as there was much work to do and my brother was too young to do heavy work. Sometime later father found out how I had finished school, but then it was too late for action.

"I was eighteen years old and soon found that I had made a mistake, so I began going to night school in the neighborhood. Very soon I could solve the problems in my arithmetic. It was easier to study when I willed to do so and when I realized what I had to know. Time passed slowly as I was anxious to be twenty-one years old. I lacked two months of this age when I decided to go West and seek my fortune. One morning I saddled my horse, threw the saddle bags across, took a long revolver and put on a pair of big spurs. Bidding mother good-bye, I got on the horse and rode away from my place of good living.

"This was in 1880 and as I rode away, putting several miles between myself and home, I reached in my pocket and took out my money. There was only $18.15, and not until I saw the small amount did I realize that I could not go very far on the few dollars in my possession. But westward I kept going just the same. The first stop was at Caldwell, where I met a friend who had stayed with us when he came from Europe. Caldwell at this time was only a small settlement with no railroad and only a few wooden buildings and the courthouse, which was also a wooden structure. I inquired about the Bohemian settlements and was told to go northeast. I mounted my horse and continued the journey.

"On the road I met Frank Skřivanek, a man whom I had known at Wesley. He did not know me, but knew my mother and father. Of him I inquired about Jan Jančik, my old friend. I went home with Mr. Skřivanek and was introduced to his wife and daughter, Terezie. When I held Terezie's hand, a peculiar feeling came over me. The Jančik home was about a mile distant and I stayed all night there. Mr. Jančik asked me to go to Caldwell with him the next day as he had some business to attend to and he could not speak English well enough to transact it. I went into the business house of Tom Hunt, and while there he looked at me and asked where I came from and if I could stay and work for him. If so, he would pay me fifteen dollars per month and board. This to me was a large offer, as on the farm a good worker got only ten dollars a month. I accepted at once.

"Terezie Skřivanek was at the time attending school at Caldwell and I met her often. I always got the same peculiar feeling when I took hold of her hand. In the course of our acquaintance I found that she was the little girl who had nailed the flag to the pole at Wesley. She was very small then and did not remember seeing the boy in the torn and shabby clothes. We were married on January 10, 1882.

"Terezie Wunderlich, step-daughter of Frank Skřivanek, was a niece of Josef Mašik, the first Czech teacher in Texas, her mother being the daughter of this pioneer. This family had come to Texas much earlier than the Holiks. The story of the coming of the Mašik family included the tragic death of the mother as the family traveled from Houston to Hempstead, these immigrants walking the distance, there being no railroad at the time.

"Sometime before the Civil War, the oldest daughter, Terezie Mašik, married William Wunderlich of Shelby, Austin County. Soon after the marriage he went to war. When the baby daughter came he obtained leave and came home to see the mother and baby. He left to rejoin his company and never returned, his death occurring near Navasota. The wife sold out and went back to live with her parents at Wesley and after the war married Frank Skřivanek.

"In the year 1882, with Thomas Krajča I went into business at New Tabor, near Caldwell. The business moved along nicely. The only thing that I did not like was that we sold liquor and some of the citizens neglected their work and business on account of drinking. As I did not want the mothers and daughters some day to tell me that I was the cause of their misfortune, I sold out and moved to Brenham. There things went along well. I received good pay, as I spoke four languages, which gave me opportunity to wait on everyone who came into our place of business. Our family in the meantime had grown and I bought a farm of two hundred acres near Caldwell. In Brenham I was admitted to the Masonic Lodge of A. F. & A. M., in the presence of Vincenc Mašik, Josef Marek, Frank Klukaň and Frank Haubelt.

"In 1887 we moved back to Caldwell, remaining until 1912. Our family consisted of seven children, four daughters and three sons. The oldest daughter, Ružena, married Rob Hofman; the second, Antonie, married Frank Lešovsky; the third, Liduška, married J. W. Šugarek. The oldest daughter died when young, leaving two small girls, who lived with us until grown and married.

About this time my brother, Charles, lost his wife and she left a two-months-old baby son, Stanley. We reared him until he was twenty-one years old.

"All the daughters have been educated in the Czech language as well as in English, but the boys, in growing up had no desire to study, and I did not have time to make them, so I bought a farm of 676 acres in 1908 and this came in handy in rearing them. But soon the oldest son, Josef C., when he was twenty-one years old, left home to make his own way. The second son, Charles W., did the same, but the youngest, William V., wanted to go to school, so he was placed in A. & M. College, where he studied electrical engineering. The daughter, Annie, was graduated from Denton College as a teacher, and thus the family grew smaller and smaller.

"Two of the boys, Josef C. and Charles W., were in the World War, remaining in Germany for nine months after the armistice in the Army of Occupation. The third son, William V., was on his way across from New York when the armistice was signed. William V. spent considerable time in travel. I once remonstrated, telling him the rolling stone gathered no moss, but he countered by saying that the stone that rolls is brighter, so I let him go. He went into the service of an electrical establishment in Boston, Massachusetts, and in that state married a Miss Eline McArthur. He was sent back to Texas with the position of supervisor of an electrical power service in Southeast Texas.

"The mother and I get lonesome. The home is so quiet. We two cannot do much noise-making, but we get pleasure from our children with their families when they visit us each year. At home I left one sister, who married Frank Mikeska, and three brothers, John B., Frank and Charles W. Brother John died in Houston. My parents died at Sunny Side, Texas. Father was seventy-seven at his death and mother lived to be eighty-three."

The Holik family home is at Chriesman.

*   *   *   *

John Jančik and family, the youngest of which was a baby boy, one year old, emigrated to Texas from Moravia in 1871 with but little money, in fact, only about two hundred dollars, but they had the courage to take passage on a sailing vessel at Bremen, Germany, for Galveston. After a voyage of eleven weeks and four days the vessel with the Jančik pioneers reached its destination.

Austin County was the mecca toward which the family journeyed, settling first at Nelsonville. After a few years residence there, they moved on a farm two miles east of Caldwell, Burleson County, and there was the beginning of the achievements that have gone down in the history of the Jančik family in Texas. During these years the baby, John, Jr., grew into young manhood, receiving his education in the schools of the county, living with his parents on the farm, helping with the farm work as his time permitted. At the age of sixteen years, he went to Caldwell where he secured employment in a lumber yard. Following this job he worked for two years in the employ of W. F. Gay & Company, liquor merchants, of Caldwell. Some time later he was married and then went into the liquor business for himself, remaining in this business for sixteen years.

In 1907 Mr. Jančik gave up the liquor business to establish a grocery and hardware store in Caldwell and soon became one of the outstanding merchants of that community. Some years after he engaged in this business he was instrumental in promoting the Caldwell National Bank of which he was a director for seven years.

The story of this Czech pioneer family does not reveal all the hardships, the unending labor, the months and the years required to bring about the success that resulted from such efforts.

In checking over the list of the things that John Jančik, Jr., had a part in promoting during the years when the city of Caldwell was in the process of development, that of helping to organize the company that built the Caldwell Opera House stands out. Mr. Jančik also had a part in the building of the residential section of the city.

As for politics, Mr. Jančik has preferred always to use his influence in behalf of his friends, having never offered himself for political office. He has held the position of school trustee for some years, devoting himself unsparingly to the interests of education and matters relative to the economic betterment of his town and community. He has always been affiliated with the Democratic party in the State, and has been also a member of the S. P. J. S. T. and Č S. P. S., two Czech fraternal lodges.

In April, 1890, Mr. Jančik was married to Miss Frances Skřivanek. The Skřivaneks came from the same part of Moravia as the Jančiks. The father of Mrs. Jančik, Frank Skřivanek, who was a farmer, had married Miss Teresa Mašik Wunderlich. The children were: Mrs. Jančik, Mrs. Antoinette Dušek, Mrs. Stannie Ripple, Mrs. Winnie Dušek, Mrs. Lillie Shiller, and Rosa, Frank and Annie Skřivanek.

There were six children in the John Jančik, Jr., family—Lottie, the wife of E. S. Dušek, connected for some time with the Caldwell National Bank; Ella May, who died when eighteen months old; John, William, Allen, Frank, Olga and Robert Lee.

John Jančik, Sr., died in Caldwell in July, 1915, at the age of seventy-seven. The children of this pioneer family were John, Fannie, wife of Paul Lukša of Milam County; William, who died at Caldwell, leaving a family; Charles, a business man of Caldwell; Mary, deceased wife of William Žalobny; Teresa, wife of Frank Krištof of Caldwell.

Caldwell of Burleson County has been fortunate in her citizenship. It is made up largely of these Czech pioneer families and their offspring, who, having come of sturdy stock and honorable and splendid lineage, have planted this spirit and influence in the land of their adoption.

An outstanding and interesting thing in the chronicles of the pioneer Czech settlements of Texas is that the geneaology of the families carries on and on. The great Texas-Czech geneological tree will not die. Always there is a live branch that will perpetuate the great trunk that has grown up from the deeply-imbedded roots.

CHAPTER XIII

The Gallia Family

Ondřej and Mary Russek Gallia sold their possessions in Moravia, Austria, all save their household goods, and with their family of young children, one a baby twelve months old, set sail for Texas, arriving after a three months' voyage at Galveston, from where the family went to Dubina by ox-team. They had come seeking a new home in a new country, following the lead of Valentin Haidušek and other friends and neighbors who had preceded them.

The Gallia, and other pioneer families found the habitation, but not the land, as described by the Prophet Joshua, who said: "I have given you a land for which ye did not labor, and cities which ye built not, and ye dwell in them; of vineyards and olive yards which ye planted not, do yet eat!"

Those early settlers found the land, but they had to plant the vineyards, build the cities and labor in order that they might eat and live.

The Gallia family was provident, having brought with them seed for their first planting. These included wheat, rye, oats, and cabbage. Flower seed, too, was not forgotten.

Ondřej Gallia was by trade a cabinetmaker, but came from the agricultural section of his native land. So, on reaching Texas, he settled beneath the protecting branches of a great Texas live-oak tree near to what is today the thriving little city of Weimar.

An agreement had been made between the Haidušek and Gallia families that one should come first to Texas and if it seemed well to remain, then the other would follow. In the event of dissatisfaction, there would be help from back home for the return voyage. Fortunately no return voyage was found necessary. The Haidušek family found the country one of promise, and when this news reached Ondřej Gallia he embarked for the new land as soon as he found opportunity to sell his property and make the necessary arrangements for the voyage.

Soon after the arrival of the Gallias the Civil War called men to arms. Ondřej Gallia took up arms in defense of his adopted state, joining the Confederate Army. His enlistment left the young wife and children alone in the new and unsettled country with barely enough to live on.

On his return at the close of the war, Mr. Gallia engaged in the merchandising business in which he continued until his death in 1876. The son, who was but one year old when the family came to Texas, after the death of his father embarked on a career of his own, first holding the position as clerk in a general merchandising store at LaGrange and reading law at night. This was in 1880. The study of law was to "acquire a good business knowledge."

Looking back over the years of his experience, and his decision not to continue the study of law after it had served his purpose, Mr. Gallia cited an incident which had at the time influenced his decision. According to the story a man accused of cattle stealing came into his office one day, in quest of a lawyer to handle his case. Getting audience with the senior member of the law firm, the accused man said: "I want you to defend me." Cattle thieves in those days usually received their punishment at the end of a rope.

This man had stolen the cattle. He admitted the theft. The lawyer asked: "How can I defend you when you tell me that you are guilty?"

"You are the lawyer. I'm here to pay you to know how, not to tell you how to do it," was the thief's rejoinder. Such confidence in his professional ability was not without its effect, and after a brief silence, during which the lawyer looked at the client, sitting in one of the rawhide bottom hickory chairs, the case was accepted.

Lowering the front legs of the chair from a tilted position, suddenly to the floor with a thud, the two men got down to business. The retainer fee was to be $1,000.00. The lawyer, after turning the case over in his mind, viewing it from its various angles and deciding on the methods to be pursued at the trial, said: "Can you bring me four good witnesses who will swear that you did not steal the cattle?"

"I can bring you a dozen," was the quick response, and with that answer the trade was closed. The case came to trial in due time. Witnesses for the prosecution swore on the stand that they saw the accused on the day of the theft in the act of skinning the cattle and later saw him in possession of the hides.

The defense attorney in his examination of these witnesses inquired: "How close were you at the time to this party you claim to have seen skinning some cattle? What kind of a horse was he riding when seen later with hides in his possession? What kind of clothes did he have on? Did the sun shine in your eyes at the time, or was the sun on the face of the man with the hides?" These and similar questions delivered in a confusing and disconcerting manner were flung at the witnesses for the prosecution.

They admitted uncertainty. They could swear to nothing for sure. Then came the valiant twelve. One by one they took the stand. They lived over Gonzales way, in the opposite direction from where the cattle had been stolen.

Yes, they swore when put on the stand, they knew the defendant. They knew him well—had known him for a long time. On the day of the crime he was with them, helping to cut out some cattle. Had been for three days helping them separate two and three-year-olds from the herd.

The verdict was, "Not guilty."

Ignatz Gallia says today, that then and there he quit the study of law. The sun in the eyes of those witnesses proved a telling weapon in the hands of that defense lawyer, and young Gallia was afraid that he might not be so fortunate in the choice of a defense should he be admitted to the bar, and have a similar case in court.

Democratic in belief, Ondřej Gallia imparted to his son the same principles—that to stand for State's rights instead of a centralized power was his duty. This party affiliation was held to be sacred. For twenty years this son of Ondřej and Mary Gallia was postmaster at Engle, Texas. This, however, was managed in connection with his merchandising business as an accommodation for his patrons, rather than because of any financial rewards. The revenue from the post office was so small that it would have been discontinued if there had been a salary to pay.

Mr. Gallia recalls having lost the post office for a period of three months during his term of twenty years. This happened because of his active support of the Democratic candidate for Congress from that district. The Republican National Committeeman took him to task for this activity, calling to his attention the matter of his holding a Federal appointment.

On election day the word went forth from Republican headquarters: "Watch Gallia and his friends." According to Mr. Gallia, looking back over the years, the Republicans got fifteen votes and the Democrats nineteen. He lost the post office but as nobody wanted it, the government handed it back to him.

An older brother became in the early days a member of one of the teamster organizations and hauled cotton to Mexico, there being at the time no Texas market. This was a commercial project, promoted by one of the pioneer business men of the period, for the purpose of not only finding a market for the cotton grown in Texas, but because the hauling paid a nice profit. Each team had five pairs of oxen and the wagon carried ten bales of cotton, the approximate weight of each bale being between four and five hundred pounds. The destination was Matamoros, and the driver started on the long trip with a strong arm and a long whip. When they went into camp at night the wagon train was arranged in the form of a hollow square for defense against Indian depredations. History records that the great Czech military leader, Jan Žižka, employed a similar method of defense for his crusading army in 1417.

The Gallia family had during those pioneer days saved money for the purchase of a farm near Flatonia, called at that time Mulberry Creek. The purchase price was $10.00 per acre, the land being bought from an old sheep-herder. It was later put under fence, this being fashioned of live-oak brush. A crop was then planted. These settlers, according to Ignatz Gallia, accepted the country as they found it on the thesis that if it was good enough for the people who were living in it when they arrived it was good enough for them. By the same token they identified themselves with the customs of their new home as readily as they could. They brought with them no ideals. They left behind the old home and its order. The patriotism, the love of native land, they kept in their hearts, and this love helped them to build a new sentiment for their adopted country. To have been born poor in the old home country meant to die poor as these courageous immigrant Czech settlers well knew, for it was a country over-populated and oppressed through centuries of warfare and political unrest.

Ignatz Gallia drank in with the Texas air out under that live-oak tree during those first years of his childhood residence in Texas, something of the spirit of the pioneer and the rugged courage of the immigrant. For three months he had been rocked on the waves of the Atlantic, his parents husbanding their store of provisions, trusting that they would reach the land of their future residence in safety. As the boy grew toward maturity, he loved his country more and more. He visioned the future when development would have put the thousands of untilled acres to the plough. He saw communities rise up from the waste and desert lands. Saw in the mental picture new methods of industry put into use.

In 1889, with Frank Russek, a member of one of the pioneer Czech families, he got a contract for 25,000 acres of land at a price of $2.65½ per acre located at what is now El Campo. The first two purchasers of land out of this colonization tract were John Melchar and Christian Bruno, who paid $3.00 per acre. Later the land was sold for $4.00 and $5.00 per acre, with ten years to pay, six per cent interest being added for the accommodation.

Soon after the project was launched, there came a heavy and continued rainfall. The lands were flooded. Those who had bought acreage, with the exception of a few, including the two mentioned, abandoned their purchases and left to settle elsewhere. The two promoters, believing in the future of the section, tried to get the necessary financial backing to enable them to hold on and carry out their development plans, but bankers and financiers could not see its possibilities. Failing to secure financial help, a new company was organized and the holdings taken over. When aid was solicited in the way of money with which to put in drainage and to build roads, the bankers, according to Mr. Gallia, laughed at them. This was not agricultural land, they said. Today El Campo bears witness to the faith of these two pioneer developers. They believed in its possibilities and they were not wrong.

Mr. and Mrs. Gallia in later years bought a home in Houston where they reared and educated their family. In 1933 Mr. Gallia was actively engaged in the real estate business, maintaining his lifelong interest in everything pertaining to state and community development.

CHAPTER XIV

Joseph Peter, Emigrant

ALWAYS in the early chronicles the name of Joseph Peter was given a place in the list of names of those Czech immigrants who came to settle and develop Texas. For sixty-eight years he lived in the new home, and during this time was a factor in the progress and development of Texas. Born in Moravia on February 2, 1845, he immigrated with his parents, coming to Texas in 1856 in company with a number of families, among whom were the Haiduseks.

This early Czech immigrant colony first stopped at Cat Springs, went thence to La Grange and later settled at Dubina, where a community was founded. The story of the voyage, which lasted for thirteen weeks, was often told when the pioneers grew reminiscent in after years. Fayette County was thinly-settled in those pioneer days. It was thirteen miles to the nearest corn mill, and school facilities were like the country—badly in need of development.

When yet but a child, the boy Joseph learned the blacksmith's trade, and at one time was the proud owner of a shop of his own at Dubina, where the pioneers were establishing homes and planting crops. Those were the days of miracles in the way of achievement. Where once had been a wilderness, came the cultivated and growing fields with smoke rising from the chimneys of the homes of the pioneers.

The home of Joseph Peter, built in this long-ago time, stands today, strong and weather-proof, even retaining its primitive appearance. The original two log rooms, with the immense double chimney of rock built between, are intact. They have been reinforced by the addition of up and down timber weather-boarding and a shed room in the rear.

The first Catholic church services were held in one of the log rooms of the Joseph Peter home. The neighbors came from far and near to hear mass in the log room set aside for the church services. Wedding feasts were prepared in the capacious depths of the chimney place and wide hearth-stone. The family meals and reunion viands were cooked in pots and ovens over the burning coals which were never permitted to die out.

The Peter family grew and prospered. The boy, Joseph, eleven years old, when he reached Texas, waxed strong as the village blacksmith, and when the years of young manhood came—1875— married Miss Barbara Vrana. Ten children were born to the couple, eight of whom survived the pioneer, whose death occurred at the family home March 26, 1924, at the age of seventy-nine.

Joseph, like his father, was an ardent supporter of the Confederacy, but was too young to enter the army. Not satisfied to remain inactive, however, he joined a wagon train which was hauling cotton to Mexico from High Hill settlement and Dubina. The destinations of the wagon train were Rancho Davis and Brownsville, a distance of some five hundred miles, the route leading through territory beset with bandits and Indians. On one of these trips the train was attacked by fourteen robbers who attempted to seize the wagons. They were beaten off, but not before they had killed one of the teamsters.

Although active in politics, Joseph Peter never sought office, but at the request of his boyhood friend, Judge August Haidušek, he accepted the nomination for Representative from Fayette County in 1890. He was elected by a large majority. While in the Legislature he was a member of various committees and active in agricultural affairs; mining and minerals; privileges and elections. He was also postmaster at Dubina for a period of six years.

No wayfarer ever passed the Peter home without enjoying the splendid hospitality of the family. The table was always laden with a bountiful supply of food and the latch-string hung on the outside. Strangers sometimes stopped for days at a time, but never a penny was accepted in payment for the hospitality. There are many happy memories held of visits in the home of this Texas-Czech pioneer.

On the occasion of the death of Honorable Joseph Peter, Governor Pat M. Neff, in a telegram addressed to a son, Dr. L. J. Peter of Schulenburg, offered his sympathy and condolence as follows:

"My Dear Mr. Peter:
"It was with deep regret and with a feeling of sincere sympathy for the members of his family that I learned of the death of your father and my friend, Honorable Joseph Peter. I want you

to know that I am thinking of you in this hour of sorrow. The State has lost a worthy citizen. With every good wish I am,
    "Your most sincerely,
        "Pat M. Neff, Governor."

Telegrams of sympathy and condolence came from friends and acquaintances in all parts of the State, including Doctors Adolph and Ferd. Herf, Messrs. Wolf, Rice and Ross, all of San Antonio. W C. Munn and I. G. Gallia of Houston, Stephen Kubala, Beeville; Honorable George Willrich of La Grange; General Jacob Wolters, Houston; and Jim Ragsdale, Victoria. Attesting the esteem in which this pioneer Texas-Czech settler was held, the press account of the death of the pioneer stated that the funeral procession was one of the largest ever known in the section in which he lived.

The passing of the pioneer was not, however, the end of the work he had started and carried on to so great a success. The wife and eight children survived. The sons and daughters bear his name to do further honor to it and to their father. The names of this family are known for their accomplishments.

The daughters, Mrs. H. W. Riebe, Strawn; Mrs. Joe Sobotik, Schulenburg; Mrs. F. Vacek and Miss Wilhemina Peter, Dubina; and Mrs. E. F. Mikeska, Taylor, and the sons, Dr. L. J. Peter, of Schulenburg; Emil Peter and Julius Peter, Dubina; are carrying on through the rich heritage left by their father.

The story of the life of the late Joseph Peter is not finished without certain comment on the son, Dr. L. J. Peter of Schulenburg, who, in addition to his profession, is the affable and genial gentleman one enjoys meeting. Always busy, he will yet find time to welcome a friend and extend greetings in keeping with the pioneer hospitality dispensed by his worthy ancestors.

Dr. L. J. Peter graduated from the Medical College, Galveston, Texas, in 1909.

CHAPTER XV

THE CHUPICK FAMILY

THE history of the Chupick family in Texas begins in the latter part of the year 1855, according to John F. Chupick of Jourdanton, Texas, one of the third generation. Mr. Chupick is a grandson of these early Texas pioneers. He says:

"The history of the Chupick family in Texas, originally spelled Chupik in the Czech language, begins with the advent of Thomas Chupick and his wife, Rozina Vitek Chupick, paternal grandparents, from Hoštalkova, Moravia, and Paul Šebesta with his wife, Rozina Paga Šebesta, maternal grandparents, from Zadveřice, Moravia, then a province of Austria. They arrived in Texas after many weeks' voyage in a sailboat. They landed at Galveston along with a number of other Czech families. These new arrivals were taken to Harrisburg on a large barge. Harrisburg in 1855 was a part of Houston, described as being 'a good-sized village.'

"The paramount reason for these Czech people coming to Texas was the desire to emigrate to a country where they hoped to better themselves in a material way in addition to having freedom, liberty and the equality which at the time they knew to be beyond the reach of the masses in Austria, especially for those of the Protestant faith, such as the Moravian Brethren Church, the Church of John Hus.

"Upon their arrival in Houston, they knew not what to do or where to turn. Finally they made the acquaintance of a German teamster who had a fleet of ox wagons in which he was hauling cotton to Houston from Cat Springs. They made a bargain with him to take them to Cat Springs. When they arrived at a point somewhere between Cat Springs and Millheim, Austin County, the teamster, who was named Schmidt, unloaded them under a motte of live-oak trees, and this became their first home in Texas. Not knowing the English language, nor the conditions, customs and habits of their new home, and having very little money, they had a hard time. To protect themselves against the elements, the men constructed huts out of logs, limbs of trees,

123

rails and moss, and in these they spent the winter. Not accustomed to this manner of living, a number became ill from exposure and some died shortly after their arrival. They eagerly awaited the coming of spring, hoping for more moderate weather.

"Their lack of knowledge of English was a serious handicap in securing employment. Texas at that time had few white people, with the exception of rich planters and slave-owners, who, having their slaves, did not care to employ any other kind of laborers. In a short time, however, the immigrants learned a little English and soon convinced their neighbors that they were really good artisans, mechanics, and workmen. The old settlers were then anxious to employ them, so that by the spring of 1856 practically everybody in the expedition had found some kind of gainful occupation. At that time this first colony broke up, the families moving to Fayetteville, Industry, Biegel, Vesely (the present site of Wesley, Texas) and various other places.

"My paternal grandparents moved to a place near Old Ulm (near the present site of New Ulm) in Austin County, where my father, John Chupick, born on May 8, 1849, was reared. It was here that he attended school for several months under the tutelage of Professor Teichmueller, who in later years became a very prominent lawyer and district judge of Fayette County. In later years, Fayette County was my father's home. Professor Teichmueller's school was located in a settlement of people of German extraction and he taught both English and German. Father took both courses and learned to speak and write both languages. He evidently was an apt student. I know that he learned German quite well, because as long as he lived, our German neighbors would often ask him to write letters in this language for them.

"It was in this neighborhood that my father remained with his parents, farming in a very primitive way, but doing the best he could. He had to use a home-made wooden plow, the beam of which was made from a crooked live-oak limb. To this was fastened a wooden hand-hewn mold board. By the time my father was fifteen years old he became expert at hewing these wooden mold boards out of live-oak logs. For many years he kept some of them as souvenirs. Their farming equipment consisted of these wooden plows, a yoke of oxen and a sled. At crop gathering time, they placed a big chest, which they brought with them from the old country, on the sled and in this manner hauled the cotton, corn, etc., from the field. They remained there until the close of the Civil War when they moved to Vesely, in Austin County.

"From their temporary home under the live-oaks near Cat

Springs, the Šebestas, my maternal grandparents, moved to Biegel, in Fayette County, and from there to Vesely, where my mother, Frances (Františka) Šebesta, was born on March 19, 1859, shortly before the outbreak of the Civil War. While up to the time of the Civil War these people were not prosperous, they were getting along, working and struggling to secure a foothold in their adopted country. Most of them had their own farms. They lived in their modest log cabins which were covered with home-made shingles. These cabins had no floors and the openings between the logs were sealed with mortar made out of joint clay and moss. Some of them had fireplaces, but most of the people cooked on the outside on an open fire and were satisfied and contented.

"When the Civil War broke out, however, things took a decided change for the worse. All men able to bear arms, from mere youth to old age, were conscripted into the Confederate Army. Those who were too young, or physically unfit, were drafted into the service to haul cotton to Mexico. My father's half-brother, Steve Elšik, was drafted into this service and made several trips to Mexico during the war, hauling cotton to Matamoros in wagons drawn by yokes of six to twelve oxen. What an undertaking a trip of this kind was through several hundred miles of wilderness, with no roads, no bridges, no towns on the way, and especially during wartime, can easily be imagined.

"Soon after the outbreak of the Civil War my mother's brothers, John, Josef and Frank Šebesta, joined the Confederate ranks. At this time my mother was only two years old and of course does not remember their departure. I have often heard her say that the first recollection she has of these brothers was when they returned at the close of the war and brought her some candy, the first she had ever seen or tasted.

"During the war things were extremely rough for the pioneers. There were practically no men folks left at home. The women had to manage the best they could. They plowed the fields, worked and gathered the crops. With the aid of Springfield rifles they protected their families and especially the girls against the aggressions, insults, and assaults of white degenerates, who were very bold in their attitude toward these people, whom they called 'the foreigners.' During the Civil War there was no coffee, sugar or flour to be had on account of the blockade of the southern ports by the Federal Navy, and if any such supplies reached Texas from Mexico, the price was beyond the reach of the people. They had to do without these necessities and lived on home-raised and home-ground cornmeal, bacon and homemade molasses and used parched or roasted and ground corn for coffee. At times even bacon and lard were scarce and tallow had to be substituted. "With the close of the Civil War our people were again looking to the future for better days. By that time my paternal and maternal grandparents were living in Vesely, which had become quite a Czech colony, and where, in 1866, they built the first protestant Czech church in America. This church was the first church of any denomination in which the services were conducted in the Czech language with the possible exception of the Church of the Moravian Brethren, who came to America before the American Revolution. This church is still standing and in the cemetery adjacent to it are buried all four of my grandparents. After the war these people got along better. From year to year they were becoming more accustomed to their environment and American ways, and their knowledge of farming had improved.

"By readily absorbing American ideas and methods they profited in a material way and most of them acquired their own farms. They moved out of their old log cabins into frame houses with wooden floors and glass windows, something very unusual at that time. The homemade tallow candles were discarded in favor of kerosene lamps, and instead of the outside open fire for cooking they now had the convenience of a cook stove in the home. Mother often told us how proud she was in her child mind when her parents put in glass windows and bought a cook stove.

"Mother spent her childhood days at Vesely, where she attended school conducted by Professor Mašik. This being a Czech school she did not learn English. Through association with a family named Connally (Senator Tom Connally's ancestors) who were large land and slave owners, she learned to speak the English language. These people took great delight in making mother happy and on one occasion presented her with a complete outfit of homespun yarn, with everything to match, including a sunbonnet. This was the first 'dress-up dress' mother ever had and she never forgot this kindness.

"When mother was about ten years old, her parents moved back to Europe, taking with them the two youngest children, my mother and her brother, Tom. The older sons, having by that time established their own households, remained in Texas. In Europe, the Šebestas bought a mill in their old home, Zadveřice, Moravia. It did not take very long for them to find out that the liberty and freedom they experienced in the United States was not to be had in Austria. During their sojourn in Zadveřice mother was confirmed in the Moravian Brethren Church. She repeatedly stated that this wonderful church building and the religious atmosphere in Zadveřice was the only thing she liked in Europe. During the World War an attempt to remove the bells from the belfry of this church and to convert them into weapons of war was frustrated by members of the church. Under cover of darkness and a penalty of death, the bells were removed from the tower where they had tolled for probably a century, buried in the field where they remained until after the collapse of the Austrian government and the birth of the Czechoslovakian Republic, when they were returned to the church. Mother, with tears of gladness in her eyes, told us how happy she was that the bells of the church in which she was confirmed did not fall into the hands of the enemy.

"After remaining in Europe about a year and a half the Šebestas returned to Texas and settled at Vesely where mother grew up. When father became grown, having heard all kinds of stories of the Old Country, and knowing nothing about it himself, he naturally became curious to know something of Europe, and to satisfy that curiosity he made a trip to Europe in 1876. He remained there for several months and when he returned to the United States he brought with him quite a number of young people who were anxious to come to Texas. Being of a studious nature he also brought back with him all kinds of books and literature, some of which are still in the possession of members of our family.

"My parents were married on February 5, 1878, in the Vesely church by Reverend Ludvik Chlumsky, who also married my father's younger sister. Reverend Chlumsky afterwards returned to Europe and for many years, until his death in 1917, was the pastor of a church in Svratouch, Počta Svratka, Bohemia. The first two years after their marriage, my parents resided at Vesely, which by this time had become known as Wesley. They then moved to Brenham, where father was employed in a retail and wholesale merchandising establishment. Two years later they returned to the farm at Wesley. Father being of a pioneering disposition and spirit, was by this time beginning to think that the country around Wesley was too old and worn out for him and he began looking for a place to establish a new home. In 1883, with his half-brother, Steve Elšik, he bought a farm of a little less than one thousand acres, a part of the Colonel Burr Jarmon plantation on the Colorado River at Ellinger, Fayette County. In 1890 he bought out his half-brother's interest. His brother moved to Moulton and then to Cistern where he died about 1920.

"This farm at Ellinger became the destination of scores upon scores of Czech immigrants arriving in Texas after father had advanced and arranged their transportation. Of all the Czech people that father helped in this manner not a single one failed to pay his debt to him, which was indeed a good recommendation of the honesty and integrity of the Czechs coming to Texas at that time. While father owned property elsewhere, this farm at Ellinger was his home until he died on December 5, 1905. After father's death mother with the younger children lived on at the farm in Ellinger until 1921 when she moved to La Grange, where she built a beautiful home and where she died on October 17, 1931. Both of my parents are buried in the cemetery of the Church of the Moravian Brethren at Ross Prairie between Ellinger and Fayetteville in Fayette County, Texas. They became members of this church when they moved to Ellinger in 1883.

"Our family was a large one: Mary (Mrs. J. H. Novosad); Fannie (Mrs. T. S. Hruška); Albina (Mrs. J. J. Sedlmeyer), who died September 24, 1930; John F., Joseph S., who died January 15, 1932; Vlasta (Mrs. George H. Kristik); Rose (Mrs. W. R. Juren), and I, John F. Chupick. I was born at Ellinger, Fayette County, March 26, 1889. I attended the public schools at Ellinger and La Grange. After graduating from the La Grange high school I took a business course and this is all the schooling I ever had.

"After the death of my father in 1905, I, being the older of the two sons, became up to the time of her death the adviser to my mother and manager of her business interests, especially her farming properties. In 1912 I was employed as cashier of a bank in Ellinger which position I held until 1915. I resigned at this time and organized a bank at Fayetteville, where I filled the position of cashier until January, 1916. Then I was appointed State Bank Examiner, which position I held until the summer of 1918. I resigned this appointment to enter an army officers' training camp at Leon Springs, Texas, and in December, 1918, I was commissioned a lieutenant.

"In December, 1920, my brother and I bought the old home farm at Ellinger. In 1923 I sold out to my brother and went to San Antonio to engage in the land and colonization business in Atascosa County. Brother sold the farm in 1924 and followed me to San Antonio. From that time until his death we were engaged in this business as partners, having offices in San Antonio and Houston. We bought, sub-divided and improved ranches and farm properties, principally in Atascosa and Brazoria counties. I married Miss Clarine Bližnak in January, 1926, and we live in Jourdanton, Texas."

CHAPTER XVI

OTHER TEXAS-CZECH PIONEERS

JOSEF RYPL came to Texas with his parents from Čermna in 1854, a baby, three years old. He was only nine years old at the time of the Civil War, which period he recalled as "hard days." "The water had to be hauled a long distance, and shoes for the family were made of wood, as there was no money to buy handmade or manufactured leather shoes," Mr. Rypl related in his memoirs of early days in Texas. "The houses were so poorly constructed that even the snow could not be kept out, and often during the winter months the family on returning at evening from a day's work, had to shovel out snow that had drifted into the house. Houses were few and far between at this time."

The Rypl family, the father, Vinc, and his three sons, hauled cotton to Houston from Victoria in those early days, making a trip about three times yearly, traveling in caravans for company and protection. They took home supplies received in exchange for their cotton. The sons of Pioneer Rypl later founded their own businesses. One became a hotel proprietor, another a cattle man, the third a farmer at East Bernard.

Josef Rypl, one of the three sons, married Marie Novosad. One daughter married Stephen Novosad, the brother of Marie. He settled at East Bernard where he is still living.

These two, Stephan and Marie Novosad, came to Texas with their widowed mother in 1871 from their native country of Czechoslovakia. Landing at Galveston, they walked the distance from this point to Ross Prairie, passing through Houston and Columbus en route. Before setting sail for Texas the family sold all their possessions to raise the money for the passage. The sale of the property netted the sum of $125.00.

They were made welcome on their arrival at Ross Prairie by pioneer Tom Hruška, who in those days kept open house for all who passed his way.

Josef Rypl, who set foot on Texas soil at the tender age of three years, found health and happiness and some prosperity in life, farming, raising cotton, corn, vegetables and poultry on his farm at Ellinger, where friends, visiting him but a few months

EVOLUTION OF A CZECH HOME

No. 1—*Novosad home as it is fifty years after its erection; John H. Novosad, his wife and parents (left to right).*

No. 2—*(Lower left) Novosad residence, Ellinger, in pioneer days.*

No. 3—*(Lower right) Same place at a later date.*

since, heard from his own lips the story of his pioneer days in Texas.

John H. Novosad and wife established the home at Ellinger in 1876, four years after they had arrived in Texas from the Old Country. Here they lived for more than half a century. John Novosad, senior, died in 1925 at the age of eighty-nine. The wife's death occurred soon after. A son, John Novosad, and his wife, own the home and since the death of their pioneer parents have continued the program of development and improvement.

A party of visitors entertained at the old home one Sunday in October, 1932, enjoyed a round of golf on the plantation "links." The barbecue pits furnished beef, lamb and chicken for the table, where the guests partook of a bountiful and elaborate "spread."

Stretching out into a magnificent orchard area were to be seen the pecan and peach trees, the yearly crop yield from which brings thousands of dollars.

The big two-story plantation house is equipped with a lighting system and running water. The radio brings the world to the fireside. The splendid system of Texas highways developed within the past quarter of a century, along with the advent of the motor vehicle, have been the means of bringing the material world to the doorway of the pioneer home.

John Novosad, another of the first settlers at Ellinger, was provident and looked far into the future, buying land when it was to be had for as little as fifty cents and one dollar per acre. On this land he built primitive shacks for tenant farmers. Often these were occupied by the immigrant families who came looking for a place of shelter or land to cultivate. In some instances the occupants of these first houses on the Novosad plantation were relatives, as in the instance of the Hruška family, who came to Texas to obtain educational advantages for their children.

The Hruška family knew nothing about Texas cotton fields to which they were told to turn their attention and their labors. Stephan Hruška, father of this pioneer family, who had brought to Texas with them $14,000 in money, had received practical scientific training in the business of meat manufacturing in his native country. In Texas he found no demand for this knowledge and experience. Beef cattle were slaughtered in the open, sometimes under the shade of a live-oak tree. The meat was hung in the open, the only requirement being that it be out of reach of the wild animals which were so plentiful in the early days.

This family, having never seen a cotton plant, started the new life in one of the tenant shacks on the Novosad place at Ellinger.

The new fields in which they were to labor stretched out and around as far as the eye could reach.

On hands and knees the members of the family planted the cotton seed, and in the same manner weeded the young plants when they came in sight through the earth. The $14,000 began "melting away," as one of the daughters described the passing of the money out of her parents' hands into that of tradesmen and promoters of the period.

"My parents were unacquainted with money values and the relative values of the articles of commerce which they were called on to buy. When they bought a wagon, or any farm implement, they took out the money and told the dealer, or salesman, as the case happened to be, to help themselves to the price of the article for payment. This method continued until the whole of the $14,000 brought from the old home country was gone.

"Mother, unaccustomed to the work in the field and to the climate of Texas, was taken ill soon after our arrival. This added to the unhappiness and the trials and discomforts of the life."

As the years passed, through their own efforts living conditions improved. Cotton growing was past the experimental stage, and crop yields were much better.

Rural school advantages came, too, in the course of the years for the children of the Hruška family. Months in the rural school were supplemented as opportunities presented themselves with night school work. Thus the nine children found places for themselves in the program of state progress and development.

It is interesting to note that three sons, J. Hruška, C. J. Hruška and Ed Hruška, own and operate a large meat manufacturing business in Houston. Here in their business they have the opportunity to use the methods which their father learned in his years of study in his native country. Another son, John Hruška, lives at Wharton, Texas.

Mr. and Mrs. Stephan Hruška, father and mother of the family of nine, celebrated their golden wedding anniversary several years ago at their home in Houston, where they enjoy comforts and conveniences which they did not even dream of in their pioneer days.

The five daughters are married and live in Houston. Mrs. F. Goettsche, Mrs. M. Kneblik and Mrs. C. L. Hurley are associated in the ownership and management of a large beauty salon. Mrs. Laurence Kristinik and Mrs. Charles Jordan also live in Houston.

A visit to Wesley during the months of 1932, and on the occasion of the visit, meeting Dr. Tom S. Hruška, son and grandson of these two pioneer Hruška Czech-Texans, Honorable Tom Hruška and John Hruška, Sr., brought to light an old manuscript, written by Tom Hruška, dealing with pioneer Czech reading clubs. This manuscript is a prized possession of Dr. Tom S. Hruška, and is dealt with in a later chapter.

We were seated in the office of Dr. Hruška, Wesley, Texas, discussing pioneer days, when the doctor opened some drawers in the old desk and took therefrom the bundle of manuscript, yellow with age; and in tendering it, said that it might add some additional interest to the history of Czech achievement and development in Texas.

The name Hruška stands out prominently in Texas, having a place in all pioneer activities. It belongs, too, with present day activities and achievements. The name in English means a "pear." It has truly been a fruitful name in the State. There are today many branches of the family and each branch has given a splendid account of itself.

Tom Hruška, a member of the first Czech family, was born in 1854 in Jablunce, near Vsetin in Moravia. He came with his parents to Texas in the spring of 1856. At this season the South Texas prairies were abloom with wildflowers. He often related how, during the Civil War, he and his brother had but one pair of trousers between them, and consequently only one of them could go among people at the same time. The one minus the "britches" had to stay at home clothed in a uniform which the mother had made from old sacks. In the later years of his life he also recalled that he was grown before he ever had a pair of shoes. These shoes were made by a cobbler from home-tanned hides. During wet weather they stretched, becoming so large that they fell off his feet. By the same token, in dry weather they shrunk to uncomfortable proportions.

Tom Hruška lived for many years at Ellinger, where he was notary public and civil engineer, not only for the county, but his work called him away from home for as great a distance at times as several hundred miles.

During the Civil War the family lived for a time at Rutersville in Fayette County. His father hauled Confederate Government cotton at the time from a plantation at Waverly to San Antonio, for which he received pay in Confederate money. In 1864, with several neighbors, he started hauling commercial cotton to Eagle Pass, for which he received eleven cents per pound for the hauling, this being paid in gold. From the first trip the father, John Hruška, Sr., brought home his earnings of sixteen dollars in gold mints. These were described as being somewhat smaller than the twenty-dollar gold pieces of the present. The gold was hoarded in an old coffee-pot in the Hruška home at Rutersville. When the pot was full enough, the family bought a farm. About this time the father came near being drafted into the army. One day an officer from La Grange came to the house. The sight of the officer frightened Mrs. Hruška. He stood in the open doorway and asked for her husband—also demanding to know his age. Without time for thinking, she replied, "fifty years." The officer said, "Very good. Have him come to LaGrange tomorrow and I will make an affidavit which you will sign before a notary public. The fee will be fifty cents and we will attend to the rest." The wife pleaded with the officer not to take her husband and as she pleaded she held one of the hoarded sixteen dollar gold pieces in her hand.

Reaching out and catching hold of the officer's hand she put the gold piece in it. At first he did not want to take it, but he finally slipped it into his pocket and told her to have the husband go to Rutersville the next morning. This was only about three-quarters of a mile from the Hruška home, so John Hruška was there at the appointed time to appear before the notary public. The outcome of the matter was that he was given a Government pass as a cotton-hauler, and by the time he returned from the cotton-hauling trip the war was over.

He brought home on this occasion $200.00 in twenty dollar gold pieces, a sack of coffee, some clothing and other luxurious commodities for family use which were not obtainable in the state for love or money. After the war the country was infested with bands of robbers which made conditions bad for the teamsters. John Hruška bored holes with an auger in the wagon tongue and therein placed the gold pieces. He then effectually covered the holes and in this way was able to bring his earnings safely home.

In the office of Dr. Hruška at Wesley are to be found memories both of yesterday and today. The primitive setting of the old building, remodeled and partly rebuilt from the original timbers, stirs the imagination and sends the thoughts racing backward to the days of early settlement. Dr. Hruška explains that once in the long ago, the office had been a two-story building, the second story being devoted to a kind of sanitarium.

The visitor had a vision of the world beating a pathway to the door of this man's house. Wesley has no railroad connection nearer than Brenham, eighteen miles away. She is content to rest in nature's favored section of fertile soil and to quietly watch the world's activities, knowing that Wesley has had her share of fame and distinction. Always the quiet and quaint little village will wear the mantle of achievement, woven through the efforts of the pioneers who valued education and freedom.

Pioneer farm homes are located throughout the whole of old Williams Prairie. The quaint little community that has been called both Vesely and Wesley in the course of the three-quarters of a century will continue to be the mecca for many who seek historic territory.

The Mikeska general merchandising business is carried on in the old frame building that has stood for many years. The Mikeska residence, situated on an eminence about a half-mile distant from the store, is in Austin County while the store is in Washington County.

Joseph Mikeska was at one time a member of the Texas House of Representatives, elected from Austin County where his official residence is maintained.

* * * * *

There belongs also in the story of Texas progress and development pioneer Frank Mikeska, who came as an orphan boy to Texas in 1862 with the Rožnovjak family, who had reared him from his birth. He was later legally adopted by Josef Kozel, farmer and cattle-raiser.

The boy had a hard time. He had to walk many miles each day in rounding up the cattle, there being no horses for him to ride. He was often forced to stop and take off his rough, hand-made boots and pour out the dew that had accumulated from the tall, heavy grass. Deciding one day that he could walk no longer, he joined the army of the Confederacy, remaining in the service for one year. This was hard, too.

"The soldiers were often without food and water and I had to walk and walk even more than I had done hunting for my foster father's cattle. Soldiers were often so hungry that they would have eaten dry wood if they could have found it," pioneer Mikeska has been heard to relate.

When the war ended he returned to his home and married Miss Anna Ječmenek. According to the records he prospered. Mrs. Mikeska was killed in an accident when the horses ran away with

a buggy in which they were riding to the wedding of the Reverend
H. Juren near Ross Prairie. Mr. Mikeska married again, his
second wife being Miss Anna Kubin of Lipa, Moravia. There
were four daughters from the first marriage, two sons and two
daughters from the second. The youngest daughter married Frank
Hruška of Ellinger. The oldest daughter married John Kachtik.
Mr. and Mrs. Frank Hruška had five children, and Mr. and Mrs.
Kachtik had eight—six sons and two daughters.

*   *   *   *   *

"On November 7, 1873, we landed in Galveston where Mr.
Reymershoffer met us and took care of us until we got on the
train that carried us toward our destination, which route was
through Columbus. We did not stop at this place, as yellow fever
was raging there at the time," wrote Mrs. Kateřina Ječmenek
of Fayetteville, Texas, in January, 1932.

"When we reached Weimar we left the train to spend the night
and the following morning continued by wagon the journey to
La Grange. On reaching the Colorado River, over which there is
today a splendid steel bridge, some of the party were much afraid
of the crossing which then had to be by ferry. The ferryman
dispelled our fears, however, and we crossed safely to the other
side. At a little distance beyond was La Grange. Here the driver
loosed two pairs of oxen from the wagon so that they might
be free to graze, there being grass in Texas at this season of the
year. We were then taken to the teamster's home where we were
given a very good dinner, the yams tasting, as I remember,
especially good. From La Grange we continued our journey on to
Fayetteville, arriving at the farm home of our uncles, John and
Joseph Bubela, located on the edge of the town.

"My father, Pavel (Paul) Slováček, was born September 13,
1834, at Horňi (upper) Jasenka near Vsetin, Moravia. His
father's name was Martin, and his mother's name Rosina, née
Trlica. My mother was born at Vsetin. Her father's name was
Jan (John) Bubela and mother's Marie, née Hřibek, or in the
Czech, to be grammatically correct as per declension, Hřibkova.

"My parents farmed the little homestead given them by my
father's parents and as they had children, and taxes were rather
high in comparison with their earnings, they had to be very
economical to get along.

"It was early in June, 1873, that they received a letter from
my mother's brothers, Joseph and John Bubela, living then in
Texas, and who had at the time made their first crop. In the

letter they advised my parents to sell their property and come to Texas. They were enthusiastic about everything pertaining to the new home and country. They promised all help in getting them established in a home near them.

"After long deliberation my parents decided to follow them, emigrating on October 9, 1873. The parting with the relatives brought tears and sadness. Our uncle Rožnovjak took us in his wagon to Meziřici where we boarded the train for Bremen.

"I do not remember the name of the vessel on which we sailed, but the voyage across the Atlantic was a stormy one, the ship rolling heavily, causing many passengers to suffer seasickness. On November 7, we landed in Galveston as previously mentioned.

"Although I was only six years old at the time, I will never forget that first evening of our arrival at the home of our uncles. After the cordial welcome we were invited to supper which consisted of black coffee and corn bread and some kind of stewed sauerkraut made from the green leaves of the cabbage. Our aunts brought us this food, sobbing as they did so. Our father was like he had been stricken dumb when he saw the food. My mother burst into tears, and sobbing, asked why they had desired that we should come, when they themselves were in such dire need. They explained that the crops had been destroyed by grasshoppers and other devastating insects that came in swarms, destroying all except the corn. At this time there were no preventions such as spraying, and so the calamity of the pests left them in a precarious condition. This they did not want my parents to know, as they were so longing to see us, and feared that if they knew of the circumstances, they would not come. Their home consisted of two rooms, one for each family.

"I recall with pleasure the joy of the first ride I had in the new country, going with my uncle to a religious service held in the home of Paul Hřibek, mother's uncle. At this time there was no evangelistic or protestant church near by. Our conveyance for the trip was in keeping with the new country, it being a crude sled about eight feet long on which stools had been placed. Mules were hitched to the sled after we children had been seated. The sudden starting of the queer conveyance tumbled all of us off on the ground. Extricating ourselves from the stools, we abandoned the sled as a means of transportation and decided to walk. This was a long hike, but put our digestive organs in good condition so that we enjoyed immensely the very good dinner which Grandma Hřibek and her daughter, Mrs. Tom Ječmenek, prepared for us.

"During this same fall we had helped to pick cotton for the

St. Dančak family, and afterward our uncles found a rent farm for us on the land of Mr. Hlavaty, Sr. The first year we farmed on halves, the crops were good, and altogether we made ten bales of cotton. Five of these were due Mr. Hlavaty, the landlord, and one-third of the other five was given to mother's brother, Paul, who had helped us produce the crop.

"Next year we had our own team and the crop again was good. We were just gathering the sixth bale when the hurricane of September 15, 1874, came and tore off all the cotton that had been left on the stalks, and we were barely able to complete the sixth bale.

"In 1876 we rented land from Mr. and Mrs. John Hruška, Sr., and again we made a good crop, but the first of November of this year my sister, Veronica, died from pneumonia, she being just seventeen years old. This brought such heavy sorrow on my parents, especially my mother, that she became ill.

"In 1877 the yellow fever raged again, both my parents being stricken with it. They continued ill during the whole of the cotton chopping season. Neighbors and a Mrs. Grossman and her daughter came to our rescue, helping us with the farm work. My brother, Paul, was only nine years old at the time, so we had to depend largely on these neighbors. After several years we enjoyed somewhat more prosperous times. Our mother died on April 21, 1886. Father later married a second time. I was married in November, 1887, to Joseph Ječmenek. My brother had previously married Miss Frances Mačuda."

These pioneer families have been long and favorably known in the Fayetteville community and the names of Mr. and Mrs. John Hruška, Sr., were connected with much of the early development in the State.

The first Protestant Czech church at Fayetteville was built by John Hruška.

* * * * *

A mighty Texas live-oak tree, the tall tops interwoven with the thick gray moss, the limbs and branches interbound with mustang grape vines, provided the first shelter for some of the immigrants as they sought to take up their residence in the new country.

In the absence of the tree, when only the open stretch of the prairie was at hand, a primitive shelter made of the long prairie grass and Texas sod, had to do until better accommodations could be had.

The "better accommodations" came. Today on the farm home

of the Texas-Czech is to be found all modern conveniences. A prominent Houston jurist, a pioneer-native of Virginia, one recent summer evening fell to reminiscing, and the conversation drifted back to the days of unscreened homes, flies and mosquitoes.

"Do you still have these to contend with in the country?" one member of the party inquired. And the Virginian in Texas said, "Well, not on the farms that belong to the Czech farmers of the State. I have just returned from a visit to one of these farms, and I have never found better comforts in any city home. There were electric lights, gas, water, telephone, radio and screens."

Once a small Czech boy poured the cold morning dew from his hard rough boots on his tramp through the Texas wilds in search of the grazing cattle. And in the years that are gone, the Czech pioneer family had to shovel the snow from the cabin home before they could kindle the hearthstone fire and then lie down to sleep. Sometimes they lighted a fire in the open near to the family shelter to frighten the wild animals away.

Tired feet were removed from the rude shoes and hands, numb and weary from the long day's toil, were folded for a brief respite from their labor, as the pioneer slept and dreamed of a future when the structure of the new home in the new country would be established.

CHAPTER XVII

Other Texas-Czech Pioneers—*(Continued)*

The story of the "covered wagon" has become an epic. But the story of John Havlik has not been written until now.

John Havlik was born in Ratibor, Czechoslovakia, in the year 1829. He married Miss Anna Trampota and in the year 1855 with his wife and two children, Katherine and Rose, packed his belongings and sailed for New Orleans. Among the fellow passengers were: Joe Malina, Joe Cajňik, Frank Malik, Joe Holec and Frank Dřevojanek. From New Orleans the party proceeded to Houston, Texas. In Houston a freighter was hired and with all their belongings piled into the huge wagon, drawn by eight oxen, they started on the journey to Cat Springs.

On a lonely prairie the wife of John Havlik gave birth to a baby girl. Unfortunately the infant lived but a few moments, and was buried there near the spot of her birth. The interrupted journey was resumed. The pioneers arrived finally at Cat Springs where they decided to settle. There was no work to be had at this place, so John Havlik went forth to look for employment.

After a search of two weeks he located a job at a sawmill in Travis, now Kenny, Austin County. With a sack of cornmeal on his shoulders he returned to where he had left his family. Again they loaded up for moving and started for Travis and the sawmill. Traveling was slow, as heavy rains which had fallen but recently flooded the creeks. While crossing Mill Creek the water rose, the wagon was submerged, overturned and everything emptied into the swollen stream. John Havlik managed to save his wife and one child, but the swirling waters with a mighty undercurrent wrested two-year-old Rozinka out of her mother's arms and carried her down stream never to be recovered. The driver lost his teams and clothing set adrift was found ten miles down the river.

John Havlik worked at the sawmill at Travis for three years. At this place a son, John Havlik, Jr., was born in 1857. Some years later a daughter, Annie, was born. After three years' work as a sawmill hand, Havlik rented a small farm from a Mr. Clements.

140

Left Panel:
Mr. and Mrs. Vinc Rypl
(Rypel)
after a lifetime of pioneering

Center Upper:
Josef J. Holik

Center Lower:
Joseph Janak
Oldest Texas-Czech native
of Texas

Right Panel:
Mr. and Mrs. Joe Rypl
(Rypel)
Son of Vinc Rypl

John Havlik, Jr., describes the adventures of his father and family during those trying years:

"Times were hard for poor immigrant tenants, as the country was owned by large plantation owners with many slaves. It was these same poor foreign tenants, however, who bought nearly all of the land in Austin and Washington counties after the Civil War. The plantation owners were either killed in the war, or so badly impoverished from its effects that they sold all their land. In 1861, father contracted to haul cotton to Mexico for the government. This arrangement left mother and we three children at home to shift for ourselves, as it took father several months to make one trip. In 1863 while he was away on one of these trips mother passed away at childbirth.

"Well do I remember the day, for after the burial only we three children, the oldest a girl of eight, were left. Soldiers came often to the house, looking for father, or any other men that might be found, to take them for service in the war. They would ransack our home, eating up what little food we had. Parched corn was used for coffee and cornmeal for bread. There was no flour, sugar or coffee.

"In 1868 my father married Eva Siptak and we moved to Hewett, now Latium, in Washington County, where he bought one hundred acres of land. After eight years he sold out to Mr. Paul Šebesta and moved to Wesley, Texas, where he bought three hundred and twenty acres of land. Here he lived until his death in 1894. He was buried in our family cemetery at Wesley.

"Sister Katherine married Mr. John Talaš and she died the year following. Sister Annie married Mr. Thomas Hruška of Fayetteville, Texas.

"In 1881 I made a trip back to Europe, visiting Germany and Czechoslovakia. After my return in 1882 I was married to Miss Johanna Bača of Fayetteville, sister of Frank Bača, the founder and leader of the famous Bača's Band and Orchestra.

"I lived in Wesley on our old home place until 1906, when I sold out to my brother-in-law, Joseph Bača, and moved to Bell County. Since then I have resided two years in Falls County and eight years in Milam County.

"My wife and I have reared twelve children. Ten are living. Four of the sons served in the World War. In November, 1932, we celebrated our golden wedding anniversary. In my seventy-five years of life I have seen many changes in the times and the conditions of our great State.

"Depressions, hard times, hard work. The passing of the longhorn cattle, slaves, and wild animals. The change from oxen to mules and then to tractors for farm cultivation. From wagons to buggies, railroads to motor vehicles and airplanes for transportation.

"I have seen the State changed from a wilderness and unbroken prairies to its present-day agricultural magnificence. But even with hardships and dangers, we had our good old times. I am thankful that I have always enjoyed good health; even at my age I am still hale and hearty."

Three-quarters of a century of life with its vicissitudes, its changes, its joys and its sorrows, is the share that John Havlik, son of the pioneer of 1855, has in the history of Texas. In addition to his own service in behalf of his State and Country, he has given ten children to carry on when he has finished his life's work. As he lifts the curtain of the past on the scene of the primitive home, where three small children are but returned from that new-made mother's grave, his spirit is calm. There is no grumbling or self-pity. It was a condition that came with the building of a State and Country. Today, as he lives peacefully at the family home in Temple, Mr. Havlik recalls the good things of life rather than the bad. The celebration of his golden wedding anniversary was the fitting climax to a long and useful life spent in helping to build Texas.

The Havlik children are leading useful, happy lives. Thomas J. Havlik married Miss Julia Halamiček, and is a merchant at Fayetteville; John V. Havlik married Miss Annie Faltisek. He is a merchant at Moulton. Henry J. Havlik lives in Waco. Oscar J. Havlik is a graduate of Sam Houston Normal, Huntsville, and also of San Marcos Teacher's College. He is a salesman, married, and lives in Temple. His wife was Miss Bettie Švadleňak. Louis Havlik married Miss Annie Maresh and is engaged in the wholesale grocery business at Temple. Miss Hermina Havlik married Walter Johnson of Temple. Miss Frances Havlik is a graduate nurse of King's Daughters Hospital, Temple. Miss Vlasta Havlik is a beauty operator in Temple, and Miss Marie Havlik resides in Dallas.

*   *   *   *   *

Martin Gavenda was one of the pioneers who came to Texas in 1867 from what is today Czechoslovakia. His family at the time consisted of four children, two sons unmarried and two married daughters, Mrs. Tom Kachtick and Mrs. Jan Slovak. They settled first at Wesley, a community which through these early pioneers has become one of the historic communities of the State.

These early settlers had a bad start, for they were without money. Two years after their arrival they, with seven other Czech families, moved to Caldwell in Burleson County. This was in 1869. The Gavendas, Slovaks and Kachticks made up the party. All bought farms, every transaction being on credit. Long dry spells in crop-making time, which lasted for several years, brought distress to the small colony. Only two of the number could speak English and this on a very limited scale. In consequence, they suffered in their business transactions. It was a struggle, not only to exist, but to hold on to their property. The burden of the debt was weighted with fifteen per cent interest.

Today they have the distinction of being the first Czech settlers in that section of the State. In 1876 they were joined by forty additional pioneer families, all settling around Caldwell. With this increase in the Czech population and the widening of influence, a school building was erected, in keeping with the primitive life, being only a small box structure. To build a church edifice at this time was not practicable, as only once or twice a year was a religious service held. At such times Reverend Adolf Chlumsky officiated. He had to travel in a covered wagon, and with a large territory to look after, his visits were necessarily at long intervals.

The lean years passed and the good crop years came. Homes were paid for, and with prosperity came happiness. The families who had endured every privation of the unsettled country, and the hardships that came from crop failures, began to look into other sections of the State for homes, thinking perhaps a change of scene would better their conditions.

*   *   *   *   *

Jan Slovak and family, after a residence of fourteen years in Burleson County, moved to Milam County, where they lived until Mr. Slovak's death in 1918 at the age of eighty-nine. The two children, a son, Frank, and a daughter, Mrs. Tom Machalek, survive. The latter lives in Temple. Frank lives at Harlingen.

Tom Kachtick, wife and four children, Tom, Paul, John and Mary, moved to Bell County where the father, pioneer Tom Kachtick, died in 1929, also at the age of eighty-nine. Two sons, John and Paul, live at Harlingen with their families. The daughter, Mary (Mrs. John Jarma), resides in Temple.

These pioneers of 1867, the Gavendas, Slovaks and Kachticks, came to Texas from Hoštalkov, crossing the Atlantic to Galveston, in a sailboat, being on the ocean for nine weeks. From Galveston they went on to Brenham in Washington County, and there on July 4, 1867, they were met by John Chupik, who took them to Wesley.

Could the years that intervene be put aside, and the scene of pioneer Texas be presented, there would be much to chronicle. The arrival of the new citizens in a new country was on the National Day of Independence. But the newcomers proceeded without formality to take up their residence. They rented farm land from John Chupik and then began those years of crop failures, sickness and privation. They had suffered much while on the sailing vessel bound for the new home and country. One quart of water was allowed them each day with an allowance of only one hardtack to each person. Parents with children were allowed no more. All were sick, and they landed in Galveston with but little money, so life had to be started on credit.

They lived in log houses with dirt floors. Jan Slovak's wife went into the cotton fields and picked cotton for a neighbor in exchange for an iron cooking pot and baking oven, a table and two wooden benches. Beds were crudely built, without springs of any kind, and mattresses were made of corn husks.

*   *   *   *   *

The lives of Martin Gavenda, Jan Slovak, and those early Czech settlers at Wesley and Caldwell are splendid examples of courage, endurance and tenacity of purpose, without which nothing can be accomplished. Today Brenham and Caldwell are thriving, progressive young cities. They stand in all their bustling activity in testimony to the spirit of those pioneers.

Today their descendants are scattered over the whole of the State. Františka, who was the wife of John Kachtick, had six sons and two daughters, Robert, John, William, Edward, Emil, Walter, Louise and Lillian. The mother was a Ječmenek from one of the old pioneer families, who came by boat to Galveston and then proceeded on foot and in ox-drawn wagons into the sections which finally became their homes.

*   *   *   *   *

Henry Ginzel, who owns about three hundred acres of land adjoining the City of Caldwell, in Burleson County, is one of the early Texans, having been born at Industry, Austin County, in 1851. His father died when he was only two years old and in consequence he does not know where he came from in the old country, or when. It must have been, he thinks, at least eleven years before he was born—as his father was a widower and owned a farm at Industry—when he married his mother, who was a widow. The father was of German descent, but the conversation in the family was always in the Czech language. The mother's first husband died soon after landing at Galveston on account of malnutrition caused from poor food and bad water. About one-half of the immigrants died either on board ship or soon after landing. While at sea there were many funerals, and the people got so used to them that they wished that they also were dead so that they might be over with the distress. His mother, Mr. Ginzel recalls, often talked about the trip and the terrible suffering.

After the death of his father, his mother remarried. The husband this time was Joseph Ripl. Today the Ripls are scattered all over Texas.

Industry at the time was considered quite a city. There were three stores. Fayetteville had only one mercantile establishment.

The settlers lived mostly in "dug-outs," or used the rail fences, especially the corners, for two sides of the house. For the roofs rails covered with grass or sod were placed on top. There were no chimneys, cooking being done on the outside. During inclement weather it had to be done in the house and on these occasions the smoke had to go where it could. There was no glass for windows or doors. For the latter slabs of white-oak were used and for the windows the same kind of material was used, the slabs being roughly held together or bound by means of primitive fastenings, there being no nails. One of the settlers had a pet deer that never waited for the door to be opened, but whenever so inclined, jumped out the window or hole in the wall. The dogs always found a hole in the wall for their exit or entrance.

In his time at Industry Mr. Ginzel recalls that the following families were residents: Two Schiller families, a Konařik, a Martinek, a Zapalač and a Polčak family. There were few wagons, only sleighs for general transportation. There was one wagon and this was owned by one of the Schillers. It was crudely made, the four wheels being cut with a borrowed crosscut saw from a thick sycamore tree. The other parts were cut and made with the aid of an axe, no other tools being available. Many wished to borrow the wagon, but Pioneer Schiller refused both neighbors and friends this favor!

Mr. Ginzel married Johanna Šupak and they had eight children—seven sons and one daughter. Three of the sons and the daughter died. One son lives in West, Texas, the three others on the farm near Caldwell. These are William, Louis and Walter. The wife and mother of the family died in 1914. The father, born eighty-two years ago in Texas, lives with one of the sons. He retains all his mental faculties. Only his limbs refuse, he says, to function as he would have them. He is an honest man, never during his long residence in Burleson County did he have a litigation or bad words with his neighbors and is loved by all.

* * * * *

Paul S. Škrabanek of West, McLennan County, Texas, son of Mr. and Mrs. Tom Škrabanek, pioneer Texas-Czech settlers, holds the distinction of being one among many Texas-Czechs who has succeeded in a chosen line of business.

The parents of Paul Škrabanek came to Texas with four children, Josef, Mary, Tom and H. J., from Czechoslovakia in 1871, settling on their arrival in Washington County, where they lived for eleven years and where three other children, Paul S., Frances and Rosalie, were born.

In 1882 they moved to Austin County where the youngest child, John T., was born and where the father of the family died in 1886. Mrs. Škrabanek, the mother and children moved then to Burleson County, where she died in 1891. The son, Paul S., attended the rural schools of the communities in which they lived and later attended a business college at Austin. About 1895 he accepted a position with a mercantile company at Temple. In 1897 he was married to Miss Mollie Rose Lešovsky, daughter of Mrs. Kubela by a former marriage. In 1904 Mr. Škrabanek went into the general merchandising business with Joe R. Schiller of Ocker, Bell County.

In 1906, when the Schiller home burned, the firm of Schiller & Škrabanek was moved to West in McLennan County. Mr. Škrabanek remained in the mercantile business until about 1920, when he was made president of a bank in West.

Mrs. Škrabanek was the daughter of Mr. and Mrs. Frank Lešovsky of Muscada, Wisconsin, where Mr. Lešovsky died, leaving his widow and two children, Mollie, aged two, and Frank, only ten days old. Mrs. Lešovsky married John Franklin Kubela and the family moved to Austin County, Texas, in 1882. A son, John W. Kubela, was born before they came to Texas, and another son, Ed S., was born in Austin County.

While the family lived in Austin County, Mr. Kubela engaged in farming, growing cotton almost exclusively. In 1883 they moved to Milam County where the family lived in real pioneer fashion in a log cabin. In 1884 Mr. Kubela bought one hundred and sixty acres of prairie land in Bell County, seventeen miles east of Temple, where two daughters, Lucy Mae and Della, were born. In 1897 the family moved again, going to El Campo, where Mr. Kubela bought land and engaged in rice and cotton growing, cattle raising, and later in the banking business. At this place two other sons, Stanley and Raymond, were born. Mr. Kubela bought more land and began the education of his children. Some of them attended college and in 1931 Mr. Kubela died at the age of seventy-four years. Three of the children are in the drug business, two being registered pharmacists.

Mr. and Mrs. Paul S. Škrabanek have four children. Three were born in Temple and one in West. The eldest, Klara, married H. B. Morgan of Waco. They live in Houston, where Mr. Morgan is connected with a trust company. Raymond E., married Miss Lois Cook of Seymour, Texas. They make their home in Houston, where Mr. Škrabanek is an architect. He had the opportunity of designing the handsome residence for his parents at West. He is a graduate of the Texas Agricultural and Mechanical College, receiving his B. A. degree in 1926. All four children are proficient in both art and music.

Pauline, the second daughter, married Gene E. Taylor of Waco, and Helen, the youngest daughter, married John Popp, a prominent young business man of West. All three daughters attended the College of Industrial Arts, Denton. Helen received her B. S. degree in 1929, majoring in Fine Arts. All three taught school in McLennan County before they were married.

In both the Škrabanek and the Kubela families there were eight children. Life in Texas in even the later pioneer years, when these settlers came, was far from easy. Mrs. Škrabanek recalls how her mother saved and practiced rigid economy. These early Texas settlers knew all the hardships that might be attributed to "depressions," according to Mrs. Paul Škrabanek, whom fate has favored in that she is the wife of a successful business man, and the mother of a family of four children who have made good every cherished hope of the parents.

It is, however, but one of many stories of similar kind that could be told, and is given by way of testimony in the chronicling of that which has come to pass because these Texas-Czech pioneers were not afraid to put their hands to the ploughshare or the sickle, the sledge hammer or the maul. They have continued the march of progress and development through the years.

*   *   *   *   *

Czech women of Texas have been developing their individuality and talent, not only in limited fields, but in every line of work. The story of their achievements may never be written in full. It has taken not the span of one lifetime to accomplish that which has been done.

In presenting a few of the great number of Texas-Czech women who are today taking their place in all professions, and in the various fields of activities, we cannot write of the present without first referring to the pioneer mother who spun and wove the cotton which she had toiled in the field to produce, that her family might have clothes to wear. The mother who gave years of her strength to the rearing of her children. Who gave of her very life that they might have the chance to progress. The educator, the musician, the artist, the technician, and author all owe their attainments to the pioneer parent. It was she who made it possible for the daughter to be prepared to teach. Through the whole list of activities, in every field of service, this influence projects itself.

*   *   *   *   *

For fourteen years the name of Mrs. S. Mikulenka has appeared on the official courthouse stationery of Hallettsville, Lavaca County, as County Treasurer. On the death of her husband she was appointed to the position which he had held, and for fourteen years she was re-elected to the same office. In the course of her duties she has signed checks for sums of money amounting to as much as $150,000 at a time. The records throughout the years she held this office have been kept in her own writing, and the heavy volumes are interesting, not only for the records of county activities, but because of the legible and beautiful penmanship.

There is to be found nowhere in the State a more cultured woman than Mrs. Mikulenka. She at all times received those who called at her office in the stately stone courthouse at Hallettsville with the courtesy of her official position, and in addition radiated that cordiality which comes only with refinement and a pleasing personality.

Mrs. Mikulenka was born at Skřivan, Czechoslovakia, a village of about two hours' distance from Praha. At the age of eight she came to America with her mother and brother, settling near Green, Kansas. The circumstances leading to her coming to Texas some years later had to do with Kansas weather. It was in the winter of 1893 that she—then Miss Bertha Svoboda, a school teacher at Fancy Creek, Kansas—was caught in a blizzard while on her way home from school, with the result that her eyes were frosted. This left them in a weakened condition, most sensitive to the cold. It being decided that she should live in a warmer climate, she accepted a position to teach school in the Chromčik School, Fayetteville, Texas.

In 1905 she was married to Dr. Emanuel Van Vettermann of Shiner, Texas, known as one of the most distinguished physicians in Texas. He had received his education and training at Charles University in Praha.

In February, 1909, Dr. Van Vettermann died. During the following month, Mrs. Van Vettermann's mother died. Mrs. Van Vettermann, with a small daughter, Columbia, returned to Kansas, but came back to Texas in 1912. In 1913 she was married to Ed Mikulenka of Bartlett, Texas. They settled in Hallettsville, where, in 1916, Mr. Mikulenka was elected County Treasurer of Lavaca County. On his death in 1918, Mrs. Mikulenka was appointed to serve out the unexpired term as County Treasurer. In speaking of her work she said on the eve of retiring from the office that she had felt the responsibility of the position keenly and in her earnest desire to do her best for the public, she had had only one vacation of a month, at which time she made a visit back to her old home in Kansas.

Believing that every one should know the language of his ancestors, and know something of the land of his fathers, Mrs. Mikulenka helped solicit names for the petition that brought about the adoption of the Czech language as a department in the University of Texas. She was later instrumental in having the language adopted in the high school at Hallettsville.

Although the work of the County Treasurer increased steadily all during the fourteen years Mrs. Mikulenka was in office, she kept the records in perfect order. In December, 1931, a Houston company audited the books of Lavaca County, and the County Treasurer was complimented on her excellent work. In fact, so accurate were her books, that the only error found was that the county owed her forty cents.

Mrs. Mikulenka recalls among incidents connected with her work in the schoolroom in Texas that the children studied aloud, and sat on hand-made benches in the Fayetteville school in 1895. Her daughter, Columbia, is the wife of T. J. Holub, book-keeper and assistant manager for a packing company at Taylor, Texas. Mr. Holub is an A. & M. College graduate. Mrs. Holub was a member of the faculty of the Hallettsville High School, and retained her position for some months after her marriage. She was re-elected in 1932 to her same position for the terms of 1932-'34, but resigned to join her husband at Taylor.

*   *   *   *   *

Wenzel Květoň and wife, Rosina Tejčka Květoň, were natives of the village of Bremzi, Bohemia, near the city of Praha. In 1852, with their family of four children, Wenzel, Jr., born 1840; Joseph, born 1843; Maria, born 1846, and Matthias, born 1849, they set out from Bremen in a sailing ship for Texas, arriving at Galveston in May, 1852. From this point they moved on to Houston, where some years later two other children were born, a son, John, in 1855, and a daughter, Annie, in 1859.

Having established himself and family in a home on his arrival in Houston, Wenzel Květoň set about to help build that community. His first work was with the first railroad that entered Houston, the Galveston, Houston and Henderson. Later he helped build the old City Market House, one of the earliest business enterprises of the city. This building, one of the old landmarks, was described by an early chronicler as a "pretentious affair," occupying an entire block from Preston to Congress Avenue, where it stood until the Civil War.

When he had thus contributed toward the construction of the first railroad, and the building of the first market house, he decided to engage in business. He established a brick-yard from which he was able to supply building material for other Houston structures. After he had made a success of the brick-yard venture, Pioneer Květoň looked out into the field of community building, and opened a grocery store which was one of the early exclusive establishments of the kind in Houston. In connection with this business, he operated a transfer and storage business, handling produce by wagon as far distant as Austin County, and a settlement known at the time as Blossom, being the English translation of Květoň.

During the year 1872 the Květoň family moved from Houston to Austin County, near Cat Springs, where farming engaged their interest. Both husband and wife lived to the age of ninety-three years.

The son, Wenzel, enlisted in the Confederate Army, being a member of Green's Brigade. He was at the Siege of Vicksburg and witnessed the surrender of that city. Joseph was at the time too young for enlistment as a regular soldier, but anxious to do his part in serving his State and country, went with De Bray's Regiment as a hostler and coach-boy. Matthias, who was just a boy, insisted on doing his bit as an assistant in the Quartermaster's Department, making bullets for the Confederate Army. All members of the family married and reared large families of their own, and all have died except the daughter, Mrs. Annie Hranitzsky, who lives near Sweet Home.

Pat Květoň, attorney, of Dallas, is the son of Matthias, the boy soldier. Like his patriotic father, he, too, was a soldier, and has the distinction of being a veteran of the World War in which he saw active service on the battlefields of France. He is past State Commander Texas Veterans of Foreign Wars. On his maternal side Mr. Květoň traces his ancestry back through many historic old families of the South, even to that of General Wade Hampton. He is proud of his Czech blood, however, and of his Czech name, which he has from his pioneer grand-parents.

* * * * *

Josef Lidiak came to Texas in 1860, just prior to the Civil War, from Moravia, and settled in Fayette County at a place known as Bluff. He immediately began farming and continued in this occupation until 1863, when he became a corporal in Martindale's Company, Confederate Army. For the most of the time of his service he was kept in the State. After the war he returned to the peaceful pursuit of agriculture in which he continued until his death in 1869, at the age of sixty-six. The wife, Anna (Pohrabač), also a native of Moravia, died in 1884, at the age of sixty-five. They left a family of four children.

John, who was a farmer in Fayette County, served in the United States Army during the Civil War. He had gone to Brownsville, hauling cotton for a neighbor who, after selling the cotton and also the team, left the boy some 365 miles from home with no means of transportation back. He met a number of his friends who were enlisting in the Union Army and was persuaded to join them. Thus it came about that, after only two years residence in the new country, father and son were arrayed against each other in the conflict between the States. The son was a member of Hammett's Company, First Texas Cavalry, United States Army.

Frank Lidiak, the second son of the family, attended his first school in Fayette County, when sixteen years of age. Later he entered a private German night school taught by a Mr. Cremer. There he learned both German and English. Having always spoken the Czech language at home, he was now able to speak three languages. He taught school at the Bluff community schoolhouse for three years, 1873-'74-'75. Following these years of work in the schoolroom, he served as deputy county clerk for three and one-half years under T. Q. Mullen, and then established the first Bohemian newspaper in the State at La Grange. This paper, *The Slovan,* continued publication for five years, when Mr. Lidiak sold out.

He was afterward given a deputy collectorship in the Third District under President Grover Cleveland's first administration, and served in this official capacity until September, 1888.

On August 19, 1890, Mr. Lidiak, with other citizens of the county, established a newspaper called the *Fayette County Democrat,* and was connected with this publication as the managing editor until January, 1891. In February, 1892, he bought the German newspaper of Fayette County which had the distinction of being the second German newspaper ever published in the section. This weekly, the *Deutsche Zeitung,* became one of the leading newspapers of the country under his editorship.

Mr. Lidiak enlarged his activities in the publishing field by establishing *The Slovan* in the Czech language. This was after the style of an American magazine, the pages being devoted to fiction, the laws of the country, customs of the people in the early days and other important subjects. In June, 1877, he married Miss Pauline Adamčik, a native of Moravia, and daughter of Frank and Rosella (Janda) Adamčik, who had arrived in Texas in 1860.

Both Mr. and Mrs. Lidiak held membership in the Catholic Church. They were the parents of seven children—Sophia, Lilie, Edna, Frank Jr., Anna and Martha, twins, and George. Frank Lidiak, the pioneer, took an active part in politics.

CHAPTER XVIII

OTHER TEXAS-CZECH PIONEERS—*(Continued)*

"A fertile soil with industry and easy
Transportation for men and things from
Place to place makes a nation strong and great."
—BACON.

LESS than a quarter of the population of the United States, according to the statistics, now live on farms. In the last ten years, we are told, every State east of the Mississippi and north of the Mason and Dixon line has lost in the number of farms.

This is not true in Texas. Only a small percentage of abandoned farm acreage is to be encountered over the State. The development of the highways has been a powerful factor in keeping people on Texas farms. One hundred years ago, the distance between Austin and San Antonio, something over eighty miles, was without a single human habitation. "The route," wrote William Kendall, a member of the Santa Fé Expedition, which left Austin in 1841, "was infested with hostile Indians." Today this route has been transformed into a modern highway, traveled daily by thousands of motor vehicles and every acre of the land is utilized. The college town of San Marcos and the industrial city of New Braunfels are both located on this route, with developed farm and pasture lands stretching between. The men of the Santa Fé Expedition rode horseback with saddlebags to hold their rations and supplies. Today airplanes span the skies where once these pioneers sought to invade an unknown region.

This illustration shows what industry, fertile soil and easy transportation has done for the State.

There had to be more than this, however. Or rather there had to be something behind it. A spirit that was dedicated to the cause of development. The Czech pioneer, well-fitted to industry, took hold of the soil when he came, and remained with the problem, in the field, at the plough handles, until results were achieved.

Today Texas is classed as an agricultural State. There remains,

153

however, even after a century of progress, thousands of acres of virgin soil, awaiting development.

Across the vast domain from what is known today as the "Big Bend" country in West Texas, traversing the section which later became the historic route leading to Old San Filipe, LaBahia and thence on to Natchez, Mississippi, we may envision through the vista of the centuries, Spanish miners crossing the country from the West, their caravans of pack mules ladened with gleaming silver bullion moulded into long, solid bars.

Passing over the intervening years, which have effaced the footsteps of these first explorers, and hushed the sound of the Indian war-cry, we take a page from an old diary kept by one of two early pioneers. They rode horseback to Texas back in 1835, coming from Alabama and Tennessee. The page, blurred with the dust of years, sheds light today on the early settlement of Fayette County, Texas, the home of so many Texas-Czechs. These young American pioneers, John Moore, later known as Colonel John Moore, the Indian fighter of Tennessee, and John Dancy of Alabama, saddled their horses early one morning and turned their faces toward Texas.

They had met by agreement at a specific starting point which chanced to be Franklin, Tennessee, young Dancy riding from his home at Decatur, Alabama, to join his companion, and from there the start was made. Each day they wrote in a diary, marking the various stages of the journey. One prophetic day in 1835 they dismounted at a place which later became the city of LaGrange. John Moore looked about him. He saw a valley set in the frame of hills with a beautiful stream, the Colorado River, winding its way along beneath overhanging bluffs and ridges.

Unsaddling his horse at the ford on the west side of the Colorado, he became a veritable Monte Cristo, monarch of all he surveyed. Young Dancy, not as yet content, rode across the river to prospect further. If its appearance pleased him, he was to stand on a prominent point and wave his hat, whereupon his companion would join him. Together then they would make coffee and eat their lunch in celebration of having founded a new home in a new country.

Young John Moore was satisfied with his choice of location. He secured a section of land out of the Baron de Bastrop league. John Dancy sought to acquire a section which had been previously granted to the Castlemans of New Orleans. The matter of securing title to the land took him back to the Crescent

City and during his absence John Moore induced several Bohemian and German families to take up residence on his land. Today the historic and beautiful little city of LaGrange stands on the Moore survey.

The site selected by John Dancy on the opposite shore of the river was just as suitable for settlement, but he was not as fortunate as his companion in securing the first settlers.

Pioneering in Texas has continued through the years and the frontier has been pushed farther away with each succeeding decade. The Czech settler on the whole has not been given to advancing frontiers, usually preferring to remain in the first place of settlement, but he has stood ready when the homestead has been developed to build cities and carry the work on into the frontiers.

* * * * *

Honorable Wenzel Matajowski, born in Nechanitz, Bohemia, in 1829, emigrated to Texas in 1850, landing at Galveston. He had received his education at the Gymnasium of Trautenau. His father, Anton Matajowski, was a merchant, also the Mayor of Nechanitz. A brother, Anton, was royal and imperial landrath (an officer invested with the powers of district judge and commissioners' court combined) of Praha. Two younger brothers were merchants in Nechanitz. Each served as mayor of that city.

On reaching Texas, Wenzel Matajowski engaged in farming on the Bernard. From this section he moved to Bastrop, where in 1852 he established a cigar factory. In 1853 he was married to Miss Christiana Dietrich of Bastrop. In 1855 he moved to Long Prairie where he farmed until 1867, when he bought the mercantile business of Robert Zapp. He became postmaster at Long Prairie, to which, in 1873, he gave the name of Nechanitz.

During the Civil War he was a strong Union man and became allied with the Republican Party. For many years he was one of the ablest Republican leaders in the county. During the years 1862-'64 he served as constable in his precinct. He was appointed postmaster at Nechanitz in 1873, serving for many years. In 1886 he was elected Representative to the Twentieth Legislature, which held its first session in the new capitol building. A large family of children were reared and have taken their places over the State in various lines of industry. One son, Edward, was for some time a merchant at Birch, Burleson County.

A daughter, Mary, married Gustav Franzc, farmer at Cummings Prairie, near Ledbetter, Fayette County. Another daughter, Otillie, married Louis Kruse, farmer and butcher, near Ledbetter. A son Gustav, was a merchant at Warda, Fayette County, Wenzel was a merchant at Yellow Prairie, Burleson County. Augusta married William Kruse, merchant, at Ledbetter. Clara became the wife of George Kruse, a stockman and farmer, near Ledbetter. Anton was a merchant near Dime Box, Lee County. Laura married Joe Dullye, farmer and stockman, near Giddings. Charles and Paul, two younger sons, for a time remained at home in business with their father. Antonio married Albert Speckles, farmer, at Giddings.

It is interesting to note that this Czech pioneer was a successful grower of tobacco in Texas. He was awarded prizes at a fair in Houston many years ago for his tobacco exhibit. His death removed a highly respected and outstanding citizen of the State.

The offspring of the large family, twelve of whom lived to years of maturity, are perpetuating the life and splendid influence of this early Czech settler.

*   *   *   *   *

Mr. and Mrs. Charles Vašek, who moved about twenty-five years ago from an old settled section, Lavaca County, westward to the vicinity of Stamford, are due credit for pioneering. At that time they bought six hundred and forty acres of land on the boundary line of Jones and Haskell counties, and began at once improving the property. As they carried on the development of this tract, other communities were benefited. At this time there were no houses in this section, and no railroad. Haskell was a settlement of but a few shacks.

Today the six hundred and forty acres have all necessary improvements of a well-cultivated and profitably-operated ranch home. The land value has been enhanced many times and today the Vašeks are considered well-to-do and prosperous ranch-farmers.

There are six children in the family, five sons and one daughter. The two youngest sons, Joe and August, are twins, aged twelve years.

Mrs. Vašek's ancestors were pioneer settlers in Lavaca County, settling in that section many years ago. Mrs Vašek is one of ten daughters in the Šramek family. This family has lived in one house in the Moravia community, Lavaca County, for over sixty years.

* * * * *

Frank Kučera of Ennis, Texas, is a self-made Texas-Czech and a prominent citizen of the State. His business at Ennis stands as evidence of the achievement of an immigrant boy in Texas. Back in June, 1881, his mother, a widow with three small children, arrived in Sherman, Texas, having first landed at Baltimore from Czechoslovakia. The widow had sold the little home back in the old country and with the proceeds from the sale had embarked with her family for America. The ticket read to Denison, but in some way the little family were put off at Sherman, a few miles south of their destination.

The two sons became "hired farm hands" in the new country. Recalling some of the incidents of the life that followed in the course of the years, Frank Kučera refused to take credit for having accomplished more than the average man would have done.

The brother died and the sister is today Mrs. Josef Bařina of Ennis. A nephew of the brother, A. W. Kučera, lives in Ennis. His father knew, loved and cultivated the Texas soil. The son knows the soil as the artist. It is with paint, pallet and brush that he gathers the harvests. On the front of a large steel safe in the Kučera store there are two pictures. One is the field in the glory of verdant and growing life. The other depicts the harvest with the shocks of golden straw, pumpkins and fruits of the harvest yield.

"I wanted a picture of an oat field on the safe with the dwelling house near by," Mr. Kučera tells visitors who comment on the colorful painting. At once the visitor and friend of the one-time Czech immigrant boy sees in the man a sentiment deep and wholesome. Citizens of Ennis and community speak of Frank Kučera with great esteem. He speaks of himself too modestly. Of Texas, however, he speaks always in glowing terms.

The late Henry A. Parma, who came to Texas with the Haidušek immigration party in 1856, has left behind a record that is an inspiration to other Texas-Czechs. In his native country he held a position of trust and responsibility as an official in the courthouse of his home town. Skilled with his pen, gifted as a linguist, he carried on his official duties expertly. The court records were kept in the beautiful and legible writing with pen and ink for which he was noted. A few of these old records are preserved by his children as souvenirs.

There were nine in the family, four boys and five girls. One of the sons, H. A. Parma, is in the merchandising business at Ennis, Texas. Another brother, Anton, is in the automobile and garage business in Ennis. Another brother, E. J., is also in the merchandising business.

H. A. Parma remembers riding, when a child, in an ox-drawn wagon into Columbus. He also remembers something of the early schools in Texas. His father taught school for a number of years in Fayette County, where the family first lived. Recalling some of the pioneer days—and these are not so long ago, for Mr. H. A. Parma is yet a man in the prime of life—and Texas has not been so long weaned from her pioneer existence, he relates an incident of his school days.

"There were many German children attending school with us in Fayette County, and I remember that they would sometimes call the members of Czech families *Boehmische Hund*—in English, 'Bohemian dogs.' One day when a schoolmate called my sister this name I hit her. The teacher, a German, called me in after school for an investigation, and on hearing the story of the cause of the fight, I was permitted to go home and a reprimand was given to the child who had been guilty of using the insult. The teacher admonished the pupils of the school, saying that we were neighbors and must be friends and should refrain from all animosity or prejudices."

*   *   *   *   *

F. W. Pustějovsky, a prominent farmer of West, McLennan County, has for the past forty years kept a record of his farm-work and the results derived therefrom. His cotton sales record for the forty years is of outstanding interest to not only Texas farmers, but to students of economic conditions of the country as well.

From the files of the West *News* is taken the story of Mr. Pustějovsky and his forty-year record.

F. J. Pustějovsky, an outstanding farmer of this section, has a unique record of his career as a cotton producer. He has farmed near here for the past forty years and has kept a complete record of the prices he has received during the period.

The figures have been kept in his memorandum book since 1892. Mr. Pustějovsky came with his parents to the farm on which he now lives on January 28, 1882, being at the time a boy of fourteen. Ten years later he made his first cotton crop of twenty bales, produced on twenty-three acres. This crop brought him $869.00. His best crop was made in 1894, being twenty bales on twenty acres, but the average price received for it was less than five cents a pound. During the first twenty years, Mr. Pustějovsky had from twenty to thirty-five acres in cotton each year, but during the last twenty years he has increased this to an average varying from forty-five to fifty acres.

On January 31, 1920, he received the highest price of the whole forty years, forty cents per pound for two bales. The lowest price recorded, November 11, 1894, was 4 45/100 cents per pound for three bales.

This forty-year record relating to the cotton crop on one farm in Texas is believed to be without precedent, and the credit is due this one of the Texas-Czech citizens for the thought and the method and accuracy with which the record as been kept.

* * * * *

The Czech settlement of Floresville, near San Antonio, was the home of another pioneer, Jan Mikulka, who relates some interesting facts concerning the trials and tribulations he underwent in those early days:

"I was born on September 2, 1854," says Mr. Mikulka, "in Palkovice, County of Frydek, Moravia. My father's name was Frank and my mother's Johanna, née Bilkova (Bilek.) There were ten children in our family, nine boys and one girl, and it is only natural that, raised under such circumstances, the girl should have been pretty much of a tomboy.

"In those days a certain kind of serfdom was in vogue in the old country. Subjects of the nobility were forced to work in their fields, and, of course, without remuneration. I remember that my father used to work at the manor of some nobleman at Frydland (Friedland.) The overseers were a hard lot, and any disobedience was quickly cared for by corporal punishment. This serfdom ended in 1848, however, thus relieving to a great extent the suffering of the poorer classes.

"I had very little schooling. In those days education was not stressed as in later years. Teachers seemed to think if you learned the Lord's Prayer and a little reading and arithmetic, you were well equipped to face the world.

"My oldest brother, Filip, escaped compulsory military service by emigrating to Texas in 1866. When the time came for me to go to the colors my father advised me to join Filip in America. So, after a touching farewell, I left home on September 5, 1873.

"With several emigrants from Palkovice, I entrained for Bremen, Germany, from which port we sailed on September 10th. A sea voyage in those days, before the advent of the modern palatial steamers, was a great trial in itself. Seasickness, insufficient and unpalatable food, bad quarters, with few comforts, all contributed to what I regard as one of the most miserable periods in my life.

"But, of course there is an end to all things, and eventually we saw a tree-lined coast, with moss hanging from the limbs, so white, that most of the emigrants thought it was cotton. Our first port of call was New Orleans. After a few hours in that city we were transferred to some kind of a cattle-ship, on which we received no food for a day and a half, at the end of which time we landed at Galveston, from which city we boarded a train for Columbus, then the railroad terminus.

"The rest of the journey was made on ox-drawn wagons, the most common and familiar conveyances of that period. Many parts of Texas were still a wilderness. Men and women traveled on horseback and usually settled as near the woods as possible, so that timber for houses and fences might be secured with little effort. Houses were not very fancy in those days, being usually made of logs, while windows were mere holes, without glass or other protection from the elements.

"In 1877 I ended my bachelor existence when I took as wife Miss Anna Vivjal. Her dowry and my total assets were two pairs of healthy, willing and industrious hands. It was very hard in the beginning; but other farmers were faring no better, and eventually things improved.

"I farmed up to my sixtieth year, then turned over my property to my children, so they would not have such a struggle through life as I had had."

*   *   *   *   *

Hearing much about the land of promise, "America," Anton Dvořak, head mechanic in a concern which manufactured fabric for men's clothing, decided to come to Texas. He was born in 1860 at Žamberk, Bohemia. His wife was born in the same city on March 8th of the same year. They sold their possessions and with a baby three months old, a girl of three, and a boy of four, landed in New York in 1893. From there they went to Houston where, in a hotel, Anton found a copy of a newspaper, *Svoboda,* in which was an account of a Czech colony at East Bernard.

That was the information he was seeking so immediately he went there.

Mrs. Frances Dvořak Chalupňik, the daughter, offers this interesting comment:

"At that time there were about a dozen Czech families settled around the railroad station in East Bernard, including John Holub (the one-legged); Paul Jochetz, Anton Polak, Frank Vašek, John Vacek, C. O. Senkel, John Stavinoha, Frank Anděl (The Fiddler), John Orsak, Frank Jaňik, John Jochetz, John Vražel, John Gallia, and Joseph Beran.

"All these people secured their land from Leveridge and Stockton who came over from Kentucky and bought the whole Boatright League. This they divided into small farms which they sold at seven dollars an acre. Outside of this league were other Czechs living closer to town. They were Louis Urbanec, Frank Toman, and Andrew Šrubař.

"My father, Anton Dvořak, was well-to-do in the old country and when he first came here, he paid cash for everything he bought, including eighty acres of land, located on both sides of the railroad, and there the town of Nottawa now stands. The Berans were his nearest neighbors and they were about five miles away. There were no fences anywhere except along the railroad and the boundary of the Boatright League. Longhorn cattle in immense herds grazed on the prairies.

"The day we came was an unusually balmy one, although it was winter. It was so warm that father declined further hospitality of the Urbanec family and decided we would live in a covered wagon until he could build a house. My father was a great reader and he brought along a great number of books. He had read much of the early pioneers and I fancy that he wanted to be classed with those of the covered wagon era, hence his insistence on living in such manner. If he could have seen just one day ahead, he would have planned differently. That night a norther blew up, which for severity surpassed anything in the memory of the oldest settlers. There we were in the middle of the prairie with nothing but a few boards propped against the wagon to break the force of the wind. Inside the wagon, mother tried to bake some bread, but the little cookstove produced more smoke than heat. We children cried from hunger and cold. The suffering of that night cannot be described. In the morning the three-months-old baby was dead. Father made a box for a coffin and buried the child in the cemetery on Holub's farm.

"The extent of the havoc caused by the cold wave that night can be measured in a way by the number of cattle frozen to death at the intersection of the League and railroad fences. They were dead by the hundreds. Every adversity has some benefit, so in this instance the hides from the frozen animals proved to be the first source of income for these pioneers.

"Needless to say that after such an experience, father rushed to completion his dwelling, a hut. We had a combination bed and table. At night the table board, which was fastened to the wall by hinges, was raised and hooked to the wall, and there was the bed. In the morning the process was reversed, and there was the table supported on the foot and head of the bed. Brother and I slept on top of the big chest in which we had brought most of our belongings across the ocean.

"Then the breaking of the land and planting of crops began. But as father was more of a mechanic than a farmer, he encountered great difficulties and the yield was not promising. To make matters worse, father was stricken with a fever, probably typhoid, in the heat of the summer. One day father fell asleep. Mother, thinking he was better, took us children into the field to pick cotton. When we returned we witnessed a most tragic sight. Father was sitting on the floor in the middle of the room in a pool of blood, exclaiming, 'Oh, what have I done, what have I done?'

"When he regained his senses, he told us how in his delirium he had fancied that he was confronted with a disgrace which he could not bear, and consequently, stabbed himself three times. One of these wounds eventually proved fatal. Mother rushed to the nearest neighbor for help. That very same day she, too, was stricken with a similar fever and brother contracted the fever a few days later. There was I, three years old, left to be the nurse for three people desperately ill. Tramps and section hands stopped by to give us assistance. As they came they filled every available vessel with water so that we at least had enough of that.

"The neighbors brought food, but as it was cotton-picking time they could not stay long. Finally, they decided that something had to be done. One day, as I was sitting astride my father's chest, in play, totally ignorant of his condition, Mr. Gallia and his son, Anton, came along and took me to their home. That was the last time I saw my father alive. Later, Mr. Vašek took the rest of the family to his home. There father died on October 2, 1894. Mother and brother were desperately ill for several weeks, but finally recovered. The problem mother had to face after this experience was most tragic. Here she was in a foreign country, broken in health, with two small children, no money, and no means of making any.

"About that time Mrs. Anton Polak died and in due time mother and Anton Polak were married; thus I had a new father and five new sisters and brothers, the oldest grown and the youngest two years older than I. After that we moved to the Polak farm. We got along very well, as Mr. Polak was kind to us. I did not like cotton-picking, but fortunately that did not last all through the year. With donations and help of the neighbors, my step-father built a community school on his land. School was taught about five months out of the year. Our teachers were poorly paid, receiving but $200.00 a year, and as a consequence they were not all we had hoped for. Usually we boarded the teachers, charging five to seven dollars a month, including the laundry.

"One teacher, Philip Janaček from Hallettsville, inspired me greatly, so much so, that I decided to become a school teacher myself. I had many difficulties to overcome, chiefly the fact that I was a girl. Mother thought that girls did not need an education. I attended the Middle Bernard school for eight years and in that time I did not learn to speak English. The teacher usually learned enough Czech to communicate with the children, and apparently was not bothered with more. They usually held third-grade certificates, but even at that, teachers were scarce. At thirteen I was graduated from this school. I could pronounce and spell some words in the Fourth Reader; I could do fractions, and even possessed a geography, but I did not know what it was all about. I hated dish-washing, but in order to learn English I hired out during harvest season to a rice-farmer's wife. There I learned English rapidly.

"After this I attended school in town. There I had a very fine teacher and at the end of two years was able to pass an examination for a third-grade certificate. My step-father rejoiced with me over my success. He died that summer, September 15, 1906. The following year, at the age of sixteen, I taught at my old home school, Middle Bernard. My salary was $200.00 for five months. I saved my money and studied and finally I was graduated from the Southwest Texas Normal at San Marcos. I also did some work at the George Peabody College in Nashville, Tennessee. Today the school in Middle Bernard is a consolidated five-teacher school. I am proud of it because I taught there eight years.

"Most of the descendants of the 1893 Czechs still live around East Bernard, respected and influential citizens. Of the pioneer men, only John Jochetz, the neighborhood wit, is living. We believe that his perennial humor keeps him young. Of the pioneer women, Mrs. Beran, Mrs. Gallia and my mother are still living.

"Out of the first marriage of Anton Polak two children are living. Frank Polak married to Victoria Macha; Mary Polak married to Joe Kovař of Guy, Texas. Both men are prosperous farmers. Of the marriage of my mother, Frances Dvořak, and Anton Polak, the pioneers, two children were born and are still living—Janie, born in October, 1891, and married to John Dvořak, son of Thomaš Dvořak and probably a distant relative, lives in Houston. William, born in April, 1900, is married to Lydia Sykora (daughter of an early East Bernard settler), and lives on the old Polak homestead.. My brother was born on November 11, 1889, in Žamberk, Bohemia, and died at East Bernard on July 9, 1910, at the age of twenty-one. I was born on January 10, 1890, in Žamberk, Bohemia. I am married to G. A. Chalupňik, a railway postal clerk. We have four children and live in Houston. My mother still owns the original Dvořak homestead and owns and lives on the original Polak homestead."

Anton Polak came from Frydek, Silisia. He crossed the ocean in a sailboat in 1882 in company with the Bezecnys of Schulenburg and the Kačiřs, of Sweet Home, distant relatives of the Dvořaks. The Kačiřs experienced a great grief during the voyage. A storm overtook them and as a result, they thought, their oldest son, John, died and was buried at sea.

*   *   *   *   *

The harrowing experiences of Anton Dvořak probably deferred the coming of some of his distant relatives to "Golden America." Thomas Dvořak, born on October 18, 1867, at Vežne, Moravia, shoemaker by trade, instead of coming to America, decided to go to Vienna where he met Miss Františka Šmejkal, born on March 17, 1869, at Janovice, Bohemia. They were married February 12, 1893. Perhaps they would have emigrated sooner, but children began arriving in rapid succession, and the trip was put off. When their last child was five years old, they decided to leave the old country. They landed in Galveston on June 24, 1910, and went from there directly to East Bernard. Later they moved to Rosenberg, then to Richmond, and now live at Iowa Colony, Texas. They have six children. Vladimir, born in November, 1893, is now in Portland, Oregon, where he is the leader of the American Legion Band. John, born in January, 1894, is a wood-turner, and is married to Janie Polak. They have two children and are residents of Houston. Frank, born on October 8, 1897, is a designer and painter of fine furniture, in which line he is an artist. He married Miss Frances Němec. They have two children and live in Houston. During the World War he joined the Czechoslovak Legion and saw service for eighteen months in France. Frances, born on October 9, 1899, is married to Frank Olexa, Jr. They have two sons, Henry, born in 1923, and Erwin, born in 1924. They, too, live in Houston. Joseph, born on February 2, 1903, is a musician and a farmer. He is married to Alvina Krampota. Rudolph, born on December 3, 1905, is a musician and painter. He is single and lives in Houston.

* * * * *

Frank Olexa, Sr., was born on June 4, 1876, at Trnavka, Bohemia. At the age of twelve, he moved with his parents to Kutna Hora. Later he went to Vienna to learn the art of wood-carving. After military training he returned to Vienna where he met and married on March 17, 1899, Miss Teresia Fendrijch, who was born on October 12, 1873, at Štemech, Moravia.

In 1900, their only child, Frank, Jr., was born.

They landed at Galveston in 1912 and went to East Bernard. There Mr. Olexa tried his hand at farming and working with a bridge gang, but a few months convinced him that this type of work did not suit his artistic temperament, so he moved to Houston, where he has since been engaged in the business of wood-carving for which he was trained in Vienna. He specializes in ornamental wood trim; also does other and beautiful wood-carving, such as mirror and picture frames. For his work he first makes a free-hand drawing. From this a mould is made in life-size from which the final work of art is carved in wood. His work may be seen in many of the leading establishments of the city.

CHAPTER XIX

The West Community

REVEREND Wenzel Pazdral was one of the pioneer Czech Presbyterian preachers in Texas, having had the pastorate of the church at Fayetteville years ago. Dr. George Pazdral, his son, is now one of the pioneer physicians of the state. He can also claim the distinction of having been a pioneer in musical activities, as he organized one of the first music clubs of Central Texas at West, many years ago. Captain Method Pazdral, his brother, is not only a lawyer of statewide prominence, but one of Texas' most gifted orators.

In the first pioneer days of settlement, when the Czech immigrants came to Texas, they found many German settlers here. They became neighbors, later intermarried. Old grievances were in large measure forgiven and forgotten, for they found many things in common in the new homeland. Words had to be coined in many instances in order to give names to products and commodities of the new country. For example there was cotton. The German immigrant settlers had named the plant *baum wolle* or, in English, the wool of the tree, *baum* in German meaning tree. The Czechs called cotton *bavlna*, pronounced "ba vulna," *vlna* meaning wool.

Some of the early pioneer immigrants, as they came in sailboats from New Orleans, mistook the long gray moss they saw hanging from the trees for cotton, of which up to this time they had only heard.

It was a new life as well as a new country for these Czech pioneers.

*　　*　　*　　*

Frank Marak, Sr., came to Texas from Czechoslovakia in 1855, settling first in Colorado County, where in 1857 he was married to Anna Stanislav. Texas at that time had been a member of the Union only eight years. Less than twenty years before she had won her independence at the Battle of San Jacinto. It was at this formative period in the State's history that Frank Marak came as a pioneer to Texas.

There were no railroads. A stage-coach line traversed a section of Colorado County, following historic routes, including the "Old Spanish Trail" or *Camino Real* as the King's Highway was called. The eagle nested in the tall oaks. The stately sycamore trees gave friendly sanctuary to the birds who sang and nested without molestation. In 1880 this early settler made a prospecting trip up country into McLennan County. At that time this was no easy thing to do. It was like a journey into an unknown land, so difficult was travel before the modern highway came. He must have been pleased with what he found, for he went back again in 1881. This time he bought one hundred and sixty acres of improved farm land at what was then known as Bold Springs, about two and a half miles northwest from what is today the thriving city of West. The land was purchased for $10.00 per acre. Raw land was selling for one dollar to four dollars per acre.

In the latter part of 1881, a son, Henry Marak, accompanied by the maternal grandfather, John Stanislav, Sr., John Santislav, Jr., and Martin Marak, both uncles of Mr. Marak of West, moved from Colorado County to the Bold Springs community, all buying land, on which they settled, establishing what was among the first Czech settlements in that part of the State.

These first families had been preceded only one year by Joe Mašek and family, John Fojt and family and Joe Svaček and family.

In 1881 the Missouri-Kansas & Texas Railroad was completed through West and McLennan County. In 1882 the railroad bridge over the Brazos River was completed. With this progress and development other settlers began to move in.

In 1885 the names of Frank Bezdek, Paul Šulak, Frank Karlik, John Mynař, the Škřehots, Grossmans and Urbanovs, all large families, settled in that section, near what today is West. In 1882 Frank Soukup, Joseph Křižan and Charles Beralek with their families added their names to the list of early Czech settlers of McLennan County.

These families have each a separate story in the history of Czech settlements in Texas.

Rudolph J. Marak, son of Henry Marak, grandson of pioneer Frank Marak, was born in 1882 on the farm his father first settled near his pioneer grandfather's home. He attended a country school which had been built on his father's land. From this school he went to West College in 1904. This institution later became a part of the West Grammar School.

Finishing his education in the public schools of Texas, Mr. Marak went to the Kansas City College of Pharmacy, and Natural

Science. The young college graduate practiced pharmacy in Kansas City until the fall of 1906 when he returned to West to engage in the drug business.

After seven years Mr. Marak sold his business to engage in the land and loan business, which has held his interest and attention throughout the years that have followed.

A recent newspaper tribute paid Mr. Marak came from the presidents of the three West banks. These men of finance said of this grandson of that early Czech pioneer settler of Texas:

"We have known Rud. J. Marak very intimately for over twenty-five years. He has been engaged in the real estate business in West for over twenty years. We can recommend Mr. Marak as honest, reliable in all his dealings with his fellowmen."

This recognition of business qualifications and integrity of character came from W. R. Glasgow, president of the National Bank of West, Paul S. Škrabanek, president of the West State Bank, and C. W. Holloway, president of the State National Bank of West.

Mr. Marak holds the distinction of being the oldest land and loan man in point of service in West.

In 1919 Mr. Marak was elected City Commissioner of West, serving in this official capacity for twelve consecutive years. He was the first Czech to become acting-mayor of West. It was in 1919, at the time of the death of one of the Commissioners, that Mr. Marak was appointed mayor pro tem. During his first term in office as City Commissioner, a change was made from horse-power to motor-power in all city equipment. Again in 1925 Mr. Marak was appointed mayor pro tem. During his administration of six years the city of West purchased the water works which had been privately owned.

The water mains were extended, the system of expansion covering almost the entire City of West, a project which cost something over eighty thousand dollars, and which brought into the city a revenue of about ten thousand dollars annually. Also during this administration a sewer system was installed to serve the entire city at a cost of sixty thousand dollars, with a revenue therefrom of six thousand dollars annually.

*   *   *   *   *

Joseph F. Janak has the distinction of being the oldest native-born Texas-Czech. He was born at the family home, Fayetteville, some seventy-four years ago. He thus has the privilege of knowing his Texas, both of yesterday and today. As a boy in   pioneer environment, he helped to twist the cotton string that went into the cup of grease that furnished the light in the primitive Texas home.

His education was begun while he was serving as altar boy with Reverend Father Chromčik in the sacristy of the early church. He helped build roads and he helped build communities. In 1934 Joseph Janak holds a place of distinction and trust, and responsibility not only in his home town community of West, but throughout the State. He is a member of many constructive organizations. He has always taken an active part in civic affairs as well as in things that have to do with politics. When and wherever in West and McLennan County, anything of constructive import is about to take place, Joseph Janak will usually be found on hand to take a leading and active part. He is usually made marshal of affairs, whether it is a patriotic parade, a benefit entertainment, a political rally or a community picnic. As an auctioneer for a charity bazaar, Joseph Janak has the reputation for getting in more money and giving better entertainment in so doing than any professional whoever stood on the auctioneer's block.

Mr. Janak lives with two daughters—Mrs. Kubela and Miss Rose Janak—in his commodious residence in West. He has accumulated comforts for the mature years and has also stored memories of the pioneer days in Texas, which makes of his life a full and well-rounded out span of near three-quarters of a century. * * * * *

The progressive little City of West is situated in the northwestern corner of McLennan County. The adjacent trade territory reaches out into Hill County, and this section is settled by thrifty farmers, mostly land owners, seventy-five per cent of whom are Czech citizens. Fifty per cent of the city property is owned by the Czech people. Both the mayor of West, Honorable James Maresh, and the city secretary, Robert Červenka, are Czechs.

Early founders of West were Vaclav Mašek and family, who moved into that section in 1874; Frank Soukup and John Fojt in 1874; Leopold Škřehot and Frank Urbanovsky in 1872; John Adam, Joe Adam and Frank Grossman in 1879; Henry Marak, Mathew Marak, Frank Marak, Sr., and John Stanislav, Sr., John Stanislav, Jr., in 1880, and Julius Pustějovsky in 1881. Following these pioneer settlers of the West community came Frank Bezdek's family, John Karlik's family, John Hromdka, John Mynař, Sr., and the Beralek family.

CHAPTER XX

*"The benefits of education and of
useful knowledge, generally diffused through a community, are
essential to the preservation of a
free government."*
　　　　　　—SAM HOUSTON,
　　　　President of Republic of Texas.

To John Amos Komensky (Comenius), born in 1592, in a
small Moravian village, the son of a miller who was a member
of the Moravian Brethren, the world is indebted for the
rudiments of education.

His "Didactia Magna," the art of readily and solidly teaching
all men all things, and his "Janua Linguarum Resartar," gate
of tongues unlocked, published in 1631, won him the recognition
and plaudits of the world. The last named book was translated
into all languages, even Turkish, Arabic, Persian and Mongolian,
and is familiar to all the East Indies. He planned and carried
to perfection a scheme for universal knowledge.

Komensky, at the age of sixteen years, began the study of
Latin. As the Jesuits used Latin as the common language of the
church, he thought also to use it as a means of instruction for
every nationality. He demanded, however, that all nations be
taught in their native tongue.

He translated the Psalms of David into his own mother
tongue. It was on account of religion that he fled the country
of his nativity in 1627, never to return. He settled at Lissa,
near the Silesian frontier, where he found employment in an
old-fashioned school of the Moravian Brethren. There he continued writing, teaching, studying.

"I care not whether I teach or whether I learn," he stated
on one occasion. The Peace of Westphalia, concluded in 1648,
with no provision being made for the restoration of exiles, left
him a wanderer.

More than a century and a half after the death of Komensky,

father of education, renowned Czech author, scientist and philosopher, the Czech immigrant pioneers came to Texas. Education was in its infancy in the new land. Schools were yet to be built.

They came seeking a new country with the opportunities for education and the complete freedom which makes for peace, happiness and contentment. They brought with them their priceless heritage, the spirit of Komensky. They held close to their hearts also the appreciation of the fact that Praha was the shrine of the first university established in Europe. What a contrast! When they arrived in Texas they found a wilderness!

When Komensky became an exile, he found refuge in the home of a Bohemian nobleman, Baron Sadowsky, and while there assisted with the education of the three young sons of the house. Some of the early Texas-Czech pioneers taught school in the homes of the noblemen who had come to win their way in the new land.

The spirit of Komensky must have lived again in those first Texas educators. Had there not been some impelling influence to urge them on, how could they have conquered the seemingly insurmountable obstacles, handicapped as they were?

As this spirit lived then in the hearts of the Czech pioneers in the Texas wilds, so it continued to live throughout the years, and to-day its influence is felt all over the State. Counting those who have gone forth from the schools to take their places as teachers in the institutions of learning, not only in Texas but throughout the United States, it must be conceded that the seed planted by the pioneers did not fall on barren soil.

The Reymershoffer family, emigrating to Texas in 1853, brought with them in their library a copy of "Orbis Pictus" (The World In Pictures) by Komensky, published in 1798. The book is printed in four languages, Latin, Slavic, Hungarian and German. The world is portrayed in all its various activities. Each picture is accompanied by numbers which correspond with the descriptions given on the opposite page.

In connection with these Czech pioneers, it is interesting to recall a statement made in 1818 by J. V. Hecke, who came to Texas with a plan to make a "new Prussia." This early German visitor, after looking the country over, wrote home that there was very little civilization in Texas, but that fifty acres of land, if fertile, was sufficient to support a family.

The soil has not changed down the years, but that "little

civilization" has continued to grow, and to the early Czech settlers credit is due in large measure for this progress.

One of the early settlers, Josef Holec, in recording history some years ago, went back to the year 1855 and the first settlers of Kašprlink (Cat Springs). "It consisted of five square miles, and at the time there were ten Czech, three Moravian and ten German families.

"There was a church building, and in this Reverend Bergman taught the children in the Czech language. He also taught German, and alternated, teaching some of the time in his home and then in the church edifice."

Mr. Holec, who came to Texas in 1848, played an important and lasting part in the development of early education in the State.

Unable to make a living from school teaching and preaching, he planted a vineyard. Also he cultivated corn, raised many kinds of herbs and gave medical advice.

"There were few children at the time, and few parents sent their children to school," wrote Mr. Holec. "The pay was small and some of it hard to collect."

This first Czech teacher, who gathered the children in his home or, on occasion, in the church houses, taught them, no doubt, to read the beloved *"Kde Domov Muj,"* and to pronounce the words that stood for home and liberty. When fever scorched the brow and the pulse ran high, the teacher became the physician and ministered from the store of his homely remedies. Those were the days when history was in the making. Holec and his small group of children stand out against the historical background.

The school children of the first Texas-Czech settlers were gathered from neighborhood and community, from hither and yon throughout the first settled places into the pioneer Czech school houses. And the early Czech schools and the first Czech school children in Texas were stepping stones in the great system of educational progress, social and economic development that has since made Texas distinctive among her sister states.

In 1859 Josef Mašik began teaching in the Czech language at Wesley. He taught first in the home of a Mr. Šupak, whose place was located some four miles from the town, in a community where there were a number of Czech families. The school was later held in the church at Wesley. It has been authoritatively established that Josef Mašik was the first Czech teacher in the United States. In addition to this distinction, the school was taught in the first Czech Protestant Church to be erected in the United States.

The pupils of this first Texas-Czech school came, in some instances, from as far as twenty miles, there being an enrollment of from fifty to one hundred pupils during the school term. Professor Mašik continued his school work for many years, even after his strength began to fail. In 1872, when he was sixty-two years old, he arranged that another Czech teacher be provided, Mr. F. B. Zdrubek, who came to Texas from Czechoslovakia to take up the work. Josef Mašik did not give up teaching altogether at this time, but continued to carry on his educational activities, slowing down gradually in the last days of his life to enjoy the results of his labors.

In the Fall of 1856, six Moravian families settled on land west of the Colorado River in Fayette County, South-Central Texas, a distance of about eighty miles from the Gulf of Mexico. The county is traversed by the river, which divides it into equal parts.

Josef Petr, Ignac Šramek, Ignac Mužny and Josef Kalig from Tiche, and Valentin Holub and Valentin Haidušek from Myšiho (Mišši) arrived as immigrants to the Texas wilderness. Only a few huts were there before these Czech settlers, and they, scattered many miles apart, were occupied by American families.

There was no thought of schools during the first year of residence. There was no time to think of anything but how to provide food and clothing.

In 1857 a school was organized in this settlement and the children of the pioneers started with their first lessons in English. Mrs. H. Simpson was in charge. This school was continued for about seven years, or until the beginning of the Civil War, when it was closed. In its place another school was organized about three miles distant from the settlement. Of the six original families who had settled the community, only the children of the Haidušek family attended the new school.

Early in 1864, Miss Anna Holub started a school in the Haidušek home. This was among the first Czech schools in Texas. With some few intermissions, Miss Holub taught the school until the advent of F. J. Pešek.

In a brief autobiography of himself Professor Pešek wrote:

"I was born March 10, 1850, in Netolic, Čechy. After I graduated from high school, I taught the fourth grade in a local school in Netolic. In 1868, when I intended going to college, I received a notice from the Government that every student had to appear for government army service. When the physician examined me I found that I would be accepted, but as fate would have it, I received a letter from a kinsman, M. Jareš, in America. He wrote that if I had a desire to come to America, that he could find me employment. It was hard for me to leave my Fatherland, but I had to choose between two evils, and rather than be a soldier I came to America."

With him came several friends. They stopped at High Hill in Fayette County.

At High Hill the young teacher and his companions were met and welcomed by the pioneer settlers, among them August Haidušek and Julius Koňakovsky.

Mr. Haidušek, having already been in Texas for twelve years, was no longer a newcomer. He had during these years encountered all the varying experiences that usually fell to the lot of a pioneer. He had labored in the fields, attended school, and in the spring of 1868 had himself begun to teach.

Following the greetings and the welcome to young Pešek and his companions, it was suggested that he teach the Czech children, who at the time were sadly in need of such training. Their education had been neglected because of duties in the fields as the families fought to wrest the land from the grip of the wilderness.

In this same year, 1868, Ignac Šramek, one of the early settlers of Fayette County, announced that an empty house was available for a school, he having previously taught in the home of the Šrameks.

It is of interest to note that just after the War Between the States, the families of Ignac Šramek and Valentin Haidušek had moved from the place of their first location, a distance of about four miles to High Hill, then a growing community but later known only in memory, owing to the establishment of the town of Schulenburg, which has grown into a prosperous and thriving little city.

From this meagre beginning, Czech schools multiplied, seven school houses being built west of the Colorado River in Fayette County, all of which were supported by the State School Fund.

Fayette County received her first apportionment from the fund in 1854. The amount was $769.42 and was doubtless in keeping with the financial requirements of the period. The highest amount received was in 1859. This the records give as $1,954.98, the county treasurer going personally to Austin to receive the money.

Land was plentiful. The founders of the Texas Republic, mindful of future generations, had provided for their education by donating large tracts known as school lands. All public and many of these lands went to the early settlers under the term of "headrights."

In the year 1867 there were in Fayette County 1,819 school children between the ages of six and eighteen, but how many of this number were from Czech families the records do not show.

Following the story of the early Czech schools in Fayette County we move to the east side of the Colorado River in the settlement known as Ross Prairie, where there were many Czech families, even before the Civil War, but no schools up to the year 1868, when A. M. Koňakovsky took upon himself the obligation of teaching the children of the settlement. There were no books, and he found himself compelled to use the newspaper *Slavie* as the text book.

The columns of this early Czech newspaper, containing such news of the times as the printer and publisher could gather with his limited facilities, would compare but poorly with our present-day text books. These children, however, were eager for knowledge. Small fingers traced the printed lines, deciphering under the patient tutelage of that zealous pioneer instructor the meaning of each word.

It is not known how long Mr. Koňakovsky taught this early school, but in 1871 local Czechs organized a lodge known as *Osvěta*. They built a hall in which to hold meetings, and this building also served as a school.

There were many children, but no teacher, a condition which came about possibly through the passing of the compulsory school attendance law. In connection with the enforcement of this law, there was another law requiring all teachers, both of private and public schools, to pass an examination in English. It is a matter of record that Augustin Haidušek was the only one who could fulfill this requirement. Accordingly, he was requested by the citizens to assume the responsibility of teacher. He complied, taking the necessary examination for a second class certificate and taught for some time. During the years that followed the Czech people built two more schoolhouses, which were supported by the State.

In November, 1868, when Mr. Pešek began teaching in the home of Ignac Šramek at Mulbery, Texas, he opened the school with an enrollment of fifteen children. A few of them brought old school books, but most of them had no books. Teacher Pešek had to copy the reading lessons for each pupil. Crayons were cut from chalk brick. In teaching them to count this pioneer teacher used primitive methods. Bits of broken chalk brick, pieces of paper on which lessons were copied from a single book, and sticks for counting comprised the school equipment. Later books were ordered from Praha, Bohemia, at a cost of $10.00 each in gold, and when they were received at Columbus, seven months later, there was an express charge of $18.35 in addition.

The school in the Šramek home lasted five months, the number of pupils increasing during this time from fifteen to twenty-five. For each child a tuition fee of $1.00 per month was paid. Some of the children came from as far as Navidad and Bluff.

No charge was made by Ignac Šramek for the use of the home and in return for his room and board, the teacher gave instruction to the children in the family.

In June, 1869, Mr. V. Holub, of Navidad, made a call on Mr. Pešek with the request that he teach school in the Navidad community. At the time there were only nine Czech families in this neighborhood. For two months the school numbered nineteen children. A night school was also conducted for the benefit of the older boys.

In the fall of 1869 citizens of Mulberry decided to retain this teacher permanently, having a sufficient number of scholars to justify regular school terms. Frank Nykel, Sr., built a two-room house near the church. One room was for the family residence, the other for the school. Here the teacher remained for two years, having an average attendance of from twenty to thirty children.

For six months during each year he taught a private school. The pay received for the teaching was insufficient for support. Mr. Pešek wrote in an early chronicle: "I was obliged to devote my spare time to farming. For this purpose I bought land adjoining Mr. Nykel's farm. This I gradually put into cultivation, and made this my permanent home."

This place, originally known as Mulberry, was later called Praha. The Praha community and Catholic Church celebrated the seventy-fifth anniversary of settlement in the summer of 1932.

After the second year another building was secured for the school, the number of children having increased to fifty. It also became necessary at this time to engage an assistant, the students being divided into two classes, one for English, the other for Czech.

In 1871 the government passed the school law, wherein it

was compulsory for all teachers to pass examinations in English
before being permitted to teach. Mr. Pešek found this requirement hard to comply with. He was without books from which
to learn the English language, and it seemed for a time that
he would be forced to give up teaching. Friends and citizens of
the community took the matter in hand, however.

The advice of August Haidušek, who was at the time practicing law at LaGrange, was sought. Mr. Haidušek asked the
School Board to permit Mr. Pešek to stand the examination in
either Czech or German in both of which he was proficient. The
request was not granted. As the assistant in the school was an
American, and capable of teaching English, Mr. Pešek was
permitted to continue.

At the close of the school term citizens asked permission of
the School Board to erect a new school building. This request
was not granted, refusal being made on the grounds that there
was a German-English school at Flatonia, and that the Praha
community should send its children there. To this plan many
of the citizens objected and, in spite of obstacles, began the
erection of their own schoolhouse. Lumber, at the time an
expensive item, had to be hauled from Columbus, a distance of
thirty miles. With the help of some of the wealthy citizens,
necessary funds were secured and the building erected.

Ondřej Gallia, one of the early settlers, donated five acres
of land adjoining the church property. Frank Nykel, Sr., offered
to erect the building. Messrs. Josef Vyjala, Josef Hajek, Filip
Buček, Frank Brabecky, Tom Nykel and several others not only
donated money but their time and effort. To these sturdy pioneers
credit is given for having made possible the first Czech-English
school in the Texas Praha.

The school was completed in the year 1872 at a cost of
$500.00, including furnishings, the dimensions of the building
being eighteen feet by twenty-four feet. By close application to
study, Professor Pešek was by this time able to pass the prescribed English examination and at the beginning of the regular
school term was granted license to teach in the new building.
The enrollment was around forty, and for three or four months
each school year the tuition was paid by the State. The remainder
of the term the school was taught privately, the teacher being paid
by the parents of the children.

For five years Professor Pešek taught in this school. At times
when the number of pupils grew beyond the one teacher, his
mother came to the rescue, taking charge of the beginners. In

1877 the number of pupils increased to seventy. This increase called for an assistant, and the services of Mr. A. Nesrsta were secured. The following year Mr. Nesrsta became a regular teacher, the building was enlarged and again the children were divided into two classes. With this arrangement the school continued for seven years, from 1877 to 1883. By this time the number of students had increased to eighty and it was again necessary to have larger quarters.

A building committee was appointed with Professor Pešek as chairman. The new school, approximately twice as large as the building it replaced, was erected in 1883 at a cost of $1,000.00.

Having taught for fifteen years, Professor Pešek felt that he needed a rest so he did not teach in the school which he had been largely instrumental in having built. He bought a tract of land five miles south of Praha, with the intention of devoting his time to farming, but as soon as he began building a residence for himself, citizens of Velehrad called a mass meeting and prevailed upon him to teach the children of the community, promising to build a new schoolhouse, the old one having burned six years before.

This pioneer teacher did not have the courage to withstand the pleadings of the early settlers. It may have been that the school room atmosphere had so thoroughly permeated his system that he could not stay away from it. At any rate work on the new school building proceeded and in the fall of 1883 Professor Pešek was back again in the school room, where he remained for two years.

The school started with fifty pupils. The salary for the term of eight months was $400.00. Living three miles distant from the school, the teacher rode to and from his work each day on horseback through all kinds of weather. It was because of this that he finally gave up the position, accepting instead a position as teacher in a German-English school at Grief, which was only one mile from his home. The pay was the same, but the work was heavier, it being necessary to teach three languages, German, English and Czech with lessons in all grades.

CHAPTER XXI

PIONEER CZECH READING CLUBS

WESLEY, Washington County, Texas, one of the early Czech settlements, holds the distinction of having had the first Czech reading club organized in the State. This pioneer literary club, "Československy Čtenařsky Spolek," (The Czechoslovakian Reading Club) was founded in 1867 and had a fairly good library which was later destroyed by fire.

The record of this and similar organizations over the State during a period of something over a decade, was kept by the late Tom Hruška, in a manuscript prepared by him some time before his death.

We have no list, however, of the books that comprised the library, which is to be regretted. The present generation would be interested in knowing what kind of books these pioneers enjoyed.

The reading club was the nucleus for a number of others of similar kind and purpose and the forerunner of the early Czech schools of Texas. The organization at Wesley had at the beginning an enthusiastic membership drawn from a scattered population. The early settlers of that community found in the reading club an inspiration for frequent social gatherings. Mr. Hruška called his manuscript, "The Origin and Beginning of Clubs in Texas." The sketch, although meagre as to detail with regard to the life, activities and plan of operation, is nevertheless far-reaching in its scope and foretells many coming events.

These early reading clubs aroused educational interest and stimulated a desire for knowledge which brought about the demand for schools.

In 1871, another reading club was founded at Ross Prairie, a settlement between Fayetteville and Ellinger in Fayette County. The announced purpose of this club was "educational and social." It also had a library. In 1872 the first hall, or lodge building, was erected in Fayette County. Later this became the first Czech-English school in Texas, where both the English and the Czech languages were taught at the expense of the State. Augustin Haidušek was the first teacher.

Credit is given by Mr. Hruška to a number of the early pioneers for the parts they played in establishing this school. Specifically mentioned are A. N. Koňakovsky, A. Haidušek, Tom Ječmenek, Josef Hlavaty and John Hruška, Sr. The club, with some seventy-five members, prospered for a time, but other interests gradually intruded, its membership dwindled, and in 1883 its activities were ended.

This club organization, known as the Československy Čtenařsky Spolek, started under the influence of the Evangelical Church congregation at Wesley. It was this same Evangelical faith which later organized the club at Ross Prairie called "Osvěta," meaning in English, "Enlightenment." Because this club and school were between the two localities, Fayetteville and Ellinger, and a large number of families subsequently moved into Ellinger, the demand grew for a school nearer than the one at Ross Prairie. In 1880 one was established at Ellinger.

The founding of the school at this place was through the efforts of zealous partiots such as A. N. Koňakovsky, Joseph Křenek and F. J. Mikeska. Through these pioneers, with the help of the other workers, the movement was carried through to the final club formation, and this organization took over the obligation of building the Czech-English Independent School. Then arose the question of what manner and kind of a club would be permanent. Past experiences had not been altogether conducive to optimism. The failure of two or more of the earlier club undertakings loomed before the educators. There was the suggestion of a club combining agricultural, reading, social and educational activities.

It was at this juncture that Mr. Koňakovsky proposed the organization of a Česko-Slovensky Podporujici Spolek chapter. Few settlers were familiar with this organization. There were only six subscribers in the State at the time to *Dennice Novověku,* the official publication of the organization, and there were many obstacles in the way of launching the movement. Some of the local citizens were antagonistic to the proposition. Bad feeling arose as a consequence, but Tom Hruška recorded many years later that if it had not been for the Č. S. P. S. Chapter, organized at that time, there would have been no Czech-English Independent School at Ellinger. We quote from Mr. Hruška's manuscript:

"We were a handful—six in number—in the vicinity of Ellinger, Texas, who were convinced that in order to preserve the Czech nationality, it was necessary to organize. The question was what form of an organization was to be founded. In order that an organization would exist permanently, it was necessary to have a sound foundation. Past experience had taught us that it was a daring thought for so few in number to attempt to overcome the many obstacles that were in the way. The work was finally accomplished, however. New members came slowly, but finally there were nine. Being informed about this time that the Secretary of the Supreme Lodge, Max Kirchman, would pay a visit to Texas to initiate the first chapter in the State, "The Texan," at Praha, Fayette County (Lodge No. 104 of the Č. S. P. S.), we made a quick decision and telegraphed Brother Kirchman to ask if it were possible that he come and also initiate our chapter. It was a bold move, we not having the required fifteen members, but on April 15, 1884, Brother Kirchman arrived, trusting that we were then prepared. On the promise that we would by April 21st have the required membership for the chapter, he consented and the chapter was initiated.

"On the night of April 15, 1884, we met in the store of F. J. Mikeska where we signed a petition for the initiation of our chapter which we named 'Čecho-Moravan.' On April 16th two more members were added, bringing the membership to eleven. The chapter was initiated as No. 105, the charter members being A. N. Koňakovsky, F. J. Mikeska, Joseph Liebich, Thomas Hruška, Joseph F. Křenek, Joseph Kabela, Ignac Křenek, Ondřej Kunetka, Pavel P. Zapalač, Joseph Ondřej, John Franta, Frank Ripl, Joseph Ripl, Stephan Novosad and John Hruška. Following the formal initiation, officials of the chapter were selected as A. N. Koňakovsky, president; F. J. Mikeska, inspector; Joseph Liebech, secretary; Tom Hruška, accountant; Joseph F. Křenek, treasurer; Joseph Kabela, inner guard; and Ignac Křenek, outer guard.

"Following the bestowing of the honorary degrees on all officials, Brother Kirchman addressed us and sincerely thanked us for the exemplary order and with a brotherly handclasp the meeting was concluded. The chapter initiation fees were $5.00. All members joining later paid $8.00 with a monthly fee of fifty cents."

The pages of the old manuscript, written in ink on white ruled paper, form a link in the chain of events dealing with the establishment of early Czech schools in Texas.

The reading clubs of the '60s, as established by Czech pioneers, were far-reaching in their influence. The student interested in research who goes to the libraries of the State will find few books that belonged to Texas at this time. With the advent of the circulating libraries, rural communities were served. The recent establishment of county libraries in several counties has marked another epoch in the cultural efforts of state and county commissioners. And yet but for the faded old manuscript prepared by pioneer Tom Hruška, the history of those early Czech Reading Clubs might have been lost to later generations. Among the books provided for the pioneer Czech Reading Clubs was one for young boys and girls, *"Orbis Pictus,"* written by the great educator, Komensky, and printed in the early 1700's. The book, of which there is a copy in the Reymershoffer library in Galveston, is instructive, even when viewed with modern eyes. The copy referred to is written in four languages, Latin, Czech, Hungarian and German. Having mastered the contents of this primer the reader would find himself equipped with the fundamentals of knowledge as they were known to the learned men of that period.

There is a movement on for the organizing of present-day Czech reading clubs over the State. Several hundred books in the Czech language have been placed in the Houston Public Library. These books are in the main the gift of local Texas-Czechs, both individuals and organizations.

Of specific interest is the Czech department in the Houston Public Library. During the first part of 1933 several hundred books were added to the Czech volumes already on the library shelves. The list given elsewhere in this volume will show something of the class of reading that has been provided.

Stephen Valčik, connected with the registry department of the Houston post office, has taken active part in securing the books for the enlarged Czech section in the Houston Library. Judge Charles Henry Chernosky, Dr. Henry R. Maresh and Dr. Frank Lukša of the Houston Czech language high school faculty, have also been interested in the movement.

East Bernard, a Czech community in Wharton County, has a Czech library, or reading club, of over four hundred volumes. Throughout the State, wherever there is Czech citizenship, a movement to sponsor Czech libraries is in progress. This is part of the work of the Sokol organization. In many localities this organization is a veritable storehouse of material for cultural advancement. In the Dallas headquarters of the Sokols are something over three hundred books on dramatic literature.

The far-reaching influence of the Texas-Czech citizenship in relationship to educational affairs may be further stressed by mention of the fact that a Texas-Czech, Mrs. E. H. Marek of Yoakum, is first vice-president and director of extension of all

Parent-Teachers Associations in the state, consisting of two thousand local units, fifty-one city councils and one hundred and three county councils.

CHAPTER XXII

Language

PROFESSOR Charles Knižek, instructor in Slavic and Germanic languages, University of Texas, 1915 to 1924, now a member of the faculty of a California college, holds the distinction of having pioneered in those languages in Texas.

In discussing his work in introducing the Slavic language into the curriculum of the University of Texas, he explained that Czech (Bohemian) is a part of the western branch of the Slavic stem of the Indo-European family of languages.

He has given the various Indo-European branches with a comparison of their development in Slavic and Germanic, Indo-European, or Indo-Germanic; also Aryan or Caucasian:

1. Italic or Romance (Latin and modern Romance).
2. Greek.
3. Celtic (Irish, Gaelic).
4. Albanian.
5. Lithuanian (Lettic. Similar to Slavic).
6. Indic (Sanskrit, also Gypsy).
7. Iranian.
8. Armenian.
9. Germanic; (Gothic, Old Norse, Old Saxon) Anglo-Saxon, English Scandinavian (Norwegian, Danish, Swedish). (Old H-G-Middle H. G., New H.G.) and Dutch or also low German.
10. Slavic; Russian, Euthenian, Czech (Slovak) Polish, Bulgarian, Slovene, Wendiah and some minor dialect.

Language is "human expression" according to the definition given by Mr. Webster. And some eminent philologists have thought that man has always possessed articles of speech.

The story of Adam, having given names to all things, has kept alive through the ages the widespread faith in the Divine origin of language.

Miklosich, the author of the Wendic grammar, declared that the old Bulgarian Slav, back in the ninth century, was responsible for Slav idioms. Saints Cyril and Methodius, missionaries of

Left:
PROFESSOR CHARLES KNÍŽEK
First Professor of Slavic
Language (1915-24)
University of Texas.

Right:
PROFESSOR EDWARD MIČEK
Present Professor of Slavic
Language, University
of Texas.

the ninth century, made a translation of the Bible in the course of their work.

The position of Czech in the family of European languages is of interest. The Czech tongue has developed for long ages alongside the Baltic tongues, even up to the Fourth and Fifth centuries. After the Fifth century it did not at first differ materially from the old Slavonic language, and in this may be found the reason why the apostles of Christianity, St. Cyril and Saint Methodius of Constantinople, should be called to Central Europe from Bulgaria in A. D. 863, and why the Czechs could speak with them in the current tongue.

The Germans, not being able to understand, were called "Němci" meaning the "mute ones." In the study of the language it is interesting to note that in the middle of the Seventh century the Czech chieftain, Samo, defeated the Avars and the Franks, and established a kingdom which included the Slovaks, who, at the time, covered the greater part of the Danubian plain. The Czechs and the Slovaks, acting as a single and undivided nation, established the Great Moravian Empire which in the latter part of the century included not only what is modern Czechoslovakia, but through a common language exercised some sort of authority from the Spree to Bulgaria.

The overthrow of the Great Moravian Empire by the Hungarians or Magyars marks the parting of the ways of the Czechs and Slovaks, covering a period of a thousand years, and yet the Czech language was preserved. The Slovaks, to all intents and purposes a captive people, remained as a separate and distinctive race. The Czechs likewise under the Austrian dominion kept their language inviolate.

In Europe today there exists two great language families, distinguished from each other by the manner in which they express the number "100." The Latin and Germanic tongues have for the number expressions similar to the Latin "centum," originally "kentum," and designated accordingly. The Slavic and Baltic tongues use for "100" expressions similar to the old Persian satem and the Indian satem. Czech belongs to the family of the satem tongues.

Noteworthy in the Czech language is the old heritage, probably from the Babylonian-Phoenician alphabet, which was syllabic in that it had no vowels.

Saints Cyril and Methodius, who were sent as missionaries into Bohemia early in the Ninth century, by the Emperor Michael of Constantinople, had already been among Slavic people in Macedonia. They brought along with them a Slavonic translation of the Bible which later became the literary standard.

One historian says: "While it is impossible to know in what dialect these Bulgarian Monks wrote, the reasonable assumption is that it was in their native Thessalonica."

The existence of a distinctive Slavic alphabet, the Glagolica, of which Cyril's alphabet was but a simplification, makes it certain that Cyril and Methodius drew from an older literary stock, composed in a language already in possession of the Czechs in Carolingian times.

The Cyrilic alphabet has forty-one characters, with few silent letters. In the Czech language there were indefinable characters and tones. These, wrote F. Marion Crawford, American novelist, "are softer than the softest of southern languages."

The consonants which are to be encountered so frequently in the Czech language are not pronounced explosively, but instead are smoothly passed over, thus giving the softness of which Mr. Crawford wrote.

There are no silent letters in the Czech or Bohemian language. There is, however, no letter "w" but the letter "v" takes the sound of both.

For instance *"Svoboda,"* meaning in English "liberty," and pronounced as if spelled "swoboda," with the accent on "bo," illustrates the absence of the letter "w."

"Dum," meaning "house" and *"novy domov"* meaning "new home," shows the similarity of the words to the French, Spanish and Latin, and bears out the statement that the language can be traced back to the old Sanskrit written by Seneca in the time of Nero.

"Vlk," meaning in English "wolf," and pronounced "vulk" shows how often the consonants are used without vowels. It is easy to run smoothly over the consonants but the vowels call for a halt, which makes for roughness.

In behalf of the Czech language it has been said that a well-educated and well-read Czech can take down a speech made in English even though he does not know a word of the English language, so readily can he produce sound phonetically.

In the matter of literature, Bohemia occupies a place of distinctive superiority. The prose literature of Bohemia after the Greek and Latin, is one of the oldest in all Europe. The three centuries from the time of Charles IV to the outbreak of the "Thirty Years' War," covers the early brilliant period in literature.

In 1843 the Congress of the Texas Republic ordered the laws of the country to be published in German. In 1844 the Texas Congress again recognized a foreign population by granting a franchise to the Hermann University. The result of this was the erection of a large two-story stone building in Frelsburg. It was used later as a public school building, but not as a university, as the German university project did not materialize.

The establishment of the chair of Slavic language in the University of Texas did not come for many years after this first recognition of the German language.

It was in 1915 that the Slavic language was made a part of the curriculum of the university. It had been previously planned to have an instructor who could teach German and also give attention to the Slavic language, but at this specific time the State Legislature, through interest of some friends of Czech citizenship, passed the law which provided for the independent department devoted to the Slavic language. In connection with the Legislative Act establishing the language in the University, provision was made for an appropriation of $1,800.00 a year for salary. Dr. A. W. Battle, then acting President of the University, appointed Professor C. Knižek instructor in charge. He remained for nine years, teaching more of German during the last three years of the time than Slavic.

The introduction of the Czech language into the public schools, first of the Republic and then of the State, has had the effect of reviving the Czech national consciousness. The Czech people can point to the glorious past of their nation, as they were wont to do in their folk-lore, "Once the Czechs Were Great."

Interest in the development of the Czech language in Texas is not confined exclusively to the Czech citizenship. Children of other nationalities, who help make up the public scholastic population of the State, are taking up the study of the language, making it in some instances the foreign language prescribed in the course of high school work.

When the public schools in Houston announced in 1931 that the Czech language had been adopted as a part of the curriculum, this interest was given an added impetus.

The name Czech, the pronounciation of which is seemingly difficult to the Anglo-Saxon, is preferable to the ambiguous term, "Bohemian," by which Czech people have been largely known and designated in America.

The correct pronunciation of the name is "Chekh." To the

ear attuned to the language and accustomed through some practice in the speaking of names, pronunciation comes easier.

According to writers who are accepted as authority on whatever subject they write, the claim has been that blood and language are tests of national landmarks. The two nationalities of the Czechs and Slovaks are closely allied in language and tradition. The language of the one is akin to the Polish and Russian and related to the Serbian and Croatian. The Czech provinces of Bohemia, Moravia and Silesia have a language preserved throughout the centuries as before mentioned and believed to be of the oldest origin.

In the country that is now Czechoslovakia, while German was spoken to a great extent for a period almost similar to that during which the Danish language prevailed in Norway, the Czech language was zealously preserved.

We find here in the United States that our own language shows the earmarks of the influence of the aborigines, whom we know as the North American Indian. The Czech scholar will remark the similarity between some of these so-called Indian names, and certain Czech names.

Dr. Morgan Callaway, Jr., of the University of Texas, who ranks second in the nation in length of service as a teacher of English, with fifty-one years to his credit, the last forty-one of which he has spent at the University of Texas, has a word to say about the Czech language:

"The generally accepted view at present concerning the Czech language is this: It is not derived from the Sanskrit, but is a member of the Slavonic branch of the Indo-Germanic or Indo-European, as some prefer to call its family of languages, and, like the other seven branches of that family (Sanskrit-Persian, Armenian, Albanian, Greek, Italic, Celtic and Germanic), is derived from a common mother tongue, now lost, often called Primitive Indo-Germanic or Primitive Indo-European."

Gradually the teaching of the Czech language has been adopted as a part of the curriculum of Texas public schools, following the lead taken by Austin and Houston. Schools at Shiner, Hallettsville, Needville, Temple, Schulenburg and Caldwell had Czech language classes in 1932.

The Czech classes at John Reagan High School, Houston, held full attendance throughout the school term at both the day and night sessions. When it was found necessary to close the night school classes to cut down expenses, the Czech class was of such prominence because of steady attendance that it was transferred

to Sam Houston High School in the heart of the city, in order
that the term might be finished.

Dr. Eduard Miček, a native of Frydek, Czechoslovakia, was
appointed head of the Slavic language department at the University of Texas in 1926. The appointment came following the
recommendation of the council of higher education.

Dr. Miček, after completing his secondary education in Europe,
had entered Charles University, Praha, Czechoslovakia, where
in 1923 he completed his course, taking high honors in philosophy
and pedagogy. Later he studied at King's College, London, and
in 1924 was awarded the degree of Doctor of Philosophy by the
Charles University, Praha.

He left Czechoslovakia in 1924 for the United States to accept
the position as instructor of the Czech language at the Harrison
Technical High School, Chicago. Under his instruction the
number of Czech students at this institution increased from 180
to 240. During his term he took additional courses at the University of Chicago, adding to his efficiency and qualifications
as an instructor.

When he took the chair in Slavonic Language at the Texas
University there were fourteen students enrolled. And now, after
seven years of work, the department of Slavonic language of the
University of Texas is the largest of its kind in the United States.

Dr. Miček is the author of two books, written since his
residence in Texas, "The Spirit of American Training," and
"American Is Learning." Both are written in the Czech language.
In addition, he has written a number of articles dealing with
American life and education for the outstanding journals of
Czechoslovakia. He has also delivered many lectures on educa-
tion, and has spoken on numerous occasions to Texas audiences
about Czechoslovakia, its history and culture.

Dr. Miček is a member of the American Institute in Praha,
an organization formed to encourage cultural relations between
Czechoslovakia and the United States, and which has been recognized as an authority by the educational world.

*   *   *   *   *

THE effort expended in getting the Czech language adopted
into the State University is an interesting story. After eighteen
years there are only a few people in Texas who remember the
details of this accomplishment.

Dr. Henry R. Maresh of Houston has the distinction of having
been the first student of the University to have availed himself

of the opportunity afforded by the new language chair. To him is also given part credit for the University having a department of Slavic language. It is not intended to claim for him the actual achievement, for this was made possible through the influence toward official legislation by personal friends who, through this young Czech student, became interested in the matter.

Former State Senator Myron T. Blalock of Marshall, Texas, who was a student in the University in 1915 and was also serving as a member of the Thirty-fourth Legislature, and Honorable Frank Burmeister of Christine, McMullen County, a member of the House, are directly responsible for the Legislative Act which provided for the teaching of this new foreign language in the university.

Henry R. Maresh and Senator Blalock were domiciled in the same boarding house in Austin. The legislator was interested in his student friend and room-mate. When the problem of needing a foreign language to secure the necessary entrance credits for the Medical College at Galveston was discussed, Senator Blalock began to ponder over what could be done about it.

Henry R. Maresh, being of Czech parentage, spoke that language fluently, as well as English. He had previously requested Dr. Battle, acting president of the university, for the privilege of taking an examination in the Czech language so that he might have the necessary foreign language entrance credit. He proposed, in addition, to take an examination in German for the additional credit required. Dr. Battle promised that this could be done, but later announced that such would not be permitted, there being no recognized Chair of Slavic Languages in the University.

It was at this time that Senator Blalock came to the rescue. There was an estimated Czech population of 100,000 in the State, and as he discussed the matter with various members of the legislature he hinted that the Texas-Czech vote and influence was worthy of serious consideration.

The fact that there were at the time seven Czech newspapers in Texas was given due recognition in the course of the discussion that followed.

In a letter written from Marshall in February, 1933, Judge Blalock wrote concerning the incident:

"I remember that my good German friend, Honorable Frank H. Burmeister, took a leading part. My participation was in giving him all assistance possible. It has been recalled that some of the legislators said that they had never heard of the Czech language, and that the Honorable Frank Burmeister told these members of the House that he could bring in tons of literature for them in the Czech language."

Texas-Czech citizens had for years sought to have Czech taught in the University, but up to this time nothing had been accomplished.

Professor Charles Kniżek, who had been an honor graduate of the Preparatory Department, Southwestern University, Georgetown, a student at Polytechnic College, Fort Worth, and later at the University of Texas, was given the Chair of Slavic Language.

Before the department actually began to function the ambitious young student, Henry R. Maresh, was ready to take his examination in the Czech language.

Half a century before at the ceremony of the laying of the corner stone of this State institution of education, the speaker, Colonel Ashbel Smith, first president of the University, disputed the claim that the institution was designed exclusively for the rich and not the poor.

In the passing of the years other speakers have had to stress the same fact, and the plea for a chance to make his way, by this young Czech university student, son of Texas-Czech pioneers, and the answer he received by Legislative Act, goes far toward proving the rights and privileges of the masses.

The *Daily Texan,* Austin University newspaper, designated as the "first college daily in the south," in the issue of May 25, 1915, carried the story of the passing of the bill, under the heading "Lawmakers Please Czech Students at the University."

A petition, which set forth the reasons why the Czechs wanted the language taught in the University had been presented in 1914 to the President of the Board of Regents of the University under the signatures of E. Mikeska, Baylor University, Waco; L. Schiller, Trinity University, Waxahachie; J. Migel, San Marcos Normal; H. Hošek, Denton Normal, and C. Kniżek, University of Texas.

The petition set forth in part:

"In the name of the Czech students of the leading colleges of Texas, we take the liberty to approach you in the matter which merits, and we trust will be accorded, a fair consideration by the University authorities. Although we must confess that in this action we are prompted mainly by motives to benefit our own people, nevertheless we believe that we are able to show that it would be an advantage, both to the University and to the State of Texas, if our desire should be realized.

"In the first place the share our nation contributed to civilization in the past calls for recognition at present. History shows that Czechs were foremost in civilization, enlightenment and progress, and even now, in spite of two centuries of oppression and persecution, they compare favorably in science, art and literature, with other leading nations of the world. Our Comenius (Komensky) was and still is the 'teacher of the nations.' Huss lived one hundred years before Luther, and the University of Praha flourished one hundred years before Columbus discovered America. Our Chelčicky inspired Tolstoy and the Bohemian exiles carried the torch of liberty and civilization to many other countries.

"In recent times the names of Zebger, Purkyne, Masaryk, Dvořak, Kubelik, Kolař, Šafařik, Vrchlicky, Palacky and their contributions to science, art and civilization, are well known.

"Secondly, the character and the beauty of our language makes the study of it desirable. In richness and expressiveness of words, variety and subtlety of structure and in many respects like the Greek, it had the advantage over Latin and other languages. It is generally conceded that Czech is the most advanced of all Slavic tongues. In this connection it may be well to call attention to the growth and progress of Czech literature in the past century. Finally the number of our people in Texas entitles us to a just consideration of our request. There are almost 100,000 of our countrymen in this State and yet many of the American Universities offer a course in the Czech language though the number of Czechs in some of these States is much smaller than in Texas. Besides many leading Universities in Europe, as far as could be ascertained, the following Universities in the United States offer a course in Czech or Slavic literature: Nebraska, Wisconsin, Minnesota and such colleges as Oberlin, Dubuque, and others. This advantage attracts many students, even from Texas, to the schools of the north."

In writing the history of Texas-Czech pioneers in Texas it is interesting to know that the first Czechs (Moravians) in the United States settled in Georgia in 1735, and six years later moved to Pennsylvania, where they established educational institutions and churches, hospitals and peaceful industries. They named the place of their settlement Bethlehem, which in its Biblical significance, means "Bread." Salem, N. C., was also founded in 1752 by Czech immigrants, this being the second colony established in the United States, and is one of the most flourishing communities in North Carolina. The school established there about 180 years ago now has over six hundred students.

A brochure, entitled "The Easter People," a pen picture of the Moravian Easter celebration in connection with the old school at Salem, written by Winfred Kirkland, tells the story of the establishment of the school in 1752 with the purchase of 100,000 acres of land, comprising the Moravian tract purchased from Lord Granville in North Carolina.

The reference made to the institution by Miss Kirkland, according to Howard E. Rondthaler, President of the College, is entirely appropriate. Mr. Rondthaler said, in 1932, that the institution itself is in "vigorous life and in great health and strength." For example mention was made of $300,000 having been invested within a period of three years in additional buildings, this being the gifts of interested friends who have known through the years the efficient life and work of Salem College.

Perhaps in no better way can appraisement of this institution be correctly determined than by the knowledge that it is accredited by the State Department of Education, the State of North Carolina; by the Association of American Colleges; by the Southern Association of Colleges and Preparatory Schools, of which it has long been a member.

The pioneer Czech schools established in Texas and the effort to preserve the "mother tongue" is but a part of the same spirit and love of culture which founded this splendid institution of learning at Salem, nearly two centuries ago.

CHAPTER XXIII

"ČECHIE"

THE LATE Eugene T. Blount, of Nacogdoches, whose ancestors were Texas pioneers, referring in a speech at historic San Jacinto Battleground to pioneer days in Texas, said:

"Only the bravest came, only the strongest could survive the hardships of the wilderness life." And he asked: "What were they fighting for?" And answered: "The ideal of democracy, self-government, individual and religious liberty."

The Czech pioneers among the "bravest and strongest" who came and survived the wilderness life, believed that an educated people constituted the safeguard of democracy and labored to that end. How well their efforts have been repaid is told in the lives of the men and women of pioneer Czech parentage in Texas.

During the 1909-10 sessions of the University of Texas, there were five students of Czech nationality: C. H. Chernosky, from Brenham, in the Law Department; and in the academic courses Miles J. Breuer of Cameron, E. E. Křenek of Dime Box, Louis Mikeska of Caldwell and Joe Kopecky of Taiton.

As the years passed these five Texas-Czech students finished their education, each in his chosen line, and took their places in the business and professional world. C. H. Chernosky entered the practice of law. He was later elected County Judge of Fort Bend County. Later he located permanently in Houston where he maintains law offices and conducts an extensive legal practice.

Miles J. Breuer of Lincoln, Nebraska, son of the pioneer Texas-Czech physician, Dr. Charles Breuer of Waco, and charter member of the Texas "Čechie" society, is today a recognized authority in the field of chemistry, having made valuable discoveries in this science.

E. E. Křenek resides at Dime Box where home and family ties hold him close to the soil and the affairs of that community.

Louis Mikeska, one of the members of the pioneer and historic Texas-Czech Mikeska family, has since his University days in Austin and the organization of "Čechie" lived in New York

194

Left to right, standing: E. E. Křenek, Joe Kopecky, Louis Mikeska;
Seated: Miles J. Breuer *and* C. H. Chernosky

City, where he is in touch with the affairs of the world, but retains his interest in Texas-Czech affairs.

Joseph Kopecky chose the medical profession, and has become a prominent physician. He has retained his interest in "Čechie" and all that it was organized to stand for. He has kept the records through the years and has treasured the photograph of the five charter members which is used in this history. Into his charge the year "Čechie" was organized was given the matter of art and its promotion and he has been faithful to the trust in his endeavors to spread the cultural and artistic influence.

Each of these first Texas-Czech students was a son of a Texas-Czech pioneer. Their parents were among those who helped to found the first Texas-Czech schools and through these gave to their children the opportunities of higher education.

On October 23, 1929, after the lapse of years, during which each one of the original five Czech University students had been busy, they met in Austin for the purpose of reorganizing the club, "Čechie," to perpetuate the memory and the influence and the sentiment of their student days. Henry Hejl of Taylor was at the time attending a business college in Austin and joined with the five charter members in the organization of the club.

The purpose of the club was to promote friendship among students of Czech origin; to study Czech music, Czech history and Czech literature; to work toward interesting the Czech children of the State in higher education, and the teaching of the Czech language at the State University.

M. J. Breuer was elected the first chairman; C. H. Chernosky was made vice-chairman, and E. E. Křenek was elected secretary. Mr. Chernosky was to be responsible for the teaching of Czech grammar in the club, Mr. Mikeska for the teaching of Czech history; E. E. Křenek was given Czech music as his especial responsibility, Joseph Kopecky was put in charge of Czech art and M. J. Breuer was assigned to the perpetuation of Czech literature.

These five students set for themselves tasks of unusual responsibility. Czech music, Czech history, Czech art and Czech literature, were in scope not only nation wide, but world wide. The meetings of the club members were bi-monthly and all proceedings were carried on in the Czech language that the purpose of the organization might be upheld.

On Thanksgiving Day, 1932, a meeting of "Čechie" was held in the main Administration Building, Texas University, Austin. Dr. Joseph Kopecky of San Antonio presided as president, and there were members present from all over the State—lawyers, doctors, teachers, writers, business men and women. Two teachers of the Czech language, Dr. Eduard Miček, Professor of the Chair of Slavic Language, University of Texas, and Dr. Frank Lukša, teacher of the Czech language in Houston public schools, were present. Dr. Miček, author of several books, and occupying a high position as a member of the faculty of the University of Texas, presented in part evidence of what has been accomplished through the efforts of the five student organizers of "Čechie."

Honorable Charles Henry Chernosky, who was made responsible in the beginning for the teaching of Czech grammar in the club, recognized no limitations in his efforts to carry on the work assigned to him. He served many years as a member of the State Board of Education. As a member of this Board he assisted in the selection of text books used in the public schools. He not only helped select the text books, but looked after the interest of all schools of the State in connection with his co-workers, the other eight members of the Texas Board of Education.

Czech music has been duly accorded recognition, not only in Texas, but throughout the United States. In Texas, Czech musical programs are broadcast daily over the various radio stations. Czech folk-songs and folk-dance music have through this medium, as well as through the many Texas-Czech musical organizations, such as bands and orchestras, been given a prominent place in State music circles. In the neighboring state of Oklahoma a regular weekly program of Czech music is broadcast, with many listeners in Texas.

The Czech language is now recognized as a major study in the University of Texas and has been adopted as one of the foreign languages in several Texas high schools.

Prior to 1860 the people of Texas were dependent for the education of their children upon private schools, organized and supported by patrons who paid tuition to the teacher. This item of Texas history in connection with the evolution of the school and educational system brings into prominence the matter of the establishing of the early Czech schools, together with the founding of the Czech reading clubs.

The founding of the club "Čechie" by those first Texas-Czech students, marks an epoch in the educational and cultural life of the State.

Czech students are annually being awarded fellowships for Charles University, in Praha, Czechoslovakia, thereby further

Class Group Czech Students,
University of Texas,
Spring of 1934

Back row, left to right: Arnošt Horak, Bennie Mikulenčak, Frank Horak (Second Semester, President); Arthur Loštak, Albert Blaha, Louis Bartosh, Arnold Kocurek, Daniel Hruška, Joe Bartoň (First Semester, President).

Third Row: Laddie Lidiak, Olga Kucurek, Emil Mazoch, Edmond Hejl, Johnny Bartoň, Albert Tieman, Emilia Zazvorka, Emil Mazoch, Irene Buček, Reuben Lešikar.

Second Row: Frances Kraft, Willie Wiesner, Raymond Novosad, Joe Skřivanek, Rosa Marek, Daniel Dařilek, Marian Chamrad, John Skřivanek, Mrs. Martha Chovanetz, Mary Kutalek, Ella Koemel.

Third Row: Earline Baier, Elizabeth Kutalek, Leona Kroulik, Emilie Bezecny, Professor Dr. Eduard Míček, Vlasta Tapal, Josie Mrazek, Ruth Ann Marčák, Carolyn Malina, Frances Kamas.

demonstrating the value of the influence which has emanated from the pioneer schools.

Texas-Czech students at the University of Texas receiving Fellowship for Charles University include: 1928-29, Miss Agnes Kolaja; 1929-30, George E. Kačir and Henry Slavik; 1930-31, Roman Jack Bartosh and Frank Lukša; 1932-33, Miss Mildred Jelinek, (Edwin Adams of Burlington attended through his own efforts, Miss Lydia Kolaja attended for a limited time and is now teaching in the Czechoslovak high schools).

In connection with the Department of the Slavic Languages, University of Texas, of which Dr. Eduard Miček is Associate Professor, there has been established a Scholarship Fund, out of which, each year, deserving Texas-Czech students receive stipends or donations to help defray matriculation fees. This Scholarship Fund is supported by donations from various organizations and clubs such as the S. P. J. S. T.; K. J. T.; K. J. Ž. T.; R. V. O. S.; $25.00 each: Laddie F. Lidiak, Elizabeth Kutalek, Mary Kutalek, August J. Watzlivick, Gertrude Urbanic, Richard Martiňak, Edmund J. Hejl, Albert Blaha, Marie Matush, Josie Mrazek, Leona Kroulik, Marie Chamrad, Emil J. Polašek, Raymond R. Novosad, John F. Halamiček, Daniel A. Hruška, Mrs. Martha Chovanetz, Arnošt Horak, Reuben B. Lešikar, John M. Skřivanek, Joseph J. Shřivanek, Annie Lee Miller, Arnold J. Kocurek, Evelyn Šulak, Rosa Marek, Daniel Dařilek, Ruth Šefcik, Johny Bartoň, Martha M. Chudej, Carolyn Malin, Frank A. Horak, Ella Koemel, and Berta Novotny.

These fellowship awards, in connection with the hundreds of members of "Čechie" scattered over the State, are important units in the march of progress.

CHAPTER XXIV

Czech Catholic Churches in Texas

"Everyone invited to be with the old mother parish, Saturday, August 15, 1932, for an annual celebration at Praha, Texas." This was the invitation extended through the medium of a printed poster and widely distributed throughout the Praha community on the occasion of this feast in the pioneer Czech Catholic Church. When the day and hour for the services arrived, a large and representative gathering of parishioners and friends were present.

Services began with the Procession at 9:00 A. M., from the Parish Hall to the rectory and thence to the church, with musicians of the "Starry Band" assisting. Dinner was served on the grounds at 11:30 A. M. and at 3:00 o'clock in the afternoon there was an address given by Mr. Vlad Malec, editor of *Novy Domov*, of Hallettsville. At 6:00 P. M. supper was served. There followed at 8:00 P. M. a Bohemian play presented by the Cistern Dramatic Club. A social entertainment concluded the day's program, given through the courtesy of the members of the Starry Band.

The Praha Catholic Church, which holds a vital place in the progress and development of the State, celebrated its seventy-fifth anniversary on this occasion. History of the church and parish has been in the making since the early pioneer days.

Located on a hill in a beautiful live oak grove, the church, with its tall steeple, may be seen for miles around. In its material structure it is typical of the members of the parish and the pioneer immigrants who came to settle in Texas. It is substantially built of solid rock. The altar is the work of a master hand. Beautiful stained glass windows represent, in their paintings, the scenes from the life of Christ. Reverend Father L. P. Netardus, one of the pioneer priests, was for many years the pastor.

The population of Praha is made up almost entirely of Texas-Czechs. The settlement started in the early fifties with M. Noval, F. Granitsky, Joseph Vyjala, George Morysek, Joe Kajak, M. Jareš, John Bača and others. The first name of the settlement

SISTERS' HOME

ST. MARY'S SCHOOL

CHURCH OF THE ASSUMPTION

WEST, TEXAS

RT. REV. MSGR. JOS. PELNAR

ST. JOSEPH'S HALL

RECTORY

Czech Catholic Institutions in Texas

Lower Center:
RT. REV. MSGR.
JOSEPH PELNAR

was Mulberry, but this was changed in 1878 by the postmaster, E. Knešek. The first Catholic church was built of wood in 1868. In 1875 a new church building was erected, and in 1891 the present handsome edifice was built.

An interesting story in connection with this new building has been related by Frank Teich, artist, sculptor of nation-wide prominence, world traveler, and pioneer German settler of Llano and San Antonio. Mr. Teich was summoned by an aged parishioner and pioneer to make a statue of the Christ for the exterior of the church building. The sculptor recalls how he searched through his material for the most beautiful piece of marble from which to carve the statue. It was not easy to obtain such material on short notice. He had one long piece of fine marble, but it was not quite as thick as he would have desired, but in using it he resorted to the skill of the artist, cutting deftly and finely. This marble Corpus was set in another piece of stone, larger and of a contrasting color, which brought out the beauty of the marble and the fine workmanship. When the work was finished and the donor of the beautiful piece came to meet the sculptor, he brought with him the money with which to pay. It was all in gold and with toil-worn fingers, this aged, loyal churchman, a Czech pioneer, took the pieces from a leathern pouch, which he first opened by untying a leathern thong. The amount was $300.00 in gold, and he gave "Gold for the King."

Czech Catholic representation from the communities of Damon, Columbus, El Campo, East Bernard, Frydek, Ganado, Hillje, Houston, Hungerford, Needville, Richmond, Rosenberg, Sealy, Stafford, Sugarland, Wallis, Wharton and Yoakum, took part in the Eucharistic celebration held at Holy Rosary Catholic Church at Rosenberg, in October, 1932. This church has gone through several stages of improvement since it was established in 1911. The present handsome edifice was dedicated in October, 1926.

Reverend Edward Hajek was one of the first priests in charge. Reverend Father Ignacious Valenta served the church in 1917 and Reverend Father James Květoň became the pastor in 1922, remaining until the celebration in 1932. Assisting Father Květoň with the ceremony upon this second annual Eucharistic celebration were Father Joseph C. Kunc, East Bernard; Father O. J. Jansky, Hillje; Father Edward Murscki, El Campo; Father A. W. Nesvadba, Frydek; Father J. J. Tydlačka, Father V. O. Svoček, Houston; Father B. L. Němec, Wallis. Father Květoň is a native of Czechoslovakia, but attended St. Mary's Seminary,

La Porte, Texas, and was ordained to the priesthood at St. Mary's Cathedral, Galveston, in 1914.

Bands from Wallis, Ganado and Frydek took part in the procession. Members of the Catholic lodges, Česka Řimsko Katolicka Jednota Žen Texaskych and Česka Řimsko Katolicka Jednota Texaska assisted also with the historical celebration. This parish is largely made up of Czech and Polish parishioners, with a smaller percentage of German, Italian, French, Irish and American.

In 1903 and 1904 several Czech families from Ellinger and Ammansville settled near Needville, a small town, twelve miles south of Rosenberg.

Reverend Father A. W. Nesvadba, formerly assistant priest to Right Reverend Monsignore Pelnař at St. Mary's Church, West, Texas, at present in charge as pastor at Frydek parish, with Bellville as a mission, contributes some early church history.

The first settlement at Needville was the nucleus of the present large Czech settlement and largest mission attached to Rosenberg. The nearest Catholic church at the time was at Sealy, about forty miles distant. Father Skoček was the first priest who visited the section. He came a few times during the year and said mass in the different homes. When Father Demel was appointed pastor of Wallis he was requested to take charge of the territory. He came regularly once a month, holding services in Foster's school, two miles north of Needville. All the parishioners were willing to do their part toward the building of a church, but were divided as to the choice of a location.

There were about thirty families scattered around Needville, where already there had been established a cemetery, one acre of ground having been donated by Mr. Paul Kulčak, one of the early settlers. He had at the time lost a son, killed accidentally while hunting. The boy was buried in the cemetery and later there had been a few additional burials, and to this first acre the donor was willing to give another for church property.

Czechs around Fairchilds, a small village in the section, included the Kneitz, the Nesvadba and Vacek families, all early settlers, and these were anxious to have a church there. Father Demel favored Needville. This location was selected and the church edifice erected there the same year.

Mr. Frank Horak donated an acre of ground for the church, and two for a cemetery. A small church building, fifty feet by thirty feet was built. At the time it was thought that this would be large enough. It was about all that could have been done, as most of the families in the parish were renters of the land on which they lived and those few who were on their own land owned it mostly on notes.

St. John's Parish of Ammansville donated its old main altar and a small bell. St. Veronica's Parish of Cameron sent two side altars. Mr. Felix Stavinoha donated a large set of Stations of the Cross. The church was dedicated on May 22, 1912, by Right Reverend Gallagher of Galveston. There were present for the ceremonies besides Father Demel, the pastor, Father D. A. Montreuil from Rosenberg; Father K. Kačir from Marak; and Father Joseph Kunc from Caldwell. Forty-eight children were confirmed at this time.

In 1916 this mission was attached to Rosenberg and has since had services twice a month. Father F. V. Lepsa gave a successful mission at the church in 1916. A life-size crucifix, a gift from Mr. Alois Kneitz, was blessed by this missionary. Some preparations were made in 1919 for a new church, but the following year and the next crops were poor, so the church remains as first erected, with eighty-eight families.

The first entries were made in the church register with the baptism of Rudolf Dubčak, son of John and Frances D. Dubčak, March 13, 1907, the marriage of Peter Sury, son of Paul and Anna Sury, and Pauline Kulčak, daughter of Paul and Pauline Kulčak, July 18, 1908, and the burial of Frances Kulčak, son of Paul and Pauline Kulčak, age ten years. Date of burial December 9, 1906.

In 1927, Reverend John E. Kalas was appointed local pastor and held services each Sunday, there being at this time over one hundred Czech Catholics living in or near Needville. In 1922 Reverend Father A. W. Nesvadba offered his first mass at this church.

* * * * *

Hungerford, in Wharton County, six miles northwest of Wharton, the county seat, was, until 1900, an open prairie. Hundreds of cattle roamed at will over the wide open spaces. Today, within the radius of six miles, there are farms, large and small, mostly owned by some sixty-five Czech families. These began the settlement about 1900. At first there were three families, one from Gonzales and two from Sweet Home. Each year others followed. The nearest Catholic Church at the time was at East Bernard, ten miles distant. Mass was said at Hungerford for the first time in the new Vienna (Viden) school, four miles southwest of Hungerford, by Father Demel of Wallis, on the occasion of the Feast of Saint John the Baptist, in 1913. Father Demel continued to hold services once each month after this and in 1915 this mission was placed in charge of Reverend E. J. Kajek, the priest then resident at Rosenberg.

The following year preparations were made for building a church. Two lots were bought in Hungerford from Mr. Vinyard of Wharton, who also donated two lots. Mrs. Buček of Hungerford donated one acre of ground for a cemetery. An unnamed lady sent a gift of five hundred dollars through the Church Extension. The Apostle whom Jesus loved was selected as the Patron Saint for the church. Twenty thousand dollars were subscribed and paid by the people. The cornerstone was blessed November 15, 1916. The church, sixty feet by forty feet, with a small belfry, was completed in February, 1917, and the first services held the third Sunday in April. A large bell was donated by Mr. Louis Matušek, Sr., one of the first settlers, and was blessed on November 28, 1917, by Father Demel; Reverend Father P. F. Němec of Frydek; Father J. F. Kaňak of Sealy; Father Havel of Ganado, and the pastor, Father I. J. Valenta.

In 1919 the church was enlarged, a sanctuary twenty-eight by twenty feet being built; also two sacristies, fourteen by twelve feet. The small belfry was torn down and a tower twenty-five feet high was erected in its place. The old building was also remodeled. New pews were installed and the whole remodeled. The church was formally dedicated by Right Reverend Bishop C. E. Byrne of Galveston, with Reverend Demel of Wallis, Reverend P. F. Němec of Frydek, and Reverend I. J. Valenta present. Sixty-three children were confirmed. There are now over seventy-five Czech families in the parish. Reverend James W. Květoň, successor to Reverend Ignac J. Valenta, has been in charge since 1922.

The first entries in the parish records are: Baptism of Cyril Methodius Brenk, son of Peter and Anna Brenk, July 22, 1913. Marriage of Rudolph Vacek, son of John and Anna Vacek of East Bernard, and Lucile Victorin, daughter of Frank and Agnes Victorin of Hungerford. Burial of Lillian Horečka, four-months'-old daughter of Emil and Emily Horečka, September, 1916.

* * * * *

Frydek, named after the beautiful and historic city of Silesia (Czechoslovakia), known for its Shrine with a miraculous Madonna, is situated in an historic section of Texas. The town is located about three miles south of historical San Felipe where, in 1833, the Convention of Texas was held and the petition drawn demanding that the State of Coahuila be separated from Texas. Again in San Felipe, in the latter part of 1836, representatives of all colonies in Texas formed a Provincial Government, by which act Texas became independent of Mexico. It was here that Sam Houston was elected general of the Army of Texas.

To this place the first Czech family, that of August Mlčak, came in 1871 from Moravia, Czechoslovakia. There was one son, Anton, still living, actively engaged in carrying on the work of his farm. Two daughters in the family, soon after their arrival, married American-born Germans, and they, too, lived in San Felipe. The Mlčak family was fifty-two days on the ocean. On arriving in Texas a small farm was purchased for the sum of $32.00, representing seventy-five cents per acre. In 1882 the family bought a better farm, paying three dollars per acre, the land being situated between San Felipe and Frydek.

In 1875 Miss Florentina, daughter of Mr. and Mrs. August Mlčak, was buried in the old San Felipe cemetery. In 1885 the aged wife of Mat Kutura and John Saha, Sr., and six-year-old Peter Saha, were buried in this cemetery.

The chairman of the first Cemetery Committee was Frank Pavliček who, in 1932, was over eighty-five years old, living at Blessing, Texas.

John Saha, Jr., who has served on the board of trustees for many years, and Anton Ležak, who has served as secretary-treasurer, have been active in the development of the community.

Among other early settlers were Mr. and Mrs. Mat Kutura and family from Czechoslovakia. They came in 1883, joining with Joseph Sodolak and family, John Pavliček, Frank Pavliček and family, Joseph Buchala and other pioneers in developing the community.

The pioneer priest, Father J. Chromčik of Fayetteville, attended to the spiritual needs of these first settlers. In 1908 a structure was erected which was used as church, school and sisters' residence.

Right Reverend Bishop Aloysious Gallagher of the Diocese of Galveston, blessed the building on May 20, 1908, thus establishing the Mission at Frydek, which was joined to the Parish of Sealy. Reverend Father William J. Skoček attended this mission until the Fall of 1911. Father M. A. Dombrowski then had charge of the work until the Spring of 1912, and was succeeded by Father J. A. Valenta, from St. Mary's Seninary, La Porte, who served until the Fall of 1912. At this time Reverend Father P. F. Němec was appointed pastor at Sealy, with charge of Frydek as one of the missions. At the end of October, 1919, in order to have the church and school more conveniently located, it was moved about a mile and a quarter further into the settlement and in the Spring of 1917 a rectory was built.

During a Diocesan retreat in 1917, Father Němec of Sealy was appointed the first resident pastor, taking charge in July, 1917.

*   *   *   *   *

The little settlement of San Felipe was located and settled twelve years before the city of Houston was founded. Governor Luciana Garcia named it as an intended compliment to Don Felipe de Garza, then commandant of the eastern provinces, and also to the colony's founder, Stephen F. Austin. Austin, with a small band of adventurous pioneers, had rested at this point for a while in 1824.

It was into this early settlement that hardy Czech settlers came, following not so many years after these pioneers had kindled fires and planted crops. It was left for the hands of Czech pioneer settlers to build a church and a school and set aside a spot of blessed ground as the resting place for the dead.

The first child baptised in the new church was Josephine Ležak, born June 15, 1908, this ceremony being performed by Father Skoček, June 28, 1908. The first marriage in this church was that of Valentin Jurek and Mary Smahel, on June 1, 1909.

The new cemetery was blessed by Father Weimer, on September 16, 1890. At the time this was part of the Sealy Parish. The old records of Sealy were lost by fire so it is not known who was the first to be buried there. Old residents claim that the first were Mrs. Aloysia Pavliček and Joseph Sodolak, who were buried in 1885. In 1888 Mrs. Frances Zbořil, Mrs. Marie Helstyn, Joseph Vechta, Mrs. Anna Buchala, Father Sodolak, Father Grmela and Charles Pavliček were all laid to rest in the old cemetery.

The Sodolak and Pavliček families were large land-owners in this settlement, having bought nine hundred acres of the land when they moved into the community, paying between two and three dollars and fifty cents per acre for it. They moved to Frydek from Fayetteville in 1883.

It has been planned to write and publish a history of the Czech Catholic parishes and churches in Texas, the book to be issued in connection with the erection of a proposed monument to the

The Bible on the opposite side is printed with the use of old German type in old "Bohemian" or Czech. The translation was made for this history by John Mikulik and Dr. George Pazdral of West, McLennan County.

ᛉ   ᛉ   ᛉ

"In the year of our Lord, one thousand five hundred forty-nine, on Thursday before Palm Sunday, this Old and New Testament, in the first place, for the glory and praise of God Almighty, and then, for the soul-saving usage of all those that are true to the Bohemian tongue and nation, was printed in Mala Strana in the city of Praha, at the house of Bartolomew Netolicky, with an unusual outlay of the same Bartolomew and George Nelantrich Roždalovsky, and thus, with much work and careful diligence, was finished. For all this, praise, honor and glory and thanks be unto Lord God Almighty, for ever and ever." AMEN.

AN OLD FAMILY BIBLE *belonging to the Parma family, Dallas, Texas;
printed from old German type, in old "Bohemian" or Czech, in 1549.
On the back side will be found a translation of the dedicatory page.*

REV. FATHER CHROMČIK, *Pioneer Czech Priest*

pioneer priest, the late Josef Chromčik, whose life labors were given to the Fayette County territory.

Reverend Josef Klobouk of Fayetteville has been appointed historian, and he will be assisted in collecting the material by the priests of the Czech Catholic churches of Texas. The erection of the monument was ordered by the Bohemian Catholic Alliance at a meeting held at Plum, Thanksgiving Day, 1931. At a later meeting at LaGrange, Fayetteville was selected as the site for the memorial. The proposed volume will deal with sections in which the Catholic Czechs have played an important part.

Christmas, 1932, marked the sixtieth year since the beloved missionary and pastor, Reverend Father Chromčik, came to Texas to begin his work in Fayetteville, which became the center of his labors.

Father Klobouk is master of the Czech language in which the history is to be written, he having been a professor of language in one of the European universities before he came to Texas, and is recognized as one of the outstanding Czech scholars not only in Texas, but the entire South.

The history, like the monument, will be a tribute to Father Chromčik, who is held in high and loving esteem by the people of his own time and by those of the present who know of his work. Chromčik School, which he built at Fayetteville, and in which he taught for fifteen years, as well as the Catholic church building there, which he restored, and which is one of the largest and most beautiful in the State, are memorials to him. He was a linguist and in addition was noted for his scholarly attainments and spiritual life. Among the highly educated it is said that he had but few equals. His thorough knowledge of several languages gave him qualifications for enlarged educational work and far-reaching missionary accomplishments. He was diocesan consultor at the synod to assist the Bishop of Galveston in ruling the whole Diocese, representing the German and Bohemian nationalities in their affairs. He was ecclesiastical judge for the clergy in ecclesiastical cases, and in addition, fiscal attorney, i. e., prosecutor and defendant in ecclesiastical cases.

Reverend Chromčik was born on January 25, 1845, at Olomouc, Moravia. He finished his studies in Olomouc and graduated there in 1866. After his ordination to the priesthood he was assistant priest at Lichtenau, Moravia. He then became administrator of the Parish of Senftleben, Moravia. Having been assigned to the Diocese of Galveston by Bishop Dubois, he came to Texas, arriving Christmas Eve, 1872. He was then sent to

Fayetteville, where he resided until his death. In 1894 he made a trip to Europe to celebrate the jubilee of the twenty-fith anniversary of ordination. On his return he brought with him four young priests, Reverends Skoček, Šebik, Mahan and Kačer.

The celebration on October 7, 1931, of the investiture of Right Reverend Monsignore Josef Pelnař of West, Texas, pastor of the Church of Assumption, in his new title as Domestic Prelate, was a distinctive recognition for Texas-Czech Catholics. The honor came to Monsignore Pelnař after his service of thirty-one years, a fitting recognition of his life of faithful labors. The ceremony was attended by people from all sections of the State, with Most Reverend C. E. Byrne of Galveston presiding. The celebration began at 10 a. m. with a procession at the Church of the Assumption and the investiture ceremony followed at the sanctuary. Bishop Byrne delivered the address in English and was followed by Reverend Vaniček of Granger, who spoke in Czech.

Dinner was served to the visiting clergy at the S. P. J. S. T. Hall with Reverend J. B. O'Leary of Waco acting as master of ceremonies. Speakers of the luncheon program were members of the visiting clergy and Captain Method Pazdral and R. J. Marak, both of West. At the same hour a barbecue lunch was served, the other visitors attending the ceremonies in the Lone Star park, under the auspices of the ladies of the parish. Music during the day was furnished by Kohut's Orchestra, an outstanding Texas-Czech musical organization. The large number of Texas-Czech citizens from over the State, who were present for this memorable event, availed themselves of the opportunity to pay tribute through their presence to Monsignore Pelnař and his good works.

The distinctive honor was bestowed on Monsignore Pelnař several months prior to the investiture celebration. The honor and recognition of his services came to him during a visit to Europe in the Summer of 1931.

*   *   *   *   *

The necessity of having church facilities of their own stirred the thrifty farmers of the virgin soil to further activities. Reverend Father Joseph Charles Kunc of East Bernard has contributed the story of Holy Cross Church and Parish of that place.

"The beginning of the new and flourishing parish of Holy Cross at East Bernard dates back to the year of 1900, when several Catholic families settled on the broad prairies in the northeast corner of Wharton County. The settlement received its name from the East Bernard River, which flows independently into the Gulf of Mexico, and in its course forms the border-line between Wharton and Fort Bend counties. Folklore holds the legend that the Indians called the stream 'The Ringing River,' but this is another story.

"The Catholic spirit of the early Czech settlers is shown by the fact that they desired to have a burying ground of their own. A meeting was held in August, 1900, for the purpose of purchasing this ground, 'God's Acre,' situated on the west bank of the river, which was procured.

"It was in 1905 that two blocks of ground were acquired in the town of East Bernard and in the same year the church was built. The pioneers were encouraged and were guided in their efforts by Reverend William Skoček, at that time pastor at Sealy.

"On account of his sacrifices in promoting the work, John Vacek, Sr., was given the honor of selecting the patron of the church and he chose the title of the 'Holy Cross,' in memory of the village church in Bohemia where he had been baptised.

"In the Fall of the same year, Reverend Father Skoček offered mass for the first time in the little frame church, which had been erected at a cost of $850.00. Father Skoček having at the time other missions, was unable to say but few masses during the year. The parishoners asked the Bishop of Galveston for a priest of their own. In September, 1906, the newly-ordained priest, Reverend Jacob Schnetzer, was appointed the first resident pastor. The old Brooks residence with two acres of ground was acquired as a residence for the priest.

"The church records show the first baptism: Maria Ludmilla Večeřa, baptised November 4, 1906, and the first marriage, Anton Brandl and Theola Armatinsky, on November 13, 1906. Father Schnetzer, being unable to speak the Czech language, resided in the parish only a few months and for about one year the church was attended from Houston. Again Father Skoček was assigned to the church, but when Wallis received a resident priest in 1909, Father Machaň, now deceased, East Bernard was made a mission of the Wallis parish, being only eight miles distant.

"Soon after this arrangement Reverend Wenceslaus Demel became the pastor at Wallis and East Bernard had regular services, which were attended no matter how bad the weather or how muddy the roads. Under the zealous care of this priest, the mission grew and prospered. Among other improvements a large K. J. T. Hall was erected in 1913 and made the nucleus of many parish activities.

"During the World War the parish sent more than its quota of young men to the army. There is a bronze tablet in the church and the following thirty-six names are on the honor roll:

"Alois Beran, Joseph Beran, Andrew Beran, Frank Fried, John Genzer, Alfred Grigar, Frank Hlavinka, Wencelas Hrdecky, John Janiš, Joe Jochec, Robert Jochec, John Kučera, Ladislas Marak, Eduard Martiňak, Charles Maywald, Raymond Morris, Herman Mueller, Joe Mueller, Joseph Petraš, John Polašek, Ignac Pustka, Frank Sašin, Alfred Štaffa, Joe Šulak, Peter Šulak, Frank Švec, John Švec, Albert Sykora, John Sykora, John Tomanek, Steven Valigura, Clement Večeřa, Frank Vitek, Ernest Walzel, Ferdinand Wojtek and Frank Zapalač. Two of the number, Alois Pustka and Joseph Tomanek, lost their lives in the service.

"As soon as it was known that East Bernard was to have a resident pastor a handsome new rectory was at once erected at a cost of $5,000.00. The new pastor, Reverend Charles Joseph Kunc, whom the Bishop, Right Reverend C. E. Byrne, had recalled from New Castle Pa., took charge on September 11, 1921. With the coming of Father Kunc, the East Bernard mission became a parish with regular services every Sunday. In the Autumn of 1922 the parochial school was opened with two Sisters of the Incarnate Word and Blessed Sacrament of Shiner, Texas, in charge. Sixty-three children were enrolled. The Sisters lived in a rented house and the K. J. T. Hall was used as a school building. A successful bazaar was held the same year and the sum of one thousand dollars was raised for the use of the school and church. The church being at this time over-crowded, it was decided to erect a new structure, and each family was asked to haul five loads of sand from the Middle Bernard River as a sign of the determination to start a new church. A big pile of good sand was in evidence on the church ground before Christmas, 1923. Cash donations were then asked and $1,500 from a parish bazaar was made the same year.

"In August, 1924, the sketch of the new church was approved and the architect was told to go ahead with plans and specifications. Another meeting was held in October, 1924, to consider bids for the construction of the building. A bazaar was held on October 27th and $3,257.00 was realized. Other donations were forthcoming and the work on the new church building started October 29, 1924. After eight months of steady work, under very favorable weather, the church stood finished and was solemnly blessed the 29th day of June, 1925, by Right Reverend

Christopher E. Byrne of the Diocese of Galveston, with twenty-five priests assisting. About 5,000 people from far and near were present to take part in the ceremonies of the dedication.

"The structure is of Spanish Colonial type, reinforced concrete and hollow tile construction, with apricot stucco on the outside. The building is fifty feet wide and one hundred and ten feet long. Ten large windows imported from Czechoslovakia are of special design, worked out in roundel glass, which makes them unique in Texas. There are also some mosaics and outside shrines and the whole has a pleasing and symmetrical appearance. The furniture was made by Joseph Svoboda of Kewaunee, Wisconsin. The Stations of the Cross are from Schmalzel and painted on copper-tin. The whole interior is tastefully decorated. Large pictures done in oil on plaster by an able artist, Pio Pizzi of Ohio, add much to the beauty of the church interior. The church as it is, complete with furniture, statues, sidewalks and surrounding wall, represents an expenditure of $50,000.00. All the money was collected in the two years following the building of the church, with no outside help, coming from about one hundred and fifty families, all of moderate means. Two-thirds of the parish families are renters.

"The old church building served two years as a school, but soon the step toward a school building was taken and also a home for the sisters in charge of the school, and in 1928 an architect was employed and the buildings erected at a cost of $28,000, of which $10,000 was subscribed and the balance borrowed. Both of these buildings are of the mission style to harmonize with the church. On September 27, 1928, Bishop Byrne went to East Bernard to bless the new buildings. The enrollment in September, 1931, was one hundred and thirty children.

"On July 11, 1929, the general convention of the K. J. T. (Catholic Union of Bohemian Men in Texas) was held in this parish. Many useful laws for its 4,000 members were enacted at this session. From March, 1930, until September, Reverend Joseph C. Kunc and Mr. Michal Prorok of East Bernard, were in Europe, Egypt and the Holy Land. On their return there was a splendid celebration to welcome them home. Mr. Prorok donated a Holy Sepulchre Shrine to the church in thanksgiving.

"In January, 1931, more ground for the cemetery was purchased from O. C. Koym. The present church trustees are: August E. Morris, Frank Pražak, J. J. Vacek and Adolph Bohaček."

The Catholic Sokol of Texas was organized in 1908 and celebrated the quarter of a century of organization in June, 1933, the occasion being designated as the "Silver Jubilee." The organization at the start was perfected in nearly all of the Bohemian Catholic parishes, there being some eighteen councils established. In 1917, at the time of the entrance of the United States into the World War, Sokol activities were largely suspended and all councils ceased to function with the exception of the one at Bluff, now Hostyn, which has continued actively to carry on the work through the twenty-five years. In 1928 new life was injected into the state organizations through the efforts of the National Catholic Union of Chicago. A Sokol from Czechoslovakia, Professor John Madl, came to Texas and helped with the reorganization work.

There are now Councils at Ennis, West, Granger, Taylor, Bryan, Hostyn, Fayetteville, San Antonio, East Bernard, Wied and Jourdanton, which belong to the Texas Unit. There are Councils in Hallettsville, Yoakum, Moulton, and Moravia, which at present do not belong to the Unit.

There are at present four hundred and forty-seven members in the Texas Unit, composed of men and women.

In several Councils of the Texas Unit there is "Youth Auxiliaries" for boys and girls from the age of six to sixteen. This is the beginning of the organization, it is said. The boys and girls will grasp the athletic part of it as they grasp their lessons in school.

This athletic work is not only for the benefit of training the body, but they are trained also in the spiritual welfare which makes for moral citizenship for the State and the Nation. Members are also trained in singing and recreation for both mental and physical enjoyment.

The main idea in the Sokol is the training of mind and body as the proverb says: "In a healthy body, there is a clear mind." The Catholic Sokol stands for higher ideals, and the main one is: "For God and Country" and always "Forward—Never backward."

The Texas Catholic Sokols have their annual meeting every year at different places in Texas at which time they compete for prizes. It generally occurs the last of June or first part of July.

Upper Left: *Reverend Adolph Chlumsky, pioneer Czech Minister.*

Upper Right: *Summer Class, 1932, Huss Memorial, Temple, Texas.*

Center: *Home Moravian Church, Winston-Salem, North Carolina, with weather vane and clock beneath; stands as built in 1769. The main hall of Salem College adjoins the Church.*

Lower Left: *Huss Memorial School, Temple, Texas.*

Lower Right: *New Tabor Church, near Caldwell, Burleson County, Texas.*

CHAPTER XXV

EARLY CZECH-PROTESTANT CHURCH DEVELOPMENT

As the religious history of Czechoslovakia is interesting, so likewise it may be said that Czech religious history in Texas is interesting, particularly in tracing the growth and development of communities and settlements.

The struggles under oppression that have gone on through the centuries, in what is now Czechoslovakia, have had a large influence on the Czech religious life that is found today in Texas.

According to available statistics for Texas, the Catholic religion predominates with the Czechs. The Moravian Brethren, as a denomination, has a large membership, as has also the Presbyterian Church. There are in addition a considerable number who refer to themselves as "free-thinkers."

It is an historical fact, that the first Czech Evangelical Church erected in Texas was at Fayetteville, built there in 1855 by the Reverend John Volanek (Zvolanek).

The right of oppressed nationalities to self-determination, as realized in Texas, the new home country, brought about no radical movements on the part of the Czech settlers. The privilege of liberty, equality, democracy and justice, found ready acceptance in the hearts and minds of the Czech pioneers as they built communities.

In the course of the development, they built churches in which to worship according to the dictates of their own consciences, and in accordance with the traditions and teachings of their own country and their forbears who were a part of it.

In giving the history of the churches and affiliated organizations in Texas, we follow close in the footsteps of the progress that has established towns and communities and built up commerce and industry throughout the State.

It may at first seem that some of the records are too near the present to be of vital interest, but the history is being made for future record, and as time marches on, the data included in this volume will belong with the past.

It is with pride that the story of each church is told; of how

211

the struggling missions started and finally became flourishing parishes and congregations.

It has been explained by such authorities as Thomas Čapek and Dr. Habenicht why Czech Evangelical immigration from Moravia was turned toward Texas at an early date, both giving similar explanations:

"Before the Austro-Prussian War in 1866, Austria was a dominating member in the coalition of the German States, the later German Empire being founded after the Franco-Prussian War in 1871 and the Austrian regiments were quartered along with the German in the different German forts, as in Mainz. Before the year 1848 there was strong emigration movement to Texas. It has been suggested that there was a certain possibility that German soldiers of the Lutheran faith were on most cordial terms with the Austrian soldiers of the Evangelical Protestant religion during their sojourn in the military service, and this has been given as a possible reason why many of the first emigrants to Texas were of the Protestant faith."

Arnošt (Ernest) Bergman, born at Zapudov near Mnichove Hradište, Bohemia, in 1797, came to Texas in 1848, having prior to emigration studied theology in Prussian Silesia. He had also been the pastor of a Czech Protestant community at Stroužne, Prussian Silesia. Through his influence many Protestants were among the early emigrants.

Continuing with Jan (John) Zvolanek at Fayetteville, who founded an Evangelical Church there in 1855, the chronology would doubtless lead on to Wesley, where Josef Opočensky founded another Evangelical Church a few years later, possibly about the year 1858.

The development of the Wesley church was continued through the years, undergoing the usual trials that came with the unsettled condition of the new country. Discord arising in the church organization during the ministry of Reverend Opočensky, not only disrupted the work, but also undermined the health of the pastor and his death occurred in 1870. In 1872 the congregation called to the church F. B. Zdrubek of Cleveland, Ohio, who was later dismissed on account of reputed heresy or irreverence. He became, according to historical records, a "free-thinker." Reverend J. L. Chlumsky accepted the pastorage of the Wesley Church in 1874.

From the very earliest immigration to Texas, there have been in the many Czech settlements and communities evangelical church organizations—in fact, these units are among the first established in the United States. Texas holds the distinction of being the first State in which the Word of God was ever preached in the Czech language. Reverend Zvolanek of Fayetteville is given credit for being the first in his work during the year 1855. He did not, however, organize any church units.

These pioneer preachers accommodated themselves to the living conditions and in addition accustomed themselves to the privations that were necessarily a part of the life.

Reverend Opočensky, recognized for his scholarly attainments and religious zeal, had to live in the home of one of his church members, Mr. Schuerer, at Wesley, who carried on in his residence a flourishing general merchandising business, with restaurant in connection. The noise attendant upon the operation of this commercial enterprise was not conducive to study and the environment was not suitable for the mental and spiritual preparation required in the preacher's ministerial work.

Building was naturally costly as building material had to be hauled from Galveston, a distance of one hundred and twenty miles. The local church members did not feel in position to incur the expense of building a church at the time, and Reverend Opočensky decided to make a trip to Europe to solicit help from friends. He failed, however, in obtaining this help and so returned to Texas empty-handed.

Meanwhile, his dream of a church edifice was to be realized through the offer of a gift of material from the Reymershoffer family of Galveston. When the settlers of the church community were told of the proffered assistance they refused it, but proceeded to subscribe money themselves for a church. To Reverend Opočensky this was a distressing state of affairs. He termed the behavior as "obstinate."

Josef Opočensky joined the Confederate Army in 1861, and after the war again took up his ministerial work, preaching at Wesley which claims the distinction of having the oldest organized Protestant United Church in Texas. Among the first members of this church unit were Peter Mikeska, Josef Skřivanek, Pavel Šebesta, Frank Šebesta Buslavskeho, Karel and Joseph Rypl, Joseph Skřivanek, Jan Žabčik, Jan Baletka, Vincent Pšenčik, Mat Rubač, Tom Chupik, Arnošt Schuerer, Vinc and Josef Šiller, Joseph Ježek and Joseph Mašik. Many of these early settlers came from distances up to twenty miles to attend the church services. So zealous were these worshipers that in 1866 a church was built at a cost of $938.00. In 1868 an organ was purchased at a cost of $106.75, that the religious singing might be better. The church, however, sold the organ in 1871.

Through these years of the evolution of the church, following the various pastorates, the church work and influence grew. When in 1874 Reverend J. L. Chlumsky was invited to come from Moravia to the church pastorate, there were forty-two families belonging to the church unit. In a short while this number had increased to one hundred and fourteen. Reverend Chlumsky was young and ardently taught the principles of the church. He received the support of the State to teach the Czech language, but he grew homesick and returned to his native land in 1881.

He was followed by the Reverend Juren from Fayetteville, who was a public school teacher as well as a preacher and taught both English and Czech. Under his pastorate it became necessary to enlarge the church. Petr and Josef Mikeska donated a bell which weighed 300 pounds and cost nearly one hundred dollars, and on which was inscribed in Czech, "*Evangelicka Cirkev Česko-Moravska,*" (Cech-Moravian Evangelical Religion). In the year 1895 a new organ was installed.

The organization of these Evangelical Texas-Czech church units continued to extend the work of the early Protestant preachers until as many as twelve different localities were being served. The work was extended to Industry, Austin County, and Shiner, Lavaca County.

Reverend A. Chlumsky wrote "Historie Česko-Moravskych Bratři v Americe," ("History of the Czech-Moravian Brethren of America.") This book, written and published in the Czech language, was later translated into English by Miss Annie Juren, daughter of the pioneer Czech preacher.

The preface to the booklet is the history of the coming of Christianity to Bohemia. The story of the Reformation under John Hus is also dealt with, and then the emigration of Czechs from the eastern part of Moravia to Texas. Reverend Chlumsky gives credit to Reverend John Zvolanek of Fayetteville for being the first Evangelical preacher, setting the date at 1855. The oldest congregation is given by this pioneer author as that of Wesley, Texas, established in 1864 by the Reverend Josef Opočensky, who had emigrated with his people from Moravia in 1858, and died in Wesley, Texas, in 1870. Reverend Louis Chlumsky, vicar in Německy, Moravia, came to Texas in 1872, and, finding more work than he could do, called in 1876 a fellow-student, Reverend Henry Juren from Čermna, Bohemia. Reverend Juren settled in Fayetteville. Reverend J. L. Chlumsky returned in 1881 to Bohemia. Reverend Juren was joined in his work in 1888 by Reverend B. Laciak, who after a few years' service in connection with Reverend Juren, died suddenly. It was in 1889 that Reverend Adolf Chlumsky, born in Bohemia in 1842, came to Texas and settled at Brenham, from which point he served his congregations.

Reverend Adolf Chlumsky was born on October 3, 1842, in Dvakočovicich, Čechy. His father was a minister of the local Reformed Evangelical Church. The standing of the tolerant ministers was not very good. Their pay was insignificant, but the gifts and the love of their followers lessened the physical shortage and made it possible to stand the oppression of the Catholic State religion. In such an adverse environment young Adolf spent his childhood. His father accepted a position in Německe, Moravia, and was replaced in Dvakačovicich by Reverend Benjamin Opočensky, later minister in Zadveřicich. There were no evangelical schools at that time so he was instructed by his father. When he reached the age to go to the gymnasium he was sent to Tešin (Silisia) and Levoč (Hungary) to study evangelism. After he finished these schools he went to Basle, Switzerand, to study theology. There he remained two years, going then to Vienna for one year to continue his studies in theology. At the same time he studied medicine, which served him in good stead, for when he came to Texas he was able to give his followers both spiritual and medical advice.

He was ordained in 1866 by Right Reverend Beneš. He became a Reformed minister in Velke Lhotě, Moravia, and remained there until 1872 when he went to Krabčic, Čechy, where he was elected first minister of the local Evangelical Reformed Church. While in Krabčic, he began editing a religious newspaper *Straž na Sionu* (Guard on Zion.) He chastized his colleagues for going to Germany, England and America. He did not want the descendants of Czech Brethren to go to foreign lands to beg and accept money. He was of the opinion "Whose bread you will eat, his song you will sing." He was very ardent in awakening the Czech Brethren. He wrote the truth, but truth is one thing many people do not like, consequently he made many enemies.

Reverend Adolf Chlumsky was a very active member of the International Red Cross, especially during the Russian-Turkish War, and for his services at that time he received in 1876 a medal of honor. In the Fall of 1915, he was asked by the Serbian Division of the Red Cross to return the medal to Serbia, so that an additional medal might be added for his services for Serbia among the people of Texas. The Order of St. Savy sent a diploma with the personal note and signature by the King of Serbia, thanking Reverend Chlumsky for his services to Serbian soldiers. The medal consisted of the image of the Serbian Crown and a cross made in blue *email-ombrant*. In the center of the cross is a cameo of St. Savy. The medal and diploma of St. Savy is said to be the same that the King of Serbia awarded to John D. Rockefeller.

In 1889 he gave up the ministry in Krabčicich and came to Texas. He bought a farm near Brenham and devoted his time to that occupation. After four years—in 1893—he came out of his seclusion and began visiting evangelical communities. The ground was prepared by Reverend J. Juren as the existing parishes were incorporated under the name of Czech Brethren. This he liked and the work increased. The people were moving away from the old parishes to new soil in distant counties, so the time was opportune to organize new parishes. This he did wherever possible. As evidence of his efforts, there are the churches at Granger, Taylor, West, Vsetin and Caldwell. He loved children; he counted much on young people.

In 1893 at a convention in Wesley, where the delegates from Wesley, Industry, Shiner, Caldwell, Ocker, Fayetteville and from other communities met, an effort was made to organize the different parishes into a Union. A temporary union was formed, a protocol was written and signed by all present with the exception of two. The people, however, did not seem to understand this beautiful and idealistic move, as there was no evidence of any activity or benefits for the ten following years. Then it was again thought the time to form a union. This time the meeting was called at Granger. Reverend Chlumsky presided. The union was formed. A protocol was written and signed by all delegates with the exception from Caldwell and Smithville. *Bratrske Listy* was accepted as the news organ, a benevolent fund was started, officers were elected and from that time on the union functioned and grew.

As long as he could, Reverend Chlumsky edited *Bratrske Listy* himself. He published the history of the Union. He wrote articles on various subjects. He was very active. Hard work, night travel, loss of sleep, worry over ingratitude, etc., affected his health. He suffered a stroke of apoplexy, but recovered. He gradually lost his hearing. Fearlessly he prepared to leave his earthly sojourn, and when the time came, February 1, 1919, at the age of 76, he was ready. He was buried in the cemetery of the Czech-Moravian Brethren Church at Granger. He wished to rest among

his faithful and he felt that this parish was loyal to him to the end.
He was born poor and died poor. He ministered to the sick and
gladly gave to the poor. He loved his friends and remained true
to them during their well-being as well as in time of adversity.
While he was minister in Velke Lhotě, he married Miss Julia
Kmin, who shared his trials and tribulations until his death.

Reverend L. von Lanyi was among the early preachers in Texas,
serving churches at Ocker and Caldwell.

Reverend Theodore Kubricht, born in Bohemia in 1864, was
called to the pastorate at Wesley in 1896, remaining until 1901,
when he left Texas for Chicago to study medicine. Returning
to Texas in 1905, he settled at Taylor, where he was ordained
in 1906 by the Union of the Bohemian-Moravian Brethren, and
became the pastor in charge of the church in that city. In 1907,
when Reverend Adolph Chlumsky's history was written, there
were thirteen organized congregations and five pastorates. In 1893
an attempt was made to unite the different congregations in Texas
into a whole, but this failed. At the beginning of 1902, Reverend
Chlumsky began the publication of a monthly paper, *Bratrske
Listy,* for the purpose of fostering religious knowledge.

Eventually the prophecy, so held of Komensky, the last bishop
of the Moravian Brethren, "that the management of thy affairs
will be given thee again, O, Bohemian people," came to pass in
the agreement to the uniting of all congregations into the one
"Bohemian-Moravian Brethren Congregation in Texas." In the
assembly held at Taylor, December 28, 1904, the denomination
was provided with a State charter.

In 1906, $32.96 was collected for home mission work. Of this
amount Reverend A. Chlumsky received $7.64, Reverend H.
Juren $14.10, and Reverend Kubricht $11.22. The result was that
Reverend Chlumsky organized a congregation in Buckholts,
Reverend H. Juren organized one in Wallis, and Reverend
Kubricht established a Sunday school in Taylor.

Reverend Chlumsky traveled throughout the whole of the State
during the years of his ministry, preaching and teaching. He
relates in connection with his ministerial labors that his sermons
were often prepared while he "shucked corn in the barn."

Reverend J. W. Dobiaš, formerly of Texas, but later a resident
of Praha, Czechoslovakia, organized the "Hus" Bohemian
Brethren Presbyterian Church in Houston, on March 28, 1915.
He remained the pastor of the Houston church for some years,
but was known for his work throughout most of the Czech communities in the State, as he traveled and lectured in the interests

of Czech organizations. He sponsored a number of organizations, such as the Komensky Club, and in addition, religious and educational projects.

During these years churches were organized at Rowena and other points over the State. The Houston church was started with but a few members, there being at the time, according to minutes of the church and other records, but three ministers of this church in the State. Dr. W. F. Fransee, brother-in-law of Reverend Dobiaš, was in charge of the church at Rowena for some time, and later became pastor of the Houston church.

Reverend Dobiaš returned to his native land after the World War to engage in the ministry in Praha.

The Texas organization of the Czech-Moravian Brethren Church has been in existence for about thirty years, having been organized in 1903. Conventions at one time were held annually, but more recently have been held every two years, on July 6th and 7th. The dates July 6th and 7th commemorate the martyrdom of John Hus, who was burned at the stake in 1415. The 1933 convention was held at West, at the Czech-Moravian Brethren Church east of the town. Reverend Anton Motyčka of Nelsonville, is president of the State organization. Reverend Joseph Bartoň of Granger is vice-president, Reverend Horak of Caldwell, secretary, and Will Baletka of Owenville, treasurer. Delegates were in attendance at the West convention from Temple, Ennis, Granger, Holland, Crosby, Nelsonville, Caldwell, Dimebox, Elgin, Taylor, Dallas, Rosenberg and other points, numbering in all about one hundred.

CHAPTER XXVI

Hus Memorial School

Reverend Joseph Hegar, M.A., principal of Hus Memorial School, Temple, Texas, in offering a brief history of this institution, gives it the distinction of being the only school of its kind, not only in Texas, but in the whole United States.

John Hus, who lived a century earlier than Martin Luther, and whose death over five hundred years ago has been commemorated in Texas, has in this Texas school a living memorial. The story of its establishment and the work of carrying on its mission, has an important place in the history of church and school development in Texas.

"When the Evangelical Unit of the Czech-Moravian Brethren was organized in Texas for the emigrants from the land of Hus," according to Reverend Hegar, "the main problem of the infant organization was the care of the youth in the Sabbath Schools and young people's societies." Reverend Adolph Chlumsky of Brenham, one of the early pastors, started the nucleus of what is today the Hus Memorial School by taking a few promising young girls into his home near Brenham, where they were given training through a course of instruction in the Bible and Sunday School principles and management. His wife, a talented musician, assisted by the daughter of the family, gave lessons in music, both vocal and instrumental, specializing on the organ. In return for this the young women helped with the work of the household. They were selected from the various congregations, so that each church might be provided with trained teachers and musicians as well as faithful and consecrated church members.

This work, begun in a modest way and nurtured with the zeal of the true missionary spirit, has continued through the years and the fine results may be found in the story of this school.

As the years passed a number of well-trained young women went forth from the Chlumsky home to fill places as organists, choir leaders and Sunday School executives in their respective congregations.

In July, 1910, two new ministers, Reverend Joseph Bartoň and Reverend Joseph Hegar, were added as active workers in the field. Reverend A. Chlumsky and his wife were growing old and did not care for the burden of having an augmented home circle which was necessary when taking the young girls into the home for training.

This work was given over to the two younger pastors. Reverend Bartoň had located at Granger, having married a musically-gifted young lady, and soon found his small home inadequate to accommodate the girls who came for training. It was at this time that he conceived the idea of calling together such girls as wanted the education and training, for a conference. The plan he formulated was for them to live in private homes of local church members while in training, teachers to be hired, so that an intensive training course might be given, thus accomplishing in a few weeks what otherwise would require months to achieve.

The first class under this arrangement, consisting of seventeen students, met in January, 1914. This class or school was given the distinction of being called, "The Hus Memorial School" (*Husova Škola*) in honor of the Czech reformer, whom history tells us was burned at the stake at Constance, on July 6, 1415. The class met regularly every day for eight weeks and in so doing inaugurated the school work and system which has continued down through the years.

The study courses include the Bible, old and new testament, Czech language, Sunday School principles and management, music, and the study of the life of the Apostle St. Paul.

The instructors, Reverend Bartoň and Reverend Hegar, his assistant, with Mrs. Joseph Bartoň in charge of musical instruction, have continued in the work ever since, with the course of instruction remaining practically the same as in the beginning, it having been found to be well adapted to the needs of the various church communities.

The school being a private undertaking, no tuition was charged and no salaries paid. The students gave to the teachers of their own accord some remuneration as a token of appreciation.

In March, 1914, the project was extended through the move of some progressive laymen of different church congregations who met at Taylor and formally organized the "Hus Memorial Association." The primary purpose and object was to help the Evangelical Units of Czech Moravian Brethren, to establish and support the Hus Memorial School in a Hus Memorial building.

At the annual convention of the "Unity" held at Shiner, Lavaca County, the school was officially accepted, and the two educators in charge were duly elected to continue the work so courageously started, financial assistance being promised. The five hundredth anniversary of the martydom of Hus, July 6, 1915, was designated as appropriate for the launching of the plan. The class not having a school building, had been meeting in the high school, in the tabernacle building, in a public hall, and sometimes in vacant houses in Granger. The classes usually assemble twice a year for an eight weeks' course, the spring term beginning in January, and a summer class in June.

During the year 1919 while Reverend Hegar was in Army Y. M. C. A. work, Reverend Bartoň, assisted by his wife, was left in charge. Plans for further expansion were delayed by unsettled conditions following the World War.

The classes of both 1921 and 1922 were held in the church building at Granger with Reverend Hegar the only instructor. Five congregations at this time were seeking the 1924 class, these being Granger, Taylor, Caldwell, West and Temple. Temple was the final selection. There was no church building in Temple at this time, and as the building first considered as a location could not be obtained, a vacant private schoolhouse, known as the Wedemeyer Academy, was rented for three months to house thirty-nine students, this being the largest class in the history of the school.

Two rooms were fitted up as a girl's dormitory, the auditorium serving as a class room. Another room in the building was turned into a kitchen, another into a dining-room, and thus the school was actually launched. When the school was in full operation and visitors came and saw the work being done, a movement was again started, led by Reverend T. H. Horak of Caldwell, to acquire the building for permanent school quarters. A committee composed of five men from Temple and near-by communities and congregations were elected and authorized to buy the property, money to be raised by donations from the members of the different church congregations. Reverend Joseph Hegar remained with the school as principal.

It was at first proposed that an academy with a regular three years' course be established, including the studies which had been taught throughout the existence of the school. This plan was dropped in favor of the continuance of the school as it had been founded.

The building was bought and paid for in less than one year. Ladies Aid societies of the different congregations furnished the building for the accommodation of sixteen pupils.

The auditorium was furnished through individual donations.

Hot and cold water and gas heating systems were installed. School desks were given by the Sunday Schools of the congregations as well as several dozen folding chairs.

Once a year, on Thanksgiving Day, the ex-students gather for a reunion. On these occasions as many as one hundred and fifty former students are present for a business meeting, followed by a banquet in the large class-room. An important feature of these reunions is the evening program, held in the main auditorium, and consisting of musical and literary numbers prepared by the committee, always with the educational idea stressed. This ex-students' association is composed of approximately three hundred members, with an executive committee of five.

The association publishes four times a year a pamphlet called "The Czech Moravian Youth," the mission of which is to keep in touch with the students scattered from coast to coast in their individual undertakings. Dr. F. E. Lukša of Houston is the editor of the *Czech Moravian Memorial*, the ex-students' paper.

There are at present, accordinng to Reverend Joseph Hegar, thirty Czech Moravian Brethren churches in Texas, not including in this number several small mission stations. The Hus Memorial School building was purchased at an original cost of $7,000.00 and was improved at a cost of about $2,000.00. Today this amount represents only about one-third of the real value of the property. The school is owned and controlled fully by the Evangelical Unity of the Czech Moravian Brethren Church which holds biennial conventions, and is supervised by the following members of the executive committee:

Reverend Anthony Motyčka, Bellville, president; Reverend Joseph Bartoň, Granger, vice president; Reverend T. H. Horak, Caldwell, recording secretary; H. J. Baletka, financial secretary, Burlington; John J. Křenek, Caldwell, treasurer.

Since 1927 the executive committee of the church has been in full charge of the school. The Hus Memorial Association, which formerly helped the church in financing the undertaking, has been relieved of this obligation. No tuition charge is made the students, the whole expense being paid out of the general treasury fund of the church. The students room in the building free, if there is room, but pay their own board and personal expenses. When the school has no vacancies in the dormitories students stay with different church members in the city, or with relatives or friends. This plan, as first applied, has been found satisfactory, giving opportunity for young students, even of very moderate means, to have the benefits of the school's training.

The class of the summer of 1932, as shown in a photograph, includes the class members as: No. 1, Joseph Adolf Hegar; No. 2, Daniel Thevdon Hegar; No. 3, Reverend Joseph Hegar; No. 4, Noemi Ruth Hegar; No. 5, Mrs. Hegar; No. 6, Mrs. Hegar's mother; No. 7, first honor student, Miss Lydia Richter, Holland; No. 8, second honor student, John Daniel Bartoñ, Granger; No. 9, third honor pupil, James Hejl, Temple; No. 10, fourth honor student, Miss Bertha Novotny, West, McLennan County.

The picture of the "Hus Home" memorial school was made several years ago and does not show later improvements to the grounds. The picture of the pioneer founder of the school, Reverend Chlumsky, is typical of the man in his serious pose. The three pictures are illustrative only in a small way of the work that has been done, and is now in progress.

There were two Reverend Chlumskys who belong in Texas history. They were brothers. The younger brother was Louis Chlumsky who came first to Texas. He returned to his native land in the early '70s, having first induced the Reverend Juren, then a young seminary graduate, to come to Texas. The older brother, Reverend Adolph Chlumsky, came to Texas in 1889, having spent more than twenty years in the ministry in Bohemia. He came, according to those who knew him intimately, with the determination to reorganize the Moravian Brethren Church and this he succeeded in doing in 1904. His death occurred in February, 1919, and he is buried at Granger. A son of this pioneer missionary, John Chlumsky, lives in Houston and a daughter, Hermina, lives in Temple.

CHAPTER XXVII

BLAZING THE TRAIL

ON a wind-swept clearing of new ground, piled high with heaps of brush ready for the torch, red swirling flames tossed themselves skyward, roaring and crackling in unbridled fury, sucking unto their fiery circle whatever came within reach.

The full skirt of a pioneer woman, swelling out with the rush of the wind over the open space of the new ground clearing, was caught by the leaping flames as they swerved with the changing course of the wind. Immediately the body of the woman was enveloped in flames.

In the land of the pioneers, in the service of homemaking, she gave her life.

Today we are told that a new nationality is being created, European in its origin, but American in its character. Houston, San Antonio, Dallas, Fort Worth, El Paso, Amarillo, Waco and other Texas cities are not communities of an established nationality, but rather of one that is in the making.

*   *   *   *

While the early Czech settlers in Texas were building for finance and industry in the State, they were also establishing their claim to recognition in the realms of art, literature, music and the sciences.

Josef Jeřabek came to Texas in 1873 from Lipa, Moravia, Czechoslovakia. He was born on March 21, 1840, and died near Seymour, Texas, September 6, 1906. His wife, Rosalie Jeřabek, was born in Břeslovicich, Moravia, February 2, 1849, and died near Caldwell, Texas, on December 19, 1886.

Before emigrating to Texas, Josef Jeřabek was in the Austro-Hungarian Army, stationed on the Dalmatian border. During this time there were hostilities between Austria and Italy, soldier Jeřabek taking part in actual fighting. It was because of political and religious reasons that this family decided to leave the native home and come thousands of miles to Texas, a foreign land, still in the wilderness stage.

Josef and Rosalie Jeřabek had a baby daughter at the time of their emigration to America and Texas—Mary, a child of

224

FRANK JOSEF MARESH *and*
MARY JEŘÁBEK MARESH

three. She was born July 1, 1870, in Moravia. On leaving Moravia they set sail for Galveston, and from this port of entry passed through Houston on their way to Wesley, Washington County. They brought with them among treasured family possessions several books which have remained priceless heirlooms throughout the years. One of the books, a large family Bible, was purchased only a short time before the family sailed for America, the purchase price being Rosalie Jeřabek's own hair which she had cut from her head. Having such a heavy suit of hair, she decided to thin it, probably in contemplation of the long sea voyage. With this the Bible was purchased. The hair was a shade of light brown and must have by its beauty of texture and color been highly valued, since only a portion of the natural suit was required to purchase the Bible.

This book was published in 1863 for the commemoration of the One Thousand Year Jubilee of the turning of the Slavs to the Christian Religion. An interesting item in connection with the book is the inscription, "Publisher and Book Buyer, Seyfried, successor to Jeřabek, in Praha, 1863."

Among the other books was one called "Kancyonal," a book of Psalms and songs from religious authors, Czech and others, written for the purpose of education, inspiration and enjoyment. The date of publication was 1753, and the volume was rebound in Brně by Jan Jiři Šastla, book buyer and publisher, in the year 1823. The second title page carries the following:

"This new Kancyonal is anew published and placed in the light, to Our Holy God for the Honor and Glory and the Holy Order of Czech Evangelists who are sincerely asking for the Pure and Redeeming Word of God and for the wise and orderly teaching of the Order of the Czech Brethren."

Another book called "Postylla," was personally edited by Vicar Josef Ružička. This is the fourth edition and was published in Praha in 1856. The original volume was dated May 20, 1746. It is said that the book was buried for years, during a period from 1753 to 1823, when it was rebound. In addition, there is in the collection a small paper-bound booklet the objective of which is the preparation of children for their first communion and confirmation. The books are naturally printed in the Czech language, but different type is used, and the bindings are in keeping with the period.

Passing from the rare old books, it is interesting to visualize the reaction of those pioneers when removed from a thickly inhabited, informed and enlightened nation, to the environment of the wild country where they were shut off by reason of an alien tongue from all current events and literature; where they were confronted with sickness, privations and want; where the sole means of obtaining livelihood was through manual labor. But the price they paid for freedom—the hardships, privations, griefs and sorrows—was not counted as being too much. They did not mind walking several miles to and from church, or riding on a sled, or going to town for provisions and possibly a few sticks of candy for the children, once in several months.

Stopping first at Wesley, a community which had been settled as early as 1851, Josef Jeřabek built there a log structure to house himself and family. For three years they lived in this primitive home, moving from this location into Burleson County, where again a log house was built, in which the family lived until 1901.

It was here, in 1886, that Rosalie, the young wife, was burned to death in that new ground clearing while helping to tend the burning of the brush. The small figure of the woman wrapped in the flames, the fire fanned by the wind as she ran screaming in her terror, is one of the most vivid of the pictures hung on memory's wall, depicting scenes from the lives of the pioneers. Rosalie Jeřabek, wife of the pioneer who had sought freedom in a new land, contributed her life to the development of the new country.

In 1901 the husband moved farther west, going to Parker County, leaving behind the scene of this tragedy. From Parker County he moved on again in 1905, still blazing the trail to the westward, settling at this time in Baylor County, where in 1906, he met a tragic death, being killed in an accident with a team of run-a-way mules.

It seemed the irony of fate that the thing he loved so well should be the instrument of his death. The mules, a fine, large well-matched pair, always perfectly groomed, were the pride of Josef Jeřabek. With him at the time of the tragedy was a young nephew, A. J. Maresh Jeřabek. The boy was too young to realize what had happened.

That piece of new ground cleared in Burleson County back in 1886 was tilled. It produced crops of provender such as corn and cotton, potatoes, rye and oats, and when these were harvested they tided the pioneers over from year to year, while progress and development came gradually to Texas.

And there was little Mary Jeřabek, daughter of the pioneer couple, who had come with her parents to the new homeland when she was but a baby. She grew to young womanhood, marrying, at the age of sixteen, young Frank J. Maresh, twenty-five years old, who had been but a year in the new country.

Twenty-four days he spent at sea, the vessel storm-tossed, a seaman washed overboard to a watery grave, but young Maresh held on to his faith in the destiny that awaited him in Texas. Frank Josef Maresh was born on September 8, 1861, in Čermne, Bohemia. He was reared in a well-to-do Catholic family. When he came to Texas, it was in quest of adventure. He made the voyage at the age of twenty-four, landing at Galveston, where he was directed by Mr. Russek how to reach Brenham by rail. Here he met Josef Holik who directed him to Josef Bednař and Ignac Hejl who lived near Industry. He then walked to Wesley, where he stayed with Josef Marek for one month, and the end of which time he found work as a helper with Josef Ježek—who was building a house.

This was his first job in America. Later he dug a well for Jan Drgač. After this he worked in a cotton gin for Emil Spiess. While there he was bitten by a copperhead snake and was attended by Dr. McClean who was in later years the family physician at Caldwell. He then worked for Jan Marek for nine months at nine dollars a month. Following this he secured a job in August Ustynik's cotton gin in Wesley at twenty dollars a month. From there he went to Burleson County where he met Frank Haisler and Frank Marek, friends he knew in the old country. They persuaded him to stay. He found work in the cotton gin of Petr Mikeska and Jan Elšik at New Tabor. While working there, in 1887, Rosalie Jeřabek burned to death. After the tragedy he worked for Josef Jeřabek. There he met Mary Jeřabek who later became his wife. It was this same piece of land that Rosalie Jeřabek helped to clear and the same log house she helped to build that F. J. Maresh bought in 1901.

The first year they lived with the Mareks near Tunis and here their first child, Frank Boleslav Maresh, was born on November 7, 1888. Mr. Maresh then purchased a tract of untilled land adjoining the Jeřabek home place. This he cleared and developed into a farm home. The three other children, Henry, Rudolph Edward, and Rosalie were born there.

Scarcity of water was the pioneer's worry in those early days, and these young home-makers had no water. The young head of the family was resourceful, however. A small dam was built across a creek, thus forming an artificial lake. Below this a hole was dug, into which the water seeped. This provided the water supply, but it was at considerable distance from the house and worked a hardship, as all water had to be carried by hand from the water hole.

There came a visitor one day, a Mr. Bernard Hejl, and on being told of the problem of inadequate water supply, he offered to locate spring water. Like a magician the visitor started on his quest. With a little forked peach-tree twig held firmly in his hands, Mr. Hejl walked slowly, step by step. At a certain place the twig bent downward, pointing to the earth. Here, near the house where the magic wand pointed, water was found. The good work of the "witching twig" was carried on also at the father-in-law's place. Following this young Maresh hired a well-drilling outfit and took contracts for making wells, Mr. Hejl locating shallow spring water in a number of localities.

After living on this farm for some eight years, Mr. and Mrs. Maresh sold out and rented for a year. They then bought a farm from Josef Jeřabek and lived on it for three years. The family, suffering from illness most of the time, decided to move to Parker County.

During a residence of seventeen years in Burleson County, according to records kept by Mr. Maresh, he accumulated only $700.00, this being due to family sickness and poor crop yields.

When Henry and Rudolph were ten and eight years old respectively, they were permitted to take a bale of cotton to the market at Caldwell. They drove the wagon first to the cotton gin, where the bale was loaded onto the wagon, then to Caldwell, a distance of eight miles. On the market square the cotton buyers were encountered and the youth of the lads with a bale of cotton to sell furnished much amusement. Further interest was aroused when the buyers began bidding against each other for the bale. When the sale was finally made, and the check presented for payment at the bank, the teller plied the boys with questions as to their identity and why their father had not come along.

Nonchalantly they answered, "Oh, he's too busy," and thus settled the matter. On the way back home with seventy dollars in cash, the boys saw along the highway nice new tin signs and getting down from the wagon they collected the signs, thinking that their father could find use for them. When they proudly displayed their collection to their mother she was much distressed and sent Henry back immediately on horseback to replace each sign as it had been found.

The early schools attended by the children were the simple country institutions of the time. Miss Nora Duckworth was their first teacher in the Postoak school, Burleson County.

Later Frank, Henry, Rudolph and Rosalie attended the grade schools during the family residence in Baylor County, these years bringing about steady advancement.

There was organized the Maresh Band, and the two older boys, Frank and Henry, were included in the company of musicians, as drum players. Not being big enough to carry their drums they would take turn about, one carrying the drum while the other beat the music. One Sunday afternoon, while the band was practicing Sousa's "Washington March," little Rudolph, acting as band-master, his stick up in the air, was going through all the gyrations of the seasoned director when the family dog, a big black fellow by the name of Pinčl, decided to join in with his melodious voice. Unfortunately the dog got in the way of the proud band leader, tripping him, and without ceremony he came down to earth. Thus the big parade ended in a riot of laughter from the onlookers.

When the three brothers ranged in ages from five to ten years, the father was in position to furnish his own orchestra for dance music, he playing first violin, the eldest son, Frank, second violin, with the two younger, Henry and Rudolph, taking their turn at playing the cello or bass violin. This instrument towered above their heads.

During intermissions these young musicians were always the center of attraction, surrounded by the older folks who listened to the old country folk-songs with tears in their eyes, and wanted as a matter of appreciation, to give something to the young musicians. Many a bright coin found its way into the hands of the two little boys. As time went by the mother discouraged the sons from devoting too much of their interest to music. It was not because she did not herself love music, but she feared that it would interfere with the pursuit of chosen vocations. She tried to teach the children more of the practical side of life, the spirit of independence.

Reared in rural communities of Texas, the three sons and the daughter of the family attended rural schools. They grew to years of maturity in this environment, which could boast of the friendliness and loyalty of its people. Social life was restricted to simple affairs and activities, consisting mainly of neighborly gatherings, where music with the native folk songs were the features. Discussions of crops and the weather and matters of community welfare, with an occasional bit of politics, accounted for a part of the time given to visiting. In all there was to be found a dual loyalty—love for the native homeland, and devotion to the life in Texas. On one occasion, a social gathering of neighbors, Frank Maresh made the statement to his friends that his children would have a college education. The neighbors and friends at the time considered the matter as a joke. One of them suggested that an old lady who claimed to be a fortune-teller be allowed to read the fortunes of the children present, as one parent had made bold to set a college education as the goal for his children.

Henry R. Maresh, one of the three sons, was called up, and the woman who claimed the power of foretelling what was to come said that he would either be a preacher or a physician. For Rudolph, the younger brother, she saw only the profession of doctor of medicine. From this time, when he was but three years old, he has been called "doc" by schoolmates and intimate friends. How well the prognosticator told the story of what was to be is indicated by the careers of the brothers who are prominent physicians in Houston.

Frank J. Maresh, the father, was from his youth a musician. He believed that the music of a nation was a powerful influence. He spent his evenings and other spare hours with his music and in teaching his friends to love music and to be musicians.

From Parker County the family moved to Baylor County. At the time this section was on a boom. Here again the water supply came as before from a hole dug below a dam in an artificial lake. The extreme drought of one year caused this supply to give out and water had to be hauled in wagon tanks from Seymour, a distance of nine miles. Through all these years Frank J. Maresh's father-in-law, Josef Jeřabek, was his neighbor. In the third year of the residence in Baylor County he was killed in the accident of the runaway team.

Following this second tragedy in the family, Frank J. Maresh and family moved back to Parker County. The four children born to them in Burleson County, Frank B., born on November 7, 1888; Henry R., born on October 9, 1890; Rudolph E., born on October 17, 1892, and Rosalie—named for her pioneer grandmother— born on September 29, 1894, grew into years of maturity, perpetuating the life and memory of the grandparents who were martyrs to the cause of early Texas developments.

Frank B. Maresh, the oldest child, was looked upon more as a partner than a child, and when he began to talk, he asked his mother, "Mary, where is Frank?" meaning his father. At the age of six, during illness in the family, he was sent to summon the family doctor, a distance of five miles; it happened to be in the night, and when asked if he was afraid as he rode through the woods, he answered, "No, I pulled my cap over my ears and rode my horse faster." His education was in country public schools. At the age of eleven, he visited an uncle who was engaged in railroad construction in Houston and was placed in charge of a large number of Mexican and Negro laborers. His uncle also maintained a small store especially for his employees. Frank received his first business training here, waiting upon customers, and at times minding the store at night alone. One night, after the doors were barred, and the lights were out, Frank became aware that some one was apparently trying to force the door. He had a gun, but could not muster the courage to fire. The door continued to creak and Frank visioned himself in the hands of an unprincipled criminal. About that time he heard the grunt of a porker outside and found that the hog had been conveniently scratching his back on the door.

At the age of seventeen he took his business training in Roberts' Business College at Weatherford, Texas. After this he went to Houston to engage in business, with the same uncle, first as a helper, later as a partner. Just as he was beginning to make substantial progress, his two younger brothers decided to go to medical school, thus leaving the parents alone to manage a large wheat farm near Fort Worth. After careful deliberation he decided to go home to help his parents. There he spent several years.

His inclination was not toward farming as a life career, nor toward commercial pursuits. His real ambition was to study law. But during this time, through illness, the family fortune was lost, making it necessary for the two brothers to work their way through school. The interval on the farm, the illness in the family, the reverses in finances, all served to dampen his ambition to study law.

He then engaged in business in Weatherford. Later he moved to Fort Worth and there opened a general mercantile store. During this time he married Miss Margie Wolfenbarger. Two children were born, Henry and Frank Josef. Later he moved to Rosenberg, where he engaged in the business of automobile sales and accessories. There his third child, Madelyn, was born.

A belief in the transmission of influence is demonstrated in the instances of the two brothers, Dr. Henry R. and Dr. Rudolph E. Maresh of Houston. Their grandmother Jeřabek, born in Moravia, had two brothers who were doctors.

The mother of these sons, herself reared in the pioneer days of Texas, had little opportunity for education, but through reading she gathered the knowledge that enriched the splendid qualifications that had come to her through heritage. To her children she stressed always the importance of reading, and that her admonition might be carried out, she provided worthwhile reading matter in the home. In addition, she created the proper home environment through inculcating high ideals. Having done this much, the mother believed that her children would go through life creditably by their own efforts.

To them she often said during the years of their youth that by their own endeavors would they progress or retrogress, and that every progress had its price—that it rests solely with the individual to create his own world.

Henry left the Baylor home in 1908 for a course in Roberts' Business College at Weatherford. After two years in the commercial world, he attended the Parker-Palo Pinto County Summer School and later taught school for one year, entering the University of Texas at Austin in 1914, on individual approval, with his teacher's certificate as eight credits. He entered the Medical Department of the University at Galveston in 1915; enlisted to serve in the United States Army for the World War in the fall of 1917, serving during the time of the war in the United States Army Medical Corps; served as senior interne at St. Mary's infirmary, Galveston, being at the time editor of the *University Medical*. He was graduated from the School of Medicine in 1919 with Alpha Omega Alpha conferred in 1922. He served interneship at Jersey City, N. J., in 1920, and began the practice of medicine in Houston in 1921. An added interest is given the account of his progress when we know that he worked his way through school.

Dr. Rudolph E. Maresh followed almost identically the same educational route as that traversed by his brother. After finishing the grade school of Baylor County, he graduated from Seymour High School in 1911 and taught school in Burleson County in 1913-14, attending the University of Texas 1914 to 1915, entering the Medical Department of the University at Galveston in 1915. From the fall of 1917 through 1918-19 he served in the United States Government Medical Corps, with senior interneship at St. Mary's infirmary, Galveston, graduating from the School of Medicine in 1919, with Alpha Omega Alpha conferred in 1922. His interneship service was at Jersey City in 1920. He began the practice of medicine in Houston, associated with Dr. Henry R. Maresh, in 1921.

Rosalie married R. A. Newman on December 19, 1925, and two children, Mary Ann and Richard August, were born. R. A. Newman has followed various lines of business endeavors and now is engaged in automobile sales. Mr. and Mrs. Newman are residents of Houston.

*   *   *   *

It seems opportune to return now to the point previously made, that the Czech pioneers in Texas, while they were building for finance and industry, were also establishing their claim to recognition in the realm of the arts and sciences. A new country is no place for weaklings and these early Czech settlers fulfilled all requirements. They were living up to the standard of great Americans, one of whom, Theodore Roosevelt, set forth three prime requisites of any progressive race—that they work hard, fight hard at need, and that they have plenty of children.

It was George Eliot who wrote:

"How is a man to be explained unless you at least know somebody who knew his father and mother."

And so in the instance of Doctors Henry and Rudolph Maresh, it is interesting to know these things about their parents and their grandparents. Interesting to know some of the things which they have done or the part they have played in the progress and development of Texas.

Josef Jeřabek was a real pioneer. He was not content to confine his work and his interests to one spot after it had been developed. If he had accepted the easiest way, he would not have pushed forward into the new territory as he did in moving to Baylor County. Always he wanted to keep forging ahead. The hope of gain did not influence him in any of his activities, but instead it was always with the thought of the development and advancement of civilization that he labored.

"Maresh" is just a name, without any special significance, according to the two brothers of this pioneer house.

To the old Czech name Mareš, the final letter "h" has been added in the passing years. This name was always pronounced as though it had the final letter "h" but the name in that form was both misunderstood and mispronounced—and so it was finally decided to spell it Maresh.

Years passed in the Maresh family home, and one day when life was in the full season of harvest, when the toil of the day was not so arduous, and the cares of the home lightened, Mary Jeřabek Maresh, wife and mother, at the age of sixty-two years, finished her life's work. On July 18, 1932, at the home of her son, Dr. Rudolph E. Maresh, in Houston, death came to the mother who had grown to young womanhood under the roof of the pioneer's log cabin. She was laid to rest in one of the beautiful cemeteries of Houston.

There seems somehow to be a magic in the history covering the years of life, when it offers forgetfulness for the finish, to hold out instead, ever fresh before the vision the picture of her who was that little Mary, who came with her parents, Josef and Rosalie Jeřabek, to Texas to make a home in a new country and to help blaze the trail for a new nationality. And then the memory of the young wife and mother, who through her influence, lives on and on, today and tomorrow even as in the years that are gone.

Left:

Dr. Henry Rudolph Maresh

Houston, Texas

Collaborator in the preparation of this volume.

Right:

Dr. Rudolph E. Maresh

Houston, Texas

Brother of Dr. Henry R. Maresh

CHAPTER XXVIII

SONS OF PIONEERS

THERE is a small blue book in the office of Dr. Henry R. Maresh, of Houston, which might well be listed with the worthy volumes of this modern age.

The heart-beat of a child, the pulse of a mother, the hour of appointment when the doctor will give his ear to the heart and his finger to the pulse, is written in this book.

There are but three subjects for the author—Life, Love and Death. Without Life the other two would not be.

"The antidote for ailment must lie in part in the mode of living," says Dr. Maresh. "The surrounding conditions, produced by the varying sources of climate, geographical location, or super-imposed environment all become factors for good or ill in the well being of man."

In contemplation of the ills of mankind, the physician sits often alone in his office, long after patients and office attendants have gone for the day. On these occasions he relaxes, and for a time is in memory a boy again, tramping over virgin Texas soil, reliving his childish emotions and griefs. The ringing of the telephone brings him back from this sacred realm, and the patient, listening at the other end of the wire, hears the calm words of the physician, "I cannot give will power in capsules."

"There was also a doctor of Physik. He knew the cause of every maladye, were it of cold or of hete; or moist or drye." Thus wrote Geoffrey Chaucer in "The Canterbury Tales."

And today there is Dr. Henry R. Maresh, who says that some day he hopes to find the panacea for all ills. He did not say this in just so many words, but his intense interest in the subject inspires the thought of the writer, and with it a possible panacea to be discovered at the end of the trail.

On entering the private consulting office of Dr. Maresh he was found seated at his desk with a tattered map of Texas spread out before him. He smoothed out the frayed edges, and held deftly together, with fingers skilled in surgery, the parts of the country threatened with separation through the broken creases where the map had been folded and unfolded many times.

235

"I have traveled over almost every section of the State," he explained. "I know the people and the communities, and I know the conditions under which they live. It is for this that I go here and there and everywhere, throughout the length and breadth of Texas. I go places that I may study not only people, but the conditions under which they live—that I may understand their environment. I want to know the source of the ills from which mankind suffers. Calomel and aspirin and quinine must have their prototypes in Nature's remedy cabinet."

Dr. Maresh knows intuitively many things which he has not found in books. Having read books, he seeks new avenues of thought. The humanization of medicine has been the theory put into practice by Dr. Maresh.

A bright yellow duck standing in a vantage point on top of his desk, holding in its stiff wooden bill a card on which is inscribed, "To a quack of a good doctor," drew the conversation of visitor and doctor from the subject of bodily ills and human frailties. A very good friend, while traveling abroad, sent him the duck.

"I came near not being a doctor of any kind," Dr. Maresh confided, as the conversation veered back to his profession.

He once thought he would be a preacher. He wanted to do the greatest good to the greatest number, and for a time it seemed that he could best accomplish this by entering the ministry. Had he not changed his mind there would have been no occasion for the yellow duck with the open bill and that message from a far-away friend.

The attention of Dr. Maresh was called to the matter of Talmadge having written: "The scientists tell us whence we come; the theologians tell us where we are going; while the fact remains for us to consider that we are here."

But long ago Dr. Maresh knew that he had chosen wisely when he decided to become a doctor of medicine. The realization of his great mission in the practice of medicine has assumed tangible form. Many of the office blue books, their pages filled, have been closed and filed safely away through the years—more than a decade—and a new book has taken the place on the doctor's desk.

Born in an atmosphere in which was blended the influence of the Old World and the new, Henry Maresh early in life became a student. Everywhere around him he found work to do.

Plutarch wrote of Pericles that he never walked in any street save that which led to the market place and the council hall.

Henry R. Maresh has walked not only in the streets of public places, where he was seen of men, but in the byways and hedges where he could lend a hand to the lowliest. He has walked in the great open spaces, where nature recognizes all men as equal, and where the great universe speaks to all men in one voice.

Years ago Henry Maresh built a stairway in the family home in Parker County. It was not only a good stairway, but an artistic one. His parents were more than just mother and father to him; they were, as he has said, "his pals." Like the stairway that started at the bottom and made its way gracefully and surely to the top, Henry R. Maresh has gone upward. And the end is not yet.

On entering the private consulting room of Dr. Maresh the visitor—or patient, as the case may be—sees immediately a miniature boat with all sails set which reposes on top of a well-filled book case. It is a replica of a quaint old sailing vessel of the pioneer days. Perchance the original may have carried some sturdy Czech pioneers into a new land. The old sailing vessel exemplifies a loyalty to tradition and a love of travel on the part of its possessor.

As his pioneer ancestors came to Texas in quest of a new home and country, with the privileges of freedom and the opportunities for progress and development, so this son of a pioneer has kept on in quest of that which will benefit the human family. He has inherited many characteristics of his people. He has the tenacity of purpose and the courage which has ever characterized the Czechs. To their country he looks with love and native pride, but to Texas he gives his life and its service, his love and his loyalty as a citizen, because it is the land of his birth, the home of his ancestors by adoption.

"It is only ignorance," he says, "that causes misunderstandings. If you understand the language of the people when you travel in foreign countries, things will not seem strange or queer or uncouth. And the same thought is applicable to conditions at home. Ignorance of things and people bring about doubt and misunderstanding."

The Blind Bard wrote in his "Paradise Lost:" "Man's first disobedience and the fruit of that forbidden tree brought death into the world, and all its woe."

Dr. Maresh would like to restore the lost paradise. His quest is in behalf of humanity, and his work largely a labor of love. To keep fit he believes in taking a Saturday afternoon and Sunday off, and on these occasions he gets in his automobile and goes into the country. He finds his greatest pleasure in contact with people in their own environment. During mid-summer he takes a vacation of from one to three months. During one of these some years ago, he made his first visit to Czechoslovakia, where he visited the places of his ancestors' birth and residence.

He claims that environment is the best teacher. That if you have eyes and can see, and an open mind and the wish to apply it, there is nothing to keep you from acquiring both education and culture.

"We become a part of everything with which we come in contact. Heredity comes first. Without this there would be a void. Then comes environment. The two work together. We inherit certain qualities and these qualities remain dormant until they are quickened by the five senses in the form of experience. Then each one of us, through endowment, effort, and circumstance, in proportion to our capacity and ambition, become what we are." Adding to this philosophy, Dr. Maresh says:

"In order to reach our goal we first have to know definitely what we want. Then we have to keep that goal positively and continuously before our eyes.

"During a period when I was between eight and nine years old, a very important incident came into my life. *Svoboda,* a weekly newspaper, owned, edited and published by Judge Augustin Haidušek, of LaGrange, Texas, was carrying among its features a serial story 'Ishmael,' by Mrs. E. D. E. N. Southworth. On the day the paper came, either mother or father would read the story aloud. I became interested, and as the succeeding chapters appeared I was completely fascinated. As I had to wait until the family gathered in the evening, and either mother or father had time or the inclination for reading, I would get impatient. I began to peep over the shoulder of the reader in my intense interest and before the story had progressed very far I was reading for myself. This incident marked two important milestones in my life. I learned to read Czech with very little effort, enjoyably and understandingly, and so quickly that when I think of it today I am astonished.

"It brings to mind the thought that when there is the incentive to do things—a goal to be reached—the greatest attainment can be achieved, for, after all, the supreme wonder in the world is man when he wills to do. The story of Ishmael impressed me profoundly and permanently."

Referring to the years of childhood and school-days, Dr. Maresh says.

"Our father inherited a musical talent and, purely for the love of music, followed the urge of this talent. When he set sail for Texas he brought with him his violin and his prayer-book. The violin is a genuine 'Stainer,' and has inside the inscription: '*Jacob Stainer in Abfam prope Oenipontum 1647.*' Jacob Stainer, the famous violin maker, lived in the village of Abfam (Absan), which was *prope* (near) Innsbruck, which is in the Greek, Oenipontum.

"After his arrival in Texas he became popular because of his musical ability, as well as because of his affable and genial disposition. Soon he found that this talent could be turned to profitable account. Beginning when we were three years old we three boys were taught to sing. We sang the old folk-songs, and later Frank was taught to play what was called second violin, while I played the 'cello. As a trio we furnished the music for weddings, home and local community dances and various other entertainments. Each of the pioneers had his or her favorite piece of music from the native homeland of Czechoslovakia and, as was the custom over there, whenever a music lover had the price of a tip, or a treat, the band was called on to play the favorite piece. This always placed the donor in the position of a man of influence and affluence. So it was in the pioneer days of Texas, but in the instance of the Maresh Trio, there was no tip expected, although we got the tips just the same, as there were many who asked for the playing of their favorite pieces.

"Father played several instruments. He organized and conducted several brass bands. In these Frank played the drum. During marches, because Frank was too small for the weight of the drum, either Rudolph or I would help carry the instrument.

"With these bands father played at 'fête days,' holiday celebrations and large weddings. He kept up his music through all the years, and today, at the age of seventy-three years, he still enjoys the touch of the old violin and finds pleasure in his music. The musical career of Frank and myself ended in 1902 when we moved away from the home in Burleson County to the new location in Parker County. Rudolph learned to play the violin with much of the skill of the artist and has not given up his music. Even today, with the stress of professional duties demanding his time and attention, he plays the violin with the touch of the master. Rosalie, the youngest, plays the piano.

"During the years when we lived in Burleson County, some member of the family was continuously sick. After deducting the doctor's fee and the cost of the medicine, there was little left of the income derived from the farm. We had chills and fever. The doctor would come with his 'pill bag.' I remember his spatula. He always called for baking soda, and then would measure by guess, soda and calomel, antifebrine and quinine. These chills and fever ailments came so often that father finally bought the drugs and measured out the doses himself. In 1900 arrangements were made to move to North Texas, but grandfather Josef Jeřabek was unable to sell his farm, so we rented a farm from Henry Ginzel near Caldwell, where we lived for one year. During this period the family suffered more than ever from illness. In 1900, at the time of the Galveston storm, sister Rosalie and I were desperately ill. At the time the wind that accompanied the storm broke a huge limb from a tree and part of it fell across the house. The next day Buffalo Creek overflowed and it was impossible to get a doctor. In time of need it seems that the Lord took care of us, and somehow we survived.

"The next year we bought grandfather's farm and moved there, he occupying an adjoining place. This year Rudolph was stricken with an acute illness, probably infantile paralysis, as it left him paralyzed from his waist down. He was taken to Marlin and San Antonio, but his condition failed to improve, but instead seemed to be hopeless. This must have been the 'last straw,' for we decided to move, and selected Parker County as our destination. We left part of the household furnishings, and all farm implements and cattle, in the care of a friend, and moved to the new location. As is usually the case, this was the last of the old home place. It was finally sold for $1,400.00, which represented the accumulations of fourteen years.

"Mother, Frank, Rudolph and Rosalie, with the few things they carried along, were put on the train and started for Weatherford. With two little Spanish mules hitched to a covered wagon, and one horse tied on to the rear of the vehicle, father and I took the overland route from Caldwell, through Cameron, Rosebud, Cleburne to Weatherford. It took us nine days to make the trip. Even then I had dreams of seeing the world, and this was the beginning of the realization.

"We stayed three years in Parker County. The first year we were about three miles, the second and third years, about twelve miles from Weatherford. During these years we rented a place from Dr. William Campbell. When a trip was to be made to town we started early in the morning and returned late in the afternoon. It required that much time. Today the distance and the same amount of business can be attended to in one hour.

"We were pleased with the move to Parker County as the country was more healthful for us. Also the prime object of the move—the recovery of Rudolph's health—was realized. He was taken to Dr. William Campbell at Weatherford, who advised immersion in hot water to which some kind of salt was added, this treatment to be for one hour at a time, twice daily. In two or three months Rudolph was walking. This instance brings to mind the treatment and cure effected in the case of Franklin D. Roosevelt who found relief and restoration of paralyzed muscles in the natural waters of Warm Springs, Georgia.

"There was one drawback here. Mother and father shared one aspiration in common: they wanted their children to have an education. While we lived in Parker County the school was five miles away, and in bad weather we were unable to attend. In spring and fall we were needed at home. Farming on a small scale, producing only corn and cotton, is not a money-making business, especially when you are operating on a rental basis.

"A new section of West Texas country was in process of development in Baylor County and offered opportunities for better conditions. One or two rainy seasons made West Texas a most promising location as the crop yields were splendid. So it was decided that we would move in the fall of 1903.

"Again by train and covered wagon the move was made. We bought a quarter section of land. Grandfather Jeřabek bought some land adjoining. But here, too, we found the disadvantages that go with the development of a new country—the exterminating of prairie dogs, the careful avoidance of rattlesnakes, and being kept awake by the barking of coyotes, being among the things we did not like. In order to save money, I bought a blacksmith's outfit and learned how to shoe horses and sharpen plowshares. Later from my uncle I learned the use of the square and saw.

"Together we built several houses and two public school buildings. Then for a time I hauled wheat. Following this I struck a bargain to haul cotton-seed from a gin to a ranch. From this work I made the most and the quickest money of any of my previous undertakings. Finally, at seventeen I had enough to take me through Roberts' Business College in Weatherford.

"In passing from the life in Baylor County I recall several incidents that made a vivid impression on my mind. Grandfather was killed in 1906 by a run-away team of mules. A few months after this tragedy in the family Aunt Theresa was bitten by a rattlesnake while she and I were working in the field. I immediately applied a torniquet above the knee, and with my pocket-knife split open the wound. This was my first piece of surgery. Up to this time I had been unable to kill a chicken or a hog. When I had given this first aid treatment I unhitched a pair of Spanish mules that I had been working, harnessed them to the farm wagon and rushed my aunt seven miles to a doctor. She was very sick, but recovered. Then I recall the first West Texas sand storm. Black, ominous clouds, rolling apparently on the earth came toward me so rapidly that I thought some dreadful calamity was at hand. These were the occasions that made you acquainted with the inside of a storm cellar.

"In those days I attended Sunday school and church because I enjoyed singing. There were also singing schools and I attended these. I learned to read and write music. In due time a singing school convention of three counties was held. I was selected as a delegate; also to be on the program to sing a duet. In those days, an event of this kind was a gala affair. Everybody attended. The program carried the announcement that there would be 'all day singing and dinner on the grounds.'

"As it happened I did not have a decent horse to drive, so I hitched one of the little Spanish mules to a buggy, and with my credentials as a delegate, drove to the convention, thinking that no one would notice my rig. When I went on the stage to sing Professor Thomas, master of ceremonies, introduced me as the Beau Brummel, and added that I was matrimonially inclined, otherwise I would not have driven a mule as a delegate to the convention. I was naturally timid and bashful, so it is not hard to imagine my embarrassment. When I tried to sing I could not find my note, but Professor Thomas kindly set me right.

"The number of days that I went to school were few, but mother looked after the 'home work,' and took care that there were always good books in the house to read. In addition she provided current weekly publications and these were regularly read and discussed by the family.

"When I left home at seventeen for my course in business college I was ambitious and anxious to learn. I took shorthand and typing, mastered the course in three months, then taught the same subject in the same school for two months, when I was offered a position as stenographer with the C. D. Hartnett Wholesale Grocery Company at Weatherford. I remained with that concern for a little over two years. Soon after I became associated with the firm I learned the principles of business; learned that in order to count profit you had to subtract from the sale price the cost, overhead and depreciation; that in order to satisfy a customer you had to deliver the goods you represented and not sell a customer merchandise which you knew he could not use. Simple fundamental business principles, but I found in after years that they apply to all human endeavors whether you are selling material commodities or service.

"Mr. Hartnett was considered the best buyer in the south. He would acquaint himself with the goods he bought, study the supply, probable big yield or shortage, past and present prices, and from this knowledge would forecast a possible demand for a certain commodity. In this manner he learned intelligently and profitably the principles of buying and selling. Thinking that I knew these principles, I tried my hand at selling, and succeeded very well. When vacation time came for the bookkeeper I was able to carry on his work.

"During my stay in Weatherford I lived with D. C. Noble and family. At that time Mr. Noble was a deacon in the Christian Church, and Mrs. Noble taught in the Sunday school. I joined the Sunday school class, became a member of the church choir, and took an active part in the Christian Endeavor Society. The minister was young and ambitious and we became fast friends. Under his guidance I had an opportunity to study the Bible. I took a course in training for the work of Bible teaching, and became a certified Sunday school teacher. Mr. Vivrett, a deacon in the church, offered as a prize a red letter Bible to any one who would read the Bible from cover to cover in the shortest time, and give the impressions the reading made in the most concise form. I was fortunate enough to win the Bible.

"During this time I had occasion to meet some highly interesting people who had moved to Weatherford from Utah. They attended the Christian Church, but were deeply interested in theosophy. They interested Mr. Noble in the study, providing an abundance of literature on the subject. I studied theosophy under this environment and influence. Mr. Hartnett was a devout and prominent Irish Catholic. Through him I met a cultured young priest. We became good friends. He gave me literature and books. Thus, during a period of about three years, I became acquainted with three branches of religious teaching—Protestant, Catholic and Theosophy.

"I took an interest in the small town social affairs, most of which originated through church acquaintances. I observed that the manner and mode of social entertainments of Weatherford were quite different from that of the country districts.

"I remained with the Hartnett Company at Weatherford for over two years, then went to one of their branch houses in Fort Worth, where I remained for over a year. By this time I had a pretty good business training. My opportunities in the business world were promising, but, regardless of prospects, I was dissatisfied. Business at that time, without fundamental educational qualifications, meant to me only the accumulation of dollars. When I went to Fort Worth, fortune favored me in that I found as a roommate a young lawyer, C. K. Bullard, who had just graduated from the University of Texas. He was kind, broadminded, intelligent, very ambitious and imbued with the vision of the great things he would do in the future.

"It was not long after my arrival in Fort Worth that Bullard took the mumps. The other roomers became frantic with the fear of contagion, and sprayed throats and held noses and ran down the stairway two treads at a time. I nursed Bullard through his illness and although I had never had mumps, I did not catch the disease. We became better friends through this contact of patient and nurse. He noticed that I liked to read and offered the use of his library which, in the main, consisted of his text books of the University. I read Blackstone with great interest. I visited court with my friend to listen to the proceedings and see at first hand the processes of the court. At this time the famous Sneed murder case of Amarillo was being tried in Fort Worth. On several Saturday nights we visited the City Hall to see the law in its first stages of action. Also I visited the 'bull pen,' where the prisoners were brought for 'sorting.'

"One Sunday I was reading a book of poems by Bullard's favorite, Robert Burns. He asked me for the book, and as it happened I had just read a poem which he had discussed in class while he was at the University. He asked for my interpretation, and on my giving it he said that I had to go to the University. I explained to him that I had never had a day in high school, and that entering the University was out of the question.

" 'Any one who can read and interpret literature as you have done is eligible to a university,' he said.

"I had given him my confidence in some part during the time of our acquaintance, but with this interest on his part, I forgot my usual reserve and timidity and confided my ambitions. I told him that for two years I had been searching diligently—weighing, comparing, deducting, both through literature and from people—trying to fit myself into the intricate scheme of life. My ambition was to do good, to help others, to do something worth while. I had no desire to gain fame or to accumulate money. That was the farthest from my idea of what life should be. I wanted to follow a rôle in life that would be equally beneficial to me as well as to the people I came in contact with. I wanted to be a teacher by force of attraction rather than by coercion. Not by precept, but by example. I had in mind four vocations to consider: Business, the Ministry, Law and Medicine. I had an intelligent knowledge of the principles of all four, just as a buyer would know his goods before he bought them. Business to me had meant only money, exchange, barter—goods for money —money for money. Should I ever want to do good in this world, it would be through money, and I realized that any real gain or benefit in life is gotten only through personal effort and that a material gift is worthless.

"The ministry appealed to me, but here, too, I had some understanding that I had gained by being intimately associated with church pastors. This had given me the opportunity of being both on the stage and in the audience. I had learned that the average person accepts the preacher on Sunday and Wednesday evenings, and abides by his teachings. But these days are set aside for this purpose and are looked forward to either with joy, or fear of the gain or the loss of favor in the public eye of society, or the hereafter. This appealed to me, however, because the environment seemed to be the best to be had.

"Law, to my mind, was a noble profession, but it gave me the thought that as a lawyer you were usually called on after the ox had gotten in the mire. I learned that you must defend with equal vehemence, both the right and the wrong.

"Medicine appealed to me most of all. I had observed that every doctor has some patients more or less who have implicit confidence in him—that his advice is accepted as being unbiased, genuine and true; that it is given for the patient's sole benefit, and if a doctor has any desire to do good, he has a better opportunity than any other individual. But, I questioned in my mind, could I follow this profession? Lancing boils and cutting people filled me with horror. It was later in life that I learned that I had the wrong perspective. Today I realize that it is conserving life through knowledge.

"That Sunday afternoon I laid my cards on the table and Bullard thought I should choose medicine. He told me how I could go through college. That I could enter on individual approval and work my way through.

"Up to now mother had been my sole confidant. She knew my

every thought, desire and ambition. She never made a decision for me, but always gave me thoughts and ideas and I dare say that many of them bewildered me. She told me that my decisions had to be in crystal form. I knew that she wanted me to study medicine, but she wanted me to acquire a vision of a complete possible future.

"I went home and told her of my decision. As I saw in her expression the confidence and satisfaction, a vision came before me as if from total darkness. I could see a clear road leading toward my goal. From then on there was no wavering. That was a momentous day for me, not because I made a decision, but because the possibilities of the decision were unfolded before me in the most vivid detail. Along this visionary road into the future, at every milestone, there was the icon of Mother. It was a kind of an apotheosis of her. In later years, when mother died, I realized that it was not so much the physical loss, but that indescribable, imperceptible something she had contributed as my pal, my confidant, my Supreme Court, so to speak, that made the loss so profound.

"Dr. Campbell, our family physician, had told mother that I would make a good doctor. C. K. Bullard, from the lawyer's viewpoint, thought that I was suited for this profession. But everyone else thought that I had lost my head in giving up a marvelous business opportunity for a try at the art of medicine.

" 'You will never make it,' I heard on all sides.

"In 1911, my brother, R. E., finished high school at Seymour. I thought it would be easier for me to have some help with the fundamental studies, so I tried to persuade him to go to college with me. But the idea did not appeal to him. He had already decided to teach school.

"We finally struck a bargain, that after he had taught one year, we would both go to the University. He did not at the time have a teacher's certificate, but he planned to get one by taking a course at a Summer Normal. In the spring of 1912 I decided to gather the subjects for a second grade teacher's certificate and read them at home. I took an examination and just before the Summer Normal opened I received notice that I had passed. Then I attended the normal with R. E. with the idea of working off the high school subjects and working up to a first grade certificate. This I intended to use as units for entrance credits to college. By the time the Summer Normal was over, R. E. had signed a contract to teach school at Shiner, Texas. A little later he found out that he could teach the school of his choice near Cladwell. But he had already signed up for the other school.

"So we struck another bargain. I would take over the Shiner school, thus making it possible for him to teach at Caldwell. In the spring we were both to go to Austin.

"This attempt on my part to learn the high school four-year course in six weeks at a Summer Normal was preposterous, considering the fact that I had never had instruction in any of the subjects. Without the help of R. E. it would have been impossible. While I made the grade, it was the hardest piece of work I have ever done. It marked the beginning of my gray hair. It was a dear lesson, but through it I realized that in a land of opportunity many things can be accomplished.

"In the fall R. E. and I went to our respective schools, armed with our teacher's certificates and nothing else. I did not know how to form classes, or divide periods. I hardly knew how many hours of instruction were to be given. I said little, kept my eyes open, thinking, feeling my way. Outwardly I tried to appear as a teacher should; inwardly I was filled with fear and dread. Nothing happened, however. I got along nicely and the pupils seemed to find no difference between the other teachers and myself. The enrollment was large and I persuaded the superintendent to give me an assistant. I have every reason to believe that the teaching and the school were successful. I worked and played with the children, and it was not necessary to administer corporal punishment a single time during the entire school term, which was a record.

"I carried with me, as I took up the work of teacher, books on adult and child psychology, ethics, logic and Emerson's Essays. I found psychology and ethics intensely interesting. I tried to put into practice, on myself and my pupils, the fundamental principles of both. I tried to convey to my pupils that my purpose as their teacher was to guide them; that they had work to do; that only that which they gained through their own efforts could be of any value to them. I gave the customary examinations, but I knew my pupils.

"After years of search I had finally decided on my goal in life. The eight months spent in teaching school were happy ones. But there was the goal ahead. When at the age of eight or nine years I had read about the volcano Vesuvius, it was my ambition to go to the top and look inside the crater, because as a child, I could not comprehend the great phenomenon of nature. And so when I got acquainted with the great mountain of science that I knew as Medicine, I also wanted to know it in its fullest sense, not just merely the manner and method of practice. I saw a pathway leading to the top of the mountain, but I knew there would be difficulty in climbing. I knew also that the point from where I had to start would make the climb extremely hard. But, I thought, what is life without the struggle? It is true that I had used school teaching as a stepping stone. I had in the work of teaching the opportunity for studying human nature. In books I studied fundamental principles of human conduct. For material I had a part of the Old World transplanted into the field of my work, to the New World.

"Shiner and Moulton, small community towns, twelve miles apart, were located at either end of a strip of rich, black sandy loam, three miles wide. A road leading through the middle of this trip connected the two towns. On one side lived Germans and on the other Czechs. Midway between these places, beside the road and on a beautifully wooded stream, was Dickson schoolhouse. Out of an enrollment of about one hundred pupils, there were half Czechs and half Germans, with two or three Americans and three or four Mexicans. That was the setting of my school work.

"Ethnologically the Czechs and the Germans were unrelated. Politically, in the Old Country, they had been life-long enemies. Both were trained in awe and veneration of the higher-ups. Each retained his respective native tongue and both acquired English.

"It was *Pane učitel* in Czech and *Herr Professor* in German, both meaning Mr. Teacher. This relationship offered a rare opportunity for character analysis—a study of American character formation, the workings of 'the Melting Pot.'

"When R. E. and I were through with our teaching, we took stock of our possibilities. We had each saved some money, but not enough to go through the University. We expected no help from home. In the fall of 1913 we headed for Austin and registered for the last one-year pre-medical course. We were told that it would be very hard because the medical schools were requiring better preparations in order to be classed. We had a lot of determination—or it may have been just the lack of knowledge—about the thing that we were after, but at least we knew what we wanted.

"Here again was a new environment, but one of undoubted fascination. To go to college and see the world. Through these two mediums I expected to gain both education and culture. I always looked upon college as the training place for body, mind and soul. I thought that when you went through college you were turned out a finished product of refinement. But I am sorry to admit that I was disillusioned to a certain extent. The instructor in English taught us that the primary purpose of a college was to strengthen our souls and broaden our minds; to teach us to associate with men and be men.

"R. E. entered the University with full entrance credits. I entered on individual approval. My teacher's certificate gave me eight units, which left me six to make up, including foreign language. I knew Czech, but that language was not in the curriculum. For the end of the term I was preparing to take examinations in agriculture, typewriting and bookkeeping. I went to Dr. Battle, then acting-president of the University, with the request that I be permitted to take Czech under the Department of German. He promised, but when the time came to take the examination said that it could not be done as it was not in the catalogue. This, of course, meant one year's delay just to make up a foreign language entrance requirement.

"At this time we were staying in the same rooming house with Senator Myron Blaylock and his brother. We were very good friends. I related my plight to Mr. Blaylock and asked what could be done. I also told him that previous, but unsuccessful attempts had been made to put Czech into the curriculum. He had a large following in the House of Representatives, and it was his suggestion that we select some other leader to present the bill and that he would line up his followers to vote favorably on it. He asked not even a mention in return.

"Honorable Frank H. Burmeister at this time was slashing appropriations for all higher education quite successfully. This was during Jim Ferguson's régime, when the governor made the statement that the people of Texas had gone 'hog wild' after higher education. At this time there were seven Czech newspapers and over 100,000 Czechs in Texas. Mr. Burmeister was politically ambitious, and could foresee the entire Czech following lined up in his support.

"He presented the bill and it passed by a large majority. Thus it came about that a chair in Slavic language was created in the University of Texas and the Legislature made an annual appropriation of $1,800.00 for its maintenance. Charles Knižek was selected to occupy the chair. I took the examination immediately and as a consequence mine is the first name officially registered in the Department of Slavic Language.

"At the end of the 1913-14 semester I made the one-year Pre-Medical course with honor grades, and was eligible for

Phi Beta Kappa, and five and one-half of the six entrance units. For this one-half unit I made arrangements with Professor Prokosh to study German at home and in the fall to take the examination. About two weeks before the examination I wrote him and he replied that he had no record of such an arrangement; that it could not be done. I looked through the catalogue and selected American History, read it, took the examination and went to Galveston.

"I derived great satisfaction from my one year's stay in Austin. My horizon broadened, my vision became clearer and I became acquainted with what we are pleased to call the 'college spirit.' It was not possible to gain much actual knowledge in such a short time, but when you ask a lawyer whether he knows what is in his huge library, his answer will be, 'No, but I know how to find what I need.' I spent a lot of time in the University Library and, like the lawyer, I learned how to find what I needed."

It was in the fall of 1915 that Henry R. Maresh first went to Galveston to enter the Medical Department of the University of Texas. After being accepted, and having registered, he went off to himself and emitted a sigh of satisfaction. The thing had been done. The great obstacle which every one had talked about had been surmounted.

The first year in the school of medicine is devoted to the teaching of hard, dry, fundamental facts.

"I learned early in life," Dr. Maresh says, "through the building trade that any good house must have a solid foundation and a secure and stable structure—that the walls and the windows, the doors, the floors and the roof could then be filled in according to taste and inclination. And I found that the first two years in the school of medicine represent the foundation and the structure of all future success. This is based on the soundness of foundation and structure.

"The third year in school was easier, as Rudolph and I were permitted to act as waiters in the student hall, and this paid for our board, at the time the biggest item we had to encounter in going to school.

"According to the usual custom of the student body at the end of each school year the election of officers takes place. There was one office with some pay attached—editor of the *University Medical*—and it was suggested that I run for this. About three weeks before the election took place, I entered the race, and won with a vote of three to one.

"Through the influence of Dr. George H. Lee, we were accorded senior interneship at St. Mary's Infirmary, Galveston. This provided both board and lodging, and we were equipped to make our way through school. But this was not the finish. We were inducted into the United States Army, and this meant going to school, training for Army service, serving as internes and still looking after the editing of the *Medical*.

"When it was all over we graduated with honors and eventually had the honorary Alpha Omega Alpha conferred."

Added to all this experience there is treasured in the memory of the two brothers the romance of living in an attic.

"I had read of the student in Paris, or of some aspiring young artist in search of name and fame living in an attic. Some times the story even went so far as to have the aspirant die of starvation. While our rations were at times rather scant and frugal, we survived and eventually were none the worse for the experience.

"Our attic was in the Reymershoffer home. True to the Reymershoffer characteristics of being hospitable and helping those in need, we were taken in and made welcome. During the time of our residence in the attic we did many odd jobs. These included clerking in stores, plumbing and acting as floor-walkers in some of the Galveston business establishments.

"In June, 1919, having served as internes for one year in Galveston, Rudolph and I were able to secure senior interneships in Jersey City. In anticipation of this trip I gathered all the literature I could about New York City. From pictures and descriptions, I knew the Woolworth Building, St. Johns, Broadway, Fifth Avenue, the elevated and underground transits, museums, parks, Brooklyn Bridge, Statue of Liberty, Hudson River and Tube, Palisades and Coney Island. This trip was the one great thrill of my life. I had not expected to be able to travel so soon. I knew, or rather felt, that I would have to practice many years before having money enough to travel that far and see so much of the world.

"We arrived in New York in the late afternoon, and stopped in one of the big downtown hotels near Times Square. At night the scene was dazzling. I had never seen anything like it. It held me spellbound. There were traffic lanes built of high banks, or walls of buildings and in the bed of the street, the flowing stream of people and vehicles. In Texas I had seen mighty rivers in flood stage, roaring and rushing onward, carrying huge logs, trees, houses and even dead animals. I had seen large tributaries flowing in, adding more water and more debris. I had seen the streams empty into the Gulf, becoming a part of a great whole. Here one found the origin, direction and destination, a kind of steadiness and harmony, but not so in this scene in New York.

"Everybody was apparently oblivious to everything but the direction they pursued. They would look at the sidewalk straight ahead. Sometimes they paused at a shop window. It reminded me of a cowboy riding the range, asleep on his horse. I found that the average New Yorker knows where he lives, knows how to get to his work, knows the way to the theatres and to Coney Island. He knows that the sun rises in New York and sets in New Jersey.

"I found that the Texan knows more about New York than the New Yorker knows about Texas.

"I have traveled much since that time, but never in three days or any number of days have I encountered so much concrete evidence of the powerful influence that Nature plays in shaping the destiny of man.

"Some may claim that all men are born equal and that man has the ability to create his own environment, but after observing some pertinent facts, one may be forced to revise the statement to the effect that all men are born to equal opportunities and the man who has the capability to adapt himself to his environment is the one who goes far and does things. In medicine we associate certain ailments and diseases with environment and social standing. It is true that certain diseases have no respect for class, creed or station.

"But going back to the subject of environment, we find in Texas spots where the soil is not rich enough to produce healthy vegetation. One might question how it can support strong, healthy, energetic people. In the rich soil country why could not man be more creative and have a better chance to make good in the world?

"In the industrial districts man certainly is subjected to more physical hazards, and how he builds his body, depends on the food he consumes. In the metropolitan area he would be subject to the ailments due to crowded social conditions and either become a cog in a wheel of a large machine or else by rare chance rise above the turmoil and become a peer.

"This trip was my first practical and most significant lesson in applied medicine. I realized that in order to be of service to my patients as human beings, both for their mental and physical bodies, I would have to know people; to know where and how they live; that my books would serve as a guide, but to really learn, understand and properly evaluate, I would have to go among them, actually be one of them."

* * * * *

It was not one day, but rather one midnight when Henry Maresh saw Vesuvius, a fulfillment of his boyhood dream.

"Traveling in company with Dr. Henry C. Haden of Houston, during a summer vacation spent in Europe in 1930, I saw Vesuvius. We left the city of Rome by train in the afternoon of July 22nd and on nearing Naples I had my first sight of the volcano. For this I had been waiting since I was a child.

"Heavy clouds of smoke were rolling from the volcano's crater. It looked majestic and complacent from a distance, but we had been told that it was more active than usual. My immediate desire was to go nearer, even to the very top.

"We stopped at Hotel Parker, beautifully situated on the side of a high hill overlooking the Bay of Naples from the west. To form a setting for the view it might be explained that the hotel was situated at the point of a 'V,' Vesuvius being at the end of the left arm and the Isle of Capri at the end of the right arm, the space between being filled by the Bay of Naples and the arms connected by a semi-circle of mountainous seashore for a distance of about twenty miles. The shore for the whole distance was occupied by towns and villages. At sunset, the sun at your back illuminating the whole with a fiery glow of radiant colors, one gets a picture beyond description.

"On the night of our arrival, at about 1:10 a. m., there was a terrible disturbance. I was almost thrown from my bed. The hotel rocked; the chandelier swung to and fro, in its range almost touching the ceiling, objects could be heard falling; also the sound of shattered glass. This 'shake' lasted continuously for forty-five seconds. We returned to bed and to sleep, not realizing what had taken place until morning.

"With the coming of the morning—July 23—I was more anxious than ever to visit Vesuvius. The manager of the Associated Tours on being told of our disappointment on not being able to visit the top of Vesuvius owing to a discontinuance of the running schedule of Cook's Railway for several days, came to the rescue.

"We wanted to go so badly, just to take a look. To be so near to old Vesuvius and not pay a call seemed like turning one's back on opportunity, turning a cold shoulder to one's cherished ambition. When the manager of Associated Tours said that it could be arranged we could scarcely believe it possible, but were overjoyed nevertheless.

"We left by boat for Sorrento and the Isle of Capri. First we went to Blue Grotto, a cave in a rock bank filled with water which gives a beautiful blue hue or reflection, due possibly to some copper salt in the water. Then we went to Capri by a funicular train and had lunch. In the afternoon we traveled over the island where many noted people, writers, families of the nobility, and recluses, have summer homes, and where is also 'St. Michele,' Dr. Munthe's famous bird sanctuary.

"For the evening and dinner we went to Hotel Tremantono in Sorrento. Shortly after nine o'clock we were taken in a private car to Mount Vesuvius, a distance of about twenty miles, traveling along the shore of the Bay of Naples. The streets of towns through which we passed were filled with natives gathered in fear of another quake. When we reached the foot of the volcano we were then about three miles from our goal. Here we were stopped at a toll-gate. Up to this time we had an interpreter and a chauffeur, but from this point on we required a special guide.

"It took considerable conversation and much argument on the part of the interpreter before this functionary was obtained. After an earthquake nobody is permitted to go to the top. After driving to the end of the automobile road, and within about one-half mile of our destination, we proceeded over a zig-zag one-man trail on the east side of the crater toward the top.

"We had no light, this doubtless to prevent being discovered. The darkness was so thick that we had to push our way through, even though we held on to the guides. In the distance below we could see the lights in the towns. At intervals when there was an eruption of the volcano that lighted up the side of the mountain, we could look down into what seemed a bottomless pit and then upward on a perpendicular wall. Our path was over loose lava-rock. Now and then a bit of the rock would be dislodged with the slipping of a foot and down it would drop into the abyss below. The path led through the Valle de Inferno, the crevice between the original and now extinct Mount Somma cone and the active cone.

"Finally we were on the inside of the crater from the east of Mount Somma side, and before us was the incomprehensible phenomenon of nature. Mount Vesuvius displays a large inverted cone. Within the top of the large cone is another and smaller inverted cone from which fire comes. The space between the outer and the inner cone, in concave form, is filled with semi-cooled lava. The distance across from rim to rim of the outer cone is about two-fifths of a mile. It is possible to climb over the rim of the outer cone and descend into the crater, and this we did, but even then we were about eight hundred feet from the fire. We did not advance any farther because of the hot and noxious fumes escaping from crevices in the lava. The grand spectacle, however, was the central cone. Every few minutes a terrible rumbling noise, similar to distant thunder, would be heard and a tremor felt. After the noise, which lasted for some thirty seconds, would come the mighty ejection of flame, smoke and lava. The flame would rise several hundred feet, illuminating the entire vicinity. From this fell burning cinders to cover the inner cone. From one side of the cone molten lava flowed. When the eruption occurred the smoke and flame would come in a succession of puffs, as if blown by a mighty bellows, each eruption lasting for about one minute. I carried with me a moving picture camera but on account of not having color filter attachment and films, the scene did not register.

"When a child I had read about Vesuvius, and I was puzzled with the information that it was so hot inside the earth that fire came from a mountain top, while in Texas, cool, refreshing water came from an artesian well. I could not solve the problem of how there was fire without wood, and the hardest of all to comprehend was how a substance as hard as stone could be heated to such a degree that it would flow like water. In childhood days I always associated the fiery furnace of Biblical lore with Vesuvius."

"Years later, when I stood within the crater of Vesuvius and watched the lurid glare of the erupting volcano it came to my mind that I was enjoying the supreme thrill of having one of my childhood dreams come true."

On September 2, 1933, Dr. Maresh was married to Miss Thelma Burnett of Houston, whose charming presence now graces the Maresh home at 2416 Riverside Drive. Mrs. Maresh, a former student of Baylor College, Belton, and of the Department of Interior Decoration, Columbia University, New York, too, is a descendant of Texas pioneers, being a member of the Daughters of the Republic of Texas.

* * * * *

Something of the progress that has been brought about during the years since the founding of the pioneer House of Maresh in Texas, first in Washington County, later in the adjoining county of Burleson, and subsequently in Parker and Baylor counties, may be found in the residence of Dr. Rudolph E. Maresh, 1627 South Boulevard, in Houston.

Into the building and making of this home has gone the self-expression of the owner—artistic beauty of the exterior and homely inviting comforts within.

In the garden where flowers grow in profusion, we find an appreciation of nature—the manifested love of the great out-of-doors which is inherently a part of Dr. Maresh, who spent his boyhood days in the free open country of the Texas plains, where Nature cherishes that which is beautiful.

Every day in the year there is to be found on the desk in the private consulting room of Dr. Maresh a vase of flowers. Another vase is also provided for the reception room where patients may enjoy their fragrant beauty.

Mrs. Maresh is an artist of splendid ability and to her Dr. Maresh is indebted for several oil paintings in his office, also in the reception room. Over his desk hangs a picture of the lovely home painted by Mrs. Maresh.

Like the great Zenger, Czech astronomer and master of physics who foretold the disaster of the destruction of Martinique, and found the sun to be a huge dynamo, Dr. Rudolph E. Maresh has found the cure for strange human ills. He is a student who never rests from his labors.

Dr. Maresh is a man who has elected to be what he is because he could not be otehwise. Texas during those pioneer days was a period when characters were built, when men and women had time and occasion to draw from the great storehouse of experience. But in the time between early pioneer days and the present there was the amalgamation of forces, with a breadth and depth of far-reaching influence, that crossed the pathway and life of Rudolph E. Maresh. One feels this when talking to him, but he prefers to let his thoughts delve into the intricacies of the cause and the cure of the ills that the human flesh is heir to, rather than talk about himself. He believes that the chief mystery in life is what makes one do things, and agrees with Leonidas of Tarentum who, early in the Third Century, said in his Greek anthology:

"Measureless time or ever, thy years O man, were recon'd."

And yet Dr. Maresh is a part of the decade when an added span of life has come to man through education, teaching people that they must help care for themselves.

Tracing the processes of his life, we find cause for the fleeing of the pioneers from an environment of oppression. For centuries behind them there had been heritages bequeathed from those who had spent a life-time in service. Dr. Maresh has the legacy that we are taught to believe comes through the transmission of hereditary influences.

His grandmother had two brothers in the old country who were physicians. The world today cannot afford to take a scientific holiday, or rather, cannot afford to take a vacation from science. In the field, by the fireside in the primitive Texas home, or when at school, young Rudolph Maresh was doubtless carrying on the thoughts once started on their way by those uncles, men of medical science.

As he watches his garden changing each day, and enjoys every bowl of flowers that is different, so he studied morning until evening in the years that are past to discover how much is the strength of man, and of all his days upon earth, their length.

There is an old oath which his uncles knew and which in due time came to the ken of the Texas son of the pioneers, and he took unto himself the philosophy of the words:

"I swear by Apollo the physician and by Aesculapius and Health, and All-heal and all gods and goddesses, that according to my ability and judgment I will keep this Oath and this stipulation—to reckon him who taught me this art equally dear to me as my parents, to share my substance with him, and relieve his necessities if required; to look upon his offspring in the same footing as my own brothers, and to teach this art if they shall wish to learn it, without fee or stipulation, and by precept, lecture and every other mode of instruction, I will impart a knowledge of the art to my own sons and those of my teachers, and to disciples bound by stipulation and oath according to the law of medicine.

"I will follow that system of regimen which, according to my ability and judgment I consider for the benefit of my patients, and abstain from whatever is deleterious and mischievous. With purity and holiness I will pass my life and practice my art. While I continue to keep this oath unviolated, may it be granted to me to enjoy life and the practice of my art, respected by all men, at all times."

It was Hippocrates, the celebrated Greek physician, who once said:

"Life is short and art is long; the occasion fleeting; experience fallacious and judgment difficult."

Dr. Rudolph E. Maresh has accordingly built his life around this deduction of the physician, contemporary with Heroditus the historian, and today life and art, occasion, experience and judgment, are hourly reckoned with as he sits at his desk in his consulting room or makes calls for the benefit of the sick.

First, we have been told in the study of history, that there must be a country, that there must be men and women and children to inhabit the country. Then it follows that to every community, every town and county, there belongs a history.

The study of the dangers and the toils of the early settlers, of their devotion of life and fortune to an ideal, to the building of a town or community, portrays to this generation what the country and its liberties has cost.

The pioneer Maresh home was considered as a "first-aid station" in the community. Neighbors when in distress of any kind always ran first to the Maresh home. Dr. Rudolph Maresh recalls the incident of a boy bitten by a snake, running as if for his life, which in fact he was, to the Maresh home. He had to cross a field of freshly-ploughed ground and he was a very tall boy and Dr. Maresh remembers the length of the strides he made across that field, for he was watching him as he ran, counting the steps he made.

Mrs. Maresh, the mother of the family, and in large measure of the whole neighborhood, was equal to the emergency and gave first-aid treatment to the boy. At this time there were no first-aid kits in the rural sections of Texas, nor did the people know about the use of serums or potassium permanganate, but Dr. Maresh recalls that often corn whiskey was used, and cactus poultices were sometimes applied. This neighbor boy was given a "stiff drink of whiskey" and taken immediately to the nearest doctor. He got well.

These were interesting experiences for the embryo doctor. The boy's mind was as a sensitized plate, on which the smallest incidents and experiences were photographed.

We may believe that ten thousand years covers the span of written history and that the vast time that man has lived upon the globe has left scant evidence for ideas of the prehistoric world, but the boy, Rudolph Maresh, was delving into the great storehouse of treasure that he found everywhere around him. Flowers that grew wild over the plains of Texas held a meaning for him. He watched the bees gather honey from the sweetest of these, saw that the cattle as they grazed left untouched some of the weeds and plants and he knew that the "loco weed," when eaten, made the animals go mad or queer, or as the natives said, "loco."

The studious and serious side of the life of Dr. Rudolph Maresh, in addition to his professional career, are manifested throughout the whole of his life. When but a small boy he wrote a thesis on the life of John Hus. That the parents of the great reformer were farmers may have interested the young Texas writer; at any rate he wrote with the interest that searches into the depth of the subject.

In writing of the life of John Hus the reformer, the boy biographer studied the history of Czechoslovakia and this he was able to put into his theme.

The lure of the open country weaves a spell over Dr. Rudolph Maresh and takes him into the fields and woodlands and by the flowing streams in which are to be found the finny tribe, waiting to be caught.

"Yes, hunting and fishing may be called a hobby with me," he admits.

Often in the evening in the lovely environment of his home, when he and Mrs. Maresh find themselves in possession of a quiet hour, he takes out his violin and it is the master's stroke that evokes the plaintive old folksong music from the strings of his favorite instrument. He has inherited not only the father's talent, but possibly it has come to him down the ages, through the generations of musicians which belong to his ancestral land.

Mrs. Maresh is an artist whose work in oils is recognized officially as well as by all those who have opportunity for seeing her canvasses.

CHAPTER XXIX

CHERNOSKY—ORATOR, LAWYER, STATESMAN

CHARLES HENRY CHERNOSKY was born on January 1, 1885, in the Rocky Creek community, near Bellville, Austin County, Texas. He was the second oldest child in the family. His father, Anton P. Chernosky, came to Texas from Vsetin, Moravia, Czechoslovakia, in the early part of 1870. His mother, Františka Schiller, was born near New Ulm, Austin County, Texas. His mother's parents, John Schiller and Rozalie Schiller, came to Texas from Čermne Čechy, three or four years after the trouble in Praha in 1848. They first settled in Colorado County, being among the early pioneers of the Alleyton community. His father and mother were married sometime during the early part of 1882. After their marriage they bought a small farm in the Rocky Creek community and settled there, rearing a family of nine children: Anton A. of Rosenberg; Charles Henry of Houston; Frank E. of New Gulf, Texas; E. E., of Houston; Lottie, wife of Theodore Lueckemeyer of Brenham; Fannie, widow of John J. Chadil of Rosenberg; Annie, wife of Fred Felcman of Rosenberg; Lillie, wife of Frank J. Juřica of Rosenberg; and Martin E., of Austin.

C. H. Chernosky stayed on his father's farm until twenty-two years of age. During this time, however, when there was nothing to do at home, he occasionally went out to work for others. When he was nine years of age he had learned to plow, to chop cotton and corn, and to gather the cotton at picking-time. He enjoyed his farm life all through these years. The country schoolhouse was more than two miles away from his home and when bad weather came it was impossible to attend school, but young Chernosky always tried to make himself useful at home. He was industrious, assisting his mother around the place. He enjoyed milking the cows, feeding the chickens, hogs, horses and helping his father about the place. Young Chernosky was fond of hunting and fishing and was a good shot, and often after school hours would prove his skill by bagging some doves, or perhaps, quail or squirrels. At that time both fields and woods

Judge C. H. Chernosky
Houston, Texas

abounded in wild game. The boy also spent part of his time fishing on Rocky and Milk Creeks.

When he was thirteen years of age his father was anxious for him to take a place as a clerk in a store so that he might come in contact with people and thus learn the ways of the business world. His first work was during the months of November and December, 1898, at Charles Rodenbeck's store, Pleasant Hill, about five miles south of Brenham. He worked there again in November and December, 1899. When there was work to be done on the farm Charles Chernosky would always be found on the job, and after the crops were harvested he would be either attending school or working in some mercantile establishment.

From January until the great Texas hurricane of September 8, 1900, he worked in the general mercantile establishment of C. G. McGregor & Company at Kenney, Texas. The hurricane swept away practically all of the crops in the coastal section and otherwise did a great deal of damage. C. G. McGregor & Company had to discharge several of its employes as a result, and young Chernosky lost his job. He felt a boy's grief over the loss, but was not discouraged. He had the courage that gave assurance of another job somewhere. From Kenney he went to the farm and decided to attend the old country school. He was by then a big boy, fifteen years old, and he suffered somewhat at the hands of other scholars, owing to his size and age. But his teacher, Professor Zettner, took a deep interest in him and young Chernosky made fine progress, ranking as one of the outstanding pupils of the school.

In the early part of 1902, he secured a position as a clerk at Paul Alberts' store at Bleiblersville, Texas. This was a promising position, but young Chernosky was religiously inclined and did not like the idea of working every day in the week, Sundays included, especially as some of his labors were in a beer saloon. He liked his employer and his work, but his hours were from six in the morning until ten or twelve at night. In the morning he had to be up early, sweep the upper and lower stories of the large building, also the saloon building, and straighten the store. Another duty was to wash the hundreds of glasses with soda for the saloon. After a hurriedly-eaten breakfast he would wait on the many early customers in the store, and divide his attention and service with the people in the beer saloon. This did not appeal to young Chernosky and he decided that he would go to a business school and learn bookkeeping.

So in the latter part of October, 1902, he went to a business college in Galveston. There he was joined by Joe Blažek and John C. Matějka, of Nelsonville, Texas. He got along nicely and could have finished his commercial course in about four months, but two or three days before Christmas his mother, his oldest brother, Anton, and the youngest brother, Martin, went to Galveston to visit him and then to take him home for Christmas.

When they returned and disembarked at the station at Kenney, they were met by their father and good neighbor, Charles Hensche. This was on the day before Christmas. The father looked sad, but had nothing to say. The neighbor did all the talking. Instinctively they knew that something was wrong, and though the mother asked a lot of questions, none were answered. Instead of going to the home place they stopped at the neighbor's, about a quarter of a mile away. Of course Charles was anxious to go home and to see his other brothers and sisters, but as he looked towards the old home place he saw that the old home was not there. The trees surrounding the home were badly burned and the house had turned to ashes. The fire had occurred about three o'clock that morning and nothing had been saved. The father had managed to rouse all the children, who escaped in their night clothes. Consequently, Charles could not complete his commercial education. He stayed on the farm to do his bit. The whole family lived for the time being in one of the two-room tenant houses. In 1903 they made a fairly good crop and Charles went back to school the following fall and finished his commercial course several weeks before Christmas of that year.

After graduating in bookkeeping, the professor in that department was taken suddenly ill and for several weeks young Chernosky was in charge, fulfilling his position of trust with both pride and satisfaction.

While at Galveston during this last term young Chernosky met a man by the name of Starnes. This man had a pleasing personality and was a successful traveling salesman, handling stereoscopes and views. He told Chernosky how much money he could make out of the proposition and the young chap became interested, so much so that instead of accepting a position offered him with the John F. Grant Lumber Company for $25.00 a month, he decided to go out on the road and sell stereoscopes and views. This work he continued for several winters.

During his minority he made his home on the farm with his

father, helping with the work, and as soon as the crops were laid by, he would take to the road and devote his energies to the sale of stereoscopes and views.

In 1904 he sold views during the months of September, October and November, and greatly to the surprise of his parents, made about six hundred dollars, all of which he turned over to his father and with which his father built a new home on the farm.

Then again in the Fall of 1905 he went on the road and made between four and five hundred dollars, but the work was hard and he became so run down in health that he was taken ill with typhoid fever at Flatonia, Texas. He was taken home by his brother, Anton. After a few weeks he recovered and again went out on the road, earning more money, which he decided to invest in an education. He was inclined to study for the ministry, his second choice being pharmacy, but his father insisted that he take up the study of law.

On or about the first of January, 1906, he entered the Austin Male Academy for the preparatory courses to equip himself for the University of Texas. He studied until June, 1906, the summer vacations being given over to the sale of the stereoscopes and views. Some time in September, 1907, he re-entered the Austin Male Academy and graduated with honors in 1908.

On the graduation day the graduates were delivered their diplomas, in an informal manner, but for some unknown reason no diploma was delivered to C. H. Chernosky. He was broken-hearted, and his professor, Stanley F. Ford, and the principal of the Austin Male Academy, while delivering the diplomas to the graduates of the school looked rather sternly at Chernosky.

In a low but commanding voice, the professor said: "Chernosky, I want to see you before you go home. Be at my office about two o'clock this afternoon." Recounting the instance in later years Judge Chernosky said: "I could hardly breathe. I was dumbfounded. I could not account for a single thing that I had done that would deprive me of the diploma, for which I had worked so hard, faithfully and earnestly." He knew that he had made good grades. Going back to his boarding place he did not eat, and when the landlady came in and asked him to have lunch he refused, with the excuse that he was not hungry. This was most unusual, because he was always a heavy eater. The good landlady inquired whether he was sick or what had happened. To the query he shook his head, but offered no explanation.

He waited impatiently for two o'clock to come. To him each

minute was like an hour or a day. He was nervous and jumpy and asked himself over and over, why he should appear at two o'clock. But when the time came he was there. The old professor, keen in his observation, had noticed that the young student looked sad and worried, and he smiled as he said:

"Chernosky, I understand that you want to take a course in pharmacy. Before you leave my school, I want to have a heart-to-heart talk with you. My young friend, you, of course, will succeed in anything that you undertake. You have good practical common sense. You are a hard worker. You have an analytic mind, and you will succeed as a pharmacist, but you have a wonderful opportunity before you if you will study law. You will make a success. You have a legal mind and I feel like I ought to tell you so. I felt that if I gave you the diploma you would leave and I would not have an opportunity to tell you this. I have been interested in you. I could not show you any partiality in the classroom. You have been a wonderful student and you have made wonderful progress, and I would like for you to take up law."

A mountain weight seemed lifted from his heaving breast. Chernosky confided his father's wish that he would be a lawyer; that he was first inclined to become a minister, but he and his father could not agree so he had decided to take up pharmacy. He did not want to take a course in law because a lawyer was looked upon by the people generally as a man who would not tell the truth, and this Chernosky abhorred. Before finally bidding his old professor farewell, however, he promised him that he would take up the study of law, and was handed his delayed diploma. The following fall, September, 1908, he entered the Academic Department of the University of Texas, to prepare himself for the Law Department.

He remained in the University of Texas from 1908 to 1912, applying himself closely to his studies. Each summer he traveled and sold stereoscopes and views as he had previously done, earning in that way enough money to pay his way through school.

The many and varied experiences of young Chernosky would fill volumes. He traveled in Texas, Oklahoma, Kansas and Nebraska. He came in contact with thousands of people of all races and nationalities and learned to know and study human nature, which contributed in large measure to his later success as a lawyer.

His father and mother, though not rich, financially speaking, offered to help young Chernosky, but he refused financial aid for the reason that there were four other brothers and four sisters to look after, saying that it would be unfair to his parents to spend money for his education and not give to the other children an equal opportunity to obtain an education. While at the University of Texas he took an interest in many of the student activities, but he was democratic in spirit and did not like the "Aristocrats," or those who belonged to the fraternities. There was always more or less friction between the students who belonged to the fraternities and those who did not. At one time this friction went so far as to cause Chernosky and many others of the anti-frats to get out a charter from the State of Texas and organize the "anti-frats" against the "frats."

Chernosky was chosen as the first secretary of this organization, whose purpose was to put some of the anti-frats into some of the offices in the student body. The frats were always organized and of course the anti-frats were not, and had no chance to get into office of any kind. He was bitterly opposed to hazing and was always behind every movement to stamp out mob violence. He was deeply interested in the Czech language, which was not taught at the University then, and with several other students of Czech extraction in the year 1909 he organized the Čechie Literary Society.

C. H. Chernosky received his law degree from the Law Department of the University of Texas on June 11, 1912. On June 13th he opened a law office at Rosenberg, Texas. His brother-in-law, John J. Chadil, was then living in Rosenberg and helped him in getting established. Chadil was a civil engineer and a successful real estate man. He sold land and through these sales Chernosky got the business of examining many abstracts of title. This specific type of practice appealed to the young lawyer and soon he was recognized as one among the leading land lawyers in that community. Within two or three years he built himself a splendid practice.

On December 24, 1912, he married Miss Vlasta Fojt, who was then attending the Southwestern University at Georgetown. After his marriage he built a home at Rosenberg and continued in his lucrative practice. At all times he took a great interest in civic progress and development of his community. He was always to be found among the leaders, sponsoring any good cause.

He became a member of the Odd Fellows, and also joined the Masonic Order. He was named elder of the Rosenberg Presbyterian Church, and also was elected Trustee of the Rosenberg

Independent School District. In 1916 he was elected County Judge of Fort Bend County, and was re-elected in 1918.

It is said of him that although he presided over hundreds of important cases, presented by some of the ablest lawyers in Texas, yet he never rendered a decision from which an appeal was taken to any higher court.

During his term of office as County Judge, the World War broke out. Judge Chernosky, always a splendid orator and able to speak three languages, was called upon time and again to speak in behalf of the various patriotic activities. He spoke in behalf of the Red Cross and the Liberty Loan, and he assisted in many other war activities. During the war he was granted special permission by the Postmaster General to issue the *Cechoslovak*, a Czech weekly newspaper, so that he could publish his addresses and views on various questions, and also to foster and promulgate the various war activities.

It will be remembered that during the war there was a ban placed on all foreign publications and that they were strictly censored, but the Cechoslovak paper was not and Chernosky and his associates did wonderful work for the cause.

Friends at the time thought that C. H. Chernosky was at the height of his glory. He was held in high esteem, respected by everyone, had a most powerful influence in Fort Bend County, and nothing of real importance was then begun until he was first consulted. These same friends have since had opportunity to watch him attain even greater things. After he retired from the County Judge's office, he moved back to Rosenberg and resumed the practice of law, continuing until August 1, 1924. During that period he was again called to a public office. He served for two years as Chairman of the County Board of Education of Fort Bend County.

On August 1, 1924, he moved to Houston to practice law. It was in Houston that the General Convention of the Slavonic Benevolent Order of the State of Texas was held and he was elected as its President for a period of four years. In 1928, when the General Convention again assembled at Temple, Texas, he was re-elected by acclamation, and again when the General Convention assembled at Ennis in 1932.

In 1929 he was named by Governor Dan Moody as one of the first nine members of the newly-established State Board of Education, which was created because of the amendment to the Constitution of Texas. He served until his term of office expired on January 1, 1933. He was reappointed by Governor R. S.

Sterling for a period of six years, but his appointment had to be confirmed by the State Senate. The Fergusons had defeated Sterling in the campaign of 1932. He sponsored Governor Sterling's campaign, and made numerous speeches in some twenty or thirty counties of this State. Because of Ferguson influence in the Senate his appointment failed of confirmation, it being impossible to get the necessary two-thirds majority. He received eighteen votes, twenty-one being necessary for confirmation.

C. H. Chernosky helped to organize different business institutions, especially in the building and loan and fire insurance fields.

He became successful as both lawyer and jurist, and has made thousands of friends in Texas and out, whose respect and confidence he commands. Truly, one may agree that his old professor, Stanley F. Ford, was right when he induced him to take up law instead of pharmacy.

To Judge and Mrs. Chernosky four children have been born— Charles Henry, Jr., Juanita Eulalia, Joyce Clarine and James Eugene.

C. H. Chernosky is an elder in the Central Presbyterian Church of Houston. He is a thirty-second degree Mason, and a member of the El Mina Temple and Shrine at Galveston. He is a member of the Odd Fellows and of the Modern Woodmen of America. He also holds membership in the Order of the Sons of Hermann, Slavonic Benevolent Order, and the Polish National Alliance. He is a member of the Harris County Bar, State Bar and American Bar Associations.

C. H. Chernosky has always been a practical, common-sense man. From a pulpit he can preach a sermon almost as well as any minister. Before a jury in a criminal or a civil case he can make a most earnest appeal. In a political campaign he can attack his opponents most bitterly. He is fearless and courageous, uncompromising, yet charitable. He can make inspiring patriotic addresses at picnics, barbecues and other gatherings. He has buried scores of members of the Slavonic Benevolent Order during the years of his official connection, and has the happy faculty of paying fitting tributes on such occasions. He has delivered baccalaureate sermons, and while he was a member of the State Board of Education he was frequently called upon to make commencement addresses. His ability as an orator, a speaker with the human interest touch, has brought him new laurels and greater esteem.

A calm dignity is found interwoven with the simple statement that Charles Henry Chernosky was born January 1, 1885, in the Rocky Creek community, near Bellville, Austin County, the second oldest child in the family of Anton Chernosky and Františka Schiller.

Texas, the great agricultural State, has grown year by year, expanding and developing her industries and her resources, because there were Texas-Czech pioneers like Anton Chernosky and his wife and their family of nine sons and daughters, who settled her territory. Her citizenship is recognized throughout the Nation as men and women who have achieved.

Judge and Mrs. C. H. Chernosky have made for themselves and family a home in Houston. The material structure is tangible evidence of success. The spacious dwelling, located in a desirable residence section, offers contrast to the home of the pioneer days in the matter of modern comforts, yet is the perpetuation of the hospitality which was a part of the old home back in the Rocky Creek community.

*   *   *   *   *

On October 18, 1887, in the rural community of Rocky Creek, near Bellville, Austin County, Texas, there was born another child to Mr. Anton Chernosky and Mrs. Františka Chernosky, whom the parents named Edwin Emil. It was an humble home located on a farm, but it exemplified all of the characteristics common to any good Czech family dependent on farming for a livelihood. The father and mother were stern but kind. They had a keen sense of righteousness, of religion, of understanding, of justice, of hospitality. The family was kept occupied with various labors so that there was little time left for mischief—a fitting place to impress upon Edwin Emil the ideals and principles so essential to the good citizen, the successful business man, the good Christian, the devoted husband, the respected father, and the noble friend and neighbor that he is.

Anyone who has been the member of a large family knows the tribulations to be endured at the hands of his brothers and sisters. The Chernosky family was no exception, and the one thing that Edwin Emil could never live down was the fact that when he was about two years of age, he set the little home on fire and it burned to the ground. This happened when he playfully pulled some burning wood from the kitchen stove and put it back into the wood-box. In after years this incident was referred to in jest, but it was quite a catastrophe to the family. It took hard work and many sacrifices to rebuild the home.

Edwin Emil entered the little rural school at New Wehdem in the Summer of 1896, and continued his education until 1904, when he had an opportunity to go to work in a general merchandise store belonging to Paul Albert at Bleiberville, Texas. Seven months of this type of work convinced the young man that clerking in a store was not his idea of success. So he withdrew from that occupation, spent the summer helping his father harvest the crops, then followed his older brothers, Anton and Charles, to Schulenburg, there to devote his time to selling stereoscopes and views.

His arrival was marked by an incident that still remains vivid in his mind. As he alighted from the train, a colored porter stepped up to take his bag. Remembering the admonition of his mother when he started on this journey not to let anyone take his bag, he clung to it steadfastly, and it was only after the repeated assurance of his older brother, Charles, that he accepted the services offered by the darkey.

The fall of 1905 was spent in canvassing the towns of Schulenburg, Weimar, Flatonia, Moulton and Shiner, and when his brother Charles became confined to his bed with an attack of typhoid fever, to Edwin Emil fell the task of visiting the rural communities surrounding these towns. Inclement weather made that business unprofitable in the winter so he went back to the farm. Through his experience in selling stereoscopic views he became interested in photography. While visiting Brenham in the fall of 1906 he noticed a photographer's tent on which was a sign, "For Sale." Being anxious to engage in that type of work he purchased the business and followed that vocation until the early part of 1908, by which time the panic of 1907 had made that business unprofitable. So he sold his cameras and tent in June, 1908, returned to his father's farm, and there divided his time between working on the farm and studying bookkeeping and commercial law.

In the early fall of 1908 he again had the opportunity to work for his old employer, Mr. Paul Albert of Bleiberville. His new assignment in the store, however, was to keep books, work in the postoffice, and to clerk only when business was rushing. He held that position until May, 1910, when he received a letter from Mr. E. Foerster, cashier of J. H. P. Davis & Company, bankers, of Rosenberg, Texas, offering him a position as bookkeeper in the bank. This was a red-letter day in the life of Edwin Emil Chernosky. In his excitement he forgot his duties, rushed to Mr. Albert, his employer, and read the letter to him.

Upon hearing the offer Mr. Albert exclaimed, "You, a book-keeper in a bank? That is the best joke I ever heard." But after a more thorough consideration, Mr. Albert advised him to accept the position, to do his best to make good at it, and assured him that if he were unable to hold the job he could come back to work at the store.

So on May 28, 1910, he assumed his position at the bank, determined to make a success of his new undertaking. His determination was rewarded. Within six months he was promoted to the position of assistant cashier. In 1919 he was made cashier of the bank, which position he held until March, 1923.

Two years after he started working in the bank—October 12, 1912—having received a promotion in the meantime, he married Miss Minnie Jasper, to which marriage were born three children, Dayle Odell, who died three days after birth, Eddie Jasper, and Velma Nancy. In the latter part of 1919 Mrs. Chernosky died and he was left a widower with two children aged five and three years. On October 16, 1920, he married Miss Hettie Klump, who has devoted her life unselfishly to him and her step-children.

While cashier in the bank, several of his friends became prosperous in the oil industry, and again desiring a change of atmosphere, he started out rough-necking with a drilling crew, experiencing the usual hardships attendant upon such a life. In the early part of 1924 a small development company was organized with the assistance of a few of his friends to drill for oil near Humble. Within a month, a 400-barrel producer was finished. Shortly after another well was started which was drilled to a depth of 1,000 feet, at which time salt water flooded the first well and decreased its production. Other complications set in and the company finally sold its assets to a few of the stockholders, and he was employed by the new organization as field manager, which position he held until June, 1926, when he resigned and moved to Houston, where he helped organize a building and loan association. He was made manager of the association in September, 1926, in which capacity he still serves.

Modest, unassuming, always kind and practical, Edwin Emil Chernosky has been a help and consolation to his many friends throughout the State.

Dr. Joseph Kopecky
San Antonio

Mrs. Josephine Malinak
Kopecky
Mother of Dr. Kopecky

CHAPTER XXX

JOSEPHINE KOPECKY

*"There's a divinity that shapes our ends
Rough hew them how we will."*

—HAMLET.

Josephine Maliňak, born in 1862, in Hrozenkov, Moravia, Austria-Hungary, the daughter of a soldier in the Austrian Army, might have fittingly quoted the words of the Prince of Denmark addressed to his friend, Horatio.

But Josephine, eldest daughter of Joseph and Anna Maliňak, not knowing what destiny held in store for her, took life as it came. From the hardships and the strenuous life of the soldier, together with the insanitary conditions prevailing in the army at the time, the soldier father, Joseph Maliňak, incurred an infection which developed into a chronic illness, finally incapacitating him from manual labor. Josephine learned to do for herself and others rather than to quote what others might have said.

The dream of the soldier was to move with his family to America, the "land of promise." Life following the Austro-Prussian War, was hard and conditions made the accumulation of money difficult. To save enough to pay the passage across the Atlantic became the great and all-absorbing purpose of this family.

In 1872, when Josephine was ten years old, the necessary amount had been accumulated. The dream was to be realized. Joseph Maliňak had sufficient money to pay for the passage on a sailing ship of himself, wife and three children. The ship set sail from Bremen, and after a voyage of thirteen weeks docked in New York harbor. By this time all the money was gone. The family was alone and destitute in a strange city in a strange land.

After three days they were picked up, along with several other immigrants by the planter, John Calhoun, of South Carolina, and taken to his plantation to work in the cotton fields. They went by steamer to Charleston and thence by rail to the plantation

271

near Abbeville. Turning the pages of the history backward three decades to 1844, we find John Calhoun, Secretary of State of the United States, in Washington, working on the Treaty of Annexation of Texas to the United States. Something like a quarter of a century later down on the plantation in South Carolina, while Josephine Malinak's parents went to work in the fields, she remained in the home of the Calhouns to take care of the planter's youngest child. There she learned to speak English. The great conflict between the States had been over but a few years, and the country was passing through the tragic reconstruction era.

For the work that this immigrant Czech family did on that plantation they were given cornmeal, molasses, bacon and milk. In addition there was a small wage which, as was the custom in the South at that time, was paid once a year. The plantation owners were themselves in direst financial straits.

Saturday afternoon belonged to the immigrants and the money earned for any work done on these half-holidays was used for the purchase of additional food supplies. Josephine, living in the planter's home, was isolated from her family, often not having an opportunity to see her parents for days at a time. A young Polish girl, two years older than Josephine, was her companion, she being also attached to the plantation household, her duties being to wait on the table and wash dishes. Only two meals a day were served, however, morning and evening, and the two young immigrant girls sometimes found themselves hungry, having for their meals only that which was left over from the planter's table—a situation not uncommon in the South shortly after the Civil War, when the food supply was limited.

The children of the planter's household had healthy appetites and often as a consequence there was little left over to appease the hunger of the rugged and growing young Josephine. Her mother and father sometimes augmented her scant menu with a roasted sweet potato, which they managed to bring with them whenever they had a chance to pass the "big house" on their way to and from their work.

Up to this period in her life Josephine Malinak had had very little schooling. While living in the home of Mr. Calhoun she was taught to spell and read by the father of Mrs. Calhoun, whom she recalls as a Mr. Noble.

Josephine's father was a devout Catholic and was anxious to move with his family to Texas, where he had heard there were settlements of Moravian Catholics, many of whom had come

from his own native village. After a stay of two years in South
Carolina, sufficient money had been saved for the railroad fare
to Texas. At this time Josephine, twelve years old, had learned
enough English to be able to interpret for the family on the
trip to Texas, through Augusta, Georgia; Birmingham, Alabama;
Memphis, Tennessee; Texarkana and thence on to Houston.
From Houston the family went to Columbus. At this point in
the journey the financial resources were about exhausted. Here,
as in New York, the family was taken to a farm to work, but
in this instance they were to be "half-renters." The farm was
located about eight miles from Columbus and Josephine was
left, as before, to work in the home of an American family. For
her services she received two dollars a month and her clothes,
which were made chiefly from those discarded by the members
of the family.

The money she earned was turned over to her father to help
support the family which by this time had increased with the
birth of another son, Joseph. The family at this time, about
1876, moved to Live Oak Hill, Fayette County, where they
farmed as renters for three years. Josephine during this period
lived at home and helped with the farm work.

In 1879 the family moved again, going to Clear Creek, about
five miles north of Fayetteville. Josephine went to Ledbetter
to work in the home of the Radford family during the winter
months, when there was little to be done on the farm, returning
home for the spring and summer, taking a hand in the fields
along with the other members of the family. For her work
in the Radford family she was paid eight dollars a month, all
of which she gave to her father to help support the family,
which had again increased by the birth of two more daughters,
Anna and Lena. The father's health had gradually grown worse,
owing to the progress of the disease, an affection of the lungs,
contracted while in the Austrian army.

Josephine had during the years been growing and developing
into a young woman of marriageable age. During the residence
of the family on Clear Creek, she became acquainted with a
young Czech farmer, Joseph Kopecky, who lived alone on a farm
close to that of the Maliňak's.

The meeting, which came seemingly by chance, was doubtless one of those foreordained incidents of fate. The mother of
Josephine, while at work in the field one day saw the youth
passing and stopped him to ask his name and from whence he
came. It developed that he was originally from a village adjoining

the one from which the Maliňak family had emigrated. Born in
1860, of a fairly well-to-do family, his father having died when
he was but a boy in his early teens, he had left home some years
later when his mother had remarried, the second husband being
the first husband's brother and Joseph's uncle.

The boy had been much opposed to the union of his mother
and uncle—had threatened to leave home in the event of the
marriage, which threat he carried out, running away when he
was nineteen years old, emigrating at this time to Texas to live
with an older brother of his father's, who had been in Texas for
some years.

Such in brief was the story told that morning in the Texas
field by the young Texas-Czech pioneer farmer as he made the
acquaintance of the mother of Josephine Maliňak.

After working for the uncle for a time, he began farming
for himself on his own account, and it was about this time—
1881—that he became interested in the young neighbor girl,
Josephine. It was two years before he finally got her consent to
marry him, but on April 21, 1883, they were married in the
Catholic Church at Fayetteville, with Reverend Father Chromčik
officiating.

The young couple lived at several places during the next few
years, farming during this time in the neighborhood of Fayetteville. The young husband learned English under the tutelage of
his wife, supplementing this knowledge through his association
with several American neighbors. After being married about
five years, he became foreman on the farm of Mr. C. H. Powell
in Fayette County.

Soon after they were married they gave up attending the
Catholic Church, and the children were all reared without having
any particular church affiliation or connection. Later in life most
of them joined the Southern Methodist Church. The mother of
the family, while she has never joined the church, attends this
church, where she engages in the various activities. Although
over seventy years of age, she is in splendid health, happy, active
and industrious. A full and fruitful life has seemingly given her
strength to carry on throughout the years, with no lessening of
interests.

The husband, Joseph Kopecky, as soon as he became a natural-
ized citizen, was a Democrat, except for the time he aided the
Clark faction in Texas after the split with the Democratic Party
in 1894. At that time he became an ardent Populist. He was for
a time a member of the Woodmen of the World, and also the

Bohemian order of "Česko Slovensky Podorujici Spolek," and was a charter member of the Slavonic Benevolent Order of the State of Texas, organized in 1897.

In 1904 Joseph and Josephine Kopecky moved to Taiton, in Wharton County, where the husband and father of the family of twelve children, died in July, 1914.

The story does not, however, conclude at this point, but instead just begins, for there were eleven of the twelve children living, and these needed training and education to take their places in Life's field of endeavor.

Having had but a few days in school herself and having gotten what education she had from observation and through contact with the English-speaking families for whom she had worked in her young girlhood, she was anxious for her children to have better opportunities. She had learned to read English in the homes of the American families where she spent much of her early life, and she had learned to read Czech in the home of her parents, but she had not learned to write either language.

Of the eleven of her twelve children surviving, ten have had more or less college training. Four of them have graduated at Sam Houston Normal and four others have studied at the University of Texas.

These children in the order of their ages are:

John M., married, lives in Houston; Joseph, married, is a physician in San Antonio; Theresa Miller, married, lives near El Campo; Amelia Gallia, married, teaches school at Woodsboro, Texas; Cyril W., married, is principal of a school at Rowena, Texas; Jerome M., unmarried, lives at El Campo; Alba Hejl, married, lives on a farm near Temple; Vlasta, married to Dr. John B. Rushing, lives at Hemphill; Ludma, a graduate nurse, works in the Texas University Health Department, Austin; Lily Hejl, married, lives at Austin; Laddie G., unmarried, lives in Galveston.

There are eighteen grandchildren in this large and representative Texas-Czech family. The mother, Mrs. Josephine Malíñak, makes her home in San Antonio with her son and daughter-in-law, Dr. and Mrs. Joseph Kopecky.

Recently Mrs. Kopecky retraced some of the steps over the old trail and recalled the happenings one by one from the day she went to live in the old South Carolina mansion of the historic Calhoun family.

"Yes," she replied, in answer to a question, "it was the same Calhoun family of historical prominence in the affairs of the

Government of the United States." The Calhoun family she knew, however, was that of the son, John C. Calhoun, Jr., Calhoun, the elder, having died on March 31, 1850.

* * * * *

Joseph Kopecky, the third child in the family of Josephine Maliňak and Joseph Kopecky, Sr., was born at the historic little community town of Rutersville, Fayette County, Texas, August 12, 1886. Rutersville was a college town away back in the '40s when Texas was still a republic.

The boy passed all his childhood and early youth on a farm, even helping with the farm work when he was only seven years old. It was because of the unfavorable economic conditions on the farms during the '90s that the boy had to be called into the fields to help his parents with the actual farm labor.

At the age of eight he was placed in school, but his school attendance was rather more spasmodic than regular, as the farm work interfered, during a period of eight years. When he was fifteen he was able to devote considerable time to study at home, and when barely sixteen he passed the examination for a second-grade teacher's certificate and started teaching school at Bordovice, a Bohemian settlement about three miles east of Fayetteville. He taught there for three years, then one year at Tours, McLennan County, and another year in his home community, Taiton. By this time he had saved enough money to be able to resume his own education, and in the Fall of 1901 entered Sam Houston Normal College at Huntsville.

From this school he was graduated in June, 1909, leading his class of over one hundred, and receiving the honor of being valedictorian. So far as it is known, this was the first time this honor had been bestowed upon one of Czech nationality or descent.

During the following two years, 1910 and 1911, he taught in the School for the Blind at Austin, one of the State's eleemosynary educational institutions. During his spare time he took courses as an irregular student in the Academic Department of the University of Texas. In this manner he accumulated enough college work to admit him to the Medical Department of the University at Galveston in the fall of 1911. Having lost most of his savings during the preceding summer through an unfortunate business venture, he was considerably handicapped during his freshman year. During the summer vacation he worked at the Y. M. C. A. in Galveston as office secretary, and during the last two years of his school course, he waited on tables at a students' boarding house to help defray expenses. He graduated from the Medical School of the University in May, 1915, ranking third in his class, and receiving an M. D. diploma. He served as interne at John Sealy Hospital in Galveston from July 1, 1915, to June 30, 1916, and on July 1, 1916, went into general practice at El Campo, Texas, where he remained until called into the service of the United States, November 3, 1917, as First Lieutenant in the Army Medical Corps.

He was first assigned to duty at Base Hospital No. 1, Fort Sam Houston, December 19, 1917, and was made battalion surgeon in the Nineteenth Field Artillery, Fifth Division, then stationed at Leon Springs. From here he was ordered to the Army Medical School in Washington for a course of instruction, arriving there on February 14, 1918. From this school he received a diploma on June 20, 1918, and was commissioned First Lieutenant in the Medical Corps of the regular army. He was then ordered to duty at Camp Zachary Taylor in Kentucky where he served as assistant camp sanitary inspector until February 18, 1919, when he was transferred to the Siberian Expeditionary Force, a service for which he had previously volunteered.

Dr. Kopecky arrived in Vladivostok, Siberia, on March 27, 1919, and from there went to Spasskoe, about one hundred miles distant to take charge of an American army hospital. During the latter part of April he was ordered to proceed with a detachment of Medical Department enlisted men to Verkhnie-Udinsk, a town about eighteen hundred miles west of Vladivostok. The trip was made by train and because of the many obstacles it took two weeks to complete the journey. At Verkhnie-Udinsk he was on duty with a battalion of American troops commanded by Colonel Morrow, and about June 7th, was ordered out on the line with Company "M," of the Twenty-seventh Infantry.

Dr. Kopecky was then sent to Station Selenga, near Lake Baikal. During that time Company "M" was scattered along the Trans-Siberian Railroad for a distance of over one hundred miles. There were some seven small posts along this line, and Lieutenant Kopecky was the only medical officer on duty. As it was his duty to see each post at least once a week, most of his time was spent riding back and forth on the railroad. During the beautiful Siberian summer, this part of the duty was considered a pleasant one by the doctor. But with the coming of winter, with the temperature at times forty below zero, traveling was neither easy nor pleasant.

During the early days of January, 1920, Lieutenant Kopecky took part in the operation against Semenoff's armored train Iztrebitel, which had attacked and killed some American soldiers at Posolskaya. The armored train was captured by a small detachment of some forty infantrymen and turned over to Colonel Morrow. On January 5, 1920, the American troops were ordered to return to Vladivostok. The trip was made during the height of winter. The Americans had their own provisions and had to carry the wood necessary for fueling the locomotives on top of box-cars in which they traveled. So many obstacles were encountered that it took six weeks to get back to Vladivostok.

The Twenty-seventh Infantry left Vladivostok for the Philippines about the middle of March, 1920. For some time Lieutenant Kopecky had felt that he did not wish to stay in the service of the regular army, and he handed in his resignation about six months before going to the Philippines. After staying in Manila for ten days, he was ordered to San Francisco and there severed his connection with the army on May 3, 1920. Returning to Texas he located again at El Campo, where he resumed the practice of medicine, remaining there until September 1, 1921.

At the completion of his interneship in 1916 he had been offered a position in the Medical Department of the State University, but at the time did not accept. Not being altogether satisfied with the type of work he was doing as a general practitioner, and anxious to be in closer touch with an educational institution, when he was again offered a teaching position in the Medical Department of the University he accepted, and on September 1, 1921, started his duties as instructor in Clinical Medicine and Clinical Pathology. At that time he was associated with Dr. M. D. Levy, Associate Professor of Clinical Medicine and Clinical Pathology. After a year Dr. Levy resigned and Dr. Kopecky was promoted to Dr. Levy's duties, with the rank of Adjunct Professor.

The following year he was promoted to Associate Professor. He spent the summer of 1923 at the Mayo Clinic, studying diseases of the thyroid gland. He spent the summer of 1924 at the Barnes Hospital in St. Louis and at the Mayo Clinic, studying heart diseases and electro-cardiography. During the summer of 1925 he went to Harvard University to study heart diseases under Dr. Paul D. White. Upon the resignation of Dr. M. L.

Graves, Professor of the Department of Medicine at the University of Texas, Dr. Kopecky was promoted to full professorship in Clinical Medicine and Clinical Pathology. During the absence of Dr. Graves' successor, Dr. Kopecky was in full charge of the Department of Practice of Medicine during the teaching session of 1925-1926.

Up to this date he had been employed full time by the University. In 1926 he effected a part-time arrangement which gave him opportunity for opening an office at Galveston, where he engaged in a practice limited to internal medicine and diagnosis. In 1929 Dr. Kopecky received the appointment from Dr. Benedict, President of the University of Texas, to serve during the summer as first Exchange Professor from the University of Texas to the National University of Mexico. He gave a lecture course at this University on diseases of the heart. When this appointment had been fulfilled on September 1, 1929, Dr. Kopecky resigned to go into private practice in San Antonio.

With all the years of service and activity which have gone into the making of the life of this son of the pioneers, Dr. Kopecky has found time for church, social, lodge and fraternal interests. He is a member of the Methodist Episcopal Church, South; a Thirty-second Degree Scottish Rite Mason; also an active member of the Czech Slavonic Benevolent Order; the Sokol Union of America, and the German order, Sons of Hermann. Is a member of the Phi Chi Medical Fraternity and of the Alpha-Omega-Alpha, honorary medical fraternity; a member of the County, District and State Medical Associations, a Fellow of the American Medical Association; a Fellow of the American College of Physicians. He holds rank of Major in the Reserve Corps of the Army, and organized General Hospital No. 127 in connection with the Medical Department of the University of Texas at Galveston. Dr. Kopecky is a member of the Kiwanis Club, and was the first president of the Czech Ex-Students' Association of Texas, which office he still held in 1933.

Dr. Kopecky married Miss Golda Elizabeth Willis of Graham, Texas, February 7, 1918, while he was in the army. She was a former student of Polytechnic College, Fort Worth, and a graduate of the Nursing Department, University of Texas.

Mrs. Kopecky remained with Dr. Kopecky during his stay in Washington before going over seas in the World War, and she was with him while he was stationed in the United States at Camp Zachary Taylor. During the time he was in Siberia Mrs. Kopecky attended the College of Industrial Arts, Denton,

Texas. On the return of Dr. Kopecky from Siberia she met him at San Francisco.

One son, Joseph Willis, born February 18, 1921, and one daughter, Mary, born June 26, 1926, have added to the life of Dr. and Mrs. Kopecky, bringing it up to full fruition, for it is conceded that there is no more delightful home in the State than that of Dr. and Mrs. Joseph Kopecky of San Antonio.

In the Kopecky family collection of old photographs there is to be found a family group picture with mother and father and eleven children made a number of years ago when some of the eleven, now all grown, were young, ranging all the way from the infant-in-arms to the children big enough to stand behind the group. It is not difficult to pick out Joseph Kopecky.

All through the years from youth to manhood, the family pictures of Joseph Kopecky stand out. The ambition which the boy manifested in those first school days for getting an education, kept him on the move. Following the chronology of events in his life as briefly listed one will find that the first teacher's certificate was but the beginning.

His experience in Siberia during the World War was but another incident. This experience has been put to good use. The opportunity he had to study not only men but conditions at a time when a world was at war, was not his by chance. He made application for it.

As a teacher in the Texas Blind Institute he studied the conditions of both mind and body under the handicap of blindness. As a teacher of the youth in the rural schools of Texas he found material which was to serve him well in the years to come.

But it is to the present that attention is drawn. For the time one may forget that this tall and dignified gentleman of imposing manner and appearance, of genial and gracious courtesy, was a waiter in his student days to help defray his college expenses. Rather does the interest center on the class at historic old Sam Houston Normal, Huntsville, when Joseph Kopecky was valedictorian of the class.

The footsteps lead to the present and up to the entrance and thence into the substantial brick building of the Medical and Surgical Clinic, San Antonio.

As the president of "Čechie," the organization of Texas-Czech University students, the interest of Dr. Kopecky is keenly alert to things educational. His family, his friends and his social, fraternal and business activities, outside of his professional service, keep him constantly fit for anything that may come up.

Left:

Mr. E. E. Chernosky

Houston

Right:

Mr. John G. Bubak

Dallas

CHAPTER XXXI

A Story of Four Generations

*"They dug his grave e'en where he lay
But every mark is gone."*

—Marmion.

Somewhere in the City of Houston there is the unmarked, unknown grave of pioneer John Bubak, Confederate soldier, grandfather of Honorable John G. Bubak, attorney-at-law, of Dallas.

Returning from active service on Civil War battlefields, John Bubak went to Houston, where he died in 1867 from yellow fever. The fever epidemic swept over the entire Gulf Coast section of the State, taking a heavy toll. Little was known of the disease or its treatment at the time. Carbolized water, according to old records, was sprinkled around the premises of stricken families, but death came in many cases, as it did to pioneer John Bubak.

John Bubak, Confederate soldier and yellow fever victim, was the son of Mike and Anna Bubak, who came to Texas from Czechoslovakia in 1853, settling at New Ulm where they bought a farm of nine hundred acres on which they lived for many years. Mike Bubak died there, and his wife died at Cat Springs. The dates of their deaths are not preserved in the family records.

The wife of the soldier, John Bubak, after his death, moved with her children, Mary, Wenzel, Ernest, Fannie, Ferdinand and John, to a farm at Cat Springs. There she worked in the field as many other pioneer women did, to provide for her family. Her life was one of primitive hardships, and few comforts.

The son, John, one of the six children born in Texas pioneer days, was married at Austin in 1890 to Anna Shiller, daughter of the pioneer, Joseph H. Shiller, whose parents came to Texas in 1853. Four children were born to John and Anna Shiller Bubak—Annie, Tillie, George and John. The wife and mother of this family died in Dallas in 1929. The husband and father of the family still resides in Dallas. And from the sire the son has had the privilege of hearing the story, reaching back into the past, then coming down through the generations to the present time.

Strange things have come to pass within the decades that have gone into the period between 1867 and 1933.

A stretch of two hundred and sixty miles of concrete highway now connects Houston and Dallas. Railroads and airplanes cover the distance—quick and comfortable transportation. Dining-cars and observation coaches, air-conditioned, affording cool comfort in the heat of summer. It was not until 1873 that the Texas & Pacific Railroad reached Dallas. Dallas had been founded in 1841, when a log cabin was built on the banks of the Trinity River. The settlement was called "Peter's Colony."

In 1850 practically all the State's population was to be found in the counties along the Gulf Coast, or along the navigable portion of the Brazos, Trinity, Neches, Sabine and Red rivers. Ox-wagon trains offered the only means of transportation inland. In 1934 Houston and Dallas are in contact through the mediums of these modern vehicles of transportation—the railway, the highway, and the airway. Over ribbons of steel, speeding passenger trains move, equipped with all the comforts of the modern home. Motor busses with such modern conveniences as sleeping facilities for night passengers, and free pillows for comfort in the day, along with a radio for entertainment, cover the distance from Houston to Dallas in seven hours. These are evidences of the progress and development that has come to Texas since 1851, when Mike and Anna Bubak landed as immigrants to have a part in the magnificent program of building a great commonwealth.

Gathering the chain of the story, with the great grandson, John Bubak, III, of Dallas, the connecting link, we find strong out-croppings of the old pioneer spirit.

John Bubak, like his paternal grandfather, was a soldier, enlisting in the service of his government for the World War. He had previously been a student at the University of Texas, had also attended the Law School at Lebanon, Tennessee, having chosen law as his profession. After the Armistice, armed with his LL. D. degree from Texas State University, the young lawyer began his practice in Dallas. He had not only to his credit his LL. D., but he had certificates of graduation from business colleges. His was an ambition not easily satisfied. The lure of the road to knowledge enticed his footsteps. He never returned empty-handed.

To the practice of law he has added a number of civic activities which has gained for him leadership in a large way in the City of Dallas. Astronomy is his hobby. He began this study when a boy out in the great open spaces with his father as his teacher. His father, also a student of astronomy, taught him to read through the stars the mysteries of the great blue canopy above. While John G. Bubak says that astronomy is just a hobby, he has been interested in the promoting of a Dallas Astronomical Society, and in the erection of a twelve-inch telescope.

The organization of "The American Czechslovak Society" by Mr. Bubak for the purpose of promoting the interest of the Czechoslovak people in the United States of America, was an outstanding achievement. Through the organization, Texas-Czech citizens have been brought together from all parts of the State in an annual meeting, held in October, during the State Fair. The officers and board of directors have been selected so that the list will cover every section of the State, with John G. Bubak, president; W. Drobil, first vice-president; T. H. Škrabanek, second vice-president; Joseph Wondrash, third vice-president; Will A. Nesuda, secretary-treasurer; Mrs. Frances St. Crico, assistant secretary-treasurer. The board of directors for 1934 are: Frank Ančinec, Houston; John G. Bubak, Dallas; Robert Červenka, West; Dr. W. A. Chernosky, Temple; E. J. Denke, Galveston; W. Drobil, Dallas; E. K. Hajovsky, El Campo; J. F. Houzvick, Fort Worth; Tom Hošek, Houston; Josef F. Janak, West; J. J. Juran, Fort Worth; Rev. P. P. Kašpar, Plum; Josef Krušinsky, Sr., Corpus Christi; V. Kučera, Dallas; F. J. Lidiak, La Grange; F. J. Marek, Temple; Frank Moučka, Ennis; Anton Němeček, West; Will A. Nesuda, Dallas; Frank Olexa, Jr., Houston; John Paclik, Gainesville; I. J. Parma, Ennis; Frank Rendl, Dallas; Eman Řezniček, Kaufman; Charles A. Sismilick, San Antonio; Joseph Siptak, Caldwell; T. H. Škrabanek, Ennis; Mrs. Frances St. Crico, Waco; Stanley Štibořik, Taylor; Josef Sumsal, Snook; John P. Trlica, Granger; Mrs. Bessie Valčik, Dallas; Štěpan Valčik, Houston; Joseph Wondrash, Caldwell; Frank Zubik, College Station.

On October 4, 1932, the president of the Society received a letter from Mayor Anton J. Čermak, of Chicago, extending an invitation to the members of the Society to visit Chicago during the "Century of Progress." The letter follows:

"Mr. John G. Bubak,
    "President American Czechoslovak Society,
    "Dallas, Texas.
"Dear Mr. Bubak:
    "As Mayor of the City of Chicago I take pleasure in extending
to the members of the American Czechoslovak Society an invitation to visit Chicago during a Century of Progress, from June
1st to November 1st, next year.
    "Chicago, with its excellent railway facilities, fine parks and
boulevards, hotels, and places of amusement, is in a position,
should the members of your Society visit Chicago, to make their
stay here a pleasant one.
    "Trusting that I may have the pleasure of greeting the members
of the American Czechoslovak Society personally in Chicago next
year, I am,   Respectfully yours,
    (Signed)   "A. J. ČERMAK,
                                                "Mayor."
    Star-gazing may be the hobby of this Texas-Czech citizen of
Dallas, but the list of club activities, civic, social, educational and
fraternal, to which he gives of his time and interest, calls for the
lion's share of his energy after deducting the regular hours
devoted to his profession. In addition to attending meetings of
the various organizations, he is called upon to make addresses
all over the State.
    In enumerating his club affiliations, the presidency of American
Czechoslovak Society should be given preference. Next comes
that of the Texas Museum of Natural History, Dallas, of which
he is vice-president. He carries the thought of it around with
him wherever he goes. The result is that already there is tangible
evidence of the existence of the museum out at State Fair Park,
where the exhibits are now housed in the old Coliseum building.
    He is president and director of the Lagow Improvement Asso-
ciation of Dallas; a member of the Sam Houston Club; actively
associated with the Boy Scouts of America, being chairman of
the committee of a Dallas group, participating in all Scout activities. He is a director of the South Dallas Improvement Association, which has been instrumental in some highly constructive
work. As vice-president of the East Dallas Drainage Association,
Mr. Bubak finds satisfaction in the fact that the organization
saved the City of Dallas a $1,500,000 expenditure in East Dallas
drainage.
    He is a member of the Dallas Astronomical Society and presi-
dent of Lodge No. 48, Slavonic Benevolent Order of the State of

Texas; a member of a Slavonic Fire Insurance Society; of the Dallas Sokols Unit, and of the Terry Improvement Association; vice president of The Dads' Club, Technical High School, Dallas; a member of the Dallas-Czech Orchestra, and of the Kessler Association, organized for the beautification of Dallas.

John G. Bubak is prophetically a man of the hour in Texas. He has proved through his efforts in behalf of his State and the Texas-Czechs, that he has in his make-up the material of a leader. He is a typical Czech as to type, with a splendid physique. He can match shoulders with any man in the whole of the United States. He recalls that when a student at the University of Texas he burned the midnight oil and, in looking back, marvels at the work he was able to accomplish. Too close application in his search for knowledge came near to causing a physical collapse, however. He made at that time a resolution that he would never keep later hours than eleven o'clock. So it has been the rule since those university days to retire when the hour of eleven arrives.

For some time Mr. Bubak has devoted his leisure moments to gathering material for a family history. His maternal grandfather, Joseph H. Shiller of Rowena, Texas, who is eighty-four years old, the oldest Czech pioneer in point of residence in Texas, has given him much valuable family history, writing the data with his own hand in pen and ink.

There were two Shiller families—cousins—who came to Texas in 1853. The name was spelled "Šiller" in Czechoslovakia, but was later Americanized by the addition of the letter "h." The two Shiller families, John and his wife, Theresa, with their children, Anna, Rosalie, John, Vince and Joseph, and the cousin's family, Charles, Vince, Frank and Bernard, settled in Austin County near New Ulm.

The Shiller families came to Texas from Čermna, Czechoslovakia, emigrating, according to the statement of pioneer Joseph H. Shiller, because they thought they would better their condition. Joseph H. Shiller was married April 27, 1869, to Rosalie Jirasek and to them was born seven children. Two died and the five to live were Rosalie and Anna, born in Austin County; John, Henry and Joseph, Jr., born in Travis County. The daughter, Rosalie, married Joseph Hošek; Anna married John Bubak; John married a cousin, Anna Shiller; Henry married Rosalie Shiller; and Joseph married Sadie Esteřak.

Rosalie had nine children; Anna, who married John Bubak, had four children, John one child, Joseph three, and Henry none. The four children of John and Anna Shiller Bubak, Annie, Tillie,

George and John, belong with the present—the fourth generation—and according to John G. Bubak are not counted in the government census as Czechs, but as American citizens. This will account for what may seem to be a rather large estimate of Texas-Czech citizenship, given as being between 350,000 and 500,000.

The children of the first Shiller families went to Shillerville school in Victoria County, the school and community being founded and named by the early Shiller families. The eighty-four-year-old pioneer, Joseph H. Shiller, has for a number of years, made his home with a son, Dr. Shiller at Rowena. Dr. Shiller is a general practicing physician in that locality. Ernest Bubak, brother of John Bubak, Sr., lives at the old home place near Cat Springs, Austin County. There are to be found many historical mementos of a silent past, such as the old seasoned hickory yokes, worn in the long ago by slow-moving ox-teams.

The Jirasek family came to Texas December 17, 1867, settling at New Ulm, Austin County, joining with the Czech settlement previously made and which had continued to grow through the years from the time of the earliest immigration.

Joseph and Rosie Barcal Jirasek, born respectively July 7, 1819, and January 27, 1825, in Čermna, Czechoslovakia, were the pioneer founders of the large Jirasek family in Texas. Joseph Jirasek died at Taylor, June 6, 1901. The wife died at Victoria. December 14, 1897. This great grandmother of John G. Bubak was the first woman to be buried in the old cemetery near Victoria. The seven children, four daughters and three sons, all married and reared families, and these have reached the fourth generation. Joseph Jirasek married Theresa Ježek in January, 1872; Ignac Jirasek married Julie Ježek, and Frank Jirasek married Mary Ognowsky. Rosie Jirasek married Joseph Shiller in 1869; Annie married John Shiller. Theresa married Joe Esteřak and Frances, another daughter of the pioneers, married Charles Esteřak.

Joseph Jirasek resides at Taylor. There is one brother living, Frank Jirasek of Gainesville, and two sisters, Theresa Esteřak of Smithville, and Frances Esteřak, Victoria.

Joseph Jirasek of Taylor had four children, Joseph A., born August 23, 1874; Hynek Jaroslav, born April 19, 1878; Frank L., born May 2, 1880; and Theresa, born in March, 1882.

The Joe Ježek family came to Texas in 1854. Other early Czech settlers arriving in 1867 included: Joe Mašik, Joseph Macas, Vinc Barcal, Vince Dušek, Joseph Marek and Karel Motel.

Members of these pioneer families intermarried and their progeny are scattered throughout the State.

In his research of family history, John Bubak, III, has found that there were only eight of the Bubak name living in 1933. He has a sister, Annie, the wife of Frank Hubik, of Dallas; another sister, Lillie, wife of Charles Janiček of Dallas; a brother, George, who married Carrie Kovař. The wife of Mr. Bubak was Miss Annabelle Parma.

John Bubak, pioneer, was one of the first playwrights of the State. In the latter '50s and early '60s, this Texas-Czech, whose grave is lost in the City of Houston, wrote many plays which were produced by the pioneer Texas-Czech theatre organizations in various Czech communities. Some of the old plays in the original manuscript are still preserved in the Bubak family.

Only a few years ago the log house at Cat Springs, where the pioneer Bubak family lives, was torn down. A more modern residence had years before been built on the plantation. There is a tradition that somewhere on the place is buried $100,000 in gold, supposed to have been hidden in an old cannon by soldiers of the Mexican Army when in retreat. Treasure hunters have failed to find the buried gold, however. The legend is but a part of the rich and heroic part from which Texas history is made.

CHAPTER XXXII

FOUNDERS OF TEXAS MORAVIA

As FAR as the eye could reach there were fields of growing corn and straight green rows of cotton yet in its first trim, stubby stand. Cotton and corn at work and at play, for it was yet springtime in Texas. April showers and April breezes called for the dance of growing things.

There was as yet no hint of maturity in the blades of the dark green corn as they followed gracefully the rhythm of the intriguing wind. Corn tassels and cotton blossoms would come, but as yet all Nature was rejoicing in the anticipation of fruition.

The meadows and the long stretches of roadsides flaunted spring's carnival colors. Wild flowers in profusion—Sweet Williams, Indian Blankets, Primroses, purple Verbenas, yellow and white Daisies, Bluebells, red Poppies and Bluebonnets—spread a radiance of color and charm, while birds sang and bees busily gathered their honey.

A typical Texas rural scene, near Moravia, Texas, where, but a half century ago there had been only the unbroken stretch of the prairies and the "flowers left to bloom unseen and waste their fragrance on the desert air." This was before the coming of Jacob Hollub, pioneer.

In 1848 Jacob Hollub, a mason by trade, who lived in Myšši, Moravia, Central Europe, now a part of the Republic of Czechoslovakia, emigrated with his family to the United States, settling near Chelsea, Iowa, where he purchased a farm.

For eighteen years they were contented in this first chosen home location, but finally moved to Ackley, Iowa, where another farm was purchased. There a son, J. M. Hollub, now a citizen of Moravia, Texas, was born in 1861.

In 1876 Mr. and Mrs. Jacob Hollub, with their family, seven daughters and four sons, moved to Texas, settling in Lavaca County, near what is today Moravia, one of the most beautiful and productive agricultural sections of the State.

On reaching Texas Jacob Hollub bought a large tract of land. He had sold the farm in Iowa for a price sufficient to buy twice

DR. AND MRS. CHARLES T.
HOLLUB

Houston

as much acreage in Texas and to have money left to make necessary improvements and on which to live while waiting for the harvest.

Soon herds of cattle grazed on the open prairies, and on other acres corn and cotton grew. The rich, undulating land brought forth bountiful harvests. Nature had been generous in her arrangement of the country, giving an eminence here and there for homesites and leaving great level intervening spaces for fields and meadows.

Jacob Hollub and his son-in-law, J. F. Jalufka, founded the settlement in 1880 and called it Moravia. There a church and school were established. Near by was a large two-story frame building on the lower floor of which a general merchandising business was conducted. Above the store was a large dance hall and community recreation center. In addition to this building there was a cotton gin and blacksmith shop. In pioneer days the dance hall was the chief place of amusement and the means of bringing together the people of the sparsely-settled country. Music and the dance afforded opportunity for self-expression and recreation. Otherwise, the pioneer country would have been a desert without an oasis.

In 1881 the son of Mr. and Mrs. Jacob Hollub, who had been born in 1861 in the Iowa home, was married to Miss Johanna Matula, born at Bluff, Fayette County, Texas. Her parents were pioneers, having come to Texas from the native home at Myšši about the year 1856, along with a number of other families. Her father had left Austria-Hungary because of the oppression the Czech people suffered there. He was a forester in the territory that is today Czechoslovakia. In Texas he turned his attention to farming, buying land for that purpose near what is now known as Bluff, seven miles southwest of LaGrange. The house in which they lived was of the primitive log cabin type, common in pioneer days, and the farming was done with oxen.

J. M. Hollub with his young bride, born and reared in the adopted homeland, set up their home in the Moravia community near where the family homestead had been established. There he has since resided, having, however, on several occasions purchased additional acreage which has been devoted to farming. He has carried on this farming under scientific methods, and has prospered throughout the years, being known today as one of the most successful and prominent farmers and citizens of that and surrounding communities. A strong believer in education, he has given each of his children, three daughters and four sons, the opportunity to progress along these lines. All are to-day well established in life. One daughter, Annie— Mrs. A. J. Pustějovsky—lives at Moulton. Agnes—Mrs. August Pustějovsky—at Schulenburg. Frances—Mrs. William Hajek— at Schulenburg, where Mr. Hajek is engaged in business. Edward Hollub is married and lives at Hallettsville; William E. Hollub is married and lives at Schulenburg; James J. Hollub. still single, lives with his parents at Moravia. Dr. Charles J. Hollub is married and lives in Houston, where he is a practicing physician.

Dr. Hollub is an American citizen and a native of Texas. He was born on October 25, 1900, at Schulenburg. His father is a native of Iowa, but his mother is a native of Texas. He has been educated both at home and abroad. He received a "graduate in pharmacy" degree from the University of Texas, Galveston; is a registered pharmacist. His pre-medical training was at the San Antonio Academy and University of Texas. His medical degree— Doctor of Universal Medicine—was conferred upon him in 1927 by one of Europe's oldest universities, the Charles University of Praha, Czechoslovakia, which was founded by King Charles of Bohemia in 1348.

In 1928, he was married to Miss Marie Jelinek of Praha, Czechoslovakia. Miss Jelinek was qualified with the attainments of a splendid education. She speaks Czech, German, English and Spanish languages and is fairly conversant with Russian and Jugo-Slavian. She spent two years in London in preparation for teaching the English language in Praha. While she was a teacher in the Czechoslovakian capital she met Dr. Hollub. After their marriage they returned to Texas to make their permanent home.

During Dr. Hollub's sojourn in Czechoslovakia, he made a careful study of the political, social and economic conditions there and in the adjacent countries. The knowledge thus acquired is expected to be of great value to him in aiding those seeking advice and information about the Czechoslovak Republic.

When United States entered the World War, in 1917, the Austrian Consul's office at Galveston was closed. Following the World War, a consulate was opened in Galveston by the Czecho-slovak Republic, but it was closed several years ago.

In recent years trade between Port Houston and the Czecho-slovak Republic has steadily grown so that by 1933 more trade has gone out of Port Houston to Czechoslovakia than from any other Southern port, and the need for a Texas-Czech consulate, located at Houston, became evident. Application through the proper channels for the appointment of an honorary Czech Consul, with offices in Houston, was made.

In 1934, Dr. Charles J. Hollub of Houston, was appointed "Consul of the Czechoslovak Republic for the States of Texas, Oklahoma and New Mexico, with official residence in Houston, Texas." The title is "Honorary Consul," a non-paying position. The consulate will be the only one in the South.

The consular offices, officially opened May 1, 1934, will be located in connection with Dr. Hollub's professional suite, 711 Medical Arts Building. Mrs. Hollub will act as consular secretary.

Both Dr. and Mrs. Hollub have made for themselves a place in Houston's educational, social and artistic circles. They devote much of their time to the development of social and educational standards.

Dr. Hollub has taken an active part in putting the Czech language into the curriculum of the Houston public schools.

He spends much of his time in the interest of things that are of vital interest to the Czech people in Texas.

Mrs. Hollub, who is skilled in art, including lace-making and hand-embroidery, conducts during a part of the Summer season a class of instruction for young girls, who meet one evening each week at the Hollub home for a lesson in needle-craft and, incidentally, to enjoy a social hour.

James J. Hollub, is an ex-service man, having received total disability government recognition for World War service. This disability forced him to give up the continuance of his university education in which he had, previous to his entrance into the World War, three and a half years pre-medical training at the University of Texas. After the World War he returned to college and completed two and a half years of medicine at the University of Colorado at Boulder, but, due to his physical condition, was forced to discontinue his studies. He lives at home with his parents on the family estate at Moravia, where he is devoting his time to writing, scientific study and research.

Mr. and Mrs. J. M. Hollub, parents of the family of seven children, enjoy the comforts of a splendid and commodious country home. Surrounding the house are the hundreds of fertile acres which have made possible the rearing and educating of the family.

Seated on either of one of two porches which extend the full length of the Hollub home at Moravia, these pioneer settlers can look out over the broad acres of cultivated soil where formerly there was not a house in sight; where the country, fifty years ago, was a wilderness and where there was no sign of the progress and development that is in evidence today.

An automobile swings gracefully through the wide farm gate leading from the highway through the flower-decked meadow. The rhythm of a towering windmill wheel, turning leisurely, lends a touch of mechanical industry to the pastoral scene. Beneath the wide spreading branches of a native oak, a herd of cattle grazes. At some little distance water flows into the drinking trough, fresh from the depths of the well.

In the commodious farm home the telephone, the radio, books and magazines bring contact with the great outside world.

At the age of seventy-one, this Texas pioneer is hale and hearty and finds pleasure, peace and contentment. The feel of the plough handles is yet one of the greatest joys of living.

*   *   *   *   *

J. E. Jalufka, co-founder with Jacob Hollub of the community of Moravia, lived at the home he established as a part of the community until his death in January, 1920. The widow, Mrs. Jalufka, sister of Jacob Hollub, still resides at the old family home. Fourteen children, born and reared in the imposing two-story house, have all gone away into homes of their own making, taking with them some heritage of the pioneer spirit which brought their parents and grandparents into a new and undeveloped country.

Across from the old Jalufka home, which stands with the calm dignity of age, is the same two-story frame building that pioneer Jalufka erected fifty years ago for a general merchandising business and dance hall. The activity of the community still centers around this building and the cotton gin across the road.

Of the large family of sons and daughters of the Jalufka family, eleven are living, three having died after they had reached the years of maturity. Mrs. Joe Chromčak, formerly Anna Jalufka, is the wife of a farmer at Hallettsville. James Jalufka is a farmer residing at Violet. Agnes—Mrs. John Retorik—is the wife of a farmer at Violet. Julie—Mrs. Emil Gieptner—and husband, live at Schulenburg. Lillie—Mrs. Frank Blahuta—is the wife of a merchant at Moravia. They own the old Jalufka building of the pioneer days. Julius G. Jalufka is a teller in a Hallettsville bank. Carrie—Mrs. Charles Ford—is the wife of an inspector of railroad cars at Houston. Jerome Jalufka is a ginner at Violet. Willie Mae—Mrs. Herman Schwenke—is the wife of a salesman

at El Paso. Miss Helen Jalufka is a stenographer in Hallettsville. Ollie—Mrs. Vernon Brauner—resides at Schulenburg. The
deceased were Frances—Mrs. Alfred Gieptner—of Shiner; Mary
—Mrs. Eugene Cravens—wife of a physician of San Antonio,
and Miss Edna Jalufka of San Antonio.

*   *   *   *   *

The pioneer settlers, Jacob Hollub and J. F. Jalufka, established a landmark when they founded Moravia, Texas. They
ploughed and they sowed, they winnowed and they reaped,
progress and development springing up along the pathway that
felt the imprint of their footsteps. The pathway widened with the
years into the highway and then a trail was blazed from the great
outside world to their very doors.

The trail today is the beaten path along which travel the children and the children's children of these pioneers, even to the
third and the fourth generations.

CHAPTER XXXIII

Josef and Mary Wondrash

FROM a long line of loyal Czechs, came Josef Wondrash and his wife, Mary (née Sopr), who have played a distinct part in the development of Czech interests in Texas during the last half-century. Oppressed in the Old Country, as were so many of their race, they eventually turned their faces toward the land of liberty, where they became devoted citizens of the American Union's largest state.

The story of Josef Wondrash's experiences, both before and after his migration to Texas, can best be told in his own words:

"By tradition, in the latter part of the Seventeenth Century, my great-grandfather Wondrasch moved to Nova Kryně from Straž, a village of Psohlavci, which is situated near Pomazlice. In former times the people of Psohlavci had a concession to guard the boundaries of Bohemia against their enemies, for which service they were not obligated to work free, "robota," for the various lords. This concession was granted to them in prehistoric times by the kings and rulers of Bohemia. In the year 1040, a church was built in commemoration of a victory by Břetislav over King Henry III near Brudek. This church was built in honor of St. Vaclav because the battle was fought on the day of St. Vaclav. The church still stands and is in good order. My grandfather, Vaclav Kotek, because his name was Vaclav, took me, when I was just a little tot, to this church once a year.

"My grandfather, George Wondrasch, was born in 1802. His mother died when he was an infant. For the second bride, his father chose a German girl from Hirshov, but he died soon after his marriage. The training of the child was left to the stepmother, who, being an ardent German, brought him up in accordance with her German feelings, thoughts and ideas. She was one of the "praying sisters" mentioned in the story "Lusy" written by J. S. Baar. She spent most of her husband's money building a cloister at Hirshov.

"My grandfather, Vaclav Kotek, was born at Velka Chuchle, near Praha. In later years, he met and married a Miss Sperl.

Later they moved to Nova Kdyňe, where Grandfather Kotek died in 1869. He was an ardent Czech and a good Czech patriot. These traits were inherited by my mother, through whom I, in turn, must have inherited my share.

"My grandfathers, one a Czech and the other a German, often engaged in friendly clashes, although they had very little love for each other.

"My mother, Rozalie (Rosie) Kotek, was a daughter of Vaclav and Mary (née Sperl) Kotek. My mother died when I was but two years old, and I was raised by my grandmother, Mary Kotek. From her father, she inherited Czech patriotism, and this she imparted to me. She was honest and upright, and I am sure that the early teaching of these ideas had a lifetime influence upon me.

"My father, Frederick Wondrasch, born in 1822, was a veterinary, a graduate of the Vienna Veterinary Hospital. I was born in the year of 1861, at Nova Kdyňe na Šumavě, Čechy. This city is close to the boundary line of Čechy and Bavaria. My father taught me to read both Czech and German when I was very young. I vividly remember one incident in my life. My sister, who was two years older, took me along with her to school, and there I saw the year 1865 written on the blackboard. Evidently I was only four years old. I also remember very distinctly the year 1866, the year of the war between Austria and Prussia. Many soldiers marched through the city and many remained stationed there. I remember the incessant beating of the drums. The soldiers were mostly Saxons with high hats.

"When I graduated from school, I obtained a position with a notary in our town as an errand boy and copyist. I stayed there a few months. Then I obtained a position in a colonial merchandise store, where I stayed for several years. Then I obtained a position at Česky Brod, but I did not like it there, so I went to Vienna, where I stayed for several months, or until I decided to go to America. I arrived in New York, on April 7, 1879, where I obtained a position with Josef Křikava, a wine dealer. Here I worked for ,several years. Mr. Křikava (surnamed Dědeček meaning grandfather), was one of the revolutionists of 1848. After the collapse of the revolution, he was exiled. He was a very intelligent and learned man, and a graduate of the Praha Polytechnic Institute. At one time he was associated with Vojta Naprstek, at Milwaukee, Wisconsin.

"When I arrived in New York, Mr. Křikava had been in this country for thirty years. I stayed with him for seven years, and during the most of this time attended night school. While working there, I met Miss Mary Sopr. We were married in 1885.

"After my marriage I first worked as a salesman, later as a clerk in various stores in New York. Then I bought a store and started out on my own. I did well. When the new Wholesale Market on First Avenue and 100th Street was opened, I went into the wholesale business. This was during President Grover Cleveland's second administration, 1892-93, when the country went through a panic similar to the one of 1930-33. I had to sell goods on thirty-day credit, and when the time came to collect, I found closed doors posted with notices of bankruptcy proceedings. As I could not collect, I could not pay my obligations, so I gave up.

"Trouble does not come singly, for about this time my brother-in-law became ill. The doctors pronounced it consumption and advised him to seek some warmer and dryer climate, so he decided to go to Texas. His wife and mine were sisters, and upon their solicitation, I went with him. The change worked wonders and he recovered completely. We both liked Texas—in fact, so enamored did I become of the State and its opportunities that when I returned to New York I was not satisfied. I could not forget the boundless prairies, the independence of the farmers and the cheapness of material. I stayed East one year and then came back to this glorious State to stay.

"For the first three years I had a restaurant at LaGrange. During this time I studied under Professor McCullough, who was principal of the LaGrange High School. I would study when the customers were few; I attended school at night, and I studied at night. After three years of diligent study during every spare moment. I took an examination for a teacher's certificate, and passed. Thus was one of my life's greatest ambitions realized. I had always wanted to do something worth while, to show others how to help themselves, both by precept and by example. Teaching, I thought, offered this opportunity. I taught school for several years. I was pleased with my work, as I came in contact with a large number of my own people, namely the Czechs. I was often called on to make speeches. After many years of teaching school, I changed my vocation and secured a position as deputy with John McCowen, County Clerk, at Caldwell, Texas. This position I filled for nine years. Then I was elected County Clerk for four successive terms.

"In 1900 I began working up the abstracts of city and county property in Burleson County. At this time there were two abstract companies. Both of these were later consolidated, at Caldwell, Texas, and I became the manager.

"My wife, Mary Sopr, was born in 1861, at Kozlany, Čechy. Her mother was Frances (née Frijova) Sopr, and her father was John Sopr. He was the oldest son and should have inherited the possessions of his parents, but during the war of 1848, an incident happened which changed his career. At this time every one had to give six days free labor to his lord. One day he was late for the "robota," and the overseer struck him with a whip. This angered John Sopr, and he thrashed the officer soundly. After this encounter, he ran away and went into hiding, as he well knew that his chances for a fair trial were very slim. Consequently, he lost the inheritance, which passed on to his younger brother. Three years ago my wife and I visited Czechoslovakia and the old home. The estate, I suppose, is the same today as it was hundreds of years ago."

During the years that Mr. Wondrash taught school at High Prairie, New Tabor, and other places, he was much sought after as a speaker at holiday celebrations and other gatherings. He spoke both in Czech and English. His speeches were inspiring, always advising his listeners to strive for the higher and nobler things in life, especially education. He admonished his fellow citizens to plan their lives in such manner that their adopted country might be proud of them.

Mr. Wondrash is an ardent supporter of education, but in particular is he interested in the teaching of Czech in the universities and schools of Texas. To this cause he has devoted much time and energy.

In 1934, each seventy-three years of age, well on into the evening of their lives, Josef and Mary Wondrash are due worthy and esteemed mention for all the charitable and worth while endeavors they have contributed toward the upbuilding of the State and particularly for the inspiration they have engendered among the Czechs in Texas.

CHAPTER XXXIV

ALOIS MORKOVSKY, EDUCATOR

Alois Mořkovsky is a Texas-Czech pioneer who likewise has given much. He is a man, however, who does not care for publicity. He insists that he has not become famous, but his work lives in the lives of many and his influence will never die.

Alois Mořkovsky was born in a suburb of Frenštat, Moravia, in old Austria-Hungary, now Czechoslovakia, in June, 1870. He was the seventh in a family of twelve children born to Josef and Theresia (Drapal) Mořkovsky. The family, through force of circumstances and unavoidable conditions, lived in distressing poverty. The father was almost wholly incapacitated for work by an affliction of the legs with which he had suffered from a time soon after marriage until near the end of his life, covering a period of thirty-five years. About eighty florins a year from day labor at a hand-loom represented the earnings of the mother and father of this large family of twelve. From this meagre sum rent, food and clothing had to be provided.

Nine of the undernourished children died in their infancy. At the age of four little Alois was taught the letters of the alphabet. The mother was fond of reading, which she indulged in on Sundays, at which time of leisure she taught Alois. While she worked she sang and conjured mental pictures in which no doubt the four-year-old son had a part.

At the age of six Alois was admitted to the second grade of a well-organized school in the community. Each year he advanced a grade until the Spring of 1881, when his mother died, and the schooling came to an end.

Two years later Alois came to Texas. An uncle, John Mořkovsky, was moving with his family to America. He induced the father of Alois to permit him to come along. The uncle had six daughters and no sons. He wanted to adopt the little nephew, but this the father refused. But he did consent to allow the boy to emigrate along with the uncle and his family.

"It is hard for you, without means, to learn a trade and I hate to be in your way. If America has a better opening for you, I bid you go and with my blessing. Be a good boy and God be with you," was the father's blessing.

In April, 1883, John Mořkovsky with his family consisting of wife, five daughters and the boy, Alois, arrived in Texas without money. Even a large bundle of the best family clothing which they had started the journey with, had been lost.

The sixth daughter, Petronyla Rainošek, was married and already settled at Bluff, Fayette County, Texas.

And thus began the life of Alois Mořkovsky, the boy pioneer. For four years he worked for the uncle, using what time he could call his own to study. He read anything he could get hold of. In the meanwhile he learned to speak German fluently, yearning, as he recalls today, for knowledge of the English language.

During these four years the uncle's worldly possessions had increased to include a pair of horses, some rather poor farm equipment and some household furnishings, the whole given a total valuation of $150.00. Two of the daughters had married by this time and the sons-in-law lived at home with the family. Alois was hoping for something better for himself.

One day a farmer approached the boy and asked if he would not work for him, offering as a wage $70.00 per year. This the boy refused, saying that as his uncle had paid the cost of his emigration he would be ungrateful to leave him. But thinking the matter over, he decided that he must begin to provide something for his future, so he went to his uncle with a proposition, setting forth his plea somewhat as follows:

"Uncle, you promised to adopt me as your son and to bequeath to me a portion of what you have, the same as to your own children. I am thankful for what you have done for me, but I do not want to share in an inheritance, and I do not want to leave you, so am asking if you will pay me $40.00 a year wages so that I may stay on and work for you."

The uncle was much incensed at the request of his young nephew and spoke of what he termed ingratitude. He agreed to pay only $30.00 per year.

Deciding that he could not afford to work for this amount, the boy left his uncle's home on New Year's Day, 1887. With him he took nine articles of clothing, his entire worldly possessions. He left without the uncle's blessing.

The uncle died some two years later. He had not found prosperity in the new country, but he had brought and left in Texas the boy, Alois. For two years Alois worked for the farmer, who paid him $75.00 a year. Sixty-five dollars of this sum was lost, however, on account of seven weeks' illness which came during the second year of his service.

"In 1889," he recalls, "a good man, Anton Nesrsta, a teacher at Praha, hired me for $125.00 a year to work his farm."

The following year he worked for an American family because he wanted to learn English. Here, after his hard daily task of cultivating sixty-five acres of land, planted to crops, and tending a herd of cattle, he studied late into the nights to learn the language. During those long night hours he frequently despaired of ever knowing English as he heard it spoken.

It was late in the Fall that he found the man to whom he had hired was not keeping his promise to pay. It was then that he took his fate in his own hands, making arrangements with a Professor M. H. Allis, who conducted a boarding school at Moulton, to attend that institution. This school had been in existence since 1874. In return for his schooling he was to work on the farm and do such yard work as might be assigned to him.

Leaving the family for whom he had worked for ten months without receiving his pay, he became a schoolboy again for the first time since his mother's death, in 1881. Here, at the age of twenty-one years, he studied spelling, geography and grammar with the third grade children, and arithmetic with the sixth grade, overcoming many difficulties by studying until eleven o'clock at night and rising from his bed at four o'clock in the morning to keep up with his other work. After a month of this strenuous labor the boy's health began to fail and he went with his problem to Professor Allis, asking what extra charge would he make for the time he was giving to the farm work.

The years of hardships suffered in the new home had not been without ill results. Ten months of hard labor on a farm, and this without pay, took the young Czech to the doors of the institution of learning. Moulton Institute, in a sad plight. Poor food and the heavy, exhausting work had depleted his strength and physical resistance. After a month and a week in the school, illness came and he was forced to give up. A severe case of yellow jaundice robbed him for a time of his hopes and cherished ambitions of becoming a scholar. After leaving school he was able to recuperate somewhat and when sufficiently recovered, he began the search for employment that would give him the opportunity for using what store of knowledge he might have and to use brain instead of brawn as he had been doing for many weary months.

He looked first for a position as a clerk in some store. Failure brought discouragement and finally, when almost in despair, he was hired again to do farm work.

Frank Jander, teacher in a Moravian school, in Fayette County, gave him the work at a salary of $10.00 per month, the contract calling for two months' work. When the time was up he was engaged for an additional four months. Watching the teacher in the evening doing some of the school work at home, the young farmhand decided that he could do the work equally as well if not better.

With a small tin lamp in the barn, he began to spend all his spare time, often till daybreak, with grammar, spelling and geography and whatever other textbooks he could get hold of. Here, in the confines of the barn, lighted by the small flame of the lowly kerosene lamp, ambition flamed and grew. Far from the place of his birth and the land of his people, alone, and as it seemed, almost friendless, he looked ahead and into the future—a future in which he staked his claim and planned his work. He decided to use what he knew to help other Bohemian children. If only he could get a license to teach school! He read Hughes' "Theory and Practice of Teaching," deciding that to be a teacher was the noblest work of all.

With this thought in mind he studied harder, and in October, 1891, he took a teacher's examination at LaGrange, receiving a third-class certificate with an average of a sixty-seven grade, with ninety-six in reading.

Moved by what he termed his "gratitude to God," he paid his older brother's passage over from Europe, "to get him out of poverty there."

A school at Radhost, a mile southwest from his first home in America, was offered him and there he began what he considered to be an exalted and noble work. His duties consisted in instructing thirty-four Bohemian children at a compensation of $30.00 per month. The public school apportionment in Texas at this time was $4.75 per child, and with the addition of private contributions he was able to teach seven months.

After the term ended he went to LaGrange to take a month's study in the public school, and at the next examination he received a second grade teacher's certificate for two years. He was invited to teach the Greive school and made the necessary contract. This took him from Lavaca County to Fayette County to teach a seven months' term for $300.00. At this school he made every effort to improve his teaching methods, also laying stress on the value of morality and diligence on the part of the pupils, teaching the while English, Czech and German. In addition to the regular pupils he had a class of twenty-two grown Czech men in a night school, and these he taught English, arithmetic and Texas history. He also directed the activities of a dramatic club at Praha for several successful Bohemian performances.

The young teacher learned that an appointment worth a monetary consideration of $54.00 was granted by State officials to the Sam Houston Normal Institute at Huntsville, where a permanent teacher's diploma could be obtained upon the completion of a three years' course. Through the help of Judge Augustin Haidušek of LaGrange, who was impressed with the worth of the young man, he received the appointment from the State Representative, Honorable Joseph Peter of Dubina, Fayette County, and immediately left for this school with his meagre savings and the determination to work.

He was received into the lowest class, but by heroic study, he succeeded in getting the scholarship medal of his class and finding great favor with the faculty. During the summer vacation he sold books to earn money for his board, and on obtaining the appointment again, returned to school at Huntsville. During this session, his instructor in history and civics, Professor Henry Estill, in collaboration with Professor Oscar H. Cooper and Leonard Lemon, wrote the "History of Our Country," and young Alois Mořkovsky was employed to make twenty-eight maps for this textbook which was later adopted for Texas schools.

During the summer vacation he was employed to teach school for two months at Old Sweet Home, Lavaca County. This enabled the student-teacher to add a few dollars to his depleted savings. He returned in the fall to the Sam Houston Normal Institute, where the principal, Professor H. C. Pritchett, again obtained an appointment for him. During the year he won first place in calisthenics. In a debate he won the affirmative question that a uniform series of textbooks would not be detrimental to State educational interests. He won a reputation as an unusual student in all his studies, including drawing, calisthenics and singing. He was awarded his diploma in June, 1896.

Only three months before his graduation he had received a telegram from LaGrange advising him that the brother, whose passage he had paid from Europe, had died from heart failure while he slept. This bereavement was a heavy blow to Alois, and for a time seriously affected his mind. He became despondent, dejected, indifferent. The brother, Josef, was the only person he had to love.

With his diploma and without a cent of money he was engaged again to teach the Old Sweet Home school. Two years later, at the age of twenty-eight, he married Miss Mary Raška of Koerth and built a home on a two and one-half acre lot he bought near that school. Two children were born to them there.

He was the organist for the new Catholic parish at Sweet Home; won in a debating society there against H. Key, a debater never before conquered. The subject was "Man's Success in Life Depends Upon Morality." He was appointed county member of teachers' examiners, which position he held seven years.

In the late summer of 1901 Mr. Mořkovsky was called to Moulton with Professor C. A. Peterson of Hallettsville to teach is the newly-erected Sam and Will Moore Institute. Here for four years he taught the fifth and sixth grades, assisting also in the high school work and teaching the Czech language. During the third year his room won three of the thirty-six prizes offered for scholarship on examination to sixty-five schools in the county by the school superintendent, F. G. Guenther. Later he helped Superintendent Guenther in devising a county course of study and an annual five-day institute for teachers.

Leaving Moulton, he moved with his family—now with five children—back to Greive school, where he had taught more than twelve years before. Here he taught six school terms of seven months each. Living in a house with a garden, rent free, he was able to save more of $500.00 a year than of the $700.00 he had received at Moulton. The school being on the county line, he attended teachers' meetings in both Fayette and Lavaca counties; gave lectures on different subjects; originated a course of study for Fayette County schools; conducted a class of ten Czech teachers monthly for half a year in Czech orthography; conducted a night school twice a week for six months at Praha (three miles north) and trained a dramatic club there.

His own children he taught in school from their fifth year in both English and Czech, and sent them to other schools when his term was out. His reputation as a teacher spread and soon pupils were sent to him from distant places.

From Greive school he moved to Vvšehrad (Smother's Creek) school, but their oldest son, Alois, Jr., being too far advanced for his classes, was sent to Hallettsville where he was placed in the seventh grade, omitting the sixth.

This moving about with the growing family created a desire for a permanent home, conveniently located; hence, after having finished that term, he bought a farm not so much for its fertility as for its location. It had a school at one corner, was two and one-half miles from the Yoakum high school, and offered a good market for produce. There they moved in the Spring of 1912 and tried to make their living.

After three years young Alois, having passed the tenth grade, expressed a desire to become a priest. The father warned him of the pitfalls in that calling, explaining because "the higher in position one climbs, the more danger there is of falling, and it is especially so in the priesthood." He recited to him from experience the good and bad examples of priestly lives and gave him a long time to think it over. Finding him later even more determined, he was sent to the Seminary a year before graduation from high school, for better instruction in Latin and other academic subjects that would prepare him for the calling; but if later he should decide that the strain of study or the anticipated life was too hard, Professor Mořkovsky told him to come home and study for whatever he liked.

The farming efforts were wasted and after five years of this, when cotton fell to six cents, Mr. Mořkovsky left for Ammannsville to take charge of a two-teacher school with one hundred and twenty-seven children. With a university-trained assistant, Professor Anton Hajek of Bryan, the term passed successfully. A hundred and forty-five volume school library was established and a sentiment for a third teacher created.

During the summer vacation Mr. Mořkovsky succeeded in getting forty-seven pupils to attend a two-month instruction in Czech reading, orthography, number work, Czech history and practical knowledge. This kind of instruction he had conducted in every school except Moulton, during thirteen summers, because he noticed that the Czech children progressed much better in English studies after having had this training in their mother tongue.

But now the United States entered the World War; there were prejudices against any except English, and his Czech instruction was never patronized after that year.

For the next term two assistants were obtained to teach one hundred and thirty-four children in eight grades. The handsome Catholic church, near the teacherage, burned down. Farmers had made no corn or feed the year before. The people of the community lost interest in many things. Mr. Mořkovsky, after finishing the term, left to take the position of a clerk in a Yoakum bank.

After fifteen months the trustees of the Praha public school begged him to take charge of their institution, because it had dwindled down to ten pupils and was in danger of being closed. That was a stab into his pedagogic heart. He left the bank and went to teach that school. In two years the attendance grew to fifty-two and the people were willing to do anything to keep up the work. The family was not making even a living on the farm, so they all moved to Praha. Mr. Mořkovsky organized and helped to maintain a local farmers' union, organized and incorporated the Engle Gin Company, but because of some disagreement in that organization he lost the Praha school and moved to Shiner. There he sold life insurance and in the following summer—1924—enjoyed two of the happiest events of his life.

His oldest son, Alois, after twenty years' of diligent study, was ordained priest of God and celebrated his first solemn sacrifice of the mass in the beautifully decorated church in Shiner, to which celebration over three thousand people came from hundreds of miles around.

A few days later Mr. Mořkovsky was engaged to teach a summer school for teachers with the help of five other instructors. He taught spelling, penmanship, English grammar, Texas history, agriculture and botany, teaching alternately seventy students, thirty-three of them religious Sisters; all being teachers, or becoming such.

During that summer another son, Johnnie L., expressed a desire to study for the priesthood. With practically the same warnings he had given Alois, he was sent to St. John's Seminary, San Antonio.

In the fall Mr. Mořkovsky was asked to become a member of the County Board of Education, which position he accepted and still holds, though opposed by several candidates and never soliciting a single vote. The February following his first appointment to the board he was requested to take charge of a three-teacher school at Wied, which was badly in need of building up. He finished the eight-month term there successfully and was requested in the fall to take charge of a three-teacher school at Komensky, nine miles east of Moulton.

After four successful terms of teaching at Komensky, Mr. Mořkovsky was urged to become editor of a Czech Catholic semiweekly, *Novy Domov,* at Hallettsville. He somewhat reluctantly consented and moved there with his family, where they reside at the present. But he writes principally for the *Lavaca County Tribune,* published at the same printery.

In the past eight years he had been urged in Lavaca and

Fayette counties to run for county superintendent of schools. At another time he was solicited for congressman; but his plea has been that he did not feel competent, and that whatever he undertook, he wanted to do excellently or not at all. During his life as a teacher, his prayers, he says, were most often that God grant him the ability and energy to lead the young students entrusted to him toward an honorable life, and that by his instruction, to help them to achievement in worth-while things. Of his pupils more than one hundred and fifty are, or have been, teachers. Some are physicians, others bankers and business men, all filling honorable stations in life. Professor Mořkovsky has now rounded out sixty-three years of life and remarks as he looks in retrospect to his early childhood and environment that there is no limit to the bounds of his gratitude to God for what He has permitted him to do.

His father had two brothers and two sisters who left no male descendants and it would appear that it has been left to this Texas pioneer to perpetuate the name and keep the branches on the family tree. Seven sons and three daughters have been born to Professor and Mrs. Alois Mořkovsky. All are living and well, the youngest past seventeen.

These children would be the pride of any family. Alois J. is a priest of God and professor in a seminary; Emil J., with a family of four children, is a custodian of the famous Mission Concepción, San Antonio; Joe A., married, is a mail clerk in a Houston terminal and in railway mail cars; Ladik A. is a secretary and bookkeeper in the United States Immigration and Border Patrol office at Brownsville; Henry J., married, with one little daughter, is a bookkeeper and assistant manager of a laundry in San Antonio; John L. is a theological student in Rome, and expecting soon to be ordained priest; Bessie T. married Professor George Kocian, taught under his principalship a year, and is now training their own little son; Marie Z. married Professor Louis F. Hrnčiř and they, with their little daughter and son, live at Nada; Alfons and Anita are at home with their parents, the former having been graduated from Hallettsville high school in 1932.

"What greater happiness or fame or honor could any man want in this life?" questions this Texas-Czech. As for himself, he says that he has been lifted from abject poverty, not to wealth, but "to a condition with plenty to eat and to wear," and his own home with its vine and fig-tree; from low degree to the most exalted position of a teacher of youth and also teacher of teachers.

While he does not lay claim to any feat or famous historical deed, yet he holds to the hope that his adopted country, Texas, has benefited from his having lived. With all his loyalty to America— and his patriotism is of a high order—Professor Mořkovsky has kept his love for his mother tongue and country and has tried to instill the same love into those with whom he has associated, asking the question "if one can love both parents and several brothers and sisters, why can't one love two or more languages and two or more countries?" He does not say, "I am for America, right or wrong," but rather tries to do his share toward keeping America from being wrong by fighting his own faults and teaching others to do likewise.

The story of Professor Mořkovsky is representative of the struggle that belonged with pioneer days in Texas. While he was not one of the earliest of the Czech settlers, yet the half-century he has lived in Texas has afforded him opportunity of standing on the threshold of pioneer life. From this footing the march has been onward, keeping step with progress and development.

CHAPTER XXXV

The House of Hanak

Ten-year-old Samuel Hanak, grandfather of a Texas-Czech, stood on the docks at Hamburg in 1840, his young face wet with tears he could not control. The vessel was about to sail away to America without him. He had made his way under great difficulties for a considerable distance to this seaport city, only to find that he could not obtain passage to the land of freedom about which he had heard such wonderful stories. Then, almost at the last minute, when hope had all but fled, he found himself in the protecting arms of a young Jewish mother, to be taken along with her own five children as one of the family on board the vessel.

And so it came to pass that the young Czech boy, whose mother had died when he was three and his father when he was five, took his place as an adopted son in the Jewish immigrant family bound for the City of New York.

Arriving in New York, the boy, Samuel, went along with his benefactors into the Ghetto where he was provided for and made welcome for two years. But young Samuel was the son of the historical tribe of Hanaks, fearless protectors of the borderlands of his native land, Czechoslovakia. The blood of his ancestors coursed through his veins, giving him the courage to dare and do in the new country, even as he had dared to stand alone in the City of Hamburg, waiting for the opportunity to sail away to the new land of promise.

His was an eventful life. His days were like those recounted of crusaders along down the ages. He was one of the "forty-niners" who, at the call of gold, set out for California. He crossed the continent in a caravan of two hundred and twenty-eight persons, frequently referred to as the Drake caravan. It was made up at St. Louis and followed the old Mormon Trail, in part, covering approximately 2,400 miles. Samuel Hanak struck gold, not once but several times, made as many fortunes and sunk them again in other ventures.

He had met one morning while attending mass in a Catholic church in New York a young Czech girl and they were married.

308

She traveled around the "Horn" in a sailing vessel to join him in California. Her death occurred there a few years later. Again he met a Czech girl, one who had been born in Vienna. They were married and this wife died years after in Houston, in the home of her son, Edward Hanak. Another son, Ben Hanak, lived in Chicago. Her people had been among the early immigrants to the United States. One member of the family, Major George Stepper, had been a West Pointer, having graduated from the military academy in 1828 with the title of major. Major Stepper is a maternal grandparent of Edward Hanak of Houston.

It has been a long trail from the dock at Hamburg, where the orphan Czech boy, Samuel Hanak, wandered up and down, sobbing at the sight of the vessel ready to leave port without him. The son, Edward, has carried on, blazing for himself a path into a fertile field—that of invention. He received his education at Stephens Institute, Hoboken, N. J., was graduated in 1891 as a mining engineer, and started work in Salt Lake City. He built, among his first big projects, a mining mill for the Preston Syndicate at Deep Creek. The story of the work in the field of mining engineering belongs within a volume of its own and will be thus chronicled and preserved by Mr. Hanak. Some years ago, looking toward this undertaking, he made a trip, after fifty years, over the same route which his father had traveled as a "forty-niner," to gather the historical material for the proposed memoirs.

To-day Edward Hanak has fifty-eight patents on his own inventions. In 1886 he invented the first "nickel-in-the-slot" telephone device ever known and used. He sold this invention for $7,000. The man to whom he sold it received $40,000 for it, and Mr. Hanak says that to-day it is worth a fortune.

Many years ago he invented the automatic scale, which is still in use and on which he has a number of patents. It was the rice-milling industry that brought Mr. Hanak south, first to New Orleans, where he became associated with that industry. The model of a five-story rice-mill which he built there was awarded the gold medal at the St. Louis Exposition in 1904. He built several large rice-mills in Texas, one in Eagle Lake and one in Houston.

Arriving in Texas in 1909, he associated himself with the Texas City Terminal Company. From Texas City he moved to Houston in 1912, where he has since engaged in business, having extensive machine shops and construction plants in operation. The Hanak conveyors are built in a number of different types, including overhead trolley systems that are universal, negotiating great distances. In one instance a conveyor has been constructed and installed for carrying barrels and cases from the railroad dock to and from the fifth floor of a bottling plant, crossing a street by means of a viaduct and passing over three buildings two and one-half blocks in length. The Hanak conveyors for loading and unloading ships at Port Houston are to be found in constant operation. Some time ago Mr. Hanak built and sold to the United States Government four unloading machines for barges operating on the Mississippi River. He is also the inventor and builder of small passenger elevators for use in private homes.

In 1925 Mr. Hanak had a tragic accident in his laboratory, an explosion costing him the loss of both eyes. Since then he has learned to carry on with his work, having in large measure overcome the obstacle of blindness through the remarkable development of an inner sight. He dictates geometrically to his stenographer, using what he terms, "the blind system," and so accurate are his calculations that a piece of mechanical work can be carried to completion without a defect, by these dictated specifications, mentally calculated.

Mr. Hanak makes his home in Houston, his office being in the rear of his residence. There he is to be found all day and on many evenings at his desk, carrying on the work of his machine plants. His telephone is one of the busy ones of Houston. He is a member of The Engineers Club of Houston and one of the charter members of the Rotary Club. Speaking one day to a visitor in his office about the Hanak family, he mentioned that while a guest at a luncheon of the Galveston Rotary Club, some years ago, he sat next to the late Father Kirwin of Galveston. From Father Kirwin he learned of the young priest, Joseph Hanak, now located at Caldwell, and through him he got the geneology of the Hanaks for 325 years. Mr. Hanak has made the geneology of the family a study for a number of years and has been able to gather the material that covers more than three centuries. Mr. Vincent Hanak, jeweler, of Hallettsville, is one of the Texas-Czech Hanaks.

Edward Hanak of Houston has been married three times. Two daughters were born in the first marriage and live in California. A son, Edward, Jr., and a daughter, Mary, are children of the second marriage, their mother having been a Miss Dana of New Orleans. The third wife is a native of London, England. Edward Hanak, Jr., assists his father in business, and is a member of the Houston Little Theater. In addition to histrionic ability, he has musical talent which includes a splendid tenor voice.

CHAPTER XXXVI

TEXAS-CZECH PHYSICIANS AND DENTISTS

ONE of the most important of the developments that has gone hand-in-hand with the progress of Texas has been the promotion program undertaken by the men of medical science in the State. Not specifically as State physicians who have exercised authority in making physical examinations, or in that of making tests and cults, but rather as men who, through the medium of their profession as doctors of medicine, are administering to the ills of a large clientele.

A fair representation of Texas doctors of medicine is to be found among the Texas-Czech citizenship. Many Czech pioneer families are represented through the third and fourth generations by those who have chosen as professions the practice of medicine and surgery.

The ills and the privations of pioneer ancestors have in many instances left lasting impressions. The story oft told of how many miles it was necessary to ride in the darkness of night, through a wild country, over roads that were but blazed trails, to get a doctor, doubtless inspired some of the sons of the pioneers to become men of medicine.

In all parts of Texas are to be found practicing Czech doctors, successful in their work—successful, no doubt, because they chose this profession in an inspired moment, when the weaver at the loom of fate ordained that they should minister to the ills to which the human flesh is heir.

These Texas-Czech citizens are traveling the road of sincerity of purpose, and their zeal will accordingly take them far along the great highway of medicine. To know the ideals and the work of each would be an interesting privilege.

Some of these have labored and passed on, leaving their work to a new generation. The late Dr. J. S. Zvesper was for a number of years located at West, Texas, and at the time of his death on January 20, 1929, was a practicing physician at Schulenburg, where his wife and eleven children survive him.

Dr. F. G. Daehne, another of the pioneer Texas-Czech physicians, died in March, 1929, he having preceded Dr. Zvesper at West. A son, Allen Daehne, is in the drug business at Flatonia.

*   *   *   *   *

Frank J. Stanislav, M. D., of Waco, is the son of pioneer settlers. His father, John Stanislav, born in Stramberg, Moravia, in 1851, emigrated to Texas during the latter '60s, settling in Austin County. There he met and married Mary Marak, daughter of pioneer Frank Marak. In 1872, soon after their marriage, they moved to Cold Springs in Central Texas, near what is now the town of West. They were among the first Czech families to settle in that section of the State. John Stanislav is responsible for much of the early development of that community. Being energetic and thrifty, he made a success of farming. He was, in addition, progressive and soon identified himself with many projects that were inaugurated for the interest and betterment of the community.

Forty years ago, when the West Cotton Mill was built, he was one of the directors of the institution, and has continued his connection ever since, holding the same official position throughout the forty years. To-day the product of this Texas textile manufactory is shipped all over the world.

The son, Dr. Frank J. Stanislav, was reared on the farm and attended the neighboring schools. In 1906 he matriculated at St. Basil's College, Waco, one of the historic Catholic colleges for young men. Three years later he entered St. Louis University, St. Louis, Missouri, from which he graduated in medicine on June 4, 1916. After graduation Dr. Stanislav took his interneship at Providence Sanitarium, Waco. He was married on July 19, 1917, to Miss Meta Loesch of Waco, and in the following year he entered the United States Army for World War service, receiving a commission as first lieutenant in the Medical Corps. He served seven months with the American Expeditionary Forces in France and Germany.

In France he was connected with Base Hospital No. 123, located at Hospital Center No. 20. After the Armistice he went into Germany and served four months at the Evacuation Hospital No. 22, Coblenz. On returning from overseas Dr. Stanislav resigned from the army to locate and begin the practice of medicine and surgery at Waco, where he has since remained. He is a member of the County and State Medical Association. He serves also on the Medical Staff at Providence Sanitarium and the Central Texas Baptist Sanitarium located at Waco. He is, in addition, connected with the Nurses' Training School of Providence Sanitarium, where he lectures and teaches student nurses.

This briefly is the story of one of the Texas-Czech sons of pioneer settlers. What he has done and is doing shows in part what is being done by the Texas-Czech citizens in the carrying on of State activities in all lines. The Czech citizenship of Waco numbers approximately two hundred families, the members of each being directly affiliated with local affairs, both in industry and commerce, and professional and artistic matters. Many of the leading business institutions of Waco are owned and operated by influential Czech citizens.

John Stanislav, pioneer, died at the family home near West on March 1, 1933, at the age of eighty-one. Surviving him are five sons, John, August, Rudolph and Joseph, all of West, Dr. F. J. Stanislav of Waco, and two daughters, Misses Bertha and Mary Stanislav of West.

*   *   *   *   *

Dr. A. C. Mussil of Granger whose parents were born in Europe, the father, Leo Mussil of French descent and the mother, a Moravian, has played a prominent part in the progress and development of Texas. As City Health officer of Granger he takes an active part in the affairs of his community. He is a graduate of the Medical Department, University of the South, Sewanee, Tennessee. He has taken several post graduate courses in medical schools of the North, and also holds a diploma from a school of pharmacy.

In the practice of medicine he has had a part in the welfare of the towns and communities of Moravia, Ennis and Granger, where his work has brought him in touch with much that is pertinent to the civic as well as the physical welfare of State, county and community.

Dr. Mussil has given to Texas and the country a large contribution in his talented family. His eldest son, Dr. Julius Mussil, was graduated from West Point in 1919. During the World War he was an officer in the Coast Artillery. Resigning from the army service after the end of the war, he studied medicine and graduated from the Rush Medical College, Chicago.

The second son, Dr. William Mussil, was also a student at West Point, but did not graduate. He later attended Texas University at Austin and Baylor Medical College, Dallas, from which institution he was graduated. He is located at Oklahoma

City, where he specializes in the treatment of eye, ear, nose and throat.

A third son, Anton Mussil, studied dentistry, and makes his home in El Paso. The oldest daughter, Miss Betty Mussil, attended San Marcos Normal College, San Marcos. The younger daughter, Miss Vlasta Mussil, took a course in pharmacy, University of Texas.

*   *   *   *   *

The paternal grandfather of Dr. L. I. Maliňak of Temple, was born in Moravia and came to Texas in 1872 and engaged in farming in Fayette County. The maternal grandfather was also born in Moravia and came to Texas in 1880. Dr. Maliňak's father was born in Fayette County on September 18, 1873. His mother was born in Moravia in 1879 and came to Texas in 1880. The father moved to Giddings, Lavaca County, in November, 1890, and engaged in farming at that place, remaining until 1920 when the family moved to Dime Box, Lee County.

Dr. Maliňak received his primary education in the country school near Giddings, took first term in high school at Dime Box, finishing high school with honors at Granger in 1925. He entered the Texas Dental College, Houston, in the fall of 1925, the course extending over a period of four years, when he obtained his degree of Doctor of Dental Surgery in 1929 as valedictorian of his class in college. He returned the following year to the dental college for a year in clinical demonstration. Since then Dr. Maliňak has been engaged in the practice of his profession. He is a member of Psi Omega Dental Fraternity, Houston Dental Society, Texas Dental Society; and American Dental Association, and during the month of August, 1932, was honored with the appointment of District Deputy, Knights of Columbus, Houston.

Dr. B. J. Čmelka's parents reside in Houston, having moved from the country to Houston some years ago. He has a growing practice and a large circle of friends. His literary and professional education followed the prescribed route for the well-educated and equipped practitioner of his chosen profession of dentistry.

Dr. E. L. Valenta of Houston was reared at Sweet Home near Hallettsville. His father, I. E. Valenta, was a private banker at Sweet Home, remaining in that business for many years.

Dr. Valenta is one of four sons, the others being A.A., L.C., and Eugene Valenta of Sweet Home. There are three sisters, Mrs. Dorothy Pavla of Hallettsville, Mrs. Estelle Hickey of Kingsville and Miss Elizabeth Valenta of Sweet Home. Reverend

Father Marcus Valenta is the nephew of I. E. Valenta, son of the brother with whom he established the banking business at Sweet Home. Father Valenta is priest at St. Ann's Catholic Church, San Antonio, Texas.

* * * * *

Among Texas-Czech physicians, widely scattered over the State, are the following:
Dr. Siptak, Caldwell; Dr. Frank Alois Somer, East Bernard; Dr. John Alfred Halamiček, El Campo; Dr. John Norman Řeznokov, 300 North Oregon Street, El Paso; Dr. C. J. Kaděrka, Fayetteville; Dr. Charles Francis Mareš, 2919 Avenue P., Galveston; Dr. Anton C. Mussil, Granger; Dr. Charles Julius Hollub, Medical Arts Building, Houston; Dr. Henry Rudolph Maresh; Dr. Rudolph Edward Maresh, Shell Building, Houston; Dr. John Kroulik, Nelsonville; Dr. Peter Zarsky, Refugio; Dr. John Jaroslav Shiller, Rowena; Dr. Joseph Kopecky, 205 Camden Street, San Antonio; Dr. L. J. Peter, Schulenburg; Dr. Frank M. Wagner, Shiner; Dr. Frank J. Kroulik, Smithville; Dr. Joseph Henry Kozar, Snook; Dr. Edward F. Mikeska, Taylor; Dr. William Amos Chernosky, 304 South 22nd Street, Temple; Dr. Frances Pacak Cepelka Spinka, Sixth and Walnut Streets, Texarkana; Dr. Charles L. Kopecky, Yoakum; Dr. Frank J. Stanislav, Fifth and Franklin Avenue, Waco; Dr. Theophilus Kubricht, Wallis; Dr. George A. Pazdral, West; Dr. George Pazdral, Jr., West; Dr. Emil Henry Marek, Yoakum; Dr. Tom S. Hruška, Wesley.

* * * * *

Prominent Texas-Czech dentists include the following:
Dr. R. L. Špaček, Temple; Dr. F. J. Křenek, Temple; Dr. H. O. Halamiček, Granger; Dr. B. J. Čmelka, Medical Arts Building, Houston; Dr. L. I. Maliňak, Medical Arts Building, Houston; Dr. E. L. Valenta, Kress Building, Houston; Dr. A. S. Valenta, Cameron; Dr. Lewis Kopecky, Eagle Lake; Dr. George Kopecky, Wharton; Dr. Charles H. Beseda, Van Alstyne; Dr. A. A. Dařilek, Shiner; Dr. Oscar Dařilek, Moulton; Dr. P. J. Hanak, Hallettsville; Dr. E. N. Křenek, Taylor; Dr. Frank Křenek, Victoria; Dr. Jos. R. Kubala, Hubbard; Dr. J. J. Menšik, Weimar; Dr. R. N. Možišek, Conroe; Dr. H. F. Stavinoha, Schulenburg; Dr. R. L. Struhal, Austin; Dr. Pete Netardus, Yoakum.

CHAPTER XXXVII

Texas-Czech Music, Musicians and Artists

THE only genuine Czech Tamburash Orchestra in the United States is at Houston, Texas. It was organized by Mr. J. Drozda, a native of Czechoslovakia, but a resident of Texas for nearly half a century.

Members of this distinctive organization responded one evening in the first week of March, 1932, to a call from the city recreation department. The occasion was an entertainment given at a suburban school, as part of the nation-wide Washington Bi-Centennial observance. On this same location only a few years before the beat of drums had ordered soldiers to their quarters, and the notes of the bugle had sounded reveille.

The old barracks and buildings of Camp Logan, where thousands of soldiers were quartered in 1916, preparatory to entering the World War, had been dismantled to make room for homes and the school building where the Czech members of the Tamburash Orchestra assembled.

The tamburash is an ancient instrument, descended from the gusla which dates back six hundred years. This instrument belongs to the lute family and probably came out of the Orient.

For many centuries traditional Slavic poetry was preserved by singing it to the accompaniment of the gusla. In commemorating the two-hundredth anniversary of the birth of George Washington, these Czech musicians played their own native folk songs on their favorite instrument. Beautiful old waltz songs, traditional marches, plaintive melodies and lilting polka numbers, inherently a part of the Czech people, composed the program.

This orchestra, organized to play and sing songs and music native to the Slav peoples, on this occasion played American patriotic airs in honor of America's first president.

The story of the Czech Tamburash Orchestra is an interesting chapter in the Czech musical activities of Texas. J. Drozda, the founder, and Mato Gjuranovic of Galveston, painter, musician and teacher of languages, explain the composition of the orchestral group.

316

UPPER PANEL: *First Czech Orchestra, organized at Fayetteville over fifty years ago*
From left to right, standing: Orsak, Frank Bača, John Jiřik, Ernest Knežek, J.R.Kuběna
and John Řek. *Front Row:* John Bartoň, Vince Šulak, Joe Bartoň, Joseph Janak, J. S.
Zvesper, later practicing physician; Frank Bača, composer, was the founder of the family
"Bača Band" that celebrated the anniversary at Fayetteville in 1932. Only three members
of the first Texas-Czech Orchestra were living in 1933. These were: J. R. Kuběna,
Fayetteville; Joseph Janak, West, and John Řek.

LOWER PANEL: *A Group of Early Czech Musicians, taken in 1895*
Standing, left to right: Bohumil Vojiek, John Kuběna. *Scated, left to right:* Joe Mazač
and Edward Mikulenka.

"There are five instruments in the tamburash group—the bisernica, kontrashic, bracas, bugarias and berda. Compared to the standard instruments of the symphony orchestra the first three would be the violins and 'cellos. The bugaria is like the wood-winds, the berda like the bass violin. Each instrument has four strings, sometimes tuned all on the same pitch, and again on two different ones. The full tamburash orchestra has practically the same range as a piano. The smallest instrument is about eighteen inches long while the berda is six feet, six inches in height. The pear-shaped sounding board is usually carved by hand from a single piece of wood.

"This distinctive Czech orchestra plays the folk-songs and the classical music of the Czech composers Dvořak and Smetana, with some compositions of the Russian composers included. Jazz does not appeal to the Czech. In the native country very little of this type of music is to be found, except it may be in the large cities. It is not heard among the villagers and the peasants."

While the tamburash was evolved some three hundred and seventy-five years ago from the older instrument, the gusla, it has been known in America for only about twelve years. It may be described as being similar to the mandolin, having, how-ever, a longer neck, with different strings and a much sweeter tone.

The Texas Tamburash Orchestra is the largest, and at the time of its organization, was the only genuine Czech orchestra of the kind in the United States. New York has had tamburash music for some years, as has also Chicago and San Francisco, but the musicians are not Czechs.

It is a difficult instrument to play, according to Mato Gjuranovic, "often taking more than a year to learn, but the Czech learns quickly."

A full tamburash orchestra has thirty-two pieces. At the organization of this Texas group there were only nine instruments, but others were later ordered from Praha.

Studewood Hall, Houston, Texas, is the frequent scene of tamburash musical programs. There the musicians gather each week for lessons and practice. Little Miss Helen Valčik, who began playing with the orchestra when only ten years old, was born in Houston and says that she does not like "jazz" music but plays expertly the bisernica, which, incidentally, is not made for "jazz."

"It is for the young people," says Mr. Drozda. "Give them something to do that interests them—something that they like— and they will not be restless and wanting to run around and away from home. We have given them the Sokol, an organization which builds both a sound body and a sound mind, and the tamburash is ideal as an added activity."

Mr. Drozda believes that the older members of the Houston Tamburash Orchestra should withdraw, since the organization is assured and going forward, and leave it entirely to the young people. This idea does not preclude there being an orchestra composed of older members. There is not a person of Czech ancestry or origin who does not have an instinctive love of music —in fact, it is such a strong characteristic of the Czech people that it is the exception to find anyone who does not have knowledge of some musical instrument.

There is no community, town or city in the State where there is not Czech musical talent and Czech musicians; one or more local bands or orchestras composed of both young and older Czech musicians.

It is interesting to note that the Czech language offers itself most readily and effectively to music. In the Czech alphabet there are sixty sounds or tones. On the keyboard of the piano there are sixty tones in the combined white and black keys. The Czech is easily adapted to the making of any known sound. It is not, therefore, strange that the Czech people are musicians almost without exception.

Bohumil Vojtek came to Fayetteville, Texas, from Europe when but a young boy. Texas was then in her early stages of development. He fell under the guidance and care of Frank Spaček of Fayetteville. Young Vojtek was naturally inclined toward music, and Mr. Spaček advised and helped him toward his goal. He soon learned to play the cornet and played that instrument in the local band. Later he joined a circus, traveling with this large aggregation of artists, going finally to San Antonio. At this time he was recognized as a master cornetist with the acclaim of the music world. At the height of his glory he was found dead one day on the streets of San Antonio.

In 1895 during the time the cornetist lived in Fayetteville he belonged to a group of young men who were inseparable pals: Henry Zdařil, nephew of Reverend Father Chromčik, a teacher at the time, now a prominent lawyer of Taylor; Ed Mikulenka, deputy tax assessor at LaGrange, later county treasurer of Lavaca County, where he died in 1918; a lad named Vaňak, who was at the time deputy tax collector at LaGrange, recognized for having extraordinary ability, and who still lives in LaGrange; the Mazik brothers, merchants, both now dead; John Kuběna, today

Left:
Mato Gjuranovic
Galveston

Right:
Mrs. Vera Prašilova Scott
Houston

a prominent business man, banker and secretary of "S. P. J. S. T."
Lodge; Joe Mazar, at the time a young clerk in LaGrange, now
deceased.

Father Chromčik, during the years of his residence in Fayetteville, which began in 1872, took an active part in all the uplifting
activities of the community, and contribued his part to the musical
life of the town and locality, playing the zither beautifully.

An old photograph showing a quartette from the group of
congenial friends and musicians of the historic town and community offers opportunity for making comparison with the past
and present style in dress. It is reproduced on another page.

All in the group are dead except John Kubĕna who is still in
the prime of life, taking active part in all its affairs, both local
and State. Mr. Kubĕna, once a violinist, and an accomplished
musician, has given up music for his business interests. For many
years he has been active secretary of the S. P. J. S. T. He has also
devoted part of his time to the mercantile business in Fayetteville
and so the old picture holds interest, showing this pioneer Czech
musician when he found time to "resin the bow" and join the
boys for an evening of music.

Mr. and Mrs. Kubĕna are the parents of ten children—eight
sons and two daughters: Jerome J., engaged in the automobile
business in Fayetteville; John A., also in the automobile business
in Fayetteville; Lad J., in the banking business in Houston;
Joe R., banking business, Fayetteville; Rudolpf R., also of Fayetteville; Lambert G., cotton business, Fayetteville. Woodrow W.,
and Edwin A., and two daughters, Julia and Anita, are at home
with Mr. and Mrs. Kubĕna at Fayetteville.

George A. Pazdral, of West, McLennan County, the son of
pioneer V. Pazdral, a musician and composer, inherited this talent
from the father through a long line of paternal ancestors. Under
the direction of Dr. Pazdral "Slavia," the musical club of West,
presents many highly interesting programs. An opera, "Bride on
Trial," written by Dr. Pazdral's father, has been presented on
several occasions.

There are thirty thousand Czech folk songs. In order to keep
them alive in Texas, a "Slavia Club" was organized in Houston
in 1933. A large number of Houston Czechs are actively interested
in making the club a success.

*   *   *   *

The picture of Mrs. Vera Prašilova Scott, made in the Vera
Prašilova Studio, Houston, by the artist of herself, is within itself

an exhibition of the exquisite and finished art of this daughter of Czechoslovakia.

Born in Kutna Hora, where the environment offers to the artist every incentive and opportunity for development, Vera Prašilova passed through the impressive years of childhood on to the years of her young womanhood when the scenes of her historic homeland drew forth the talent of the artist.

She began the study of photography in the city of Praha, using in connection with the artist's ability her sentiment and love of the home place, to transfer to the sensitized plate the scenes of Kutna Hora. These pictures have been exhibited in art museums throughout the whole of the United States, receiving in every instance blue ribbon recognition. So perfect is her art that pictures done in sepia tints on rich cream backgrounds are like etchings of the old masters.

Her studio in Houston has an outlook on a "patio" where ancient flagstones and a fountain lend an old world atmosphere in keeping with the skill of the artist whose ancestors belonged with the centuries that have given, not only to Kutna Hora, but to Czechoslovakia, its history and traditions, its music and art, its priceless heritage of turrets and towers, halls and castles.

She is the wife of Dr. Arthur Ferdinand Scott, member of the faculty at Rice Institute, Houston. They have made their home in Texas for some years, both having found the opportunity for using their talents in behalf of the development of the State. The work of this artist illustrates something of the characteristics of a people who are not satisfied with anything less than the best.

Even though she is not a Texas-Czech pioneer, Mrs. Scott is doing her part in behalf of the people and the State of her adoption.

Photography has been brought to the highest development in the Czech studios of Texas. Mr. and Mrs. Dan Urbanovsky, artist-photographers of West, belong well up on the list. Throughout the whole of the State are to be found Czech artists in photography. The work being done in these studio-workshops may be equalled, but not excelled. The Maresh Studio at Ennis, and the Herzik Studio at Schulenburg, hold places of distinction. At Schulenburg father and sons have developed much that is new and worth while in their work.

Retouching and coloring is a specialty. Many young Czechs are turning their attention to this branch of photography.

The Houston Museum of Fine Arts, in which Mat Gjuranovic had a special exhibition in 1932, has also acquired an oil painting

"Velična on the Orava" by Marta Rosankova-Drabkova, Czecho-slovakian landscapist. The subject of the painting is a street scene in a Slovak village. It was among twenty oils by Mrs. Rosankova-Drabkova which the Houston Museum brought to the United States for exhibition.

Texas is herself yet young in art and naturally most Texas-Czech artists have not been sufficiently developed to have found statewide recognition, but the trend is toward the more serious development of artistic talent among Texas-Czechs.

Miss Minnie Chlumsky, a daughter of one of the early Czech pioneers, has devoted her attention to art and as a result has accomplished some creditable work in oils. Her paintings hang in some of the representative homes in Texas.

The appreciation of art on the part of the Texas-Czechs is responsible in large measure for the preservation of much in the way of early Texas history that otherwise would have been lost. This may be more fully appreciated when attention is called to the fact that so many old and historic pictures are to be found in every Texas-Czech home. An old custom, that of having the pictures of bride and groom made immediately after the wedding ceremony, has remained through the years.

CHAPTER XXXVIII

CZECHS IN THE MODERN SCENE

John Rachač of Houston worked twelve and fifteen hours a day for a period of years to become proficient in a chosen trade— a life that is worth while. The father of the apprentice was Mathew Rachač, a building engineer. He died when the son was only seven. When he was seventeen he had received his diploma. He had made a piece of furniture complete from the raw piece of wood. It was examined by the officials in charge of the establishment and pronounced perfect. Three months' additional service had to be given as a final test of ability. John Rachač had satisfied every requirement and in 1898 was given his diploma. At the conclusion of one year's work as a cabinet-maker, he asked for an application to go through the University, which is free except for room and board. Twelve of the officials met and examined the record of young Rachač and found him worthy of the scholarship, so he went to Praha and took a three months' course in the University, receiving a regular diploma.

Then followed the fulfillment of an ambition, a tour of the countries of Europe. Through the cities of Germany and Russia the tour carried the student. He tarried to work and study in a number of the big factories where he put his skill to the test. He visited museums where he saw the woodwork of those who had labored in past centuries. He traveled in most part through the country, walking from place to place, sleeping in the open, passing over hills and the mountains.

One journey carried the young student to Trieste, at that time the chief Austrian port, from which city the traveler journeyed into Italy, to Como and thence to Berne, making the trip partly by train and partly on foot. Onward the journey led to France and Paris. At the French capital the Austrian Consul took up his passport. Young Rachač was twenty-one years old, the age when every man was called for three years' military training.

He failed to pass the examination at this time, however, and again worked at his trade until it was drafting time again, when he passed the examination, and at the age of twenty-two started

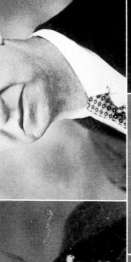

Left to right (upper) :

JOHN H. SHARY, Sharyland,
Magic Valley, Texas

J. KOVANOOVITCH
Dallas

GEORGE ADAMČIK
Dallas

Left to right (lower) :

LAMAR FOLDA
Corpus Christi

J. A. KOŠAŘ
Corpus Christi

MRS. B. MIKULENKA
Hallettsville
*County Treasurer, Lavaca
County, fourteen years*

RUDOLPH J. MARAK
West

army service. Being released for a time, he returned to work and married Frances Hron from Žirovňic. They day after he married, John Rachač started for America, but at Bremenhaven officers were waiting and returned him to his home and army service. Once again, in May, 1906, the start for America was made, and this time all went well. Leaving his wife and two small children, a son and daughter, with the wife's parents, John Rachač set sail. There were on board the vessel eight hundred passengers, and after twenty-eight days the vessel docked at Galveston.

On the way over John Rachač tried to study the English language from a Czech-English dictionary. His thoughts were back with his family, but his plans were on the problem of getting them over with him in the new land, where they could have a home and be happy together.

For two weeks immigrant John Rachač walked the streets of Galveston, getting acquainted with the city, and then began the hunt for work. There was nothing to be had in his line. But finally he encountered agents who were taking men for work on a railroad that was under construction out of Sour Lake. So John Rachač whose hand had been trained to cut and carve and to mix the colors for the rich staining of the wood as it was worked into beautiful pieces of furniture, this man who had worked in the factories of the world wherein the product was renowned for skill of workmanship, was taken along as a day laborer.

Years of hard labor followed in Houston railway shops; until finally patience was rewarded when he secured work with a large furniture concern. Back to the labor he loved and which, by intensive training, he was fitted to do.

Soon he was able to send for his wife and children and later they moved into a comfortable modern home. Of the world war period Mr. Rachač says:

"During the World War the Czechoslovaks worked hard for the American Red Cross. My wife knitted socks, scarfs and sweaters. In Europe my countrymen fought for their freedom. My wife had three brothers fighting. I had four. One of my sister's sons, only fourteen years old, was also fighting for his country, they having gone into Russia along with thousands of other soldiers at the beginning of the war."

Toward the development of modern Texas John Rachač has contributed his part.

*   *   *   *   *

Mr. and Mrs. Frank Hrnčiř, residents of the Moravia community in Lavaca County, have seventeen childen and every member of this distinctive family has a specific interest in life, and a part in the plans that have built the family holdings. The parents of Frank Hrnčiř came to Texas in 1859 from Lichnova and settled in the High Hill community, Fayette County, where they engaged in farming and agricultural pursuits. Mrs Hrnčiř was Julia Hollub, one of the seven children of the pioneers, Mr. and Mrs. Jacob Hollub who came to Texas in the late seventies from Iowa, settling near what is now Moravia. The landed interests of the Hrnčiř family are located in this same community which was organized in 1880 by the Hollub and Jalufka families.

The personnel of the Hrnčiř family is as follows:

Mrs. Annie Hrnčiř Hilscher, wife of Emil Hilscher, farmer at El Campo. They have three children.

Rudolph E. Hrnčiř, farmer at Robstown; Mrs. Celia Hrnčiř Berger, wife of Ed Berger, farmer near Moravia, with three children. Emil R. Hrnčiř, farmer, resides near Hallettsville and has two children. Mrs. Julia Hrnčiř Brown, wife of Ruel Brown, New Orleans. James Hrnčiř, owner of a garage, Hallettsville; Mrs. Lucile Hrnčiř Hilscher, wife of Frank Hilscher, farmer at El Campo. They have three children; John L. Hrnčiř operates a garage at Hallettsville and has nine children. Mrs. Stacie Hrnčiř Juren, wife of Jerome Juren, farmer near Moulton. They have two children. Gus Hrnčiř, accountant, resides at Sugarland. Mrs. Hrnčiř was a Miss Červenka of Moravia. They were married early in 1932.

Henry Hrnčiř is unmarried and at home with his parents, engaged in farming. Mrs. Helen Hrnčiř Krause, wife of James Krause, contractor at Schulenburg. They have two children. George Hrnčiř, farmer, at Moravia, has four children. Miss Ida Hrnčiř lives with her parents at Moravia. The three young sons, Erwin F., Willie E., and Stanley F., also reside with their parents.

There are twenty-seven grandchildren in the family. The picture of the family group was made some years ago and the small children in the picture, Erwin F., and Willie E., are grown. Stanley F. was not in the picture at the time and is shown in the insert at his present age of sixteen years. Mr. Hrnčiř, the father of the family, was born at High Hill in Fayette County, October, 1865, and is today yet in the prime of life.

Texas progress and development through the past century has been made possible by families like this. Thousands of cultivated Texas acres and other allied business interests have been made possible through efforts and the energy of such Czech families.

Family of Frank Hrnčíř,
Schulenburg, Texas

It is true that families of nineteen members are not the rule, but large families among the Texas-Czechs are not unusual. Some years ago Mr. and Mrs. J. Pechaček of Elk, McLennan County, were photographed with their eleven children.

* * * *

S. P. Studney of Houston, native of Praha, Czechoslovakia, but a citizen of Texas for more than a quarter of a century, is a newspaper man by profession, also a skilled machinist and when the newspaper business failed to pay sufficient dividends, he literally "put his hands to the wheel."

A student of the people, a linguist of no mean ability, Mr. Studney has a philosohy drawn from the text, "charity is kind." He presents the thought that we are a mixed people and that we should not attempt to draw the line of prejudice between ourselves and what we may be pleased to designate the "foreigner."

"Who is the foreigner? is a question not easily answered, especially in Texas. But when the question is propounded of who are the Czechs, the answer is ready:

"Progressive, loyal, home-loving citizens. As a people, provident, charitable and light of heart. Lovers of music and dancing."

* * * *

Born on the twelfth day of the twelfth month. Enlisted May 12, 1917, in the Navy of the United States for service in the World War. Trained at Newport News. Spent a week in August at Washington with a brother who was already in the United States Marines. Boarded a receiving ship in the Brooklyn Navy Yard and set sail for "over there," September 12, 1917, to be taken off transport vessel in New York, ill with mumps on February 12, after having made six round trips transporting United States soldiers, and finally to receive his discharge from the Navy at Detroit, Michigan, on October 12, 1919, John Riah of Houston, son of pioneer Czech settlers, believes that the twelfth day of the month belongs to him.

His parents, Mr. and Mrs. Frank Riah, were among the first settlers of Lavaca County. The mother of the family was a native of Tynnad Vltava, Bohemia, meaning "the town over the river Vltava." Her mother was of a family in line for receiving a title, owing to service rendered the government. The father came from the village of Protivim, Bohemia. The name in English means "defiance." The children of these Texas pioneers were given the advantages of education. They were sent during the early years to the parochial school of the community, the parents being devout Catholics.

The boy, John, youngest of the family, developed early the desire for knowledge which has continued through the years. He was not only a student of books, but of nature. Always a thinker, he would not accept a thing simply because time and custom had sponsored it.

During the World War, John Riah was Chief Yeoman in the paymaster's corps, National Navy Reserve. He reached the station of "petty officer" by promotion from plain "landsman."

While stationed on the flagship *Black Hawk* at Inverness, Scotland, with the mine laying force in 1918, Mr. Riah had opportunity to watch the German Fleet at Scapa Flow.

Speaking of family history and settlement and development of Texas, Mr. Riah asked that all the credit be given to his parents.

"My father settled in Lavaca County when there was but little other than wild land there. He was a man who attended strictly to his own affairs and the rearing of his family. He bought the land, cleared and cultivated it. He did his part in whatever was to be done in behalf of the community. Both he and my mother believed in right living. They would have countenanced nothing in their children that was dishonorable."

The seven are all living. Frank Riah lives at Sweet Home; Joe Riah is in business at San Antonio; one sister is in a convent at Corn Hill. Mrs. Mary Kasper, Mrs. Annie Tasler, and Mrs. Lizzie Henkhaus are all married and live near Shiner.

*　　*　　*　　*

S. L. Kostoryz pioneered in large Czech colonization projects in Texas. He was a man of scholarly attainments in addition to his business ability. To these qualifications were added the charm of a magnetic personality. The vision of this scholar, gentleman and business man was strongly felt in the taming of a wild domain and in the building of thrifty communities. After traveling over much of the western half of the United States and Canada for the purpose of finding suitable lands and localities for Czech colonization, Mr. Kostoryz was prevailed on in 1904 to stop off in Nueces County, Texas.

Purchasing a ranch of some 7,800 acres, he had it surveyed and subdivided, naming it "Bohemian Colony Lands," which name it has since retained. During its development the colony has progressed from wild waste lands to settled and intensely cultivated farms.

In 1910 Mr. Kostoryz added 2,300 acres of land from the Robertson Ranch adjoining the Bohemian Colony.

His prophetic mind saw instead of thousands of acres of chaparral, cultivated lands, farm homes, and community centers where the prosperous and happy colonists would gather for social and educational purposes. In the course of development he threw wide the big ranch gate and designated the trail he had blazed as a boulevard. Today this boulevard is a part of the splendid "Hug-the-Coast Highway," leading westward to El Paso and southward to Brownsville.

S. L. Kostoryz was the first man to bring Czech settlers to Nueces County, and through his enterprise he was responsible for the coming of many new people to the county. Previous to his advent he taught school and published a Czech newspaper, *Pokrok Zapadu,* in Nebraska.

*   *   *   *

In 1906 Longin Folda, a Nebraska banker, made his first trip to Nueces County. He did not at this time invest in Texas or Nueces County lands, but returned in the fall of 1914, bought a tract of land and had it cleared during the same year. In 1916 he bought a second tract, clearing it during the following winter and spring. The two tracts, amounting to 2,100 acres, were both purchased from S. L. Kostoryz. In 1921 Mr. Folda purchased the balance of the Kostoryz land holdings, amounting to 3,700 acres, most of it still in the "brush" stage. Much of this land has since been sold to Czech farmers who have built homes.

In 1923 Longin Folda died and his son, Lamar Folda, took over the management of the property. During the next few years the balance of the brush land was cleared and settled with Czech farmers, the Foldas having put into cultivation altogether about 4,600 acres.

*   *   *   *

In February, 1907, J. A. Košař came to Nueces County from Kansas where the Košař family was engaged in farming on a large scale. He stayed about two years in the county, buying and developing a small tract of land.

After returning to Kansas he continued to make frequent trips back to Nueces County to look after his property, and the additional land which had been acquired during this time by him and his father. In 1920 he came to take up permanent residence in Corpus Christi. Several other members of the Košař family

have also moved to Texas from Kansas. Mr. Košař owns several
fine farms, all worked by Czech tenant farmers.

To Pioneers Kostoryz, Longin Folda and Košař are due the
credit for the agricultural development that has come to Nueces
County.

*   *   *   *

In 1920 Joe Krušinsky moved to Nueces County. During the
World War he had been active in the interests of the Allied
Nations. He traveled over the entire State, making speeches for
the cause in all Czech localities. After the war he was similarly
engaged in the interests of liberty for Czechoslovakia. In 1932
he was active in Texas politics. Mr. Krušinsky is an influential
citizen, an accomplished speaker and is well known and highly-
esteemed by the Czech citizenship throughout the State.

*   *   *   *

"My parents came from Praha, Bohemia. My father's name
was spelled 'Šary,' with the accent over the 'S,' same as 'sh.'
When he came to America he adopted the letter 'h,' " says John
H. Shary of Mission.

The adoption of the letter "h" followed a precedent which
had been set by others whose names had not been given proper
pronunciation when minus the keynote letter.

The father of John H. Shary came to America during the
Revolution in Austria and settled first in Wisconsin, moving
in 1850 to Nebraska, where John H. Shary was born.

Before emigrating to America Mr. Shary's father was a
student at the University of Praha. At the death of a brother
he inherited a large geological collection. It was later presented
to the Museum at Vienna. It is claimed that some objects of this
valuable collection found their way to the United States where
they are housed in one of the museums, but all efforts on the
part of Mr. Shary to locate the objects have been unsuccessful.
This uncle was a member of a scientific school in Paris, and was
a great leader in industrial affairs, so much so that he was elevated
to nobility by Emperor Franz Joseph. This brother during his
life offered many inducements to the brother in America to
return to Europe, including the gift of great wealth, but the
brother remained in the new home and country of his adoption.

The achievements in industrial and scientific undertakings in
Texas has brought John H. Shary the plaudits not only of Texas,
but the whole of the United States as well.

The development that has taken place in the lower Río Grande Valley as a result of his efforts has placed him in the forefront in all matters pertaining to the agricultural and citrus fruit industry of the section.

In 1931 the Shary Cotton Plan was given wide publicity through the press of the State. Mr. Shary suggested a plan whereby cotton farmers would be financed by the banks in removing one-third of the 1931 cotton crop from the market for a three-year period. He proposed that the cotton growers be loaned the full market price for one-third of their crops at a three per cent interest. It was to be stipulated that the loan could not be repaid within the three years, unless the price of cotton reached twelve and one-half cents a pound. According to Mr. Shary the plan would have taken approximately 5,000,000 bales of cotton off the market for a definite period and the result would have been an increase in price.

The Texas Fruit Growers Exchange, of which Mr. Shary is president and also the organizer, has done for the citrus fruit growers in the lower Río Grande Valley what Mr. Shary had in mind for the cotton farmers of the State. This organization, capitalized at $300,000.00, has solved the marketing problems of the industry.

Mr. Shary is a frequent contributor to the press of the State, and with his pen preaches the doctrine of progress and development. In choosing the Río Grande Valley for his home he naturally placed his faith in that locality.

In the Valley one of the greatest and most successful of the irrigated sections of the United States has been developed to a point where a half million or more acres are supplied with irrigation facilities. To Mr. Shary belongs in large measure the credit for this splendid achievement. In fact there is always a "Shary Plan," when there is the demand for some new development. The Shary Plan for social stabilization, provides for transferring the idle millions of the cities to the land where they can produce their living out of the soil.

CHAPTER XXXIX

PROGRESSIVE TEXAS-CZECHS

HISTORY is studied from documents. There is no substitute. No documents, no history. Texas does not support an historical society to collect and publish its material. The historian must depend almost entirely upon contemporaneous sources. A beginning has been made by the library of the University of Texas toward collecting the materials necessary for the study of Swedish, Irish, French and German immigration and of the early diplomatic relations between Texas and these countries. No mention is made of the Czech settler or of his emigration to Texas in pioneer days. So in the matter of gathering Czech history from documents many difficulties were encountered. It seemed that, being no documents, there would be no history.

One day, several years before the writing of this history was undertaken, I chanced to be walking across the campus of the University of Texas. A latent breeze rushed out and over the grounds and buildings, snooping into open windows with small reverence for the dignity of "profs," and from one room purloined a sheet of paper which was tossed flippantly at my feet.

Twenty-three lines, written with a pencil on the ruled paper, met my eyes. The page started with a broken sentence:

"Wonder under what circumstances the Americans live to be so free, prosperous and happy. The natives of other countries cannot understand the circumstances under which the average American family lives because those natives have never been given the rights and privileges that are so common in the United States. The foreign people are not so interested in the rights and privileges of the American people, but they are more interested in the advantages which these rights and privileges afford the citizens of the United States. The average citizen of every country is exceedingly interested in the personal opportunities, the personal freedom and the personal welfare of the people, and for that reason the conditions existing in the United States are highly respected."

There the page ended. Something over five thousand young

students are enrolled each year for the regular term at the University, many of them the children of foreign-born parents. This fragment of a theme written by one of them reveals their trend of thought.

Hundreds of Czech boys and girls attend the University of Texas and other state institutions of higher education. Hundreds of them have taken their places in the school rooms of Texas as professors and teachers, and the study of this phase of the history of the Czech settlement and citizenship of Texas is not necessarily derived from "documents." It is to be had from the lives of the people who are making it.

* * * * *

August J. Watzlavick of Schulenburg, was an honor student at the University of Texas in 1932, winning, in addition, a prize for the best essay dealing with his major subject, "Pharmacy." Joseph and Mary Petr, the grandparents of the young student on his maternal side, came to Texas in 1874, landing at Galveston, going from there to Fayette County. At the early settlement of Dubina they spent their life farming. The grandfather was born at Opava, near Vienna, in 1814, and died in Texas in 1896. The grandmother, Mary, was born at Frenštat, Moravia, in 1815, and died at Dubina in 1911. The grandparents on the paternal side were born in Texas, but the great-grandfather came to Texas in the early days of settlement. The paternal grandfather, who resides at Blessing, does not read or write English.

August Watzlavick is studying to become a graduate pharmacist that he may take his place in business with his father at Schulenburg.

Charles D. Rutter, of Columbus, Colorado County, recognized as being the youngest county attorney in the State and as candidate for the office of County Judge of Colorado County in 1932, again held the distinction of being the youngest candidate for a judgeship in Texas.

Mr. Rutter was born in a log cabin in historic Fayette County in 1907. When he was but a mere lad he wrote an essay dealing with early Texas history and won a prize offered by the Daughters of the Republic of Texas. He is the son of a Czech tenant farmer and attended the Columbus public schools, graduating from the high school of that city in 1927. Later he attended John Tarlton College, Stephenville. He attended the South Texas School of Law in Houston during the term of 1928-29, working at various odd jobs in order to defray the expense of the law course.

Following this school term young Rutter took his ambition with him to the farm, where he worked as a day laborer. In the factory and in gravel pits he also found work and in the meantime prepared himself for teaching. He secured a teacher's certificate, but continued the study of law and finally secured the license to practice at Eagle Lake. It was there in 1929 that he was elected County Attorney of Colorado County. He announced his candidacy for the office of County Judge June 4, 1932, and received in the first Democratic Primary, July 23, 1932, a plurality vote.

This ambition to achieve is not confined to the few, but rather to the whole of the young Czech boys and girls of Texas. Through their efforts and their determination to succeed at whatever they undertake, they are setting a splendid example.

A. F. Urbanec of East Bernard held the distinction of being the youngest Justice of the Peace in the State when elected to this office in 1927. When a student at the State Teachers' Normal College, Huntsville, he won recognition for a thesis on the "History of Education." The father of this young Czech officeholder and student came to Texas from the Old Country.

Professor G. W. Kopp, for fifteen years a member of the faculty of Blinn Memorial College, Brenham, has cited for recognition in history Joseph William Tryanowski, whose splendid record at Blinn has been kept in the memory of his professors.

The story of this young Czech who wanted an education and went after it with so much determination is typical of the younger generation and a shining example to his fellows.

Joseph William Tryanowski was born in Brenham, Washington County, on February 16, 1895. When he was four years old his family moved to Austin County where he attended the rural school. After completing the course at this school he entered Blinn Memorial College at Brenham, working his way through. Due to the death of his father, he was forced to quit school and support his family.

Later he again entered the sub-college department of the Southwest Texas State Teachers' College at San Marcos. He finished his high school course and had started on his college career when he was again forced to quit school on account of the World War. At the end of the war he again re-entered the Southwest Texas Teachers' College, and after obtaining a teacher's certificate, taught commercial subjects in high schools. Later he again returned to the Southwest Texas Teachers' College, earning his way through the institution as an assistant in the Auditor's office. He was graduated in 1925.

After teaching three years in high school he entered the University of Texas and was graduated in 1929 with an M. A. degree. After teaching three years in Junior College, he re-entered the University of Texas in 1932 to work on his Doctor of Philosophy degree. Both parents of this young Czech educator came to America shortly after the Civil War, the mother landing in Galveston, the father in New York. A few years later Tryanowski, senior, came to Texas, where he married. Mr. and Mrs. Tryanowski spent their lives in Texas.

Young Gabriel Fransee, the sixteen-year-old son of Dr. and Mrs. W. F. Fransee of Houston, has won distinction as a musician of ability. In September, 1932, he was called to Bryan where he was given full scholarship in Allen Academy, a preparatory school for boys, where, in addition to his literary studies, he conducts the Academy Band, and trains the young musicians.

Gabriel Fransee, six feet and one inch in height, comes of a family of musicians. His grandfather Fransee was a musician of note in Czechoslovakia. His father, Dr. W. F. Fransee, teacher of piano and voice and all stringed instruments as well as brass, has long been connected with musical affairs in Texas. He was for some time a concert violinist and director of several large musical organizations in the north.

Miss Vera Fransee, the seventeen-year-old daughter, has been given recognition as a violin virtuoso. She played before the famous Czech Chorus from Praha, which toured Texas in 1929, and was tendered an ovation by these musicians. She plays also in the Houston Symphony Orchestra, one of the outstanding musical organizations of the State. Both she and her father are Houston Symphony artists. The Fransee Trio, father son and daughter, are heard frequently over radio.

Dr. Fransee is not only a musician, but he is a linguist, speaking in addition to Czech, his native tongue, German, French, Italian, Spanish and English. He is a scholar, a student of the peoples of the world, as well as of languages.

Marak, a Czech community in Milam County near Cameron, was settled over fifty years ago by three brothers, Thomas, George and Steve, sons of the Texas-Czech pioneer, Frank Marak. He had six sons, three of whom were born in Texas. The native-born Texans are the settlers of Milam County. They bought large tracts of land in that county, and began a development more than half a century ago, which has grown into the community called Marak.

There were three young Boháč sisters who came to Texas from Czechoslovakia as pioneers, with an uncle and aunt, the

Holubs. They married the three Marak brothers, Thomas, Steve and George, and with them settled the Marak community.

Thomas Marak still lives on his three-hundred-acre plantation at Marak, where he cultivates corn and cotton and other farm products. One brother, George, is dead. Steve lives at Cameron. The three sons of Thomas Marak, born on the farm at Marak, have families of their own. R. A. Marak has a position with a bank in Cameron. J. L. Marak is Assistant County Tax Collector of Milam County, and J. V. Marak lives in Houston where he is connected with a newspaper.

The three Marak brothers have thus, in establishing a community, helped to make Czech history in Texas.

L. O. Hošek of Guy, Fort Bend County, Texas, was a charter member of the National Association of the Roosevelt Czechoslovakian Clubs of America, organized in 1932 through the efforts of Honorable John F. Kroutil of Oklahoma City.

The purpose of this organization was to foster enthusiasm among Czechoslovakian citizens of America who have the right of franchise in the support of Franklin D. Roosevelt for President. Those elected on the board of directors included a Texas-Czech, L. O. Hošek.

Within a radius of some ten miles of Guy approximately eight hundred Czech families reside. Some of the older of these settlers have been in the county for nearly half a century, having gone through all the hardships of the pioneer settlers.

In this locality are five or six Czech lodges with their own halls or buildings. In addition there are two mutual fire and tornado societies, two Catholic churches and one Sokol Gymnastic Union. All of the second generation of Czech settlers in this locality speak English in addition to their native tongue. Many of the pioneers also speak English.

Mr. Hošek came to Texas in 1907 as a young man, having been born and educated in Vienna. He first settled at Ennis and later moved to Dallas, going from there to Guy in 1931 to engage in the general merchandising business.

Frank Tesař, of Houston, a resident of Texas for a quarter of a century has, in addition to helping in community development, had an active part in the growth and progress of a wholesale furniture manufacturing company of Houston. Mr. Tesař, born in the old country, learned the cabinet trade when a young man from the felled tree to the finished product. Today in Texas he has a part in helping supply the world with furniture. Not only is Texas wood used in the manufacture of the furniture, but material is secured in many other states.

Industrious, provident and careful in his business transactions, Mr. Tesař has been able to accumulate a competency and with his wife and two young daughters, wields an influence in educational, fraternal and social matters of his city and community. He finds recreation after business hours in his garden where he puts into practice the same painstaking methods with his plants that he does with his business during the day.

"Before I came to the United States," Mr. Tesař relates, "I was in the army—the cavalry—and I was required to always take care of my horse first, to see that the animal was properly fed and watered even before I had my own food and drink. I was told that without care the horse could not do his part. I have found that this holds good with other things. The seed that is not properly planted and cultivated afterward will not bring results."

Mr. A. R. Hamusek has established a suburban home estate near Houston. On fifteen acres located on the "Airline Road," ten miles from the city, Mr. and Mrs. Hamusek and family of seven children have a modern home. A fish pond, fruits and vegetables, poultry and flowers, go far toward making this an ideal farm-home. Mr. Hamusek was born in the old country, but Mrs. Hamusek is the daughter of a Texas-Czech pioneer. Her father, Tom Zajiček, as a boy of seven, came to Texas with his parents. The family settled first in Washington County. The father of Mrs. Hamusek has made his home for many years in Milam County, where he has engaged in farming, growing staple products, corn and cotton. He is nearly eighty years old and hale and hearty, living with some of his sons on the farm. He had ten children. One of his daughters had ten children also.

A large territory in the trading radius of Houston is settled with a Czech citizenship, and in consequence these communities have grown and developed rapidly during a period covering some ten years or more. A. R. Hamusek is a musician of ability and takes part in many of the musical programs furnished by the Tamburash Orchestra of Houston. He has a philosophy which teaches that when a citizen is a good Czech, one who loves his fatherland and his native tongue, then he is a good Texas citizen as well as a good American.

The old log house, built in 1854 on the Leshikar plantation near New Ulm, remains in livable condition, nearly eighty years later. It is owned by Mrs. John Štalmach (Theresie Leshikar), granddaughter of the pioneer builder.

A large native Texas pecan tree, spared by the clearing axe of pioneer Leshikar in 1856 because it bore large nuts, is still living and bearing each year the same heavy crop. The tree stands firm and strong in the soil of its nativity.

Grandchildren and great grandchildren of the Czech pioneers gather the nuts that fall from the lofty branches, spared to them by a pioneer who helped to build Texas.

John F. Goebel, wife and family, who reached Galveston from the old country in the year 1903, upon landing on Texas soil immediately took a train for West, in McLennan County, where they saw their first cotton. After working in the cotton fields a few months, they moved to Waco.

After a residence of eleven months in Waco, not having found satisfactory employment, Mr. and Mrs. Goebel moved to Dallas. Knowing very little English they were naturally handicapped.

Goebel found employment as a cabinet maker and during a period of six years' employment became a skilled wood-workman. At the end of this time, however, he was determined to become a farmer "on his own." He had not found conditions as favorable and prosperous between the years 1904 and 1910 as he would have liked, so the family moved to Robstown in Nueces County, where they cleared land, broke the wild native prairie soil with the plow, and made it ready for the planting of cotton and corn. This particular tract of land was on the edge of a hundred-acre forest, at that time the undisputed lair of wild animals. A flood came and destroyed the crop before the harvest time.

Discouraged, the Goebel family moved to Sugarland. Before the year had gone, just at Christmas time, the Brazos River reached the overflow stage and the waters piled up into a solid wall some ten feet high, destroying both crops and property.

Soon after Christmas, 1915, the Goebels moved again, this time selecting Richmond, Fort Bend County, as the place to make another start. Transportation was limited, bridges were in bad condition, the flood waters having washed out the road bridge at Richmond.

The mother of the family with her three small children went ahead of the moving caravan to find, on reaching the Brazos River at Richmond no means of crossing except to walk step by step the ties of the railroad bridge. Having started, there was no turning back, so with her children she moved cautiously and steadily out on the first of the long stretch of cross-ties.

Beneath were the swirling, muddy waters of the river, lashing furiously at the steel structure. A strong, fierce wind was blowing, threatening with every gust to blow mother and children into the debris-filled waters below. But they made it safely across. The year at Richmond proved no better than the previous one. A hurricane, which wrought great havoc at Galveston and elsewhere along the coast, swept inland and touched Richmond, laying waste all the crops of the section. Discouraged and practically homeless in 1916, the family moved to Girard, where Mr. Goebel accepted a position with a ginning company in the Texas Panhandle.

Girard was a shipping point for the cattle interests of the territory. But this was a drought year and on one occasion a herd of cattle being kept overnight at Girard awaiting shipment, stampeded toward dawn, having scented drinking water kept in barrels at the gin. Cowboys, however, were on hand and got the cattle under control before any damage was done. From Girard the Goebel family moved back to Dallas in 1917. Up to this time Mrs. Goebel had borne eight of a family of nine children. Two of the number had died before the family left Czechoslovakia. The ninth child was born in Dallas in 1918. Of the seven born in Texas, five survive.

One of the children is a daughter, Evelyn, who was graduated with honors from the Dallas High School and accepted a position of responsibility with the Dallas *News,* continuing with that newspaper for eight years, during which time she was assistant to the secretary-treasurer of the organization and secretary to the publicity director.

Miss Goebel was a contributor both to the news columns and magazine section of the *News.* She aspires, so she says, to become a full-fledged author.

Without the Goebels, the Bubaks, the Kovandovitchs, the Tobernys, the Stranskys, the Kučeras, the Valčiks and the Merliks, the large Dallas-Czech citizenship would probably not have been what it is today. This citizenship which has been in process of development for only about a quarter of a century, is the subject of another chapter.

CHAPTER XL

DALLAS CZECHS

IN THE City of Dallas live approximately two hundred Texas-Czech families, making a Czech population of some five thousand. While Dallas does not claim the distinction of being a pioneer Czech settlement, records reveal the fact that the first Czech settled in Dallas as early as fifty-seven years ago.

A great metropolis has been developed and built on the Trinity River during more than half a century, and Czech pioneers have had a part in the program of progress.

Joseph Zelenka, a shoemaker by trade, a Confederate soldier who served in Lee's Army, was the first Czech to settle in Dallas. He arrived in 1876. Pages missing from the life of this first Czech settler would no doubt be highly interesting. Joseph Zelenka was killed by a railroad train in 1905. His wife survived, dying years later in Ellis County. They left no children.

Alexander Polaček, a goldsmith, went to Dallas in 1878, but remained only two years. Nothing is known of his later life, or place of residence. He devoted two years, however, to Dallas development.

John Veverka, a blacksmith, went also in 1878. He, too, remained but two years, passing on and out of the record.

In 1885 Joseph Kovandovitch, a boy of fifteen, arrived in Dallas, having come to Texas from Czechoslovakia when he was thirteen. He remained and is the head of one of the two hundred Texas-Czech families. He married a Miss Wokaty, daughter of Frank Wokaty, at the time a resident of Dallas. They have six children. To Joseph Kovandovitch goes the distinction of being the oldest Czech in point of residence in Dallas. He has been a close observer of life and often writes for the English press.

Not until the years 1886 and 1889 is there further record of Czech settlement in Dallas. Settlers in 1886 were Edward Janke and Frank Janke, saddlemakers, and J. R. Polak, General Agent of The Commercial Union and also an insurance adjuster; in 1888, Michael Huss, a railroad man and Jacob Jonaš, wood

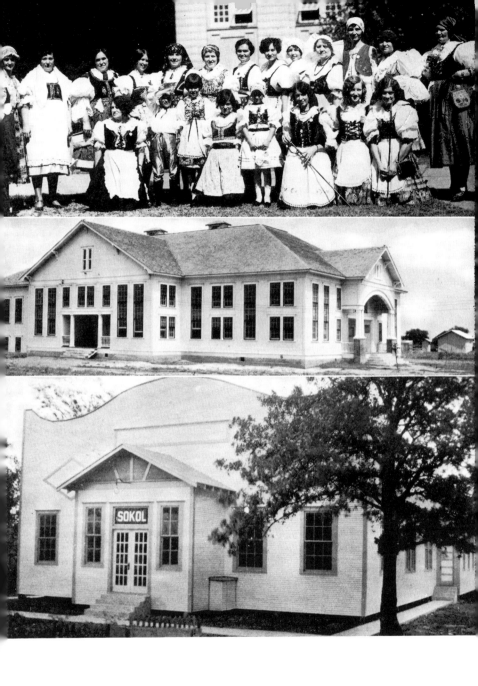

Top: *A Group in National costume, who participated in the program on Czech Day at the Texas State Fair, Dallas, October, 1928.*

Center: *School Hall, Ennis, Texas.*

Lower: *Žižka Gymnasium Club House, Dallas, Texas.*

merchant; in 1889, Frank Loecek, machinist. From 1889 to 1900 there is another interval. At the beginning of the year 1900 many Czechs took up their residence in Dallas. John Harris came from New York to engage in business, and in 1933 was one of the increasing number of Dallas-Czechs. In 1902 John Černoch arrived, and then the list grows: Josef Goebel, John F. Goebel, E. Jelinek, W. Drobil, A. Jež, J. Podhrasky, John Filipec, Frank Nestrole, Robert Duroň, Frank Linka, John Vančura, Frank Berlik, Jerry Zazvorka, Joe Zazvorka, Joe Ondrušek, John Ondrušek, Frank Rubish, P. H. Květoň, August Malik, Anton Konderla, Frank Parma, Frank Stransky, Josef Stekly, Joe Vavra, Vinc Verunač, V. Kasal, Frank Houzvička, Joe Czedzivoda, R. Kollar, Frank Rendl, John Bartošek, William J. Resek, Josef Smoldas, D. Smoldas, Josef Tuma, Adam Jessick, John Čebek, S. Hulovec, James Kotak, Štěpan Mařinik, Dr. Josef Vlček, John Žebek, Josef Zadrojel, John Prašifka, Anton Kartouš, V. Kartouš, Josef Herran, Frank Merlik, Frank Koza, F. L. Kallus, John H. Kučera, Frank Rolisek, Josef Taborsky, S. Taborsky, Anton Pavelka and many others whose names the records fail to show.

John Bubak, Sr., wife, Annie, and four children, John G., George J., Annie T., and Tillie A. Bubak, moved to Dallas in 1915, having lived prior to this time in Austin and Travis counties. From this date the Czech citizenship of Dallas grew rapidly, and during the ten years from 1923 to 1933 has made wonderful progress in all lines of business, as well as social and educational activities.

With the growth of the Dallas-Czech population came the desire for self-expression and organization. On February 20, 1910, a subordinate lodge of the Slavonic Benevolent Order of the State of Texas was organized as "Pokrok Dallas Lodge No. 84." The following were charter members: John Filipec, W. Drobil, Štěpan Mařiňik, John Bartošek, Josef Herran, Frank Merlik, John Vančura, Frank Koza, F. L. Kallus, John H. Kučera, Emilie Bartošek, Frank Rolisek, Josef Taborsky and V. Kasal. The first president of the lodge was Henry Fischl, and the first secretary John Bartošek. The president for 1933 was John G. Bubak and the secretary Frank Vodička.

Another subordinate lodge, "Jaro," No. 130, was organized on January 7, 1917, with the following charter members: John Filipec, John Vančura, John Kebrdle, Frank Rendl, Annie Pavelka, Z. Kebrdle, Anton Pavelka, Mary Filipec, K. Pavelka, Rosa Valčik, Agnes Rendl, Mary Merlik, and J. Sachar. The first officers of the lodge were John Filipec, president; John Vančura, secretary. Officers for 1933 were Frank Parma, president; Jerry F. Bouška, secretary.

The Dallas branch of the Slavonic Mutual Fire Insurance Association, Inc., of Texas, was organized September 3, 1926, the first officers being L. O. Hošek, president; W. A. Nesuda, secretary. Officers for 1933 were Frank Parma, president, and W. A. Nesuda, secretary. Many Dallas-Czechs have their property insured with this company. As has been stated, Texas-Czechs have been successful organizers. They believe that they can handle their own money investments in both fraternal and business organizations to good advantage through their own associations and companies presided over by Czechs selected to fill the official positions.

The American Czechoslovak Society was organized by John G. Bubak on May 25, 1930, the charter members being John G. Bubak, W. Drobil, both of Dallas; J. E. Křižan, of West; Anton Němeček, of West, McLennan County; W. A. Nesuda, Dallas; I. J. Parma, of Ennis; Eman Řezniček, of Kaufman; Anton Tobola, of Fort Worth; John P. Trlica, of Granger; and Joseph Wondrash, of Caldwell. These were also elected first directors of the Society.

The following were elected the first officers of the society: John G. Bubak, president; W. Drobil, first vice-president; Anton Tobola, second vice-president; Will A. Nesuda, secretary-treasurer; I. J. Parma, assistant secretary-treasurer.

Any chapter dealing with Dallas and Dallas-Czechs must, because of his dynamic personality and constructive influences, bring the name of John G. Bubak to the front. This Texas-Czech attorney of Dallas was instrumental in perfecting The American Czechoslovak Society of Texas, with headquarters in Dallas, early in the year 1930. This organization, established for the purpose of promoting the welfare and interests of the Czech people in Texas, as well as in the whole of the United States, has primarily for its mission the sponsoring and holding of conventions for the Czech people, regardless of religion or creed, fraternity or class. It is non-partisan and without prejudice, according to the rules and regulations as set forth by Mr. Bubak.

The membership is naturally restricted solely to those of Czech origin, but the society is strictly for the better Americanzation of the Czech people. There is no other agency of this character, it is claimed, with the ideals incorporated into the constitution and by-laws. Since the creation of the organization, much has been accomplished toward bringing about a better understanding between the American people and those of the Czech nationality who are citizens of Texas. A further mission of this organization is to have Czech days each year at the Texas State Fair. By bringing together Texas-Czech ciitzens the organization promotes good fellowship and harmony. The organization was perfected in May, 1930, but Mr. Bubak had previously been working for some time toward this end. Six Czech days had been held at the Dallas Fair, with an attendance of Czech people from all over Texas and other states.

On Czech days at the Fair visitors came from points as distant as St. Louis, Chicago, New York and San Francisco, but large representations from Texas-Czech localities over the State help to make the occasion a successful one. Feature of Czech days include entertainments, given under the auspices of the Texas-Czechs in the magnificent new auditorium, one of the Fair Association buildings; folk songs, and folk dances, in native costumes, to music; costume drills, native songs rendered in the Czech language by young Texas-Czech men and women which kindle the flame of sentiment, inborn native pride and love of ancestry in the hearts of the large audiences.

Prominent Czechs throughout the state have addressed the large audiences on those occasions. They always mention with pride in their addresses the great progress that has come about— a progress in which the Texas-Czech citizenship has played a vital part.

President Bubak comes of a long line of pioneer ancestors who helped to settle Texas and then carry on the progress and development. The Shiller family, among the first settlers of Texas, at New Ulm, Austin County, has been in Texas for over eighty years. The grandfather of Mr. Bubak, pioneer Joe H. Shiller, aged eighty-four years, is still living.

The line of demarkation setting up the boundary wherein are to be found Dallas-Czechs is not easy to place. Texas-Czechs from a wide surrounding territory make Dallas headquarters for many things. In every walk of life and in every line of business the Texas-Czech is to be found in Dallas. In some instances they have come as visitors and frequently these sojourns have stretched out into permanent residence.

There are the Kučeras. Five members of this family are actively engaged in professional and commercial activity in the city. John Kučera, one of six brothers, and one of the five located in Dallas, is city ticket agent for one of the large railway systems. Ernest S. Kučera is a Dallas attorney; Henry P. Kučera in 1933 was Assistant City Attorney; Joseph Lee Kučera is in the insurance business; A. E. Kučera is a member of the firm of R. L. Dixon & Brother, cotton brokers, Dallas Cotton Exchange. Louis A. Kučera, a sixth brother, graduated in 1933 from Texas University, Austin. There are twelve children in this family. The father, John Kučera, lives at the family home at Fayetteville. The mother, whose maiden name was Štefek, has been dead some years.

George Adamčik, son of pioneer John R. Adamčik, of La Grange and Fayette counties, has for some years held a position as freight agent in Texas for a northern railway system. In addition to his extensive knowledge of railroad business Mr. Adamčik has been admitted to the bar to practice law. He is a member of several Dallas civic organizations, taking active part in their regular programs. Mr. Adamčik is one of a family of eight children. A brother, E. A. Adamčik, is an aviator at March Field in California. Otto, the youngest brother, lives on the family plantation at Victoria; Jerome lives at LaGrange and Robert at Schulenburg. There are three sisters, Mrs. Gus Petraš, LaGrange; Mrs. Bertha Hluchaňek, Weimar; and Miss Mary Ann Adamčik, LaGrange. A son, Henry, was killed in an accident in 1931.

Before taking the position with the railroad, Mr. Adamčik spent a number of years in various allied branches of work. A graduate of St. Mary's Seminary, La Porte, and also of St. Edwards University, Austin, he was well equipped for business. During his residence in Austin in 1917 he was employed in the Supreme Court during the official term of Judge Nelson Philips, well known Texas jurist and statesman. In 1920 he was in the city of Washington connected with the Interstate Commerce Commission.

George Adamčik was born on a farm at Holman, Fayette County. The old family homestead was located at this place. His father, a pioneer farmer, owns several large pieces of Texas acreage.

The Adamčiks, members of the second and third generation, are to be found in various business enterprises throughout the State, in every instance the effort expended is in behalf of new enterprise and greater development. A cousin of George Adamčik, Jerome Adamčik, holds a position with a railroad at Smithville.

John Benda, another Dallas-Czech, is connected with another large railway system as traveling freight agent. Charlie Zedniček of Dallas is traveling freight agent for another line.

Czech pioneers have contributed continuously through these many years constructively and progressively to this program of progress in Dallas.

CHAPTER XLI

Slovanska Podporujici Jednota Statu Texas

The Slovanska Podporujici Jednota Statu Texas, S P. J. S. T. (Slavonic Benevolent Association of the State of Texas), one of the largest of the Czechoslovanic fraternal organizations in Texas, as well as in the United States, had its beginning in the meeting of twenty-five Czechoslovak citizens, members of the Č. S. P. S.

The Č. S. P. S., Česko Slovensky Podporujici Spolek (Czech Slovanic Benevolent Society) had been in operation for a considerable period of time prior to the foundation of the exclusively Texas-Czechoslovakian fraternal benevolent organization. This earlier organization was founded by the Czechoslovaks of the industrial centers of the Middle Western and Northeastern states, later extending the scope of its activities all over the United States.

At LaGrange, Texas, on December 28, 1896, a meeting of the Texas Czechoslovakian citizens was held for the purpose of founding an exclusive Texas-Czech fraternal organization. At this meeting a committee of three members, J. R. Kubĕna, Augustin Haidušek and F. Čihal, were entrusted with the work of drawing up suitable by-laws. Judge Haidušek later resigned from the board and C. V. Vaňek of LaGrange was elected in his place. This committee became an executive board and compiled suitable by-laws for the proposed organization. Following this, a convention of delegates from all existing lodges of the S. P. J. S. T. was called. This convention was held at La Grange on June 29, 1897. In attendance were delegates representing twenty-two lodges with a total membership of 496.

The S. P. J. S. T. started to function properly on July 1, 1897, when lodge activities were launched with the election of officers. I. J. Gallia, at the time a resident of Engle, was made president; Fred Breska, vice-president, and J. R. Kubĕna, secretary and treasurer.

The second convention was held two years later on June 19, 1899, at Flatonia, the third at Fayetteville, Fayette County,

TOM KRAJCA, Caldwell, Texas.
FRANK ŠTEFKA, Granger, Texas.
Eng. POLLACH, Caldwell, Texas.

Pav. MALINA, Temple, Texas.
J. E. KŘIŽAN, Galveston, Texas.
R. ČERVENKA, West, Texas.

HLAVNÍ ÚŘADOVNA

JOSEF DUŠEK Jr., předseda, Caldwell, Texas.
JOSEF MIKESKA, místopředseda, Wesley, Texas.

K. PAZDRAL, právní rádce, West, Texas.

J. J. FRNKA, pokladník, New Ulm, Texas.

*Officers Grand Lodge
S.P.J.S.T., 1914*

Seated, front row: M. Pazdral, Attorney and Counseler, West; Josef Dušek, Jr., President, Caldwell; Josef Mikeska, Vice-President, Wesley; J. R. Kuběna, Secretary, Fayetteville; J. J. Frnka, Treasurer, New Ulm.

Standing, rear: Eng. Pollach, Caldwell; Frank Štefka, Granger; Tom Krajča, Caldwell; R. Červenka, West; J. E. Křižan, Galveston; Pav. Malina, Temple.

in 1902. Other conventions followed at intervals of about four years. The most recent—the eleventh—was held at Ennis on August 2 to 5, 1932, attended by delegates from 149 lodges, one woman being included.

The presidential chair of the organization has changed its occupant, but J. R. Kuběna has remained uninterruptedly in the office of secretary-treasurer to which he was elected when the lodge was founded, his official duties extending over a period of more than thirty-five years.

I. J. Gallia, the first president, was succeeded by J. J. Holik, and Mr. Gallia was in turn elected a second time, succeeding President Holik. The fourth president was Joseph Dušek. The fifth, and present occupant is Judge C. H. Chernosky of Houston, who has been elected for three consecutive four-year terms.

From the very humble beginning, with the original twenty-two lodges and 496 members, the organization has grown into one of the strongest of the Czechoslovakian fraternal benevolent organizations in the United States, numbering at the end of 1933, 152 lodges, 11,141 adult members, besides having in the children's branch, 621 members. The life insurance in force totaled $10,-736,180.00. The assets of the adult association totaled $2,721,-935.53 and the children's branch $3,032.10. Its solvency is given as 105.51 per cent. It is one of the foremost fraternal organizations to show this rating.

The chief aim and mission of the organization among the Czechoslovaks in Texas is the benefit in the case of death, monetary of course, being paid to the beneficiaries of the deceased. It also pays a sick benefit.

The purpose and mission of the lodge goes further. The benefit to the living members has a potential value that can hardly be estimated. This is to be found in the propagation of the mutual acquaintance of scattered Czechoslovaks over the State, and in cultural, national as well as benevolent endeavors.

Lodges of the organization are to be found in every section of the State where there are Czechoslovak settlements. Many of these lodges have erected commodious, attractive, well-furnished lodge buildings of their own, usually on spacious grounds, where centers the cultural, social and fraternal life of the Czechoslovaks in the respective communities and near-by settlements. It is quite impossible to estimate the value of these properties, but the sum total of the 152 S. P. J. S. T. Lodges will aggregate a handsome figure.

The lodge halls are furnished with facilities for promoting

the social and educational life of the communities. Well-equipped stages offer opportunities for developing dramatic talent. The size of the auditoriums allow floor space for dancing, and the grounds that belong in connection with the lodge buildings, are suitable for outdoor entertainments such as picnics and open air musicals. The lodge hall is the social center of every community. During its existence of over thirty-five years the S. P. J. S. T. has gone diligently about fulfilling its mission, reaching out into many avenues and over a large territory. It has paid out hundreds of thousands of dollars in death benefits, has extended its help toward the saving of numerous homesteads for the orphans; has helped its members by lending them money on their properties whenever they have been in need of this assistance, and always the organization, through its personal agencies, has been interested in educating its members in the duties of citizenship. S. P. J. S. T. lodge members rate as substantial, respected, law-abiding citizens. Through their lodge affiliations they feel the responsibility of the duty they owe as citizens to the State and country. The distinction of being members of an organization which ranks as the largest Czechoslovakian fraternal benevolent association in Texas, and among the largest and financially soundest of its kind in the United States, is within itself an inspiration for the highest ideals.

From the very beginning, and during the whole period of its existence, the S. P. J. S. T. has been ably and economically managed, and to this, with the hearty coöperation of its members, the success of the association may be attributed.

Much credit is due to *Věstnik,* the official publication, for the help given toward the accomplishment of these splendid results. This publication, first a monthly newspaper, edited by F. Fabian, was later changed to a weekly and for the sixteen years was published under the editor-management of Joseph Tapal at Fayetteville. In January, 1933, the publication was moved to West, Texas, where Messrs. August Morris and Joseph Hlasek publish the paper.

Officers of the S. P. J. S. T. Lodge at the time of publication of this history were: C. H. Chernosky, president, Houston; Josef Mikeska, vice-president, Wesley; Engebert Jelinek, vice-president, Granger; J. R. Kubĕna, secretary, Fayetteville; Edward L. Marek, auditor, Fayetteville; Josef N. Vavra, treasurer, Caldwell; August Kačir, attorney, Temple. Auditing Committee: Robert Červenka, West; W. Nesuda, Dallas; Štĕpan Valčik, Houston. Inspectors: J. H. Hurta, Temple; T. H. Škrabanek, Ennis; F. Ančinec,

Houston. Editing Committee: Karel Lažnovsky, Ennis; John Gajevsky, Orchard; Josef Krušinsky, Corpus Christi.

When Judge Chernosky was re-elected president by acclamation, and stood before the large audience to deliver his address of appreciation, he was for a moment overwhelmed with the sentiment that he felt for his people.

As he stood on the rostrum, his arms folded, his tall figure erect, the splendid physique of the man in stately poise, the convention in a body arose to greet with cheers their president and leader who had served for eight years, and was to continue for another four years in the same capacity.

The eloquence of President Chernosky's address, delivered in the Czech language, was recognized, even by the visitor in the hall, not familiar with the ancient tongue of the Slavic people.

J. R. Kuběna, who has served as Lodge Secretary for so many years, when called on for a speech on the occasion of his own re-election by acclamation, expressed his appreciation for the honor and took occasion to say that the President, Judge C. H. Chernosky, had expressed his own sentiments for him more ably than he himself could do.

In reading the names of the S. P. J. S. T. Lodges, it is interesting to note that they are well scattered over the State. The counties of the Gulf Coast section, in which most of the early Czech settlement occurred, have splendid representation in these Czech lodge organizations. By way of contrast we find that Gainesville, up in Cooke County on the Oklahoma border, has "101" Pokrok (Progress) Lodge.

The cities of Dallas and Fort Worth have lodges. In Baylor County there is a Sam Houston Lodge. Wichita Falls has Lodge No. 76, some six hundred miles from the south Texas Czech settlements. Knox City in Knox County, on the border of the "panhandle," has a lodge. And thus the Czech settlement of Texas has spread. First settlers of Fayette, Austin, Colorado and other South Texas counties, have representatives throughout the State. The names of these lodges are interesting.

"Osvěta," meaning in English "enlightenment," or in some instances, "the dawn," was given to some of the first organizations. "Pokrok" (Progress), denotes something of what the lodges stand for.

The S. P. J. S. T. Lodge is non-sectarian. It has been said that the membership includes many "free thinkers." There are also Presbyterians, Moravian Brethren Church members, and some Catholics to be found in the list of members. The Czech

Catholics of the State, however, have strong lodge organizations of their own.

The eleventh quadrennial meeting of the organization was held in August, 1932. This meeting, coming after a lapse of four years after the tenth quadrennial, created widespread interest in the 149 lodges over the State. There was in attendance a representative Texas-Czech citizenship, who for the time had left business of the home behind that they might meet together as Czechs. The business of the convention was transacted in the Czech language.

Preparations had been made in advance by Czech citizens of Ennis where the convention was held. The large home of Volna Čechie Lodge, located about four miles from Ennis on a large open space of ground, afforded adequate space for the accommodation of the several thousand visitors in attendance.

The main auditorium of the lodge hall was equipped with portable chairs which were removed for dancing in the evenings. Mezzanine balconies on either side of the big auditorium afforded convenient room for committee meetings. The Lodge has its own lighting system.

Both the National and Texas colors were used in the decorations as well as the Czech and Lodge emblems and colors.

With the festive atmosphere of gay-colored bunting depending from the high ceiling and the Nation's flag prominently displayed, the S. P. J. S. T. Lodge began its eleventh session on Monday, August 1, 1932. Dr. Joseph Kopecky, of San Antonio, was acting president of the convention.

Judge C. H. Chernosky, president, and J. R. Kuběna, secretary-treasurer, presided officially throughout the meeting.

Delegates representing the 149 Texas lodges filled the big auditorium. Also there were many visitors throughout the five days.

The convention was conducted without the aid of a parliamentarian, and almost perfect order was maintained on the floor.

The secret ballot was used in but a few instances. The work of putting the business of the convention through was effected by the viva voice method, or the up-lifted hand. With many motions being put before the convention, this method expedited action.

With the accumulated business of four years coming before the lodge, delegates representing a membership of approximately twelve thousand, there was naturally much to come up for consideration.

There was abroad everywhere during the days of the convention a spirit of harmony and good will. Everybody was happy and there were no strangers.

Delegates ate at long tables in the big dining-hall, which seated one hundred and twenty-six. The barbecue pits were under the direction of skilled meat cooks. Pickles and preserves, pies and cakes, salads and vegetables were there in abundance, prepared as only the Czech housewives know how to prepare them. Telegrams began arriving soon after the convention convened from towns over the State, inviting the twelfth quadrennial convention, in 1936. East Bernard was chosen.

The delegates, officers and visitors were from every walk of life—politicians, statesmen, lawyers, doctors, philosophers, newspapermen, farmers, merchants, bankers, salesmen, artists, musicians and men of industry and commerce.

* * * * *

With the successful organization and operation of this order of S. P. J. S. T. there came discussion and consideration of a similar association which would offer fire insurance protection. On July 1, 1926, the Slavonic Mutual Fire Insurance Association was founded. The first convention was held in June, 1927, at Houston, where all the work pertaining to the writing of the insurance policies and other business of the association had been transacted during the year of 1926 by the Houston branch of the organization, with the help of members in Bryan, Crosby and Rosenberg.

The first directors of the Association were Frank Ančinec, Anton Bily, Judge C. H. Chernosky, Stephen Valčik, M. Bubac, Frank Bečan, John J. Kelarek and Tom Hošek. The same officers were re-elected at the Houston convention in 1927.

From that time, following the first convention, the Association began to grow, until in January, 1933, there were thirty-two branches with some 1,175 members, $24,618.92 capital and $2,250,000.00 insurance in force. There was paid out on losses during the year of 1931, $9,118.69.

Houston, Ennis, Granger, Rosenberg, Bryan, Dallas, Crosby, Needville, East Bernard, Fort Worth, Penelope, Temple, Dime Box, Fayetteville, Schulenburg, San Antonio, Megargle, Jourdanton, Taylor, Hallettsville, West, Cameron, Flatonia, Buckholts, Caldwell, Waco, Shiner, LaGrange, Ganado and Weimar all have branch associations.

The successful operation of this Czech benefit organization in Texas goes far toward demonstrating the effective methods of conducting organized business on the part of the Slavonic citizenship of the State.

The careful handling and safe investment of money, where this is deemed a wise business transaction, is a big factor in the carrying on of Czech organizations, whether fraternal, social or, as in the instance of the fire insurance association and the building loan organization of Texas, under Texas-Czech ownership and operation.

Domiňik Naplava of Houston

First Texan killed in the World War

CHAPTER XLII

Dominik Naplava, First Texas Boy Killed in World War

"Oh, Mother State—Oh, Native Land,
Oh, Sacred Flag—Again
We pledge you sonship, yea and sword
In sight of God and man."

Across the margin of a page yellowed with age had been written in pencil these lines of Wordsworth's:

"A child, more than all other gifts
That earth can offer to declining man
Brings hope with it and forward looking thoughts."

The book was old, the page worn, but the penciled lines were distinct.

Dominik Naplava, more than all other gifts, brought hope and with it, forward looking thoughts. He was born in the little village of Zadovice, Moravia, on January 11, 1892.

The house of his nativity stood on historic ground, a part of land comprising the property of the Bohemian crown, and these were the lands of the kingdom of Bohemia, the Margravate of Moravia and the Duchy of Silicia. Here he was sheltered in the home which the great Roman poet, pausing by the wayside more than 2,000 years before, may have had in his mind when he wrote in his journal:

"A piece of ground not over large, and near to the house a stream of constant flowing water, and beside these some little quantity of land."

Here, amid the environment of land not over large, the stream of constant flowing water, the verdant fields, the flowering and fruiting trees of the orchards, the native hills, the child, Dominik Naplava, grew up and had instilled in him, as he said in later years, "the love of home and country."

In the fertile soil of his homeland, the potatoes and the sugar beets and the barley and the rye were planted and harvested from year to year. The plums, pears, apricots and peaches grew, ripened, and were gathered in season to be marketed fresh, or to be canned or dried. The over-ripe fruit found its way into the family wine vats. The beet pulp from the sugar mills was not wasted. Provident hands carted it away to be stored for stock feed in winter.

Time was budgeted, and Domiňik Naplava had his days and years in the village school. The road from school led young Domiňik into the coal mines near the village. Here by the hour he dug out coal from the heart of the hills. Bending to his task, pick and shovel in hand, he found time for thought, and, thinking, dreamed of the future—always a future when his country would be free.

The influence of a life and the lives of those who were never cowardly, nor easily discouraged and disheartened, the pioneers who sailed the stormy Atlantic in small ships to settle Texas, and the boy patriot, Domiňik Naplava, who came years later, have left a proud heritage.

Because of this hallowed past, and because, as Domiňik Naplava said, "The glory of the present is to make the future free," the little red book, tumbling from the silent recesses of the high shelf, sets in motion a current of thought.

The space in the bookshelves from whence fell the small book remained. It was a vacancy which no other one of the books could fill. The companion volumes stood erect, not expanding to usurp the niche, while on the floor, face upward it lay, open at Chapter One, with the words written on the page margin:

"A child more than all other gifts."

The pride in ancient and illustrious origin, and the passionate desire for liberty which characterized the Czech people throughout the centuries, was an inborn trait of Domiňik Naplava. He learned in his earliest youth the history of his people; heard that oldest choral composition extant, which contains the pathetic invocation to the patron saint of the country, St. Vaclav, duke of the Bohemian land: "Do not let us perish nor our descendants."

It was early in the year 1914 that Domiňik Naplava came to Texas. He had made a previous voyage to the State, coming, on this former occasion, with an older brother, for a visit to another brother who had been a resident of Houston for some years.

Industrious and provident from his youth, the boy was financially in position to make a second trip. The decision to come back to Texas had been made after serious consideration.

Filled with enthusiasm for the venture in the new country, and holding in his heart love and patriotism for his homeland, the departure for Texas was made an occasion for a bon voyage, with the patriotic note given emphasis.

Accompanied on board the steamer at Bremen by a number of friends who had with them their musical instruments, young Domiňik was the central figure in the group gathered for the program of parting. The boy accepted the moment as opportune for making an offering of his own feelings as he said good-bye to his homeland and friends. Just as the music was to start, he held before him a poster on which he had written in Czech the words: "To the Czech Nation, liberty—good luck."

With the memory of the music and the parting wishes of his friends, linked with the sentiment of the occasion never to be forgotten, Domiňik Naplava sailed for Texas, his new home, to which he offered his loyalty and his services.

He had written his brother in Houston to meet him at Galveston, but in the letter had failed to give the date of sailing, or the name of the vessel, so it was without greeting that he set foot on Texas soil.

It was a matter of only a couple of hours, however, before he was at his brother's home in Houston, where he found awaiting a cordial welcome.

It was not to be idle that Domiňik Naplava came to Texas. Shortly after his arrival he was at work. His first job was with a railroad bridge building crew, the work taking him to the Houston Ship Channel district.

And so the boy—for Domiňik Naplava was scarcely more—chose for himself labors to test a man's metal. As a coal miner he had laid his hand unflinchingly to the task that called for might and brawn. As a bridge builder he wielded both in behalf of progress and industry, driving the rivets that bound steel together and offered the way for the onward march of commerce and industry.

The bridge-building job finished, young Naplava found a position as pantryman at the Houston Country Club, one of the outstanding social organizations of the city. Here the young Czech found employment that took him into a new field of endeavor.

It is to his credit that he made friends among the club membership. When he announced his intention of resigning the position after having held it for a number of months, he was urged to reconsider. He was happy in the work, it was not that he was dissatisfied, but there was in his heart a potent force, fanning into flame an inherited patriotism.

Soon after his arrival in Texas he had taken out his first citizenship papers. Full citizenship is not granted, however, until the completion of the required term of permanent residence, which, according to the State law, is five years. Prior to the entrance of the United States into the World War, he had tried to enlist in the United States Army, but because he did not have his full citizenship papers, he was not accepted.

Having thus failed in his effort to serve the country of his adoption, he went to Winnipeg, Canada, in 1917 and there enlisted in the Canadian Army.

It was for this that he had resigned his position at the Country Club. Only a few friends in Houston knew of his intentions. He had not even confided in his brother, John Naplava, because he feared the brother would try to dissuade him.

The first news of his enlistment came through the letters written to the brother. They give an insight into the boy's character which might otherwise have never been shown.

Domiňik believed that national defense is a basic duty which every citizen should be ready to perform. He thought of the service not wholly in the sense of being a noble duty, but because of a deeper urge.

War had been declared between Austria-Hungary and Serbia on July 28, 1914.

"The hour has sounded," he said to his brother, "when the sacred dream of our fathers will be realized. Bohemia will be born again."

Domiňik Naplava had read of the climax that followed the four weeks frenzy and fruitless negotiations between powers of Europe after the assassination of Archduke Franz Ferdinand and his wife, Sophie Chotek, duchess of Hohenberg, at Sarajevo, in Bosnia, on that fateful day.

Reading, he thought of the beloved, picturesque, historical city of Praha, and from the picture of the impressive city, his thoughts turned to the little city of his childhood, Zadovice. There, in memory, he saw the little schoolhouse, the home where he was born, the field where he had followed the furrow, planting in seed time, and helping with the harvesting. Here, he recalled and recounted, historical and cultural traditions of his native land. Under the spell of the recollections, he pictured again, as he last saw her, the mother who to him was ever the guiding light of his life.

Nationalistic passions were aroused. President Wilson had sent a message to the five important nations enmeshed in the toils of the conflict, offering to act in the interest of European peace. "Too late," came back the reply. Russia, Austria, France, Germany and England advised that mediation was not desired.

In January, 1917, the allied governments replied to another message of the president, setting forth their war aims, disclaiming all guilt of war, placing it entirely upon the shoulders of the Central powers, declaring it impossible to obtain peace that would assure reparation and restitution and such guarantees to which they believed they were entitled.

Domiňik Naplava, reading these statements, said to himself that Texas had within her bounds one man who belonged in the battle for the rights of humanity.

"To leave one's hand lastingly upon time with one tender touch for the mass of toiling people that nothing can obliterate, would be to lift oneself above the dust . . . and stand upon a giant staircase that Sampson could not overthrow."

Domiňik Naplava may never have read these words of Dickens, but in his heart he held the same creed, the same sentiment.

He had the inborn urge to fight for his country—to offer himself quickly as a defender of the ideals and principles inherent in him. The memory of the past, coupled with the inspiration of the present, carried him into battle.

It was not genius that counted in the crucial moment, but inexorable will inculcated through the generations whose sufferings, sacrifices and yearnings were at last to be expiated.

And today, the name of Domiňik Naplava is written in bronze. It is to be found on the Gold Star Honor Roll. The name preserved in the great bronze memorial tablet is set against the background of the Texas granite monument erected in front of the City Hall in Houston, that future generations may read.

Domiňik Naplava was the first Texas boy killed in action in the World War. "Killed in action on the morning of November 12, 1917." Thus came the message from the Canadian Government to John Naplava in Houston.

Such a short span between the little village schoolhouse of Zadovice and his sacrifice for the cause of liberty. So short a time since he had gone singing each morning to his work in the coal mines of his native country. And so brief the life all told, and yet who is there with wisdom enough, with the knowledge and understanding sufficient to fathom the depths, or to grasp the breadth of influence, somewhere accorded to that life?

In a few words the Canadian Government told the story in the report sent the brother in Texas.

"He was out on a work party under L. D. G. Sheratt, digging a ditch to drain the water off the road east of Kansas Cross. While returning to billets along the Duck Walk, (R. Track) a German airplane dropped three bombs on the party, wounding the officers and several of the soldiers, including private Naplava, who was struck on the back of the head by a piece of one of the bombs, and died instantly, at about 11 :00 A. M., November 12, 1917."

He died with whatever knowledge, and understanding, he had of the great World War. In the war record as given to those whom he loved, and held first in his affections, he was only "No. 294,914, Sec. D. of Unit 107 Battalion."

Less than twelve months later there might have been seen one misty morning in the city of Praha people hurrying along the streets of the city, to their places of work, with visible expectancy of something long hoped for, about to happen.

In a whisper the Sokols were asking:

"Is it really going to happen? Is the new state of Czechoslovakia to become a reality?"

The United States of America had acknowledged the right of Czechoslovakia and the South Slav Nations to independence and had particularly recognized the Czechoslovak National Council as a de facto government.

Dominik Naplava, who dug coal from the depths of the hills in his beloved Czechoslovakia, did not die in vain. And because of this, his name will stand forever on the Gold Star Honor Roll. His letters written from the soldier's camp back home to his loved ones in Texas, are sacred things that link past with present. Their sentiment is in keeping with the ideals and traditions which the boy carried in his heart.

Nobly he lived and served, and gloriously he died. As he wrote, "We care not how we shall emerge from the conflict, be it sound and well or be it wounded. Or finally should it be that our bones will rest on French soil, or any other soil, just so our dear Czech country emerges a free land from the conflict. The dove of peace must take its flight over our beloved land. Would it be that our mother could know that her son is again in Europe and in battle."

Through these letters we are privileged to view the heart of the boy soldier and patriot. In reading there comes the feeling of trespassing—of stepping on hallowed ground. They do not conclude a chapter, but instead, they begin a story, for through them is transmitted something of the spirit of the pioneers who came to settle Texas. The story of the boy, Domiňik Naplava, who held in his heart so great sentiment, love of liberty, loyalty to home and country, and withal the courage to do that which he felt to be his duty, might well be a foreword to the history of the Czech settlement of Texas.

CHAPTER XLIII

Czech Legionaries in the World War

On Tuesday, July 15, 1919, eleven hundred and four Czech Siberian World War heroes passed through Houston en route home to Czechoslovakia.

These Czech soldiers who had organized themselves in Russia and volunteered their services to the Allied Army, had tramped through Siberia, enduring every privation and hardship as they pressed forward toward their goal.

The Texan, a Czech weekly newspaper published in Houston, carried at the time the story of the arrival and entertainment in Houston of these Czechoslovakian Volunteers.

The Texan is printed in the Czech language and credit is due Mr. S. P. Studney of Houston for the translation and notes which follow:

"Friday's local newspapers brought the news that a detachment of Czechoslovakian Siberian heroes, consisting of 1,104 men, will stop on their homeward journey, at Houston. Our Czech populace was aware of their arrival at San Diego, California, a few days ago. Their next destination is Washington, D. C., and from there they will entrain for Newport News and thence through France to Czechoslovakia.

"As soon as this news spread, our countrymen worked feverishly to be able to tender them an enthusiastic welcome and the American Red Cross promised through its representatives that it will provide refreshments for them. Even our city, Houston, did not want to lag behind in the welcoming of the veterans and promised us a band of musicians for this occasion. The following Sunday the local lodge of the Benevolent Slavonic Association of Texas, Pokrok Houston, held a huge meeting at its hall, and there was worked out a reception program, and it was resolved to borrow $1,200.00 and to dispense this amount as a gift from the Czechoslovakians of Texas, among these heroes.

"It was also decided to present the coming Legionaires with a banner of the Czechoslovakian Republic, as they did not possess one, and for this memorial gift the flag of the local branch of the

Čechoslovanske Narodni Šdruzeni (Czechoslovak National Alliance of America), was chosen.

"According to the reports of the Sunday's local newspapers, the detachment was due in Houston, Monday morning at 6:00 o'clock and therefore to tender the sturdy fighters the most hearty and magnificent reception, the Houston Czechs proclaimed that Monday be a National holiday and long before the scheduled time of their expected arrival at the Grand Central Depot, Washington Avenue and its vicinity, was surging with crowds, including those who came from the neighboring towns and settlements. After an hour's waiting, it was announced by the railroad authorities that the first train had met with some accident which would cause a delay of the other trains and the expected train would not be due in Houston until about eight or nine o'clock that evening. After this report the waiting Czech women folks conceived the idea to bake up for the Czech soldiers as much as possible of 'Kolače' and 'buchty,' this product of the culinary art being well-developed among the Czech women.

"It was to be a pleasant surprise for these Siberian warriors, and they made haste to their kitchens. Mr. Louis Rulik, prominent Czech, Houston business man, took several of them to the Czech bakery shop of Messrs. Becke and Hauft who gave them their shop to use at their own disposition, and in addition donated all the necessary supplies. The others at their homes got busy too and before the evening set in, there were over 10,000 of the delicious cakes ready. At the same time, Czechs from Brookshire, Richmond, Rosenberg, Galveston, Moulton, Ennis and other near-by places reached Houston to share in the ovation to the men who fought for the Czech independence. Mesdames Miča, Hanka and Vychopeň made ribbon insignias in Czech tri-colors, which were eagerly bought by the waiting Czechs. Their sale brought $30.00.

"For the flag to be donated to the Siberian detachment was selected a red and white ribbon as an adornment and on which the Texan Printery and Czech graphic establishment, embossed the inscription:

" 'Našim Legionařum-Čechoslovaci V Houstonu.' (To our legionaires—the Czechoslovaks of Houston.) When the time was nearing eight o'clock there was another disappointment. The train was again delayed, and was supposed to be due at ten o'clock. Then again we were told that it would come at eleven o'clock. In the meantime the musicians were coming one after another, and then again another report that the train will arrive at 1:30

A. M. Tuesday. Finally at two o'clock the whistle blew and coaches with sleeping heroes were rolling into the depot.

"The clamorous greeting rolling out of the throats of the multitude of congregated Czechs: 'Na Zdar—Vitame Vas;' (to success —we welcome you) awakened the slumbering boys.

"Wearing the uniform of the United States Army, having only the caps of their former regalia (the uniforms worn being donated free by our government), the veterans were almost bewildered, not expecting such a hearty welcome. Red Cross attendants began to distribute coffee, sandwiches, ice cream and cigarettes, and at the wagon loaded with numerous gifts from the Czech war women's organization, 'Včelky' (Little Bees) stood Mrs. Čcrny in charge of dispensing the gifts among the soldiers. When the gifts were being divided the legionaires, with tears in their eyes, thanked every one profusely.

"A delegated committee composed of Messrs. Langer, Rulik, J. Kratky, J. W. Dobiaš, F. Ančinec, J. Miča, J. Drozda and I. J. Gallia, went in search of the commander of the detachment, Major V. Jirsa, who was still asleep in one of the rear coaches. As his aide had informed him that he was wanted by the committee, he sent reply that in a moment he would be ready for the audience, and appearing shortly after, he was greeted by them and by the representatives of the city of Houston.

"Editor Grossman translated the address of the city's representative to Major Jirsa and he in return expressed thanks for such a hearty and cordial reception. Judge C. H. Chernosky of Houston interpreted the speech of Major Jirsa. After this formality Major Jirsa, accompanied by Major Hoblikan, infantryman Slovaček, who had saved President Masaryk's life in the Bolshevik revolution, having on this account enjoyed certain privileges, was led to the Red Cross canteen where he received more ovations.

"Major Jirsa was requested to convey the greetings of Houston and Texas Czechs to the young republic, to which he heartily agreed. Reverend Dobiaš then asked him to accept the Czech revolutionary flag as a token of Houston Czechs' devotion to their former homeland.

"The flag, made of the finest silk, was accepted by the major who thanked them in the name of the Legionaires. Judge Chernosky then lauded the Legionaires for their bravery and loyalty to the cause. The trumpeters' signal sounded, penetrating the early morning air and the soldiers began to entrain, and at this time the music of the Czech National hymn, 'Kde Domov Muj' (Where Is My Home) stirred the hearts of the great throng.

"In the meantime the boys in the coaches of the first train were given loads of those delicious Czech cakes and other numerous gifts from the Houston Czech women. The committee then presented to Major Jirsa a part of the $1,200.00 as a gift of the Houston Czechs for distribution among the brave legionaires under his command, at the same time bidding him and the whole detachment farewell. As the train began to move, the heroes interrupted the grinding noise of the wheels with their shouts of profuse thanks, calling out as they were moving onward, 'We will never forget Texas and Houston.' More greetings, and the train was carrying them to the next destination, and thence to their hearthstones and to their families and loved ones, some of whom they had not seen for five years.

"This train carried 1,076 men, twenty-four officers, two Bohemian and two American nurses and four American army officers who were in command of the troop train on its trip. This expedition sailed from Vladivostok, Siberia, on June 15th and upon its arrival at San Diego had been tendered also a surprising reception by their countrymen living there."

The legionaires formed part of a volunteer corps composed mostly of Czechoslovakian soldiers who had formerly served under the Austrian colors and who had either deserted or been made captives by the Russians. Some of them had served also in the Russian Army, but after the collapse of the old Czarist government were advised by the Czech provisional government, headed by Professor Masaryk, not to get entangled in Russian internal affairs and to remain neutral. Some of them managed to get out of Russia, and joined the ranks of the Allies, but a great number of them had to remain in Russia, unable to move. In spite of the neutrality which they tried to preserve in the struggle for power in Russia, there had occurred many clashes, chiefly with the Bolsheviks, who were from the beginning of the revolution antagonistic to the remaining Czech legions in Russia. Then they began their epochal march across Siberian Russia, being constantly harassed by the Red Army.

They had repelled all attacks, and were able to preserve their unity without sustaining any serious losses until finally when the negotiations were closed between the Czech government and the Allies, their transfer from Russian soil to their country began.

It should also be mentioned that there were Czech volunteers serving in French, English, Canadian and Italian armies.

It was chiefly the Czechs' opposition to war waged against their Slavic brothers and their determination to emancipate themselves from the Austro-Hungarian government, antagonistic to the Slavic population of this empire, which had hastened the internal dissension and numerous desertions of Czechs and other Slav soldiers on the fighting fronts, from Austrian armies, and heralded the collapse of the dual empire.

Two weeks before the Armistice was signed the Czechs seceded from Austria, proclaiming a republic on October 28, 1918. This event passed without serious trouble. There was no bloodshed, for the Czechs were well-prepared and well-disciplined. The provisional government chose Professor Masaryk, the man who had led in the fight for national independence, for the President. While in other lands after the war there were many disorders and other numerous troubles, the Czech Republic showed a remarkable orderliness, adapting itself quickly to the changed conditions, the régime having full support of the populace. The economical conditions were soon favorable enough to help the nation to emerge from the post-war distress and put the republic on a solid foundation.

Though there are in the Republic other national animosities, they are not in any way oppressed, but enjoy the same rights and privileges as the Czechoslovaks themselves and the Constitution of the new Republic is patterned after the Constitution of the United States, having besides some modern ideas of the governmental duties with the demands of the present industrial era.

The facts concerning the Czechoslovak Legion are interesting:

On January 13, 1916, the Czechoslovak Legion entered the Russian Army.

On April 3, 1915, the twenty-eighth Regiment of the Austrian Army, known as the Praha's Children, deserted on the Eastern Front and joined the Russian Army.

On July 10, 1918, the Czechoslovak Legionaires took possession of the Siberian Railway.

On February 2, 1920, the first Regiment of the Siberian Legionaires arrived at Praha.

These Czechoslovakian troops, after their desertion to the Russians, Italians and Serbians, reorganized their forces into a dauntless army, fighting effectively on the side of the Allies in Siberia, Russia, Italy, Serbia and France. The world awoke into amazed admiration and interest in the intrepid fighters for freedom. This same world had formerly known these same people under the name of Bohemians and Slovaks and did not at once recognize the national name of Czech-Čech for the individual and Čechy for the country which had borne the Celtic name *"Boü,"* Boiohemum, for centuries.

Bohemia's endeavors at world peace date back into the early centuries, when the idea of an universal peace and of an international tribunal to settle differences and grievances between princes and nations appeared for the first time during the middle ages.

The patriotism of Texas-Czech citizens was manifested materially in 1916 with the organization of patriotic clubs known as "Č. N. S." (Česko Narodňi Sdruženi) Czech National Organization for the purpose of raising funds for the Red Cross and to aid the land of the fathers, Czechoslovakia, to regain her long-lost independence.

Appreciating and cherishing the freedom of their adopted country, these Texas-Czech citizens held in their hearts the sympathy and love for the land of their ancestry. Even those of Texas birth, of the third and fourth generation, had the inherent love which forbade that they ever forget the land of their forefathers.

To do something to express this sentiment and affection was in the hearts and minds of each individual.

In his message to Congress April 2, 1917, Woodrow Wilson expressed the sentiments of Texas-Czechs when he said:

"We are to fight for the thing nearest to our heart, democracy, for the rights of those who should have a voice in self-government, for the rights and freedom of small nations, so that liberty and fairness should rule over all nations and freedom should be all over the earth."

And again in his message to Congress, January 10, 1917:

"The purpose of the Allies is to arouse the affairs in Europe so as to insure stable governments based upon the rights of the various nations—to forever insure liberty and welfare of nations both great and small. We wish to liberate the Italians, Slavs, Roumanians and Czechoslovaks from the oppressions of others."

The young and abled-bodied Czech men of Texas did their share by volunteering their services in the United States Army. In only a few instances did they wait for the draft. There were others who joined Czechoslovak units to fight on the battlefields of France.

The remaining Czech citizens, through the Č. N. S. organizations, sought to further the cause by generous offerings of financial assistance. There were altogether eighty-nine of these patriotic organizations over the State of Texas, and through the combined efforts of the membership, over $100,000 was raised, mainly through individual contributions.

Something of the methods of operation is to be found in the records gathered and published in a book called *"Pamatník"* (Memories) at Ennis under the auspices of Č. N. S. This was printed in the Czech language and the extracts used are translations made by Dr. Rudolph E. Maresh of Houston, whose name together with that of his brother, Dr. Henry R. Maresh, is to be found listed with the hundreds of young Czech volunteers for service in the United States Government during the World War.

"Early in the year 1916, the Czech citizens of Ennis, Texas, tried to find means to aid Czechoslovakia to gain freedom. The first financial contribution of $321.00 was sent to Chicago. On June 6, 1916, at a social gathering, the Ennis Auxiliary of Č. N. S. was founded with a membership of fifty-one, and the officials chosen were Josef Buňata, chairman; Frank Moncek, secretary, and L. O. Hošek, treasurer.

"At a Fourth of July celebration, sponsored by the Ennis Lodge of S. P. J. S. T., some twenty-five additional members were added to the Auxiliary, and the proceeds from the celebration, amounting to $98.00 were donated. In addition the two Ennis Lodges S. P. J. S. T. contributed $55.00, making altogether $205.00 which was sent to the central committee at Chicago.

"Later the matter was taken up with the Catholic citizens and through the efforts mainly of Kovaska, a Catholic organization, the Č. N. S. Auxiliary of Texas was founded. In November a Catholic celebration was held and the sum of $158.00 was contributed and a membership drive for this one Auxiliary resulted in gaining three hundred members.

"About this time at a state convention of the S. P. J. S. T., held at Galveston, J. J. Frnka, of New Ulm, was chosen treasurer for the Č. N. S. of Texas, and the sum of $383.00 was forwarded to him.

"On January 7, 1917, at a state meeting of the Auxiliary, Č. N. S. attended by forty members, it was decided to give a masked ball. From this, one of the first benefit entertainments, the sum of $89.00 was realized. No more meetings were held until June 24th of that year, but in the meantime a fund of $500.00 was raised through various entertainments.

"At another meeting announcement was made that the Sokols desired to give a state-wide bazaar and asked the Č. N. S. to take the matter in hand. The suggestion was accepted, and immediately an arrangement committee was appointed. This movement stimulated the interest of the people throughout the State, and soon gifts began to arrive from every section. In some communities farmers would donate a certain amount of seed cotton, leaving it at the gin. In this way two bales of cotton were contributed. The cotton was sold at auction, and then again donated, netting the Auxiliary the sum of $1,144.00. The money was equally distributed between the American Red Cross and the Č. N. S. Auxiliary.

"In connection with the bazaar, three young women were nominated in a contest for the queen of the State Bazaar, and a voting contest inaugurated. This netted $525.00 with Miss Rosalie Houdek the winner, having 24,130 votes as compared with her nearest opponent, Miss Vlasta Krutilek, who had 20,882 votes.

"Articles donated for the bazaar netted the sum of $638.00 and the names in the 'Golden Book' added another $200.00 to the fund. The total collection for the bazaar amounted to $4,444.00 with $3,000.00 of the sum clear. Of this amount $2,000.00 was sent to the Č N. S. and $1,000.00 given to the Red Cross.

"It was found impossible to hold another meeting during the year but collections kept accumulating, until at the end of the year a sum of $305.00 was on hand to be sent to the State Treasurer, Mr. Frnka.

"The Ennis Auxiliary raised during the year 1916 a sum total of $589.00 and during 1917, $2,825.00 with a total expenditure of $37.50 to be deducted. This was used mainly for the traveling expenses of speakers. In 1918 there were organized at Ennis two other auxiliaries. These, however, drew somewhat upon the membership of the original organization, but through the activity of the membership, $1,323.00 was raised."

Throughout the State the work of this Texas-Czech organization was carried on through the years of 1916-17-18, resulting in thousands of dollars being contributed for use in humane and reconstruction work. Thus Texas-Czechs were never found wanting when emergencies demanded patriotism and drastic action.

*　　*　　*　　*　　*

The "Sokols," founded in Praha, over seventy years ago, has had a distinct part in this cultural influence. The founder had in his mind the theory of the brotherhood of man, with world-wide kindliness toward one another, as a structure, a fundamental principle being that if men can play together, then they will not want to kill each other.

It has been said of the Sokols, one of the strongest Czech organizations in the world, that it is in harmony with the old Greek conception of life, which combines music, literature and artistic culture for the mind and systematic training for the body. The moral and physical discipline of the organization is expressed in its motto, "A Sound Mind in a Sound Body."

At the seventieth anniversary of the founding of the Sokols, held in the city of Praha in July, 1932, President Masaryk of the Republic who is over eighty years old, rode horseback in all the parades. It was in 1862, in Praha, then in Austria-Hungary, that Dr. Miroslav Tyrš founded the organization.

Shortly before the World War the French historian, Ernest Denis, devoted one of his works to the study of the Czechoslovak national character. He wrote: "There is no higher learning than morality, no better law than truth, no power stronger than that of tolerance, no more valuable fortune than right, and no life without love."

And so it is said that these are the very principles upon which has been built the great and expanding structure of the Sokol organization, which has no equal in any land, as far as originality and numerical strength is concerned.

It has been found that the Sokol ideal appeals to all professions, and every strata of society, in that it stands for both the physical and the spiritual education of the people. The membership is taught to raise the nation to the highest possible perfection of mind and body; to insure true liberty and freedom and to develop a practical utilization of its typical racial characteristics.

Few people know that Komensky originated the triangle of the Body, Spirit and Mind, today so well known in Y. M. C. A. activities. This thought as demonstrated by the greatest scholar of the ages, who was born in 1592 and who died in 1670, would seemingly be the Sokol ideal presented several centuries before the organization of the Sokol organization by Dr. Tyrš.

The seventy-five enthusiasts of that first meeting in Praha seventy years ago, did not realize that they were laying the foundation for an organization which, in less than a quarter of a century, would become the largest society of its kind in the world. The organization, or "Union," as it was first called, gave itself the name of "Sokol," which means a falcon, and symbolizes its lofty ideals. The members in the beginning always met each other with the salute, "God greet you." Later this was changed to "Good Luck." The watchword of the society is "Be Fit."

Many branches of the organization have been established in Texas, with a membership drawn from all professions and walks of life. Dallas, Ennis, West, Houston, East Bernard, Guy, Corpus Christi, San Antonio, Floresville, Crosby, Galveston, Seaton, Taylor, are among the towns and cities represented.

CHAPTER XLIV

The End

TEXAS-CZECHS are building. The dauntless courage of the pioneer ancestry lives today as in the yester-years.

The Texas-Czech population is approximately 500,000, which means that recognition must and will come.

Over fifty years ago when John Ireland, a pioneer Irishman's son, born in Kentucky, was elected Goevrnor of Texas, there was a bill before the Legislative body to have ten thousand copies of the governor's inaugural address printed in the Czech language for the convenience and interest and enlightenment of the Texas-Czech population, but this bill was not favorably acted upon. There were, however, several thousand copies of the address officially printed in German. Governor Ireland was elected to the office of Governor in 1882 by a majority vote, over 50,000 Texas-Czechs voting solidly for him.

With the passing of the years have come the changes which have brought the opportunity of education, and with it the immigrant's knowledge of the English language. Strange how the pendulum now swings backward. The sons and daughters of these Czech pioneers must go to the public schools and universities of the State to be taught the language of their ancestors.

Today the Slav in Texas is in the ascendency. Free and compulsory education and a Democratic government, with suffrage, and the almost unlimited opportunities of civilization, social, industrial and commercial, have given the pioneer immigrants that which they came for—freedom and the chance to live their lives as they wished. There is no forbidden ground, either in politics, religion, society, industry, art, science or profession.

Under the American system, which is to judge by the character, capacity and the achievements of individuals, the path lies open and leads on and on, even to the seat of the highest office of the whole country, that of the President of the United States.

Andrew Jackson, the first president to come from the common people, spoke of America as an "asylum where the wretched and the oppressed could find refuge and support." A new country without tradition became for the Czech pioneer the soil into which he planted his love, sentiment and ambitions. Today it is as he helped to make it.

In the recounting of these and other incidents which have to do with the life and interests of the Texas-Czech citizens, the historian retrospectively follows the trail backward through the century of progress only to retrace the route forward again to make mental note of the milestones along the way.

Living for a time with them through the medium of historical research, lingering appreciatively in the mellow vale of the yester-years with the pioneers, has given a clearer vision, a deeper appreciation of what they have encountered and what they have endured while they labored to accomplish the results that are so outstanding today.

To the Czech pioneer the magnificent area of fertile soil in Texas was as a haven of refuge—a promised land of golden opportunity. Pioneer Czech immigrants who soon after their arrival came into conflict with the difficulties that beset them in the new home, never let up in their labors until they established the home and helped build a community.

And now in retrospection we view the result.

We see on a great canvas a story in action. The play is a magnificent dramatization of the lives of the Czech pioneers. Texas-Czech lawyers, physicians, statesmen, business men, artists, educators, musicians and scientists, along with the men of commerce and industry, keep in motion the procession started one hundred years ago by those intrepid immigrants who reached port in Texas and moved inland with ox-team caravans.

The great loneliness, the heartaches, the incurable homesickness of these early comers to Texas, has been distilled in the crucible where all great passions of the human heart and mind are consumed in the process of producing the sentiment and tradition which makes great nations.

Czechs in Texas at the beginning of 1933 holding county and State offices, included in the list outstanding citizens from all sections of the State.

Judge C. H. Chernosky, Houston, had been a member for some years of the State Board of Education, to which position he was appointed by Governor R. S. Sterling. He had previously been elected, and served, as county judge of Fort Bend County.

Honorable Joseph Kopecky, newspaper publisher of Hallettsville, had been for a number of years, director of the Board of Regents of the Agricultural and Mechanical College, College Station.

Honorable Gus Russek, banker, of Schulenburg, a member of

the Texas Senate, having served his senatorial district for many years, and for the "Forty-third" regular session of the Legislature, which convened in January, 1933, was made Chairman of the Committee on State Banking and was also appointed one of the committee of five members of the Senate selected to serve with a like committee from the House, to canvass the votes for Governor Miriam A. Ferguson and Lieutenant-Governor Edgar Witt, received in the general election, November, 1932, and also to make plans and arrangements for the inaugural ceremonies January 17, 1933.

Honorable L. J. Šulak, LaGrange, appointed by Governor Miriam A. Ferguson a member "Board of Regents University of Texas," 1933, was accorded one of the highest honors in the State.

In the House of Representatives, James Pavlica of Flatonia, was a member, having been elected in the Democratic primaries in July and August, 1932, and in the general election that followed in November.

Lavaca County has had a number of Texas-Czechs in office. Included were Mrs. Mikulenka, who was county treasurer for fourteen years; Judge C. L. Stavinoha, attorney at Hallettsville, was county judge of the county for some years. The list further includes: J. F. Božka, county clerk; V. J. Prašek, tax collector; J. F. Holubec, auditor; Frank Matula, Hallettsville and O. E. Kuběna, Moulton, county commissioners.

Thomas Jefferson, during the founding of the Nation, announced that all men were created equal and were endowed with the inalienable rights of life, liberty and the pursuit of happiness— a government to serve men and not masters.

To this great America, the land of promise, with doors open wide to the man or woman, no matter what their birth, with opportunities to make good, these Czech pioneers who have made history, came. And it is as though a great company, resounding in unison through the decades, as one mighty voice, says, "Never will we be in rebellion, or in discord with the land of our adoption."

The Texas frontier is gone in the sense that the pioneers knew it; when land could be had almost for the asking and when the new government fostered the undertaking of home-making through land grants, but there are other and newer opportunities which have come with progress.

Texas-Czech leaders have developed, and these are focussing their vision on the future and the greater opportunities that lie ahead. In organization the Czechs are not excelled—their success in constructive work through organization is to be found all down the years, ever since the establishment of the first Czech schools in Texas when a few neighbors banded themselves together in behalf of the movement. During the one hundred years from 1833, when Anthony Michael Dignowity, the first historically recorded Czech, came to Texas, and the year 1933, there has been achieved magnificent results in Texas-Czech organization movements over the State.

It has been said that Texas, up to the year 1933, had not developed a Czech leader as prominent as the late and lamented Anton Čermak, mayor of Chicago. It is, however, conceded that Texas-Czechs have no boundary line, or line of demarkation as to what they may claim for their own in the way of honors and distinctions in achievement in the open field of art, science, commerce or industry. No Czech boy or girl is content with an education short of a "degree." In fact many rural schools in Texas have young Czech teachers who have degrees from the State University, or some college. The Texas-Czech newspaper editor is a wielder of influence and a moulder of sentiment. The columns of his paper offer a medium for the dissemination not only of news, but also of that intangible commodity which we call "influence." While this influence is not to be valued too lightly, yet the Texas-Czech of the present is much given to reading and not being bound by the provincial. He thinks for himself.

The modern highway and automobile, telephone and radio, together with the free rural delivery of mail, has not only put the Czech farm home in direct contact with the outside world, but has brought the world to the doorway of the rural family. The circulating library plays its part. The Texas-Czech reads not only the classics, but in addition material covering a wide field of literary endeavor. He reads with the satisfaction of knowing that he, as a member of his people, had a part in bringing about these things. Hundreds of Texas-Czech men and women are employed in printing establishments as operators of machinery, proofreaders, writers and binders. They have a part in the delivery of the mail throughout the State, over the highways which they have through their taxes and by their labor helped to build. As members of the boards of county commissioners, they have been instrumental in providing funds to carry on the circulating libraries.

*　　*　　*　　*

The small sailing vessel, rocking on the storm-tossed waves, bearing to Texas the early Czech pioneers. The desolation of the undeveloped country that awaited them. The privations that offered not a single comfort. Famine, pestilence and warfare that followed to take heavy toll of the pioneers, pass in review.

A tear blots a page, falling in sorrow for the pioneer mother, lost in the wilderness with her baby dying in her arms. Fifty years later a young granddaughter of this pioneer mother attends grand opera in the city of Houston. It is the fulfillment of the hopes and plans and heart's desires of those who came to blaze a trail. The attainment of the things which go toward the making of happiness.

And one may look down the long vista of futurity to see an "empire" in extent, unequalled in advantages, a valuable part of the continent. And this extended empire, inhabited by the sons and daughters of Czech pioneers, inheriting the will and the purpose of the pioneer ancestors to maintain and carry them on.

Owners of the soil on which they live, and with interests in institutions which they have labored to establish and uphold. The waters of an ocean laping the shores of the great State, bearing on its bosom the commerce which the labors of the Texas-Czech citizens have helped to develop.

It has been difficult at times to gather these chapters from the lives of pioneer Texas-Czechs, who came to a wilderness and helped to blaze the trail to civilization; but the records have not been confined to the few yellowed documents or fragments of the written page, but are exemplified in the lives of the children of the pioneers, and their children's children, even unto the third and fourth generation.

And because of these things the historian has found inspiration to write—and, having written, offers no apologies, but rather, finds the courage to believe that all is well; that this history, as it is written will in the truth of it live and not be without its mission.

THE END

APPENDIX

SOURCES

For the chapters on Texas and Czechoslovakia, the author acknowledges indebtedness to contemporary volumes dealing with these subjects.

Other subject matter, pertaining almost exclusively to the Texas-Czech pioneers and their descendants, has been gathered over a long period of time from many sources. In the majority of instances, this material has been secured by personal contact with a few of the older generations, most of the second, and many of the third generation.

Through the courtesy of these Texas-Czechs, old records and letters were placed at the disposal of the authors, and from these sources the pictures of pioneer life in Texas have been drawn.

It is manifestly impossible to include between the covers of a single volume, *all* of the interesting matter pertaining to the subject; hence a careful selection was necessary, so that the more important incidents might be recorded, with sufficient minor incidents to give as complete and varied a picture of the Texas-Czechs as possible.

In many instances, stories were so filled with human interest that it was considered advisable to reproduce them exactly as narrated to the authors; hence the many chapters told all, or in part, in the first person.

Incidents in this volume have been carefully checked for accuracy, even legendary matter wherever possible; but because in many instances sources were very meagre, and memories rather dim, it has been impossible to verify all matter presented here as facts.

COAT OF ARMS OF THE REPUBLIC OF CZECHOSLOVAKIA

The Coat of Arms of the Republic of Czechoslovakia gives symbolic evidence of the conditions under which the state originated.

As the Republic is made up of Bohemia, Moravia and Silesia of old Austria, Slovakia of old Hungary and the autonomous territory of Carpathian Ruthenia, each of these were entitled to recognition in the Coat of Arms and are represented generally by certain historical events.

The Republic uses three Coats of Arms, each having its own peculiar significance and use.

It consists of two shields, one of which is superimposed upon the other. The central or frontal shield consists of a two-tailed lion on a red background. The lion is a symbol of noble-minded strength protecting the integrity of the state. The back, or surrounding shield, is divided into four quadrants, each containing the symbol of one of the component states of the Republic.

Facing the picture in the upper left quadrant are three mountain peaks with a double cross against a red background. This is the emblem of Slovakia and its position is considered to be one of honor.

In the upper right quadrant two figures are to be seen. The figure on the left is composed of three golden beams on a blue background. On the right is a red bear on a silver background. The bear faces toward the left. These two figures constitute the symbol of Carpathian Ruthenia.

In the lower left quadrant is seen a crowned eagless, checkered in red and white. The head is turned toward the left. This figure, upon a blue background, represents Moravia.

In the right lower quadrant is a crowned black eagless, looking toward the right. Across the breast of the bird is a small silver sickle with a three-leaf clover on either end. There is a small decorative cross at the center of the sickle. This figure, on a golden field, represents Silesia.

In tracing briefly the history of these component parts of the Czechoslovakian Coat of Arms it is found that the central figure represents the famous old Kingdom of Bohemia, a nation whose history dates back for more than one thousand years. In the Twelfth Century the Coat of Arms consisted of a silver-lion with two tails. The lion was later placed against a red background, succeeding the much older one used by King Venceslav. The king's emblem at the time was a fiery black eagless.

The State of Moravia possessed a Coat of Arms which consisted of a red and white checkered eagless on a blue background. When the Moravians joined the Bohemian kingdom they brought their Coat of Arms with them. Before the Fifteenth Century the

Silesian principality had numerous Coats of Arms, but during the Fifteenth Century the entire Silesian State placed itself under the crown of King Venceslav. At this time the Silesian Coat of Arms consisted of a black eagless with a silver sickle on its breast superimposed on a golden background.

Inasmuch as Slovakia was under the rule of Hungary for something like one thousand years, it had no sovereignty of its own, and hence no Coat of Arms. However, Czechs and Slovaks had for many years considered that part of Hungary's emblem consisting of the three mountain peaks, crowned by a double patriarchial cross, as their own. The three mountains reminded the Slovaks of "Tatra, Matra and Vatra," which were peaks within the original Slovak territory. The double cross reminded them of the two saints, Cyril and Methodius, who brought Christianity to their country.

Carpathian Ruthenia, like Slovakia, had long been a subjugated nation, without a Coat of Arms. Therefore, when Ruthenia annexed itself voluntarily to the Czechoslovakian Republic, it was found necessary to create an emblem for this group. The Coat of Arms thus created consists of two essential portions, the first being made up of three parallel golden beams, superimposed on a blue background. The second portion consists of a red bear on a silver background.

The State colors of Czechoslovakia have been evolved somewhat after the manner of the Coat of Arms. Before the Sixteenth Century the Czech flag consisted of a white lion on a red field. This flag was replaced by the one used in Bohemia, consisting of equal parts of red and white paralleling each other. These colors perpetuate those used in both the Coat of Arms and the old flag.

When the Republic of Czechoslovakia was formed the color of blue was added in honor of Slovakia, being taken from the Slovakian Coat of Arms depicting the three mountain peaks previously referred to. The flag in use comprises three colors—red, white and blue.

When suspended from a flagpole there are equal parallel stripes of white and red, the latter color being placed at the bottom. A triangular piece of blue extends from the center of the red and white field to the flagpole in such a position that the base of the triangle is attached to the pole and the apex runs to the center of the red and white. The flagpole is decorated with red, white and blue stripes, the blue stripe being one-half the width of the red and white.

SPEECH OF JUDGE AUGUSTIN HAIDUŠEK DE-LIVERED AT TEXAS COTTON PALACE, WACO, ON BOHEMIAN DAY, NOVEMBER 10, 1910

THE Bohemians not only of Texas, but of the United States, feel highly honored because the directors of the Cotton Palace permitted them to call one day of this great festivity as their own. It gave them an opportunity to come in closer contact with the people of other nationalities, and thus affords them an occasion to improve their knowledge of their fellow citizens.

Who are the Bohemians, whence have they come, and what induced them to come to this country? Some historians tell us that the Bohemians are the descendants of a race of people that 750 years B. C. inhabited a scope of country northeast of the Adriatic Sea, between the Baltic and the Black seas, and extending into Asia beyond the Ural mountains. Of their pursuits and domestic habits, Herodotus, the Greek historian, in substance says: "That stock-raising and tilling the soil were their main pursuits of life; that they introduced agriculture and bread among their German neighbors; that those residing on the shores of the Baltic were engaged in amber traffic with the Phoenicians and the Greeks; that they were industrious, economical, upright, kind-hearted and peaceable, but intrepid and quick in resenting injuries; that they were fond of amusements, and for that purpose would assemble in their forests; that they never resorted to arms except in the defense of their homes and their liberty, but, that when they were forced to take up arms, they fought to conquer or to die; that they were opposed to slavery, hence they never enslaved their prisoners of war; that their hospitality was one of their most prominent characteristics."

Such are said to have been the Slavs whose descendants today number about one hundred and fifty millions. Of these about six millions inhabit the western continent, most of whom reside in the United States of America. The one hundred and forty-four millions inhabit the Eastern continent, of whom about one hundred million are Russians, and the remainder are the Servians, Croatians, Bosnians, Montenegrins, Slavonians, Malmations, Bulgarians, Slovaks, Serbs, Polanders, Bohemians and Moravians. All are the subjects of four great powers: Russia, Turkey, Austro-Hungary and Germany. Their creeds vary according to the government of which they are subjects.

Writers differ concerning the meaning of the word, "Slav." Some Latin and German writers claim that "Slav" means servitude—slavery. But those writers who have traced the word "Slav" to its origin tell us that it is derived from "Slavo"—a word meaning "people of the same race." The original Slavs spoke a language of which the Russian, Polish, Slavonian, Serbian and Bohemian are the principal offsprings. The Bohemian is spoken by both the Bohemians and Moravians.

It is a language of monosyllabic roots, which are susceptible of various compositions, and on this the grammar and construction depend entirely. The leading principles governing the formation of words are of verbal and pronominal roots, which, in their combination, form the body and soul of the language. It is said that the Sanscrit type is more faithfully preserved in this langauge than in the Greek or the Latin. Like the Sanscrit it has three numbers, three genders, seven cases, a perfect system of prefixes and affixes, and an unlimited power of forming compound words. Dankorsky says, "Of the three sisters, one kept faithful to her mother tongue—the Slavonic; the second gave to that common heritage the highest cultivation—the Greek; and the third mixed the mother tongue with a foreign idiom—the Latin." The Bohemian comprises all these elements only in a higher degree, having been improved very much within the last century. Philologists admit this language to be as perfect as any of the living languages. It is much more composite and flexible than the German. It has nine parts of speech, seven moods and seven cases. The termination of its nouns, adjectives and verbs determines the number, gender, person and case. Its verbs are indefinite, simple, frequentative and perfect. Some of these verbs constitute complete sentences. Many of its sounds are as melodious as the Italian; but some are even harsher than the German. Any person understanding this language thoroughly has no trouble to learn other languages.

Bohemia and Moravia are in Central Europe, adjoining each other. They are a part of the Austro-Hungarian empire. But at one time they constituted an independent kingdom and were governed by their own people. "They were the first people that attained a commanding position among the cultured peoples of central Europe," says a reliable authority. When they settled upon the lands they occupy today no historian has stated with any certainty, but tradition says that they came there about the middle of the fifth century. At the beginning of the Christian era the country was inhabited by the Boii, a Celtic race. From this race the country was called Bohemia. Boii were forced therefrom by the Marcoman, a powerful race that was led by Marobud, who established there a kingdom, which lasted until Attila with his horde overran Europe, in A. D. 445. About that time a branch of the Slavic race, headed by Čech, came into Bohemia, drove the Marcomanni away and settled there permanently. Moravia, deriving its name from the river Morava, was also the home of the Boii, afterwards was inhabited by the Germanic Quadi, who were succeeded by the Heruli, then the Lombards and finally the Slavs.

These newcomers into these countries were at first much disturbed by their German neighbors, with whom they were almost constantly at war. But in A. D. 622, under their leader, Samo, they vanquished completely their enemies. Samo was then elected their ruler with delegated powers, and he laid the foundation for the first Slavo-Bohemian dynasty, which he governed until his death in 658. For a time thereafter the Bohemians governed themselves. Their political institutions were purely democratic. It is said that they believed that no man derived his power to govern others from any unnatural source; that all such power emanated from the people. The management of their government was entrusted to their elders whom they selected from thir midst because of their superior wisdom and knowledge of public matters. They knew nothing of Christianity; but they believed in one supreme power, and regarded it as the Creator of light and the world. At the same time they worshiped good and evil spirits, and to them made their offerings. But with all this, they believed in the immortality of the soul, and eternal reward for good and punishment for evil deeds.

Some years after managing their governmental affairs, they selected Krok, a descendant of Samo, as their ruler. He governed them until his death. Having died without male issue, he requested them that his daughter Libuša be chosen to direct the government. She took charge, but the people soon became dissatisfied with her, claiming that it was not becoming a woman to rule men, and they demanded that she have a husband whom they would entrust with their government.

Though she was a wise and just ruler, yet to satisfy the people, she sent a deputation to Přemysl, who was plowing his field with oxen, and requested him to come, that she would take him as her husband. He came, took charge of the government, and founded the second Slavo-Bohemian dynasty which became powerful, and was governed by his lineal descendants from 732 until 1306, during which time there were carried on many bloody wars with the Germans and the Franks in most of which the Bohemians were victorious.

Charlemagne invaded their country several times, but never subjugated them. Libuša founded Praha, the capital of Bohemia. Among the women she was popular—she defended their rights of equality with men. After she died the women of her court refused to be governed by Přemysl. They took possession of a fortified castle from which they tried to subjugate the men. Vlasta, a daring maid, commanded them. She addressed them thus: "My Sisters! We have lost our mistress who never allowed men to mistreat us, nor that we should permit them to lord over us. Now, we are being mistreated, it behooves us then to resist the mistreatment or the men will enslave us. Stand by me, I shall assure you of our independence." In a battle which followed, the women were conquered, but not subjugated.

Among the descendants of Přemysl were several great rulers; they had at heart the welfare of the people; they builded many cities and promoted various material enterprises: In 1241, Vaclav I defended Europe successfully against a Mongolian invasion, routing the Mongols completely in battle in Moravia. Ottocar II extended largely his domains by conquest, and thus became a formidable rival to the German Emperor.

Up to about the middle of the Ninth Century, the Bohemians were pagans, but they readily embraced Christianity when it was preached to them in their own tongue by the two Slavonic Apostles, Cyril and Methodius, who came among them from the East at the request of Rastislav, a Duke of Moravia. Bohemia prospered, and doubtless on this account jealousy and dissensions prevailed in the ruling family, resulting in the assassination of Vaclav III, the last Přemysl. This terminated the Přemysl dynasty. The Germans, who were very anxious to govern Bohemia, took advantage of the dissensions and induced the Bohemians to elect and crown Rudolph of Hapsburg as their king. In 1310 he was forced to leave the kingdom as he proved himself incapable of performing his duties. John of Luxemburg, a son of Emperor Henry, having married a Bohemian, was elected king of Bohemia. He was succeeded by his son Charles, called "the father of his country," who, by the electoral princes was placed upon the imperial throne of Germany and known as Charles IV. He was the best ruler that ever governed the Bohemians. In 1348 he founded the University of Praha, it being the first in Europe. It had over 5,000 students of different nationalities.

Historians tell us that "that was a lustrous period; the glory of Bohemia was revived and it surpassed its former splendor. Bohemia then stood first in the world in power, wealth, progress, literature, science, art and liberty." But the Slavic race seemed never to have valued properly prosperity. The people invariably became profligate and dissentious, whenever they were prosperous. Such proved to be the case when King Vaclav IV took the reins of the Bohemian government. In addition to that, the Hussite reformation brought on a protracted war, lasting many years, producing, at times, fratricide among the Bohemians and devastating the country.

John Huss, the reformer, was a Catholic priest, very pure and an avowed Catholic. But as he was imbued with the teachings of John Wickliff, the English reformer, he preached and wrote morality, justice and uprightness, always using the Scriptures for his text. Besides he was a true patriot, striving to revive the glory of Bohemia and remove the shackles of tyranny from the general people. He was accused of heresy, tried by the council at Constance, found guilty and adjudged by civil authorities to be burned alive. Before his execution he was promised his life and liberty if he would recant what he had been teaching. Refusing to do so, he was burned alive July 6, 1415, at Constance. The burning of Huss enraged the people of Bohemia, and they condemned the action of the council.

In the meantime, Jerome of Praha, a co-laborer of Huss, was arrested and brought to Constance, found guilty of heresy and burned alive in April, 1416. The council is said to have claimed that by the burning of the two heretics the people would again submit to the Roman church. But the effect of the burning of these men was contrary to what was expected. The people, though Catholics, refused to obey the authorities of the church, which resulted in religious factions among the people; some adhering to the doctrines preached by Huss, others submitting to the church authorities. These factions soon became hostile, which resulted in a war between them. In July, 1419, the Hussites assembled on Mount Tabor, numbering over 42,000, to consider their future course. King Vaclav, who was opposed to them, took steps to suppress the hostilities, but he failed. The people were too powerful; they were headed by an experienced warrior, John Žižka, who incited them to revolution, which broke out Sunday, July 30, 1419. They stormed the King's palace and threw seven officers out of windows to the enraged populace that tore them to pieces. King Vaclav died September 16, 1419, was succeeded by

Sigismund, who tried to stop the revolution. Failing to do so, he called to his assistance his German neighbors. They came with vast armies, and in 1420 besieged Praha, the seat of the revolution. It is said the army had over 300,000 men.

When the Bohemians saw that they had to face their common enemy they consolidated and, under the leadership of Žižka, dispersed the enemy. Thereafter followed destructive operations, which were not confined to Bohemia alone, but extended into neighboring countries, whereby the dominions of the kingdom were enlarged. Žižka, though totally blind, continued to lead the Bohemians until October 11, 1424, when he died. He introduced new tactics in warfare, which proved destructive to the enemy. It is said that Žižka never lost a battle. After his death the war was continued until 1434. The Bohemians gained what they had been fighting for; the Emperor offered a treaty, permitting them the use of the cup in the Eucharist, which was the principal cause of the war. In addition they were granted general amnesty and a confirmation of all their privileges.

Thereafter the Council of Brazil was assembled and entered into an agreement, which is known as "Bohemian Compactata." It fully ratified the treaty. But it is a part of the Slavic nature to be contentious and therefore, bitter strife continued among the Bohemians, principally between the aristocracy and the general people. The former were trying to enslave the people as the Germans and Franks were doing, but the people resisted, claiming that it was repugnant to the Slavic customs and destructive to all personal liberties. For a time a great confusion prevailed, but when in 1452, George Padĕbrad was chosen ruler, and in 1458 crowned king of Bohemia, which he governed until 1471—order, good feeling and prosperity prevailed for years, even after his death. But at the beginning of the Sixteenth Century conditions changed; the people were crushed into serfdom by Louis, their ruler.

After his death Bohemia passed into the hands of Ferdinand of Austria, who treated the people in a most despotic manner, and in 1517, declared Bohemia a hereditary possession. It became such. Thereafter most of the liberties of the Bohemians were suppressed. But when Ferdinand of Syria took charge of Bohemia, he capped the climax in despotism and tyranny. He made an era in history and caused more bloodshed, ruin and devastation than any other ruler in modern history. More than two-thirds of his subjects were Protestants, yet many of them were ordered to leave his domains. But in 1618 he was crowned king of Bohemia. The

Protestants rejected him and selected a German prince palatine, Frederick V, as their king.

The acts of Ferdinand so outraged the people that they took Martietz and Slavata, Ferdinand's councilors, and threw them out of a window in the second story of a castle in Praha. In the meantime Ferdinand was preparing his armies to invade Bohemia to exterminate the Hussite blood. He amassed a large army, invaded Bohemia, and on November 8, 1620, was fought at White Mountain near Praha, a battle in which the overwhelming numbers of Ferdinand's army, after fighting a whole day, annihilated the Bohemians. This was the beginning of the Thirty Years' War, and the extinction of the Bohemian kingdom, which included Moravia as both were parts of the Austrian empire, and are such today, of which empire the Roman Catholics are the principal inhabitants.

While the battle of White Mountain was raging, the Bohemian King Frederick was feasting at Praha, but when he heard of the defeat of his subjects, he deserted his post of duty and fled in the utmost consternation to the Netherlands. The Bohemians, being unable to resist longer, were treated most unmercifully by Ferdinand. Twenty-seven of the first nobles were beheaded and their heads stuck on posts in the city, and their property confiscated. Ferdinand ordered that no subject who would not conform to the Catholic faith would be permitted to remain within his domains. Thereupon 36,000 families, because they would not renounce the religion of their ancestors, were forced to leave their native land and seek homes in foreign countries. Many of them came to America, settled in North Carolina and Pennsylvania, and were known here as Moravian Brethren. Their descendants took an active part in the war of American independence. Even the renowned educator, John Amos Komensky, the last bishop of the Moravian Brethren, was compelled to leave his country. He went to Holland, and while there, was offered the presidency of Harvard College as appears in "Ecclesiastical History of New England."

Some years after the fall of Bohemia, Augustin Heřman came to America and established a Bohemian Manor in Maryland. He was a warm friend of Lord Baltimore. He distinguished himself as a valuable citizen of this country. In the old world, for many generations after their defeat, the Bohemians were hardly known because they were even robbed of their mother-tongue. Maria Theresa, the Empress of Austria, ordered that the German be used and taught exclusively in all the schools. Emissaries were sent among the people to confiscate and destroy all Bohemian literature. Many Bohemians then thought that their mother-tongue would become extinct—they were ashamed to use it. But thank God, the peasants remained faithful and continued to speak the Bohemian language. Besides them there were a few patriotic spirits, among whom were the monks of a Slavonic monastery of Sazova, who preserved the language in its purity. Prior to the battle of White Mountain the Bohemian literature was very rich. In the Ninth Century Cyril, the Slavonic apostle, translated large portions of the Scripture. Dlimil wrote his Rhyming Chronicles of Bohemia, 1314, and soon thereafter a complete translation of the Scripture was made, which is preserved at Nikolsburg, Moravia.

Then followed many renowned writers—Štitny, the moralist, Duba, the jurist and Flaška, the poet. About the time of John Huss the Bohemian literature was superior to that of any other nationality, but all was destroyed afterwards by the government. At the close of the Eighteenth Century appeared many able writers; Count Kinsky, Pelcel and Bablin. Later came Prochazka, Jungman, Šafařik, Kollar, Palacky and many others too numerous to mention. The Bohemian literature of today, in many respects, is equal to that of any other nationality. It is increasing rapidly in all branches.

In 1862 was organized in Bohemia the Sokol, which means a falcon. It was an organization composed of the best men, ostensibly for physical development, but primarily to unify the Bohemians. The organization is in existence today. Similar organizations have been inaugurated in this country, and even in Texas. It is doing valuable service in the way of good citizenship. The national spirit in Bohemia was much revived about 1848 and since then has been making good progress.

The Bohemians are very prominent in music. John Kubelik is said to equal Paganini. We have several excellent composers of music and plays. There are many artists and scientists of renowned ability. Journalism and periodicals of all kinds are well developed. Also distinguished poets and novelists are numerous. All of this is the result of education, in which the Bohemians compare favorably with any other nationality. Many prominent English, French and German authors have been translated into Bohemian and some Bohemian authors have been translated into other languages.

Reliable authority indicates that the main emigration from Bohemia to the United States commenced about 1848, and it has been steady since then. There are about one million Bohemians in the United States, counting those that are of Bohemian descent. Most of them are in large cities; New York, Pittsburg, Cleveland, Chicago and St. Louis. Chicago is said to have about 125,000 Bohemians. The States of Iowa, Wisconsin, Nebraska, Kansas, Oklahoma and Texas have a large Bohemian population. All are making a living and many are rich.

There are many good Bohemian newspapers, six large dailies, several semi-weeklies and weeklies published in the several states. The first Bohemians that came to this country, came here because of the political conditions in their native land. Others followed to better their material conditions. Texas has about 80,000 Bohemians who are domiciled in about 100 counties, of whom over ninety-five per cent till the soil. They are good farmers. The first came here about the fifties, and from that time they came every year except during the Civil War. While we are generally known as Bohemians, yet more than seventy-five per cent of those that came here, came from Moravia, the others are from Bohemia. Over seventy-five per cent are Catholics, the balance are Protestants. There are also some atheists among them. Our people prefer to live close together so as to have the facility of enjoying the benefits afforded by closer settlements. They are fond of music, vocal and instrumental, and other amusements, and for that purpose have frequent social gatherings. In every large neighborhood is a spacious hall for that purpose. A neat schoolhouse and an elegant church are in every settlement—schools are taught by efficient teachers and the Word of God is preached by learned and pious men.

There are several fraternal orders among our people, the membership of which is increasing because these orders are proving beneficial to the people. We have six newspapers in Texas: *Novy Domov, Obzor, Bratrske Listy, Texan, Buditel* and *Svoboda*. Besides, papers published in the Northern states have subscribers here. The *Svoboda*, published semi-weekly in La Grange, has the largest circulation in Texas. Of late some of the English papers in this county, and maybe elsewhere, commenced to publish supplements in Bohemian.

The medical profession is well represented; there are many good doctors here of Bohemian nationality. As we are a law-abiding people, there are but a few lawyers among the Bohemians. We have a great many merchants, most of whom are doing well. Several Bohemians have been members of the state legislature. Three were elected for the next legislature. In the counties of Burleson, Fayette and Lavaca, Bohemians were elected to some of the county offices. We had representatives in congress from Chicago, lieutenant governor in Wisconsin, and several minor offices during Cleveland's administration. There are many mechanics among our people, but most of them prefer farming to pursuing their trade. In politics our people are active locally, and nearly all vote the democratic ticket. They are democrats from principle, not for office or gain. They believe that democracy is based upon principles, permitting every man to do what he pleases so long as he does not injure others, and securing to him the fullest measure of his liberties. A large number of our people came here without any means, but in a few years they have saved enough to get them a home. When they arrive here, they generally cultivate rented land until they are able to make one payment, and then they buy a home. When they like a piece of land, they never squabble about its price. I am safe in saying that our people own the best farms in the neighborhoods in which they reside. However, some of them own very poor land, and yet they get along.

It is said of our people that they will get rich cultivating land on which a German can make barely a living, and an American will starve. Our people cultivate their lands well, and fertilize them if necessary. They diversify their crops, change seed for planting, and raise all sorts of truck. They raise their meat, chickens, eggs, turkeys, ducks and geese, and have plenty of milk and butter. Of all these things they sell enough to buy their groceries and other necessary articles. Their good wives are a great help to them, for they manage domestic affairs and also help to cultivate and gather the crop. Nearly all our people have comfortable dwellings, and well improved farms. Some of them are wealthy. Even many tenants, in my portion of the state, have money deposited in banks. All have good teams and comfortable vehicles for their use. The sentiment of our people is voiced by my saying, that they are doing well in Texas. It has been said that foreigners are not desirable citizens, that they are too clannish and cling too much to their native land; that as such they are not safe enough guardians of our republican institutions. That as they have been brought up and educated in countries whose governments are monarchical, for that reason they never grasp the principles upon which are based our institutions. For over forty years I have taken part in public life and it has been my experience that foreigners guard personal liberties, which are the basis of free government, better than the native-born citizens. The foreigners, understanding the operations of monarchical governments, are in a better position to appreciate our institutions than are the native citizens. A true value of anything can be ascertained best by comparison. The general people in the old country are fully awakened and are striving to rid themselves of tyranny, whereas here the people are in the clutches of corporations and monopolies, whose acts are even more tyrannical than those of monarchies.

A few words concerning myself—I was born in Moravia and came to Fayette County, Texas, with my father in 1856, and have lived there ever since. For forty-one years I have lived in La Grange, the county seat. When we came here, we settled on raw land on the East Navidad, about fourteen miles from La Grange. The country was not settled except by six families that constituted a Bohemian colony. We lived in huts made out of poles covered with grass—later built log cabins. The Americans came long distances in carriages to look at us. They tried to talk to us, but we did not understand them. By their bringing us meat, bacon, chickens, eggs and even some clothing, they evidently thought that we were objects of charity. Money was offered them for those things, but they refused it. Some of them tried to show us how to cultivate our crops. They thinned some corn and cotton for us, but we thought they were trying to destroy our crop. We left two stalks of corn to a hill about a foot apart, and cotton the same way. The result was that the six families made one bale of cotton and a lot of shuck instead of corn. The next crop was good—we learned better.

In 1860 a large number of Bohemians came to this country, and many came to our colony. Among them was Valentine Gallia, the father of the Gallias in our section of the state. He looked at our log cabin and said to my father: "Valentine, you had a better house for your hogs in the old country than you have for yourself and family here." My father replied: "I rather live in this log cabin and be a free American citizen than to reside in a palace and be a subject of the Austrian government." I had him explain the meaning of his reply to Mr. Gallia, and it made a lasting impression on my mind.

When the war broke out my older brother went among the first volunteers, but he never returned. His remains are resting under the sod near Brownsville in Cameron County. I went later, and I returned because I ran every time danger was approaching. For that reason I am here today enjoying the festivity of your great and prosperous city.

In conclusion permit me to say that we, the Bohemians, are

here today to pay homage to King Cotton because of the benefits that he bestows upon all who comply with his demands. It is cotton that makes us prosperous in this, our adopted mother-land, which we love as dearly as our lives because it gives us ample sustenance and homes in which we can live happy.

LIST OF CZECH BOOKS IN THE HOUSTON PUBLIC LIBRARY

Arbes: Feuilletony. *Baar:* Jan Cimbura, Počtař. *Baar:* Pani komisařka, Skřivanek, Lusy, Žolinka, Osmačtyřicatnici. *Beneš, Edv.:* Světova valka a naše revoluce, 2 svazky. *Beneš-Třeb:* Souhrn spisu, 2 svaz., Kralovna Dagmar, Z ruznych dob. 3 svaz. *Čech-Straň:* Chuda holka, 2 svazky, Mamon. *Čech. Svat:* Basnicka dila, 10 svazku, Pestre cesty po Čechach, Ruzna prosa, 4 svazky. *Čapek:* Krakatit, O věcech obecnych. *Čapek-Chod:* Jindrove, Turbina. *Dostal:* Vlnami života. *Durych:* Na horach, Sedmikraska. *Erben:* Pohadky. *Fastrova:* Gospar Niko, Tři mladenci, Zlaty kroužek. *Hanek:* Žive rany. *Herites:* Křemen a hlina. *Holeček:* Naši, Prvni tři dily. *Hrnčiř:* Obrazkove dějiny česke. *Javořicka:* Nebeska krupěj, Potok, Vrak rodiny Tomanovy. *Jedlička:* Dějiny českeho pisemnictvi. *Jirasek:* Bratrstvo, F. L. Věk, 5 dilu, Poklad, Psohlavci, Skalaci, Stare pověsti česke, Temno, V cizich službach. *Kalal:* Nevěsta z Tater. *Karafiat:* Broučci, Broučkovy pohadky. *Karas:* Smil Klat. *Klecanda:* Matčino vitězstvi, Pater Vojtěch. *Klicpera:* Jindra. *Klosterman:* Mlhy na Blatech, V raji šumavskem, Z dobreho srdce, Ze světa lesnich samot. *Konrad:* Čim srdce, čim jsi zhřešilo. *Kopta:* Třeti rota, 2 svazky, Třeti rota na magistrale. *Kosmak:* Cestopisne obrazky. *Krejči:* Filosofie poslednich let. *Křen:* Stryčkovy rozumy, Z hanackych rodin. *Machar:* Kriminal. *Majerova:* Naměsti republiky. Nejkrasnějši svět. *Masaryk:* Nova Evropa, Rusko a Evropa, Světova revoluce. *Medek:* Pout' do Československa, 3 dily. *Milota:* Kašparkovy pohadky. *Neruda:* Arabesky, Malostranske povidky, Studie kratke a kratši, 2 dily, Žertem do pravdy, 4 dily. *Němcova:* Babička, Uplne česke pohadky, 4 dily. *Němeček:* New Yorku, Zamlženo, Nove Obzory, Ročnik I. a II. *Olbracht:* Podivne přatelstvi Jesenia, Žalař nejtemnějši. *Panyrek:* Kdo zvedne kamen? *Pittnerova:* Jindra, Mlyny, Mušketyruv syn. *Polaček:* Hlavni přeličeni. *Rais:* Čteni o Havličkovi a Třebizskem, Horske kořeny, "Kača," Kalibuv zločin, Lopota, Paničkou, Pantata Bezoušek, Potměchut', Rodiče a děti,

Stehle, Trochu veršu, Zapad, Zapadli vlastenci. *Rozek Dolensky-Kosina:* Obrazkove dějiny narčsl., 2 dily. *Roden:* Irčin romanek, Irča a Lexa. *Řehoř:* Valečne tajnosti pražske, 2 dily. *Sezima:* Dravy živel, V soumraku srdci. *Sokol-Tuma:* Celibat, 2 svazky, Na kresach, 2 svazky, Valašska světice. *Sova: Toma Bojar. Stašek:* Na rozhrani, ve 2 knihach, V temnych virech. *Světla:* Křiž u potoka, Posledni pani Hlohovska. *Svoboda:* Řeka, ve 4 svazcich. *Svobodova:* Milenky, Černi myslivci. *Šalda:* Loutky i dělnici boži. *Vachek:* Sup. *Vančura:* Utěk do Budina. *Vrba:* Boži mlyny, Dolina, Zlaty kliček. *Wenig:* Podivuhodne přiběhy barona Prašila. *Zahradnik-Brodsky:* Až květy vykvetou, Bile světlo, Evangelium života, Chram usvitu, Jan Vladyka, Jaci byli, Jezero, Jarni sněhy, Jiskra v krvi, Noc jeho života, Trosky. *Zeyer:* Jan Maria Plojhar, Ondřej, Černyšev. *Župan:* Pepanek nezdara, 3 svazky. *Baudyšova:* Převraty. *Bilianova:* Pod selsky krov, 2 knihy. *Hais-Tynecky:* Pod Emausy, 3 dily. *Martinek:* Jakub Oberva.

Česke překlady cizojazyčnych knih

Beach: Ničema, Volani lasky. *Caine:* Laska a svedomi, Věčne město. *Crawford:* Bila sestra. *Connor:* Černa skala, Pod Skalistymi horami. *Curwood:* V božim kraji. *Dreisser:* Americka tragedie. *Essad:* Stalin. *Glyn:* Jeho chvile. *Grey:* Jezdci purpurovych stepi, Tajemny, jezdec. *Grinko:* Pětliteka. *Hugo:* Bidnici, Dělnici moře. Devadesat tři, Muž. ktery se směje. *Galsworthy:* Bratrstvi. *Knickerbock:* Rudy obchod hrozi, Rudy obchod laka. *Marden:* Splněni všech přani. *Marlitt:* V sovim zamku. *Hulford:* Dar ducha, 6 svazku. *Sabatini:* Kapitan Blood, Mořsky luňak. *Sienkiewicz:* Quo Vadis? *Sinclair:* Kral uhli, Penězoměnci. *Stevenson:* Ostrov pokladu. *Tolstoj:* Vzkřišeni. *Twain:* Přiběhy Toma Sawyera, Frantik Finn. *Wells:* Stručne dějiny světa. *Wodehouse:* Lupič z ochoty. *Zweig:* Spor o seržanta Grišu.

BOOKS ADDED IN THE SPRING OF 1934

Benešova: Uder, Podzemni plameny, Tragicka duha. *Čapek:* Hordubal. *Dreisser:* Americka tragedie, 2 svazky. *Dumas:* Tři mušketyři, 2 svazky. *Fallada:* Občanku, co ted'? *Frank:* Ze tři milinou tři. *Herrmann:* U snědeneho kramu. *Jahoda:* Povinnost, 2 svazky. *Jeřabek:* Dobyti Podolan. *Martinek:* Plameny, Země duni. *Medek:* Ohnivy drak, Velike dni. *Mrštik:* Pohadka maje. *Novy:* Chceme žit, Samota Křešin, Srdce ve vichru, Tvaři v

APPENDIX 389

tvař. *Olbracht:* Nikola Šuhaj. *Pfleger:* Pani fabrikantova. *Sinclair:* Boston, 2 svazky; Jatky, Wall-Street. *Sokol-Tuma:* Na šachtě, 3 svazky; Pan zavodni, 3 svazky; V zaři milionu, 3 svazky. *Tilschova:* Haldy, 2 svazky. *Vachek:* Bidylko, Cham Dynybyl, 3 svazky; Muž a stin. *Welzl:* Třicet let, Trampoty.

DIRECTORY OF THE SLOVANIC BENEVOLENT ASSOCIATION OF TEXAS (S. P. J. S. T.), WITH THEIR OFFICERS

C. H. Chernosky, Houston - - - - - - - - *President*
Josef Mikeska, Wesley - - - - - - - - *Vice-President*
Eng. Jelinek, Granger - - - - - - - - - *Vice-President*
J. R. Kuběna, Fayetteville - - - - - - - - - *Secretary*
Ed. L. Marek, Caldwell - - - - - - - - - - *Treasurer*
Aug. Kačir, Temple - - - - - - - - - - - *Attorney*
Robert Červenka, West }
W. Nesuda, Dallas } - - - - - *Auditing Committee*
Štěpan Valčik, Houston }
J. H. Hurta, Temple }
T. H. Škrabanek, Ennis } - - - - - - - - *Inspectors*
F. Ančinec, Houston }
Karel Lažnovsky, Ennis }
John Gajevsky, Orchard } - - - *Editing Committee*
Josef Krušinsky, Corpus Christi }

1. Pokrok Texasu, Jan Horňak, Fayetteville, Texas.
2. Kopernik, Jos. Pokorny, Route 1, Fayetteville, Texas.
3. Novohrad, A. J. Mika, Route 1, Moulton, Texas.
4. Karel Havliček, Anton Holy, Hallettsville, Texas.
5. Tioga, Charles Hejny, Tioga, Texas.
6. Mor. Bratři, J. A. Hegar, Abbott.
7. Rovnost, Frank B. Dušek, Route 1, Box 152, Caldwell, Texas.
8. Prapor Svobody, Adolf Barta, Route 7, Schulenburg, Texas.
9. Slovan, Dr. Jos. H. Kozar, Route 2, Somerville, Texas.
10. Texasky Mir. Aug. Madala, Route 2, Box 102, Yoakum, Texas.
11. Svojan. J, Hořelica, Route 1, Box 57, Flatonia, Texas.
12. Dubina. C. A. Habernal, Weimar, Texas.
13. Texaska Orlice. Vinc Marek, Dime Box, Texas.
14. Veseli. Ed. G. Vavra, Route 8, Brenham, Texas.
15. Svornost Jihu. L. S. Světlik, Route 3, Rogers, Texas.

16. Bila Hora. Frank Menar, Route 1, Sublime, Texas.
17. Novy Tabor. Jos. Siptak, Route 3, Caldwell, Texas.
19. Velehrad. E. V. Gallia, Route 6, Hallettsville, Texas.
20. Komensky. Jno. P. Trlica, Granger, Texas.
21. Fr. Palacky. Chas. Jalufka, Route 4, Box 159, Schulenburg, Texas.
22. Jiři Washington. W. Renz, P. O. B. 335, Eagle Lake, Texas.
23. Nova Morava John Trlica, Route 5, Schulenburg, Texas.
24. Česky Prapor. Chas. Navratil, Route 4, Temple, Texas.
25. Ennis. W. J. Hejny, Route 2, Box 129, Ennis, Texas.
26. Slovan Jihu. Julius Šumbera, Route 1, Skidmore, Texas.
27. Pokrok Moultonu. J. Zavesky, Route 3, Shiner, Texas.
28. Karel Jonaš. John Holeček, Route 1, Wallis, Texas.
29. Praha. Frank Kolenovsky, Route 2, Box 43, Taylor, Texas.
30. Hvězda Jihu. Edw. Polinsky, Taiton, Texas.
31. Pokrok Slovanu. E. E. Bushek, Nat'l Bldg., Yoakum, Texas.
32. Našinec. F. J. Shiller, Route 2, Box 78, Victoria, Texas.
33. Hvězda miru. Jos. F. Mikeska, Route 3, Bellville, Texas.
34. Slovanšti Bratři. J. G. Charanza, Route 4, Caldwell, Texas.
35. Nove Květy. Adolf Mach, Route 1, Axtell, Texas.
36. West. Jos. Holasek, West, Texas.
37. Nova Vlast. J. M. Zapalač, Route 1, Sealy, Texas.
38. Světlo. Jos. F. Slavik, Kirtley, Texas.
39. Bedřich Smetana. John Homola, Route 5, Bryan, Texas.
40. Čechoslovan. E. K. Hajovsky, El Campo, Texas.
41. Nova Ratolest. Vlasta Charbula, Port Lavaca, Texas.
42. Moravan. John. Machač, Route 1, Brookshire, Texas.
43. Bratrska Podpora. Fr. Dressler, El Campo, Texas.
44. Cešti Bratři. Fr. Langer, Star Route, New Ulm, Texas.
45. Vlastenec. J. H. Elšik, Route 2, Yoakum, Texas.
46. Volnost. Žofie Hluchaň, Box 354, Sealy, Texas.
47. Hvězda Texasu. Jerry Dana, Route 3, Temple, Texas.
48. Vyšehrad. Anton Michalik, Box 165, Holland, Texas.
49. Pokrok Roweny. Vaclav Kvasnička, Route 1, Rowena, Texas.
50. Pokrok Pierce. Jos. Bartoš, Taiton, Texas.
51. Věrnost. Petr Pončik, Route 2, Fayetteville, Texas.
52. Osvěta. Chas. Vyvjala, Smithville, Texas.
53. Česky Lev. T. A. Pophanken, Route 1, New Ulm, Texas.
54. Jaromir. Emil W. Popp, Route 2, Abbott, Texas.
55. Hvězdnaty Prapor. Louis Svačina, Route 1, Box 55, Penelope, Texas.
56. Anton J. Čermak. A. B. Janošek. Clarkwood.

57. Jan Hus. Jakub Cižek, 214 St. Paul Street, Gonzales, Texas.
58. Columbus. A. L. Matušek, Route 1, Wharton, Texas.
59. Bratři Jihu. J. J. Frnka, New Ulm, Texas.
60. Bratři Svornosti. J. M. Vašina, Wallis, Texas.
61. Vesmir. Frank Vontur, Route 4, Box 207 A., Floresville, Texas.
62. Rozkvět. E. J. Denke, 1217 Avenue A, Galveston, Texas.
63. Pokrok Sweet Home. Joe N. Morris, Sweet Home, Texas.
64. Pokrok Plumu. Louis M. Matocha, Route 1, La Grange, Texas.
65. Prapor Magnolie. Mrs. Albina Balcar, Sheldon, Texas.
66. Slovanska Lipa. Jos. Narovec, 122 South Fourth Street, Waco, Texas.
67. Bratři Svobody. Frank Holub, Route 7, Box 16, Schulenburg, Texas.
68. Vesměrnost. B. W. Schiller, Route 3, Bellville, Texas.
69. Nova Osada. Hy. Dušek, Roger, Texas.
70. Laskavost. John J. Zemanek, Needville, Texas.
71. Novy Raj. Tom Přikryl, Penelope, Texas.
72. Pokrok Jihu. R. J. Guzner, Route 1, Cameron, Texas.
73. Sam Houston. Joe Wašek, Route 3, Seymour, Texas.
74. Svatopluk Čech. Jos. Franta, Hallettsville, Texas.
75. Svoboda. Joe Pacha, Route 3, Box 18, Bartlett, Texas.
76. Neodvislost. Chas. Křižan, 2409 Eighth Street, Wichita Falls, Texas.
77. Hvězda Praporu. Raymond Přibyla, Route 2, Bombarton, Texas.
78. Dobrota. Mrs. Hermina Vrana, Dobrovolsky, Texas.
79. Corpus Christi. Karel Holasek, Route 2, Corpus Christi, Texas.
80. Tyrš. Tom Hunka, Route 3, Holland, Texas.
81. Rozkvět Ruže. Arnold L. Franěk, Route 2, Needville, Texas.
82. Čechu Domov. Vaclav Strunc, Route 6, Ennis, Texas.
83. Srdce Jednoty. Jos. Hruby, Columbus, Texas.
84. Pokrok Dallas. Frant. Vodička, 2107 Second Avenue, Dallas, Texas.
85. Pokrok Haskell. Adolf Havran, Route 1, Knox City, Texas.
86. Slovansky Svaz. O. V. Vaniček, Route 4, Temple, Texas.
87. Hvězda Svobody. H. H. Hejl, 816 North Second Street, Temple, Texas.
88. Pokrok Houstonu. Frank Olexa, 252 Malone Avenue, Houston, Texas.

89. Ružovy Dvur. Anton Uličnik, Route 1, Box 101, Rosebud, Texas.
90. Slovanske Sdruženi. Frank Pustějovsky, Box 76, Tuxedo, Texas.
91. San Jacinto. R. J. Lošt'ak, Box 306, Crosby, Texas.
92. Svaz Cechoslovanu. Albert Silhavy, 2218 Loving Avenue, Fort Worth, Texas.
93. Karnes. F. L. Pustějovsky, Hobson, Texas.
94. Dennice. Jos. Blažek, Wheelock, Texas.
95. Česky Den. Ant. Holub, Bomarton, Texas.
96. Krasna. John Marek, Route 1, Rosenberg, Texas.
97. Placedo Joe. L. Elšik, P. O. Box 105, Da Costa, Texas.
98. Vitěz. Ant. B. Šemjkal, Route 1, Box 311, Victoria, Texas.
99. Radhošt'. Eddie Neuvar, Route 4, Hallettsville, Texas.
100. Pokrok Mladeže. Tom Elšik, Route 2, Somerville, Texas.
101. Pokrok Gainesville. Mrs. Agnes Paclik, Gainesville, Texas.
102. Hvězda Mladeže. Jos. F. Machu, Box 44, Coupland, Texas.
103. Pokrok Flatonie. F. J. Fojtik, Flatonia, Texas.
104. Texasšti Bratři. Aug. Černota, Route 2, Yorktown, Texas.
105. Hej Slovane. John Plašek, Route 1, Box 104, Chrisman, Texas.
106. Čechomoravan. Frank Dočekal, La Grange, Texas.
107. Rozkvět Zapadu. E. Mičulka, Floresville, Texas.
108. Jiři Poděbradsky. J. J. Vyvial, Richmond, Texas.
109. Gen. Radeckv Em. Fojtik, Route 4, Granger, Texas.
110. Jan Rosicky. Frank Rofnovec, Route 2, Kaufman, Texas.
111. Jaroslav Vrchlicky. Stěpan Valčik, Alief, Texas.
112. F. B. Zdrubek. Rozi Mikeska, Guy, Texas.
113. Pokrok Beasley. J. F. Lukašik, George West, Texas.
114. Vyzovice, Marie Kaděra, Rout 1, Box 42, Richmond, Texas.
115. Pokrok Garwood. F. J. Bouška, Garwood, Texas.
116. Rozkvět Cooks Point. W. J. Drgač, Route 3, Caldwell, Texas.
117. Robstown. Jan F. Veselka, Route 1, Robstown, Texas.
118. Kingsville. F. J. Elšik, Kingsville, Texas.
119. Slovanska Přiležitost. F. L. Gregor, Route 1, Brookshire, Texas.
120. Pokrok Deanville, Jos. Balcar, Route 1, Caldwell, Texas.
121. Spravedlnost. Jos. F. Novosad, Route 3, Shiner, Texas.
122. Nova Doba. Jos. F. Felcman, Route 1, Box 84, Wallis, Texas.
123. Všeslovan. E. V. Janečka, Route 3, Box 56, Cistern, Texas.
124. Slovansky Dilworth. Anton Hanzalik, Dilworth, Texas.

125. Touha. Louis Lukaš, Box 36, Westhoff, Texas.
126. Dubovy Haj. Josef Foit, Route 1, West, Texas.
127. Pokrok Kenedy. H. W. Marcak, Kenedy, Texas.
128. Bratrske Spojeni. Frank Vaněk, Route 5, Mart, Texas.
129. Ladimir Klacel, Frank Zikeš, Wheelock, Texas.
130. Jaro. J. F. Bouška, 5536 Richard Street, Dallas, Texas.
131. Alamo. Hy. Sladek, Jr., Route 2, Box 82, Thrall, Texas.
132. Svatopluk. Joe Košt'ak, Route 3, Waller, Texas.
133. San Antonio, Louis Dresler, 122 Dulling Court, San Antonio, Texas.
134. Bratřejov. Chas. Machač, Crowell, Texas.
135. Volna Čechie, Jos. Vytopil, Ennis, Texas.
136. Liberty. Frant. Kalenda, Route 2, Dayton, Texas.
137. Lilie. Anna V. Kubala, Louise, Texas.
138. Vytrvalost. C. M. Šrubař, Ganado, Texas.
139. V Boji za Svobodu. Miro. Svoboda, Danbury, Texas.
140. Rozkvět Svobody. J. F. Michna, Hallettsville, Texas.
141. Čechoslovak. Jos. Taška, Route 1, Sealv, Texas.
142. Štefanik. J. J. Kelarek, 5348 Nolda Street, Houston, Texas.
143. Přimoři. Leo Krause, Jr., Route 1, Inez, Texas.
144. Slavie, Robert Skuča, Nada, Texas.
145. Moravska Orlice. Frank Hegar, Penelope, Texas.
146. Woodrow Wilson. Mrs. Anna Von Rotz, 3910 Avenue O ½, Galveston, Texas.
147. Vesela Osada. Tom Ventrček, Route 2, Box 66, Jourdanton, Texas.
148. Elmaton. Frank Hložek, Blessing, Texas.
149. Tom. Jefferson. Fr. Truksa, Alvin, Texas.
150. Mrs. A. Strouhal, Woodsboro, Texas.
151. Miss Leona Holešovsky, P. O. Box 513, Wharton, Texas.
152. Pokrok Agua Dulce. J. R. Bartoň, Route 2, Box 116, Alice, Texas.
153. Pokrok Benview, Albert V. Franek, Benview, Texas.

DELEGATES TO THE ELEVENTH QUADRENNIAL
MEETING OF THE S. P. J. S. T., ENNIS,
AUGUST 2-5, 1932

1. Jos. Ťapal, Fayetteville
   J. R. Kuběna, Fayetteville
2. Karel Hilscher, Fayetteville
3. Oldřich Motal, Moulton
4. F. K. Buček, Hallettsville
6. Jan Pavlas, Abbott
7. Jos. Dušek, Jr., Caldwell
8. Boh. Pokorny, Weimer

9. Jos. Kulhanek, Weimer
Wm. F. Rubach, Somerville
10. R. B. Kroulik, Yoakum
11. Jar. J. Michal, Flatonia
12. C. A. Habernal, Weimer
13. Jos. L. Kocurek, Dime Box
14. Jos. Mikeska, Brenham
15. Vilem Kužel, Rogers
16. Karel Holy, Sublime
17. Jos. N. Vavra, Sublime
Jos. Siptak, Caldwell
18. Frant. Janota, Elgin
19. Fr. Juřena, Hallettsville
20. Jos. H. Huser, Hallettsville
Eng. Jelinek, Granger
21. Hy. Rosenaur, Schulenberg
22. Ed. Batla, Eagle Lake
23. Fr. J. Olšovsky, Schulenberg
24. Chas. Navratil, Temple
Ed. L. Marek, Temple
25. T. H. Škrabanek, Temple
W. J. Hejny, Ennis
26. P. K. Mikeska, Skidmore
27. Rud. Mičulka, Shiner
28. Jan Holeček, Shiner
Jan Gajevsky, Wallis
29. Tom Drozda, Wallis
J. H. Tuček, Taylor
30. Jan Socha, Taiton
31. Rud. Hanyš, Yoakum
32. Jan Hošek, Victoria
33. Tom Mikeska, Bellville
34. Pavel Mynař, Caldwell
35. Ad. Mach, Axtell
36. Jos. F. Holasek, West
37. J. M. Zapalač, Sealy
38. J. C. Leshikar, Kirtley
39. Jos. Horňak, Bryan
40. A. L. Trojčak, El Campo
41. Jos. Marek, Port Lavaca
42. St. Vavra, Brookshire
43. Fr. Dressler, El Campo
44. Jos. Zaněk, New Ulm

45. Robt. Mikuš, Yoakum
46. L. Hluchaň, Sealy
47. F. E. Hejl, Sealy
J. H. Hurta, Sealy
48. Ant. Michalik, Holland
49. Jos. Kudlaček, Rowena
50. Fr. Rod, Taiton
51. J. F. Chupik, Fayetteville
52. Fr. Kulak, Smithville
53. Leop. Shimek, New Ulm
54. Robert Červenka, West
55. L. Svačina, West
57. Jak. Čižek, Gonzales
58. Ostoja Muniza, Wharton
59. J. J. Frnka, New Ulm
60. Inc. Minks, Wallis
61. Fr. Vontur, Floresville
62. E. J. Denke, Galveston
63. A. M. Bordovsky, Yoakum
64. L. M. Matocha, La Grange
65. Jac. Konečny, Sheldon
66. V. A. Žebro, Waco
67. Fr. Holub, Schulenburg
68. B. W. Schiller, Bellville
69. Hy. Dušek, Rogers
70. J. J. Zemanek, Needville
71. Tom Přikryl, Penelope
72. F. A. Marek, Cameron
73. Thos. Siptak, Seymour
74. Tom J. Pešek, Hallettsville
75. L. Havelka, Bartlett
76. Otto Stehlik, Wichita Falls
77. L. Pavliček, Bomarton
78. F. Křemenek, Jourdanton
79. J. Krušinsky, Corpus Christi
80. Jan Šumbera, Holland
81. A. L. Franěk, Needville
82. Jos. Ťoupal, Ennis
83. Jos. Hruby, Columbus
84. V. Drobil, Dallas
85. Jos. Červeny, Knox City
86. Jan Maruna, Temple
87. W. A. Chernosky, Temple

Jos. Zvolanek, Temple
88. Tom. Hošek, Houston
F. Olexa, st., Houston
89. Ant. Uličnik, Rosebud
90. Karel Vašek, Tuxedo
91. R. J. Lošak, Crosby
92. Jos. Juran, Fort Worth
93. F. L. Pustějovsky, Hobson
94. C. L. Novosad, Fort Worth
95. Ant. Holub, Bomarton
96. (Not present)
97. J. H. Mikeska, Bloomington
98. B. F. Shiller, Victoria
99. Kar. Španihel, Hallettsville
100. F. F. Šebesta, Lyons
101. Jan Paclik, Gainesville
102. F. J. Dlouhy, Gainesville
103. F. J. Fojtik, Flatonia
104. F. Rohan, Coupland
105. Jan Plašek, Chriesman
106. Fr. Dočekal, La Grange
107. Jos. Bayer, Floresville
108. A. A. Urbish, Richmond
109. Ant. Zrubek, Granger
110. Jos. Řezniček, Kaufman
111. Vilem Haisler, Alief
112. Fr. Vrla, Guy
113. C. H. Chernosky, Beasley
114. Jos. Kaděra, Richmond
115. Fr. Bouška, Garwood
116. W. J. Drgač, Caldwell
117. F. J. Moravek, Robstown

118. Jos. Elšik, Kingsville
119. Jos. Kašpar, Brookshire
120. Jos. Balcar, Caldwell
121. Rud. Myška, Shiner
122. Fr. Klečka, Wallis
123. Dom. Vydržal, Flatonia
124. (Not present)
125. J. C. Eineigl, Westhoff
126. J. J. Husak, West
127. K. E. Marčak, Kenedy
128. Fr. Vaněk, Mart
129. Leon. Lys, Wheelock
130. Wm. Nesuda, Dallas
131. Hy. Sladek, Jr., Thrall
132. L. Mikulenka, Waller
133. F. Maly, San Antonio
134. Hy. Machač, Crowell
135. K. Lažnovsky, Ennis
136. Jan Němy, Dayton
137. J. J. Kubala, Louise
138. J. B. Strouhal, Ganado
139. L. Pechaček, Danbury
140. Jos. Mladěnka, Hallettsville
141. Jos. Taška, Sealy
142. Jan Šulda, Houston
143. Theo. Charbula, Inez
144. (Not present)
145. L. Vanduch, Penelope
146. Jos. Vesely, Galveston
148. Jos. Zemanek, Blessing
149. Hedvika Truksa, Alvin

INDEX

A

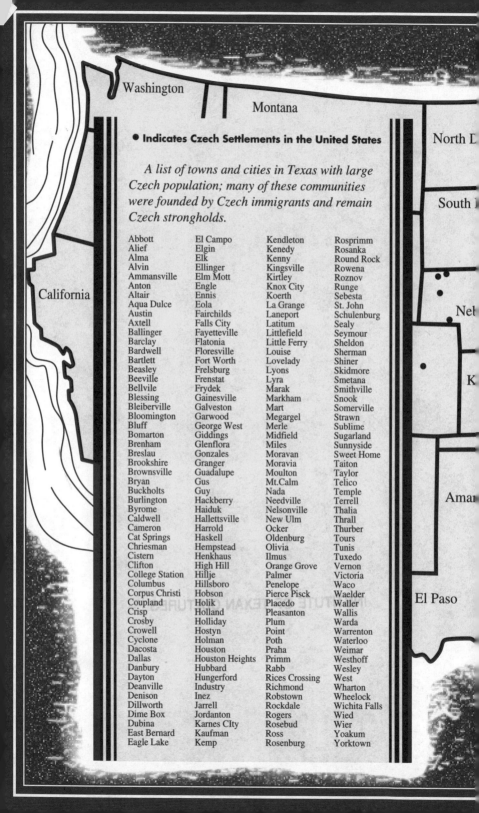

Washington

Montana

California

North D

South D

Neb

K

Amar

El Paso

● Indicates Czech Settlements in the United States

A list of towns and cities in Texas with large Czech population; many of these communities were founded by Czech immigrants and remain Czech strongholds.

Abbott
Alief
Alma
Alvin
Ammansville
Anton
Altair
Aqua Dulce
Austin
Axtell
Ballinger
Barclay
Bardwell
Bartlett
Beasley
Beeville
Bellvile
Blessing
Bleiberville
Bloomington
Bluff
Bomarton
Brenham
Breslau
Brookshire
Brownsville
Bryan
Buckholts
Burlington
Byrome
Caldwell
Cameron
Cat Springs
Chriesman
Cistern
Clifton
College Station
Columbus
Corpus Christi
Coupland
Crisp
Crosby
Crowell
Cyclone
Dacosta
Dallas
Danbury
Dayton
Deanville
Denison
Dillworth
Dime Box
Dubina
East Bernard
Eagle Lake

El Campo
Elgin
Elk
Ellinger
Elm Mott
Engle
Ennis
Eola
Fairchilds
Falls City
Fayetteville
Flatonia
Floresville
Fort Worth
Frelsburg
Frenstat
Frydek
Gainesville
Galveston
Garwood
George West
Giddings
Glenflora
Gonzales
Granger
Guadalupe
Gus
Guy
Hackberry
Haiduk
Hallettsville
Harrold
Haskell
Hempstead
Henkhaus
High Hill
Hillje
Hillsboro
Hobson
Holik
Holland
Holliday
Hostyn
Holman
Houston
Houston Heights
Hubbard
Hungerford
Industry
Inez
Jarrell
Jordanton
Karnes CIty
Kaufman
Kemp

Kendleton
Kenedy
Kenny
Kingsville
Kirtley
Knox City
Koerth
La Grange
Laneport
Latitum
Littlefield
Little Ferry
Louise
Lovelady
Lyons
Lyra
Marak
Markham
Mart
Megargel
Merle
Midfield
Miles
Moravan
Moravia
Moulton
Mt.Calm
Nada
Needville
Nelsonville
New Ulm
Ocker
Oldenburg
Olivia
Ilmus
Orange Grove
Palmer
Penelope
Pierce Pisck
Placedo
Pleasanton
Plum
Point
Poth
Praha
Primm
Rabb
Rices Crossing
Richmond
Robstown
Rockdale
Rogers
Rosebud
Ross
Rosenburg

Rosprimm
Rosanka
Round Rock
Rowena
Roznov
Runge
Sebesta
St. John
Schulenburg
Sealy
Seymour
Sheldon
Sherman
Shiner
Skidmore
Smetana
Smithville
Snook
Somerville
Strawn
Sublime
Sugarland
Sunnyside
Sweet Home
Taiton
Taylor
Telico
Temple
Terrell
Thalia
Thrall
Thurber
Tours
Tunis
Tuxedo
Vernon
Victoria
Waco
Waelder
Waller
Wallis
Warda
Warrenton
Waterloo
Weimar
Westhoff
Wesley
West
Wharton
Wheelock
Wichita Falls
Wied
Wier
Yoakum
Yorktown